Anne Griffin

CANADA AND THE UNITED STATES

CANADA AND THE UNITED STATES: TRANSNATIONAL AND TRANSGOVERNMENTAL RELATIONS

Edited by:

Annette Baker Fox, Alfred O. Hero, Jr., and Joseph S. Nye, Jr.

Columbia University Press/New York and London/1976

Library of Congress Cataloging in Publication Data

Main entry under title:

Canada and the United States.

Bibliography: p.
Includes index.
1. United States—Foreign relations—Canada—Addresses, essays, lectures. 2. Canada—Foreign relations—United States—Addresses, essays,
lectures. I. Fox, Annette Baker, 1912– II. Hero, Alfred O. III. Nye,
Joseph S.
JX1428.C2C3 1976 327.73′071 75-45495

First published in book form by Columbia University Press in 1976.

Printed in the United States of America.

TO

LELAND M. GOODRICH

CONTENTS

PREFACE

This volume is addressed to two audiences in particular—people who are interested in enlarging their understanding of transnational relations by acquiring knowledge about specific cases and those who are concerned about Canadian-American relations. The book developed from an opportune confluence of factors and circumstances. Joseph S. Nye, Jr., and Robert O. Keohane, who were active in developing the body of theory and concepts pertaining to interactions of intergovernmental and transnational relations and in their empirical testing and application, organized a special issue of the scholarly quarterly *International Organization* in 1971 around that theme.[1] Subsequently they helped organize another special issue that would apply this perspective, largely developed from other contexts, to the most extensive and intensive case of transnational and transgovernmental activity, that of Canada and the United States. This second issue appeared in the autumn of 1974. *International Organization,* now published by the University of Wisconsin Press, has been sponsored primarily by the World Peace Foundation since the establishment of the journal in 1947.

The World Peace Foundation has for over two decades devoted a significant part of its attention and modest financial resources to United States relations with its northern neighbor. Two members of the Board of Trustees who were particularly interested in this domain, Leland M. Goodrich and Joseph S. Nye, Jr., were also members of the Board of Editors of *International Organization.* Another member of the Board of Editors, Alfred O. Hero, Jr., is director of the Foundation. As a coeditor of the volume, he could bring to its organization his special familiarity with and concern about Quebec and French-Canadian thought. The special issue was made financially possible by funds generously appropriated by the Board of Trustees of the World Peace Foundation. Annette Baker Fox, of the Institute of War and Peace Studies, Columbia University, was chosen as a coeditor because of her scholarly interest in Canada and experience with Canadian-American

---

[1] Robert O. Keohane and Joseph S. Nye, Jr., eds., "Transnational Relations and World Politics," *International Organization* 25 (Summer 1971) ; also published as a book by Harvard University Press in 1972.

relations. Throughout the planning and execution of this enterprise, the three coeditors profited from the counsel and active involvement of an editorial committee of the Board of Editors composed of Leland Goodrich, Robert Keohane, and the then editor of the quarterly, David A. Kay.

The coeditors and their editorial committee were determined from the beginning that the volume should be written from diverse frames of reference and academic disciplines, yet connected in one respect or another with Canadian–United States transgovernmental and transnational activities. The editors and their associates believed that authors would need to be carefully selected not only for substantive knowledge and political sensitivity in regard to the phenomena in question, but also for their competence and willingness to approach their topics in terms of the common objectives and conceptual orientations of the volume as a whole. Moreover, they would require focused initial guidelines and continuing suggestions and comments on successive outlines and draft articles from the coeditors and the committee. In addition, each contributor would engage in discussion with the other authors and the committee together, preferably before the organization and content of their drafts had jelled and perhaps again over the drafts themselves.

We were very pleased that we could involve able authors, most of them with many conflicting commitments, in such a demanding process over almost two years, at but token remuneration. All were initially provided with guidelines concerning the concepts to be tested, some specific questions and suggestions pertinent to their topics, and a tentative table of contents of the volume as a whole. They were also requested to submit outlines of their projected contributions for circulation to the editorial committee and the other authors for discussion in a two-day working session of as many as could participate at the Center for International Affairs at Harvard University, 23–24 March 1973. Following this meeting, each author received supplementary guidelines and further specific suggestions. Pursuant to ideas generated at the meeting, additional manuscripts were solicited to fill some of the remaining gaps in the projected volume.

The resulting draft articles were circulated to all authors, the editorial committee, and others invited to a meeting at Carleton University in Ottawa, 8–10 November 1973, sponsored jointly by the School of International Affairs of that university, the Canadian Institute of International Affairs, and the World Peace Foundation.[2] Our

[2] We particularly appreciate a generous grant from the Canada Council to Carleton University and supplementary grants from the World Peace Foundation and the Canadian Institute of International Affairs, which helped to make this meeting possible.

Canadian cosponsors secured additional papers to fill gaps in the coverage of manuscripts prepared for the special issue and to develop other aspects of these and related topics. The editorial committee met several weeks afterward to consider ideas generated at those sessions and sent further suggestions to each author for consideration in revising the drafts. Upon receipt of the resulting redrafts, the coeditors, in consultation with the editorial committee, sent still further suggestions to a number of authors to help them put their manuscripts into final form for more detailed editing by Irene D. Jacobs of the *International Organization* editorial staff.

Our committee and the coeditors decided at the outset that it was impractical to examine analytically all of the critical issue areas and other phenomena pertinent to this volume's transnational and transgovernmental perspective. Instead we chose to concentrate on quality at the expense of inclusiveness. As we note below and in the concluding article, some rather glaring lacunae will thus be apparent. We searched without success for contributions in the following domains: (1) the critical, complex area of transnational cultural influences through formal primary, secondary, and university education, the arts, literature, mass media, advertising, impacts on local communities of United States–controlled branch plants, and tourism; (2) immigration, emigration, and other population movements and demographic factors; (3) land ownership and utilization; (4) agriculture, including both food and such industrial resources as forest products; and (5) science and technology.

Furthermore, although Alfred Hero had relatively wide contacts with francophone intellectuals in Quebec, the coeditors were able to secure only one contribution by a French-Canadian observer. This article is written from but one of several plausible alternative perspectives that are current among influential Quebec elites—that of an eventually politically sovereign Quebec under more or less the current moderate leadership of the Parti Québécois. As this and several other articles in the volume suggest, attitudes and behavior pertinent to important aspects of the focus of this volume among francophone Québécois probably diverge importantly from those of their anglophone and recent immigrant compatriots. Though interesting comparative observations are advanced by several of our nonfrancophone authors, it would have been useful if qualified francophones had written comparative articles in perhaps two or three of the issue areas in which Québécois thinking seems to diverge significantly from that of other North Americans, for example: education, mass media, the arts and literature, or cultural aspects generally; direct private investment, including its social and cultural implications; trade unions; and maybe defense and collective security, However, the editors were unable to engage appropriate francophone authors for such contributions within the time available.[3]

We hope that these omissions as well as the more hypothetical, speculative, and controversial observations to follow may motivate others to do empirical research in order to remedy these shortcomings in knowledge, interpretations, and understanding. Canadian–United States relations generally, and their transnational and transgovernmental aspects particularly, intrinsically warrant much more systematic attention by American and other non-Canadian Ph.D. candidates and more experienced scholars. Though few are likely to devote their careers primarily to United States–Canadian affairs, they could examine the North American context to produce substantively and theoretically important, as well as readily accessible, comparative case studies. These could relate to a wide gamut of theoretical, methodological, and politically significant interests of political scientists, political sociologists, economists, and other social scientists in areas heretofore neglected. In many fields American scholars could locate able and potentially interested Canadian collaborators, including francophones. We hope also that this volume will stimulate similar research on transnational and transgovernmental relations between or among other countries that have complex and intimate ties comparable to those between Canada and the United States.

This volume is appropriately dedicated to Leland M. Goodrich, who became an honorary member of the Board of Editors in May 1974 and Trustee Emeritus of the World Peace Foundation upon attaining retirement age in September 1974. As director of the Foundation in the mid-1940s, he was primarily responsible for the establishment of *International Organization* under the auspices of that institution. For a decade after his return in 1946 to academic pursuits, initially at Brown University and later at Columbia University, Leland Goodrich helped to guide the development of the journal in the key role of chairman of the Board of Editors. Largely owing to his leadership, *International Organization* rapidly became the central vehicle for serious research and speculation in its domain and one of half a dozen leading periodicals in the general field of international affairs. He has since continued

---

[3] For four later analyses of implications of alternative scenarios of Quebec nationalism for relations with the United States, see François Bouvier and André Donneur, "Relations Québec-Etats-Unis: perspectives d'avenir"; John Holmes, "La portée du nationalisme québécois dans les relations canado-américaines"; John H. Sigler, "Vers une plus grande entropie: la question du Québec dans une perspective continentale et globale"; and Alfred O. Hero, Jr., "Le nationalisme québécois face aux Etats-Unis: un point de vue américain," in *Le nationalisme québécois à la croisée des chemins*, special issue of *Choix* (Québec, P.Q.: Centre Québécois des Relations Internationales, Institut Canadien des Affaires Internationales, Université Laval, 1975).

as a particularly active editor, solicitor and constructive critic of manuscripts, and author for the quarterly. Leland Goodrich brought to the planning and development of this symposium not only his wide knowledge and thoughtful judgment in world affairs, but particularly his perceptive concern for Canadian–United States relations, for the roles of the two countries in international institutions, and his recent experience of two years in Canada as visiting professor at the University of Toronto.

August 1975

Annette Baker Fox
Alfred O. Hero, Jr.
Joseph S. Nye, Jr.

NEW BRUNSWICK

St. Croix River

ST. ANDREWS   LORNEVILLE

EASTPORT   Passamaquoddy Bay

MAINE   Campobello Park

Bay of Fundy   NOVA SCOTIA

BAFFIN ISLAND

VILLE PENINSULA

LABRADOR

Hudson Bay

Churchill River

NEWFOUNDLAND

COME-BY-CHANCE

Placentia Bay

James Bay

Gulf of St. Lawrence

QUEBEC   PRINCE EDWARD ISLAND

St. Lawrence River   Strait of Canso

BAGOTVILLE   NEW BRUNSWICK

SENNETERRE   NOVA SCOTIA

ONTARIO   QUEBEC CITY   HALIFAX

St. Lawrence Seaway   MAINE

MONTREAL   PORTLAND   SABLE ISLAND

Ottawa River   Lake Memphremagog

UNDER BAY   OTTAWA

Lake Superior   CORNWALL   Lake Champlain

DULUTH   Lake Ontario

                       OSWEGO

SUPERIOR   Lake Huron TORONTO

                       Niagara Falls

Lake Michigan   NEW YORK

            DETROIT   Lake Erie

            Detroit River WINDSOR

CHICAGO

PART I

INTRODUCTION

INTRODUCTION: THE COMPLEX POLITICS OF CANADIAN–AMERICAN INTERDEPENDENCE

Robert O. Keohane and Joseph S. Nye, Jr.

The United States and Canada have now entered a new and more difficult period in their relations with one another. The "Nixon shock" of August 1971 struck Ottawa as well as Japan; conversely, Canadian reluctance freely to supply energy, particularly oil, to the United States has jarred Americans used to taking access to Canadian resources for granted. The extremely high degree of societal interdependence between the United States and Canada ensures that Canada will be strongly affected by American policies. As the two societies experience rapid socioeconomic change, there are bound to be struggles over how to adjust and who pays the price of adjustment. Government regulations are likely to increase on both sides of the border.

One purpose of this volume is to provide enlightenment about Canadian-American relations in this period of difficulty and conflict. We believe that this can be done most effectively, and in a manner that does not simply duplicate treatments of the subject elsewhere, by approaching them through a broader perspective than is normally applied. The state-centric approach that underlies most analyses of world politics and international organization makes two powerful simplifying assumptions: (1) that governments are the only significant actors in world politics, and (2) that governments are unified actors. Analysts with a broader perspective, by contrast, relax these two assumptions and inquire, on the one hand, about the role of non-

Robert O. Keohane is a member of the Board of Editors of *International Organization* and is associated with the Institute for Political Studies at Stanford University in Stanford, California. Joseph S. Nye is a member of the Board of Editors of *International Organization* and is at the Center for International Affairs, Harvard University, Cambridge, Massachusetts.

governmental actors in world politics and, on the other, about the possibility of transgovernmental relations. Terminology can be confusing. In this volume, *transgovernmental* refers to direct interactions between agencies (governmental subunits) of different governments where those agencies act relatively autonomously from central governmental control. *Transnational*, which is used in several different senses in contemporary literature, here refers to interactions across the border in which at least one actor is nongovernmental. It is our contention that the use of this perspective will contribute to our knowledge of Canadian-American relations. If we look at United States relations with Canada in state-centric terms, we may see merely another case of bilateral relations between a great power and a much smaller neighbor. If we look at North America in a transnational perspective, however, we see a fascinating and complex set of systems and coalitions that crisscross national boundaries. Even though we regard governments as the most important actors, an understanding of transnational and transgovernmental relations will help us to comprehend more fully the context within which they act.

The other purpose of this volume is to look at the Canadian-American relationship as a useful testing ground for notions of what the politics of interdependence among advanced industrial societies are likely to be. It is precisely in relations of high economic and social interdependence that transnational and transgovernmental relations will be most important, although less in isolation than in interaction with governmental behavior. This was a basic proposition of our earlier volume, *Transnational Relations and World Politics*.[1] Testing that notion with respect to the Canadian case cannot confirm our hypothesis; but if the following essays had found few instances of transnational or transgovernmental relations, it would have been refuted. The Canadian–United States relationship is therefore a most likely case for our hypothesis holding true, and a proper place to begin analysis of the conditions under which these patterns of behavior are significant.[2]

Confirmation of the importance of transnational and transgovernmental relations is not the only significant task of the following essays. The Canadian-American case also helps to illustrate how issues arise, how they become politically important, what strategies

---

[1] (Cambridge: Harvard University Press, 1972). The definitions used here have been slightly changed from those used in the earlier volume. For elaboration, see Robert O. Keohane and Joseph S. Nye, "Transgovernmental Relations and International Organization," *World Politics* (October 1974).

[2] Harry Eckstein, "Case Study and Theory in Political Science," in Fred Greenstein and Nelson Polsby, eds., *The Handbook of Political Science* (Reading, Mass.: Addison-Wesley, 1974).

actors use, and what factors seem to affect the outcomes of these processes. One of the outcomes that is sometimes assumed to follow from a high degree of socioeconomic interdependence and the rapid growth of transnational interactions among advanced societies is development of attitudes favoring further political integration. This does not seem to be true in the Canadian-American case. Indeed, as the article by John H. Sigler and Dennis Goresky in Part II indicates, rising transnational interactions and rising Canadian nationalism have gone hand in hand. Obviously, transnational relations are not the only source of tensions in the relationship; and the essay by John W. Holmes spells out some of the alternative sources of changing Canadian attitudes and of the interstate agenda. Part IV of this volume deals with questions of integration, conflict, and joint institutions in some detail, and follows the essays in Part III, which analyze the Canadian-American relationship by issue areas. The volume as a whole should be taken as a tentative testing and illustration of a fairly loose set of hypotheses that may provide us with a better start toward understanding some of the problems of politics among highly interdependent advanced industrial societies.

ANALYSIS BY ISSUE AREAS

In our earlier volume, we argued that intergovernmental policy issues could be useful starting points in analyzing world politics because the actors, their power resources, and their network of coalitions often differ from issue to issue. Thus we would not expect the Canadian-American relationship to be a seamless web. Different issues are handled by separate bureaucracies, frequently without central coordination from foreign offices or politically responsible officials. Some issues involve active participation by transnational organizations such as multinational enterprises or transnational trade unions. Some cases involve large-scale economic effects or important political symbols. Other issues, however, may have quite different characteristics. We expect that different types of issues lead to different intergovernmental processes, and to different outcomes. One of the intellectual challenges of this volume, only imperfectly realized, is to explore the extent to which issues that involve different types of transnational relations in different areas of activity lead to different types of governmental processes and outcomes.

An issue centered point of view has much to offer, but what is a *policy issue?* The answer is more elusive than at first it appears to be. Issues are not the same as objective problems, such as whether there is enough usable energy available to keep industrial society humming past the year 2000. Issues are problems about which people are concerned. Thus a problem only becomes an issue when people perceive it, and a *policy* issue only when the people concerned about it believe that it has relevance for public policy. (Whether Bobby Orr is a greater hockey player than Bobby Hull may be an issue that exercises many minds, but it is not a policy issue in our sense.) A policy issue becomes intergovernmental when communications about it take place between agencies of different governments.

A given phenomenon need not give rise to the same policy issue in different periods of time. The chief policy issue involving direct foreign investment for the Canadian government in 1950 was how to get more of it, whereas Canada is now trying to control foreign investment and the issue for many Canadians is how to reduce the extent of American control over Canadian industry. The intergovernmental policy issue involving oil and gas flows between Canada and the United States has gone through two cycles. At one stage the policy issue was whether the US would export as much as Canada wanted, then whether the United States would import as much as Canada wanted, and now whether Canada will export as much as the United States wants.

We group our discussions of various issues according to *issue areas,* which are sets of policy issues that are linked not merely by outside observers on the basis of objective criteria but by participants on the basis of their subjective understanding of their environments. Frequently the division of responsibility between various government bureaucracies or the frame of reference of different international organizations will define issue areas in the minds of government officials.

It is evident, therefore, that what an issue is will depend on what people think it is. If everyone calls the dog's tail a leg—and worries over what can be done to make the tail an effective participant in walking—this becomes an issue even if the people involved are clinically insane. As economists are fond of pointing out, economic issues between governments may sometimes arise because of misconceptions about the reality of economic relations carried around in the heads of politicians. Yet this hardly makes the consequences of actions any less real. Thus the analysis of issues properly begins with what people, particularly those in power, think and do, rather than with the "real" problems of which they may be blissfully or fretfully unaware. In one sense this characteristic of issues facilitates the task of political scientists, as well as distinguishes them from economists—even where the subject matter is the same. Our principal method of analysis is to focus on questions about which some controversy has arisen, and to examine political behavior on those questions.[3]

This still leaves the problem of structural situations that prevent certain problems from becoming policy issues. How should we analyze situations of structural bias in which certain types of alternatives, or issues, do not arise? How do we deal with *nondecisions*?[4] If it is difficult to identify issues, it is almost impossible to pinpoint nondecisions. Which of the infinity of nondecisions should be singled out remains dependent on the values of the analyst. Yet the issue of structure, particularly in formulations of structural imperialism or dependency,[5] is important and the various authors have tried to deal with it in a number of the essays that follow. For example, Robert W. Cox and Stuart Jamieson describe the transnational organization of labor as a structure adversely affecting Canada, but the basic cleavage seems to be primarily internal to Canada and the issue has not become an intergovernmental one.

ISSUES AND INTERDEPENDENCE

We have referred above to *interdependence*, but we have not yet defined it. Oran Young's general definition may provide a good beginning. For him interdependence refers to "the extent to which events occurring in any given part or within any given component unit of a world system affect (either physically or perceptually) events taking place in each of the other parts or component units of the system."[6] It is clear that interdependence thus defined can be more or less intense, and can be more or less symmetrical. The US-Canada relationship is relatively intense and quite asymmetrical. Canada is affected much more strongly by its economic dealings with the United States than is the United States, but each country is very important for the other. Canada remains the single largest trade partner of the

[3] This is not meant to imply that the political analyst can ignore objective reality. Presumably, political actors who misperceive reality are likely to fail to achieve their goals unless they adjust their perceptions. In the long run, therefore, some congruence can be expected between perceptions and reality. Nevertheless, it is on the basis of perceptions, not on the basis of an objective reality that no one understands in a definitive way, that actions are taken. For a given situation, we *begin with perceptions;* to predict outcomes, or future perceptions, it may be highly useful to have further information about the reality being perceived.

[4] Peter Bachrach and Morton Baratz, "Two Faces of Power," *American Political Science Review* 56 (December 1962) : 947-52.

[5] Johan Galtung, "A Structural Theory of Imperialism," *Journal of Peace Research* (Oslo), 8 (1971).

[6] Oran R. Young, "Interdependencies in World Politics," *International Journal* 24 (Autumn 1969) : 726-50.

United States and the country with the largest amount of US direct foreign investment.

Yet even when the intensity and asymmetry of a relationship is specified, *interdependence* remains a vague term. We can clarify some points about it by making a distinction between societal interdependence and policy interdependence. Societal interdependence refers to the extent to which events in one society (not necessarily controlled or monitored by governments) affect events in another. American and Canadian societies are obviously very closely linked, socially as well as economically, with Canada affected more by events within the United States than vice versa. Policy interdependence, by contrast, refers to the extent to which governments are affected by one another's policies so that they react to changes in policy by the other side.

This distinction is crucial in understanding the politics of interdependence. During the past half century, governments have become increasingly sensitive to societal interdependence. As governments attempt to control larger areas of social and economic life, they are less tolerant of disruptions in those patterns of behavior caused by foreign events. Governments, for example, have become increasingly sensitive to changes in interest rates abroad and to transnational flows of funds. Thus even a constant (not to mention a growing) level of societal interdependence is likely to be accompanied by increasing levels of governmental involvement.

The first government to intervene effectively in a transnational system (such as flows of capital or energy across borders) may gain an advantage by being able to rearrange transaction patterns to its benefit. Countervailing action by other governments, however, may nullify that advantage and create a situation of *policy interdependence*, in which the success of each government's efforts to control transnational flows is dependent on the actions of the other government. Succumbing to policy interdependence may be the price one pays for attempting to control societal interdependence. The paradox of complex interdependence is that actions to decrease one type (societal) may lead to increases in another type (policy).

Here the question of political power comes to the fore. Efficacy in achieving governmental purposes under conditions of complex interdependence does not depend simply on devising the proper techniques to cope with nature or with nongovernmental activities. It also depends on being able to persuade or coerce other governments to act in desired ways. How is this determined?

One can think of power in interdependent relationships as stemming in part from patterns of asymmetries in policy interdependence. When actors are asymmetrically interdependent, we expect that the less dependent parties will be able to use their *relative* independence as a source of power. Insofar as negotiations take place within the boundaries of issue areas, patterns of asymmetry, and therefore of relative power resources, may be quite different from one issue area to another. When issue areas become linked, governments may bargain advantages in one issue area for payoffs in another, and outcomes in different issue areas may become much more consistent with one another.

Asymmetrical interdependence is not alone sufficient to explain outcomes, since the actors may be differentially motivated, with some more willing to suffer deprivation than others. Or they may adopt strategies of varying efficacy. For instance, while Canada is more dependent than the United States upon mutual trade (11 percent of GNP compared to 1 percent of GNP), Canadian trade is sufficiently important to the United States (one quarter of US exports) that Canada has a potential weapon for retaliation. The deterrence value of Canada's ability to inflict pain upon the United States would depend upon Canada's will to suffer great pain itself. And this may be the case because of asymmetrical salience—the relationship is more important to Canada than to the United States. Thus asymmetrical interdependence is not a perfect predictor of actors' successes or failures. Nonetheless, it does provide an indication of bargaining advantages initially available to each side.

When we analyze the politics of an issue area, therefore, we want to know (1) what the issues are, (2) what the sources of the issue are and, in particular, whether transnational relations are important in this, and (3) how intense and symmetrical policy interdependence is, given patterns of societal interdependence and the policy goals of the governments concerned.

The last point raises an important issue, since a government may not agree within itself about what its goals are, particularly if the question is not the subject of top-level attention. Indeed, certain governmental subunits may discover that their purposes are closer to the purposes of particular subunits of another government than they are to the goals of other agencies within the same government. As Roger Frank Swanson indicates, American and Canadian military officers and defense officials have often had common interests not shared by civilian agencies in either government. To achieve their goals, they may have to be more concerned with what their own budget bureaus or treasury ministers can do than with the actions of each other.

Thus for each issue it is necessary that we ask where the most important and most persistent lines of policy cleavage are: between governments negotiating more or less as units, or between informal coalitions of agencies in different governments with similar goals. In the latter case, the patterns of interdependence that will determine outcomes will largely be those *within* governments, rather than between them, and questions of bureaucratic power will become of utmost importance. The evidence in the essays in this volume suggests that in energy and direct investment, the basic cleavages are most frequently domestic; in oceans and capital movements, they are most frequently intergovernmental; in environment, they are frequently transnational; and in defense, they have often been transgovernmental.

If policy cleavages run along other than strictly intergovernmental lines, the analyst must investigate communications and coordination patterns particularly closely to see whether transgovernmental relations are in evidence. To what extent are these agencies acting autonomously from central governmental control in their dealings with one another? In Canadian-American relations, direct contacts between subunits of governments are very frequent. The Merchant-Heeney report listed some 31 US federal agencies and 21 Canadian counterparts as "dealing directly with each other," [7] and thousands of direct contacts, in person or by telephone, take place yearly between Canadian and American officials outside of regular embassy channels. We therefore have grounds to suspect that common agency interests may often be realized and acted upon. The essay by Kal J. Holsti and Thomas Allen Levy surveys some of these.

Within the category of transgovernmental relations, it is important to recognize a distinction—which becomes blurred at the margin—between transgovernmental policy coordination and transgovernmental coalition building.[8] The former refers to a range of behavior, from informal communication of working-level officials of different bureaucracies to regularized patterns of policy coordination and consultation. Although there may be no major contradiction between this behavior and central policy positions, a sense of collegiality among officials from particular agencies may develop that affects attitudes, and therefore policy, over a period of time. Communications channels may develop that promote the dissemination of certain ideas and retard the flow of others.

Transgovernmental coalition building, on the other hand, involves the joint use of resources by subunits of different governments (and/or intergovernmental institutions) to determine the outcomes of governmental decisions. To improve their chances of policy success, governmental subunits may attempt to bring actors from other govern-

---

[7] "Canada and the United States—Principles for Partnership," *Department of State Bulletin* 53 (July-September 1965) : 193-208.

[8] For further discussion, see Keohane and Nye cited in note 1 above.

ments into their own decision processes as allies. Given the diversity of interests in the two countries, the analyst can conceive of a large number of potential coalitions (transnational, transgovernmental, and mixed) across the border. In some cases, the potential alliances are so poorly coordinated that we can only speak of tacit coalitions, but in other instances they become active coalitions. For example, on the politics of the trans-Alaskan pipeline discussed particularly by Ted Greenwood, there seems to have been a tacit coalition between some US ecologists, ecologists from British Columbia, and midwestern US consumers favoring the Mackenzie River alternative opposed by the United States executive and some Canadian nationalists. The transnational activities of British Columbia's Member of Parliament David Anderson helped to make at least part of this tacit coalition an active one. It is clear that such behavior constitutes a major deviation from patterns assumed in conventional ways of analyzing world politics.

So far we have been discussing patterns of interaction (intergovernmental or transgovernmental) and possession of political resources (particularly, the direction of asymmetries of interdependence). But it is also necessary to focus on the political process, and particularly on the strategies that actors use in it. Our focus on issues that begin with transnational relations and our intention to conduct analysis by issue area make two questions central to our discussion: (1) How do problems or situations become politicized? (2) To what extent and under what conditions do actors draw linkages between issues, whether within a given issue area or outside of it?

Politicization is an easily misunderstood term, partly because the reality it describes is complex. We must distinguish first between the level of politicization of an issue at a given time, and the process by which an issue may become more or less politicized over time. Secondly, we must distinguish between hierarchical and public aspects of politicization. An issue is more highly politicized in an hierarchical sense when more attention is paid to it at higher levels of government; the measure of public politicization, on the other hand, is the degree and scope of controversiality within the politically relevant strata about what the government should do about it. It is clear that these two dimensions are distinguishable in practice as well as analytically. Defense issues, for instance, may involve hierarchical politicization without significant public politicization, particularly when secrecy is tight, whereas other questions, such as the Trail Smelter issue of the interwar period, may be highly politicized in a public sense before being taken up at high levels of government.

Hierarchical politicization may result simply from governments having inconsistent policy goals on a problem on which their policies are interdependent. Thus, as Gerald Wright and Maureen Appel Molot point out in their article, the United States politicized the capital linkage between the United States and Canada by the measures it took in the 1960s, beginning with the Interest Equalization Tax, to control outflows of capital abroad. Since these measures as originally interpreted conflicted sharply with Canadian aims, a very important intergovernmental policy issue was created. Hierarchical politicization may also stem, however, from the dissatisfaction of top officials with the actions of their subordinates dealing with one another. Swanson's article discusses some issues such as these in the defense area.

Public politicization may very well accompany or follow hierarchical politicization, as in the case of capital controls. Yet in a case such as the issue of American investment, public controversy in Canada preceded and stimulated increased governmental attention. The sources of a publicly politicized issue usually lie not so much in conflicts between governmental policies or government officials but in differences of viewpoint, interest, and ideology among the public at home.

The way in which an issue becomes politicized may be very important in determining how it is handled by the actors concerned. Issues that develop as a result of growing public pressure in one country may be characterized by quite different policies than issues that appear as a result of one government unilaterally taking action that runs counter to the interests of the other. Issues that become politicized as a result of dissatisfaction by top officials with the effects of lower-level governmental or transgovernmental activity are likely to be handled quite differently than either of these. In general, however, it seems plausible to hypothesize that as issues become politicized, transgovernmental relations tend to be inhibited. Higher-level officials will now be involved in the relationship, or parts of the public will be more attentive, or both. A sense of the need for national cohesion may develop. For example, growing controversiality and top-level attention seem to have curtailed transgovernmental interactions among Organization for Economic Cooperation and Development (OCED) countries on monetary policy during the 1960s,[9] and between the United States and Canada on oceans policy as described by Ann L. Hollick in this volume. There were fairly well confirmed reports in 1971, furthermore, that the Nixon-Connally New Economic Policy of 15 August had been accompanied by efforts by Connally and his close associates to restrict the transgovernmental communications between the American and Canadian bureaucracies.[10]

[9] Robert W. Russell, "Transgovernmental Interactions in the International Monetary System," *International Organization* 27 (Autumn 1973) : 431-64.
[10] Personal interview, Ottawa, February 1972.

We also expect that politicization will be important in answering our second principal question about political process: To what extent and under what conditions do actors draw linkages between issues, whether within a given issue area or outside of it? In general, we expect that increased politicization—particularly in the form of greater attention to an issue by high governmental officials—will lead to attempts by one government or the other (or by actors within governments) to link issues to one another. The temptation to draw linkages seems particularly strong for officials of a powerful state, confronted with difficulties in a particular area of concern, as we have seen in American efforts to link military and monetary questions in Europe.

One of the interesting aspects of Canadian-American diplomacy, however, is the relative absence of overt linkages between different issues. A 1971 effort by the US Treasury to link United States acceptance of Canadian oil to Canadian willingness to renegotiate the auto pact was as striking in its rarity as in its ironic timing. In part, this reflects the fact that lower levels of bureaucracies where day-to-day affairs are handled are limited in the scope of issues within their jurisdiction. The absence of overt linkage may also reflect the diversity of interests and actors involved in situations of complex interdependence. Threats of retaliation on an extraneous issue involve mobilization of different sets of actors. Moreover, as Holsti indicates below, the absence of overt linkage seems to be a strategy favored by Canada as a means of limiting American overall preponderance. This avoidance of linkage also helps to explain Canadian wariness about strong bilateral institutions as places where linkage might occur.[11]

If outright linkages are rare, however, implicit linkages are not. The overall structure of relations is scored in decision makers' heads, and there is often a concern for the interaction of issues that are proximate in time (e.g., the auto pact and the magazine tax discussed in the Nye article below) as well as a concern for the effect on the general climate of relations. The linkage process exists, but it is largely an informal one.

Thus far we have discussed actor behavior as well as the nature of the issues and the resources available to actors on those issues. But we are also interested in outcomes: Who gets what? It is very difficult to ascertain benefits accurately, since they depend on the policy

---

[11] The International Joint Commission (IJC) is an interesting exception to this rule because it has developed a tradition of rarely dividing by nationality, a tradition well suited to the transnational pattern of cleavages on many boundary water issues. Thus Canada frequently requests that issues be referred to the IJC, but the US is sometimes unwilling to have issues handled by an institution with a tradition that diminishes US power advantages.

goals one favors. Did Canada "succeed" in negotiations to exempt itself from capital controls, or did the sacrifice of autonomy imply a Canadian defeat? In one sense, Canada won great gains from the 1965 auto pact. But one can also view the auto pact as a tacit coalition between the Canadian government, Canadian auto workers, and United States auto companies on one side and Canadian consumers and some US auto workers on the other side. As Senator Paul Douglas said in favor of an amendment supported by the United Automobile Workers (UAW) requiring a reduction in Canadian automobile prices in 1965, "You may well say that it is none of our business to protect the Canadian consumer . . . but if we don't get an increase in Canadian demand as a result of a lowered price, this increase in Canadian production will have to be shipped across the border to the United States." [12] When this national legislative remedy failed, the UAW took a direct transnational route to discourage the export of jobs to Canada by bargaining with the companies for wage parity across the border. Canadian auto workers profited, but it is not clear that other Canadian workers did. And Canadian nationalists regretted the loss of autonomy for Canadian subsidiaries of the multinational auto firms. Or as Greenwood points out in his article on energy, the Canadian nationalist and the Canadian continentalist currently have very different views on whether Canada will benefit from one arrangement or another for trades in energy.

To summarize, the questions with which readers should approach the essays in this volume if they are interested in understanding the politics of highly interdependent advanced industrial societies include at least the following:

1. What are the chief policy issues between the United States and Canada? To what extent do these arise from transnational relations? And to what extent do the relevant cleavages separate governments as units rather than separate sets of agencies of different governments?
2. What patterns of interdependence, particularly with regard to symmetry, are discernible on these issues, and to what extent are these used as sources of bargaining power by the actors involved?
3. To what extent and under what conditions are transgovernmental relations important between the United States and Canada on these issues?

[12] US Congress, Senate, Committee on Finance, *United States–Canadian Automobile Agreement, Hearings Before the Committee on Finance on H.R. 9042,* 89th Cong., 1st sess., 1965, p. 155.

4. In what ways and under what conditions do issues become politicized, and what effects does this have on transgovernmental relations and on linkages between issues drawn by actors?

5. What seems to be the relative success of the actors involved—governmental, transnational, or subgovernmental—in achieving their purposes on these issues?

Although we attempted to provide guidance to authors, our guidelines did not pose the questions exactly as they are posed above. Furthermore, the facts rarely follow analytical schemes as closely as one would hope, and quite naturally each author has his or her own particular interests and predispositions. Thus we have an imperfect fit between our questions and the data in the articles. Nonetheless, we believe that the following essays have been written from a perspective that sheds a different light on the substantive problems of Canadian-American interdependence, and that presents the Canadian-American case as a fruitful one for thinking about the politics of complex interdependence among advanced industrial societies.

PART II

NATIONAL ATTITUDES

IMPACT OF DOMESTIC POLITICAL FACTORS ON CANADIAN–AMERICAN RELATIONS: CANADA

John W. Holmes

The major difference between Canadians and Americans on the subject of their relationship is in the intensity of their perceptions. There is bound to be conflict between a people who regard the relationship as critical and those who have scarcely noticed the other country. Firmly fixed in the Canadian view is the idea that a *special relationship* has come to an end. When the British contemplated the end of their special relationship with the United States, they were interested in an alternative—association with the European Economic Community (EEC). The problem for Canadians is that no alternative association seems clear, attractive, or promising. In light of their relative comfort in the energy crisis of 1973, however, the need for any special relationship has seemed less urgent.

THE SPECIAL RELATIONSHIP

There has been a notable Canadian ambivalence about the special relationship, and it is not surprising that some outspoken Americans are telling Canadians that they can no longer have their cake and eat it too. That means specifically that they cannot ask for special treatment on the basis of a continental relationship and then reject that relationship when the United States wants to talk about, for example, a continental resources policy.[1] When President Nixon spoke in Ottawa in April 1972, he picked up the fashionable Canadian formula with disturbing alacrity. He said it was time for both peoples "to

John W. Holmes is with the Canadian Institute of International Affairs in Toronto.
[1] Canadians generally regard the proposed Burke-Hartke bill as a menace, but when the Canadian section of the United Steel Workers of America discussed the subject, what they demanded was exemptions for Canada, i.e., protection on a continental basis. *Globe and Mail* (Toronto), 1 June 1973.

move beyond the sentimental rhetoric of the past" and recognize "that we have very separate identities . . . and significant differences," that American policy toward Canada "reflects the new approach we are taking in all our foreign relations" and "that doctrine rests on the premise that mature partners must have autonomous, independent policies." [2] Shrewder observers in Ottawa realized that he was not so much recognizing the Canadian right to independence as proclaiming an American independence of special obligations.

What Canadians forget too readily in the present debate is the terms of their own existence. Canada is an adventure of various communities that did not want to join the United States, a collective experiment in American living under different auspices and with different rules. From the beginning this was recognized as a risky experiment based on "unnatural" economics. It was and remains a defiance of the United States. Americans have come to take a reasonably civilized view of this perverse determination of Canadians to live unto themselves, but Canadians too often give the impression that there is some historic American obligation to support the project. Political annexation seems a dead enough issue, but, given the American belief in the removal of barriers to free enterprise, especially governmental, the boundary must seem to most of them a regrettable anachronism.[3] Canadians can expect Americans to play the international game more or less according to the United Nations Charter which they so strongly recommend for others. Within those rules, however, the United States will pursue its own interests and Canada may pursue its interests as it sees them. Competition and conflict are natural and perpetual. The basic facts have been concealed, especially in the years of alliance, by the stress on common interest. The sense of alliance partnership, the belief that the competition must be moderated by fair dealing and good neighbourliness, is a product of the last half century. Before the Boundary Waters Treaty of 1909 and the establishment of the International Joint Commission, the game was exceedingly rough. The Nixon administration may well lack magnanimity toward Canada, but Canadians may well compare Mr.

[2] Canada, House of Commons, *Debates*, 28th Parliament, 4th sess., vol. 2, 1972, p. 1328.

[3] US Assistant Secretary of State for Economic Affairs Thorp and Undersecretary of State Lovett, 8 March 1948, on a proposal under secret discussion to eliminate trade barriers between the United States and Canada: "The present may offer a unique opportunity of promoting the most efficient utilization of the resources of the North American Continent and knitting the two countries together—an objective of United States foreign policy since the founding of the Republic" (US Department of State, *Foreign Relations of the United States 1948*, vol. 9: *The Western Hemisphere* [Washington, D.C.: US Government Printing Office, 1972], p. 406).

Nixon's pledge to Mr. Trudeau in 1971—that the United States did not insist on a surplus trade balance—with the remarks about Canada's lack of a future made not only by Mr. Seward in the 1860s but by Mr. Taft in 1911. Canadians who make a villain of John Connally and Senator Hartke have forgotten those nasties of the thirties, Smoot and Hawley. On the other side, statements of Canadian politicians about Yankee greed and immorality were in the not too distant past a good deal more devastating than the somewhat restrained regret expressed by the Canadian parliamentarians over the bombing of North Vietnam in 1973. Plus ça change, plus il n'est pas exactement la même chose.

Even if one regards the present situation as a cyclical phenomenon, it is necessary to look for new factors. Because the two countries are less isolated from each other and the world at large, the proportions of the problems are enormously greater, and quantitative factors may have become qualitative. Among the differences the following may be noted.

END OF THE ATLANTIC TRIANGLE

Canada is now a more independent country than it was during previous periods of confrontation. A feeling of aloneness, of being the outer one, has been an important aspect of the Canadian political perception in recent years. For a century or more Canadians have had an ambiguous attitude toward the United States—seeing it as protector and as threat. They regarded themselves as an integral part of an Anglo-American world that guaranteed them security and some prosperity. Within that world their powerful protectors checked each other. British power was a counterweight that deterred the United States, even if the British on occasion sacrificed pieces of Canadian territory in the broader interest of preserving this special relationship between Republic and Empire. The movement of Britain into the EEC may or may not have important economic implications for Canada. It has had psychic effects. The British percentage of Canadian trade declined to such an extent in the last decade or so that the actual move into the Community was less worrying than had earlier been expected, but it was the fact of that decline that increased the Canadian feeling of alienation. The idea of the Atlantic Community was for Canadians an extension of the concept of shelter in the Anglo-American world. And Western Europe was seen also as the counterweight that Britain and the Empire once provided. Ottawa officialdom still clings to the idea of Europe as a counterweight in economics and in international diplomacy. Most Canadians would welcome such a factor if they could believe in its strength. Japan and other Pacific countries are looked at wistfully. Trade with all these areas does increase, but not in percentages compared with North American continental trade. The sense of being left dependent on a giant, especially a giant who may be altering his familiar personality, tends to polarize Canadian opinion. In a minority it induces a determination for drastic steps toward autarky, and in another minority it induces a disposition to give up resistance. Most Canadians are still looking for broader internationalist arrangements, aware, however, that the old triangular pattern is inadequate and they are more than ever obliged to fight for themselves in a chaotic world.

INCREASING STRENGTH AND VULNERABILITY

Another change of importance is the sheer economic strength of Canada at a time when this is a more salient factor than military power. This strength is seldom grasped by Canadians or others because it is always juxtaposed against that of a superpower rather than estimated with its peer group. Its GNP, projected at over $130 billion in 1974, and a total international trade one-third that of the United States make it one of the major commercial powers in the world, with a considerable voice in international monetary questions as well. Being a responsible member of the small community of states that can influence decision making, realizing more and more that Canadian interests in the world are unique, coincidental often with those of the United States but not sufficiently so to justify absorption into a bloc, has encouraged, at least in official circles, a new and tougher internationalism.[4] The shift of international priority from security to economics increases Canada's influence and its solitude. On many issues of the seventies, the seabed, maritime pollution, foreign investment, and the control of multinational corporations, Canada's major antagonists are more likely to be its military allies than its assumed military antagonists with which its economic relations are relatively uncomplicated. The need to find allies all over the world on an ad hoc basis to strengthen the Canadian hand in such matters has encouraged a new boldness in Canadian diplomacy vis-à-vis the United States.[5] As

[4] See, for example, Allan Gotlieb and Charles Dalfen, "National Jurisdiction and International Responsibility: New Canadian Approaches to International Law," *American Journal of International Law* 67 (July 1973): 229-58. In the currently fashionable anxiety to emphasize, as in the United States, that Canadian foreign policy is being dictated now by tough-minded national interests rather than by soft-minded internationalism as in the past, the extent to which the national interest was in fact subordinated to do-goodism by previous governments has been considerably exaggerated. The same argument may well apply in the United States, but the two mythologies are political forces nevertheless.

[5] For a contradictory aspect of this situation, however, see p. 616.

this is undertaken in defence of identifiable national interests about which Canadian politicians are concerned, this boldness is likely to have a stronger political base than past challenges to US policies on broad international issues such as China or nuclear weapons.

The paradox for Canada is that its strength increases its vulnerability. Maintaining its greater industrial power makes Canada all the more dependent on factors beyond its control.

This vulnerability, however, is more vividly perceived in economic than in military calculations, where a sense of dependence is probably decreasing. The Canadian contribution to collective defence has been maintained in principle, but in practice it consists of token contributions abroad and increasing emphasis on defence of the vast home base as a part of the whole alliance area. The feeling of dependence on the United States for protection, however, has been counteracted by a declining awareness of a military threat. The view that Canada is indebted to the United States for its defence is less persuasive than it was, partly because of an increasing alienation from United States military operations and partly because of the shift of a new generation to the view that nuclear deterrence is a game, played by superpowers with each other, which allows powers that cannot defend themselves anyway to stop spending money uselessly trying to do so. The almost unchallenged assumption of twenty years ago—that if the United States were at war, Canada would be at war—has lost credibility, largely as a result of United States unilateral activities in Indochina. Because of the decline in the value of Canadian soil for the defence of the United States in a missile age, defence pressures from the Pentagon are less than they once were. It is a situation, however, that is not necessarily permanent. Technological changes may well alter the Pentagon's concept of the part Canada could and should play in North American defence. A challenge over the new Air Warning and Control System could come shortly in fact. Current assumptions about détente could also be shattered by shifts or accidents in the configuration of powers, and in a time of fear there seems little doubt that Canadians would return to the instinct to find shelter with friends. In times of crisis, they would as usual want to play honourably their own part, and as usual they would probably have to start again from close to scratch, their military capacity having again been reduced to the barest minimum. It is even harder politically for a country like Canada, whose military power is bound to be supplementary, to maintain that power in a time when détente is assumed than for a country like the United States with the capacity for decisive military power. However, although the assault on alliance mindedness has been loud and righteous in recent years, it does not seem to have shaken the convictions or instincts of political leaders or a majority of their electors. Cooperation with conventional weapons continues. Neither withdrawal from NATO or of more troops from Europe nor disbandment of the North American Air Defence Command (NORAD) are under serious consideration in Ottawa.

The Canadian vulnerability is, like the Japanese, largely economic. The more prosperous it becomes, the more it depends on foreign trade and therefore the more vulnerable is the high standard of living. The increasing dependence on the United States market, and in particular on the auto pact, is a constant concern that conditions a great deal of Canadian foreign policy. It is probably a more important inhibition than the foreign investment on which the nationalists concentrate. It would be wrong to suggest that Canadian policy on, for example, service in the International Commission of Control and Supervision in Vietnam was decided by this concern over the vulnerability of the Canadian economy to American action. However, it was a factor much discussed at the time, and it is a factor for consideration in weighing the advantages and disadvantages of many issues. There are always voices in Parliament saying out loud or more often *sotto voce* that Canada should put its own direct interests in Washington ahead of international obligations. Herein lies a dilemma for any Canadian government. It must bear in mind the danger that can be done to Canadian interests by a hostile Congress or administration in Washington, but it must maintain the posture of a government pursuing a strong and independent Canadian policy. Its critics can be counted on to denounce it for one sin or the other. It is not only vis-à-vis the United States that the government of a major commercial power has to exercise discretion. Arab oil producers and Chinese wheat buyers require more consideration than in the days when Canada could be the free middle spirit in the UN.

CONTINENTALIST PRESSURES

On economic questions Ottawa's position is still aggressively internationalist. The spirit of Article 2 of NATO is strong—the conviction that the Western alliance will founder if its members do not restrain their competition—and Henry Kissinger is regarded as an important convert to the traditional Canadian position. In practice, however, this almost doctrinaire approach is undermined by suspicion that the Europeans and the US Congress will not play that way. The idea of Canada as martyr to its high principles is a vision seen more clearly in Ottawa than in Washington, Brussels, or Canberra. As a fallback from internationalism there is some sense of defensive continentalism in the country at large. The Canadian business community is susceptible to prevailing winds of opinion in the American business community. The hostility that this US community and its political spokesmen feel toward the Japanese, the Europeans, and other people who, by means of cheap labour and other un-American activities, are threatening the good folk on the North American continent has its appeal. Japanese trade with Canada is now second only to that with the United States, but it is open to even stronger criticism in that Japan rejects Canadian manufactures and soaks up Canadian resources. The idea of a common front in Fortress America has its attractions in Canada. The Ottawa establishment resists it in favour of wider internationalism, and there seems little doubt that the continentalist implications run contrary to what articulate Canadians would like. However, if the going gets rougher, more Canadians may decide, although reluctantly, that this is the option to back. And so, as the sense of standing together against a military threat from the Communist powers has diminished, a new concept of continental defence in the realm of economics, a realm, incidentally, where Canada could have a more influential role than it could ever have in defence, may take its place. In such an atmosphere the pressures for continental management, particularly in the resources sphere, could become less resistible.

The extent to which transnational integration has gone in practice without any government direction makes Canadians nervous. A fear that the situation is out of control tends to discourage governments' efforts to try, but the feeling that the Canadian community is being burrowed away forces them to see what could be done. The idea that Canadian citizens are being locked into a computer web that puts their personal lives on file for instantaneous transmission to Pittsburgh or Chicago or San Clemente did prompt efforts in Ottawa to preserve some national privacy in the computer industry. The Ontario government is investigating the transmission of information from private security companies to their United States head offices, and it has shown some interest in seeing that school children are reared on Canadian textbooks. After much agonizing consideration the Trudeau government came up with a proposal for an agency to review foreign take-overs of Canadian companies. However, as the minister of finance assured a New York audience, "It's not a dam, it's a filter." As the time for action has come, both federal and provincial governments are facing the bewildering complexities of unraveling the cobweb.

One form of continentalist pressure that has traditionally conditioned Canadian calculations is diminishing somewhat. This is the fear that the Canadian standard of living can never be allowed to fall far below that of the United States lest Canadians pack up and move south. New factors are affecting the balance. Even in periods of depression and considerable inequality, Canadians were sustained in their long experiment by loyalty to their own political tradition and the desire to maintain what seemed to them, if not to others, a reality —their own way and quality of life. The flow of immigration has in fact altered. In recent years more Americans have moved to Canada than Canadians to the United States.[6] The brain drain flows in both directions. Whether this reversal is attributable to factors associated with the Vietnam War remains to be seen.[7] The United States, even in turmoil, retains its fascination for many Canadians who find even its sin and conflict big-time compared with their own pale imitations. Nevertheless, the advantages of living in a less turbulent country at slightly less pay are now more obvious. There is also a rejection of American values which, ironically, is largely inspired by Americans criticizing their own country. The fact that Canadians, although to a lesser extent than Europeans, tend to lump together as American the features of modern society that they do not like is grossly unfair but politically significant. The more bucolic image of Canada, both among Americans and Canadians, is partly myth, but it has its effect. Racial strife and other factors in the United States have increased the differentiation between Canadian and American cities in fact as well as in fancy. Living in Toronto and living in Cleveland are not as much alike as they once were. Windsor is less a suburb of Detroit because Windsorites are afraid to cross the river.

THE NEW CANADIAN NATIONALISM

Contributing to this differentiation is a wave of Canadian nationalism different from anything previous. For one thing, it is for anglophone Canadians unilateral Canadianism untempered by multilateral imperial loyalties. For Quebeckers it is often not tempered even by Canadian loyalties. It is fiercest among the young. It ranges from a heightened awareness among the moderates of the values of the Canadian tradition and a desire to strengthen it against unattractive pressures not only from abroad but also from within to an irrational Americanophobia which is less in the Canadian tradition. In fact, the more neurotic Canadian nationalism has a distinctly American accent. Much of its dogma is, in the most colonial tradition, mindlessly transplanted from the American Left. Denunciations of the United States in the glottal tones and arid verbiage of lesser American graduate schools become, simply by hopping the border,

---

[6] For statistics, see footnote 17.
[7] Certainly the popular assumption that most recent American immigrants to Canada were draft dodgers has been widely exaggerated.

nationalist rather than antinationalist. Even less neurotic Canadian nationalists have always been affected by the cultural impact of American style nationalism, transferring the same credos, pledges, and convictions about government to a Canadian flag and an unwritten Canadian constitution for which they are peculiarly unsuited. The new manifestations are more intense and intolerant and directed toward rousing ill will rather than good.

Out of this confused nationalist debate, however, are emerging some genuine Canadian values. Some of these are excessively historical-romantical and some needlessly reject an American cultural heritage that has been shared rather than imposed. Nevertheless, there is a better understanding of the Canadian way of life, based perhaps on a recognition that the political identity of Canada is clear even if the cultural identity is perhaps subsystemic. The Canadian confederation was not an imitation of the American but a response to the American Civil War. It has developed more directly from its British roots and has its own strengths and weaknesses which make even good American examples inapplicable. The loose nature of the Canadian federation is its weakness, but it is also being perceived as its strength in an age when government is becoming colossal. It is the urban challenge and the challenge of regional governments, not only Quebec but the western provinces as well, to the federal structure that have forced Canadians into an argument about their own way of government, thus producing a curiously unifying effect. The debate does emphasize the frontiers between the provinces and between the provinces and the federal government, but because it is a demicontinental rather than a continental preoccupation, it draws an even heavier line along the 49th parallel. The greatest danger to the Canadian identity is a preoccupation with American issues to such an extent that Canadians lose sight of their individuality. The problems of Canadian federation force Canadians to concentrate on issues for which the United States experience is largely irrelevant.[8]

THE FEDERAL-PROVINCIAL FACTOR

Division of responsibility between federal and provincial governments, particularly in such important areas as resources and invest-

---

[8] For example, the move to integrated schools has been a great goal of liberals in the United States. In Quebec, Ontario, or New Brunswick, any threat to the right of the English and French to their own schools would be regarded as reactionary. Paradoxically also, it is the factor of the United States as an outside challenge that makes the problems of the Canadian confederation so different from those of the United States, which has no such challenge. The argument for governmental control of communications, for example, has no counterpart in the United States.

ment, and the relative decline of federal power are widely believed to have weakened Canada considerably in its effort to manage a national policy that could guarantee independence. There is justification for this view. The federal government is constantly being told that it must have a resources policy, an industrial policy, and a population policy if it is to play its cards intelligently vis-à-vis the United States and in the world at large. The government is apparently weakened by two factors. In the first place there are the divisive interests of the provinces. In the second place the regionalization of Canadian issues in politics has resulted in an almost chronic situation of minority government. The incapacity of a minority government to take bold risks in the long-range interest is obvious. In the present nationalist mood of the electorate, at least as diagnosed by the rhetoricians of all parties, a posture of resistance to the United States must be maintained.[9] A problem, however, is that the need to maintain such a posture makes difficult the constructive compromise, conceding minimum disadvantage for a greater advantage, regarding continental relations not as a zero-sum game but as a process of bargaining and manipulating for mutual profit.[10] Yet Canadians are adjusting, as many Western Europeans have, to minority government, which has been for some years and is likely to be for many more the normal way of holding together a sprawling people. The crisis over oil exports in the autumn of 1973 revealed inevitable conflicts of interest between the oil-producing and oil-consuming provinces and differences of attitude toward sales to the United States. However, the need for the government to put together an acceptable national policy was all the more clear because it had to be conciliatory to stay in office.

It has become conventional to say that Canadian nationalism is largely confined to Ontario, that it is the expression of a confident and sophisticated industrial area which feels capable of standing on its own feet, and that it is resisted by less favoured provinces that want foreign investment, growth, jobs, industrial development, and all those things they think can come from welcoming United States capital. There is truth in this assumption, but there is a danger now of its being repeated as an absolute truth. Among intellectuals, nationalism

[9] Not to be confused with genuine anti-Americanism. Resistance to the United States is a sine qua non of the existence of Canada. It does not require a belief that the United States is sinful or intentionally hostile. It emphasizes differentiation rather than superiority. Anti-Americanism is more ideological, a conviction of the far Left or far Right or far liberal that the United States is based on false premises or has grown degenerate.

[10] There is evidence, for example, that the government could improve the Canadian-US relationship on trade questions by conceding certain safeguards of the auto pact that have ceased to be meaningful but it does not dare risk accusation from the opposition parties of giving in to US pressure.

is as strong in Edmonton as Toronto. Apart from Ontario there are various regional or provincial assertions of nationalism, directed partly against Ontario but not basically continentalist in thrust. Alberta and British Columbia have been regarded as the provinces with the strongest American orientation. But they are under new management. So, in fact, are all the provinces. The old set of demagogic provincial premiers ("provochial," they have been called) has in the last few years been replaced by a set of pragmatic, managerial types, more disposed to pay due regard to the national interest than were their predecessors. Three of the four western premiers, where continentalism is believed to be most rampant, are from the New Democratic party, which is the most anticontinentalist of all the parties. Premier Barrett (NDP) of British Columbia, it is true, went direct to Washington to talk with the authorities there, but with the intention of defying them on the Alaska pipeline rather than snuggling closer. He has taken a tough line about the export of British Columbian water to Washington State. Premier Lougheed of Alberta, a Conservative, challenged not only Ontario but to a greater extent the United States with his insistence on more returns for Alberta's energy resources. He has struck a nationalist note with an Alberta accent and showed a willingness to accept a national priority. The Social Crediters, who have been thrown out of power in Alberta and BC, were far more American and continentalist in their philosophy.

The north-south industrial ties seem to be growing stronger, but there is a countervailing force. It was once the St. Lawrence system, extended to the Pacific by the railways, that created a Canadian economy. The east-west ties of trade and people are deeply rooted. The phenomenon that now holds together Canadians (to some extent against their will) may be less the St. Lawrence route than the extraordinary phenomenon of Toronto, one of the fastest growing metropolitan areas in the world, whose economic vitality retains its magnetic effect on businessmen and industry, on the professional and nonprofessional labour force from Vancouver to Halifax. To a lesser extent this is true in the arts as well—for Anglo-Canadians. Whether Toronto is the capital of an independent system or a subsystem attached to New York and Chicago, it is of some consequence that it is still to a considerable extent a transcontinental system of its own.[11] The relative decline of Montreal, however, exacerbates internal tension. The greatest threat to Canadian independence is that its divisions should increasingly associate themselves with regions in the

---

[11] When the United States went on year-long daylight saving time in January 1974, the other provinces waited for Ontario's decision, and when Ontario decided not to follow the US example, British Columbia reversed its decision to do so.

United States so that for all practical purposes the continent is divided not into two countries but into subdivisions of an essentially continental society and economy.[12] (See Gilpin's essay in this volume.)

FEAR OF AMERICAN NATIONALISM

The provinces, and particularly the poorer provinces, have as much as Ottawa to fear from the rough attitude taken by members of Congress and by Washington officials toward Canadian federal and provincial policies to widen the geographical base of industrial development within Canada. When special tax concessions were given to the Michelin Tire Company to build a plant in Nova Scotia rather than in central Canada, the United States Treasury Department imposed countervailing duties on its export of tires to the United States. The rules of the game seemed unclear, or unfairly applied, since the United States Congress had already passed legislation in 1971 authorizing Domestic International Sales Corporations (DISC). Under this law comparable tax incentives were made available to American companies to increase exports if they met certain conditions. American officials have made it very plain to Canadians that they are not prepared to take a benevolent view of what they call Canada's "industrial strategy" if it is contrary to their perception of the American national interest. As the "industrial strategy" that the Canadian electorate increasingly demands includes regional development as well as corporate taxation and foreign take-over legislation, there could well be a basic confrontation and a trial of strength.

Canadians have been able with some success, particularly in the postwar years, to argue with American officials that they should restrain their power so that a more prosperous good neighbour could establish itself as a trading partner. That plea is less likely to be heeded when those officials regard Canadians as prosperous enough to look after their own interests. When Americans talk about a more mature relationship, the message reaches Ottawa loud and clear. One aspect of this mature relationship seems to be a greater disposition on both sides to shift the argument into multilateral forums where no special relationship applies and where allies from other continents can be enlisted by both sides.[13] This is notably the case over the sea and seabed controversies (see Hollick in this volume).

---

[12] A straw in the wind could be the agreement between premiers and governors of the Atlantic provinces and the New England states, meeting in August 1973, to press their respective governments to allow a free flow of power, generated in Canada, between the two regions. *Globe and Mail* (Toronto), 17 August 1973.

[13] See particularly a report on United States tactics in the *Globe and Mail* (Toronto), 27 June 1973.

The shift toward nationalist positions on almost all fronts in Canada in the early 1970s has been to a large extent a response to what Canadians widely regarded as an assertion of nationalism [14] in the United States. Members of the Canadian business community who, in Toronto and elsewhere, have on the whole deplored economic nationalism as a left-wing aberration have been shedding some of their hopes and expectations about partnership. It is less easy to argue now that the best way for Canada is the way of economic integration, because the United States looks less prosperous and much less disposed to share anything but its shortages with a partner. There is hardly a consensus in Canada on this much debated subject, but consensus may be a little closer. The fortunes of the extreme nationalists of the "Waffle" Left have declined considerably, but the bourgeoisie are being radicalized, in a moderate Canadian way of course. They are not disposed to find socialism and nationalization the key to Canadian independence. They are impressed, however, and alarmed by the roughness of the Nixon administration. The special relationship they have favoured seems to have been ruled out by the current leadership in Washington. Many business leaders are pressing the government toward toughening its bargaining position, even though this is seen within the framework of a civil continental association rather than the noisy confrontation encouraged by the more leftish nationalists.

THE CONCEPT OF NORTH AMERICA

The Canadian problem is partly semantic. For instance, a Dutchman can call himself a Dutchman and a European without confusion. A Canadian is unable to use the term *American* to describe the cultural community of which he is a historic part rather than a subjugated victim. Too much identification with North America, on the other hand, submerges the Canadian individuality. *Continentalism* is a pejorative term in Canada whereas elsewhere there is a wide, if not very well based, belief that it is the blessed wave of the future. Even those in Canada who would like some joint management of resources, perhaps a North American free-trade or common market area, are wary about being called continentalists. Statements by Mr. Nixon and others that they would like to discuss with Canada a continental resources policy are regarded as sinister. Americans think of such proposals as equitable because they have in mind a fair division of

---

[14] It is a word Americans tend to use only about other countries, but Canadians do not see much difference between the increasing emphasis on US interests and what Americans pejoratively call nationalism in Canada.

resources. They do not realize the system's bias inherent in any scheme of sharing when one element is ten times larger than the other. Canadians realize this with their historic instincts. Americans have been vague about what they mean by a continental resources policy, and Canadians are so frightened by the concept that they do not want to be seen considering what may be under any other rubric sensible proposals.

The strong Canadian preference remains for bodies like the International Joint Commission, which has equal representation and is relatively apolitical (see Holsti and Levy's essay in this volume). Its function is to find formulas for mutual advantage and recommend these to the two sovereign governments rather than to impose them. The complexity of border issues, pollution in the Great Lakes for example, is raising the frequent question of whether the time has come for international authorities that can impose their will. Many of these subjects come under provincial or state jurisdiction and would seem to provide opportunities for ad hoc, bilateral, transborder agreements that do not challenge the Canadian resistance on the federal level to continental institutions (see Holsti and Levy in this volume). There are usually ramifications, however, that affect federal control over national resources. Canadian resistance to extending the institutional framework is reinforced by the worry that federal power is itself disintegrating. This fear may have made Canadians rigid when there is a requirement for imaginative improvisation and experimentation with national and even continental institutions. Canadian unity has been one of the false gods of Canadian politics of late. The flexibility achieved in Canada by the growing responsibility and competence of the provincial governments should be seen as an assertion of the Canadian way of life. It provides grass roots interest in Canadian independence and a stronger disposition to preserve the sacred Canadian constitutional principle of looseness against the centripetal forces in the continent. It is in the Canadian tradition for citizens to want to preserve the Canadian framework in order to live more securely as Quebeckers or Nova Scotians or British Columbians.

A problem for Canadians on the world scene, however, is presented by an increasing tendency in Europe and elsewhere to regard North America as an entity. The EEC presumptuously considers itself an entity called Europe. Being primarily interested in the United States but vaguely conscious of Canada, the EEC posits an entity called North America that it assumes, for convenience and in the interest of symmetry, speaks with a single voice because it has a common interest. Canada has many interests coincidental with those of the United States—freer entry to the Japanese and EEC markets being among them. But on a large number of important issues, from maritime regulations to foreign aid or relations with India or Vietnam, its position varies from contradictory to divergent. In many trade and other questions its relationship with the United States is competitive. In official or unofficial discussions involving, as is so often the case at present, Europe, North America, and Japan, Canada must resist being lumped as North America not from a petty desire to show the flag but because it would be a sacrifice of Canadian interests to allow the Washington government or any group of private Americans to speak for North America. There is not and cannot be a Brussels in North America. As far as culture and society are concerned, there are sound reasons for talking about North America as there are for talking about Europe. There is an unfortunate tendency, however, to ignore the difference between common issues and values and coincidental issues and values. What matters most in this context is not the similarities of accent and dress but the difference in national interests of two countries and the fact of two separate governments with no common institution. It cannot be taken for granted, for example, that Canadian interests would be served by a North American position on Middle Eastern oil, although on this or other subjects there is always the possibility of working out a common front on an ad hoc basis with the United States as with Japan or Australia.

So while international pressures and the mood of the times drive Canadians toward a continental identity, they also stimulate resistance. The rise of nationalism in the sixties has been partly a felt need to reject the conventional wisdom of the rest of the Western world and of Manifest Destiny in the guise of Frankenstein. A problem of the seventies is that an odd man out risks being regarded as a tiresome bore. He is alienated from his friends because his problems are so often very different from theirs.

QUEBEC

Most of what has been said here about popular attitudes describes English-speaking Canada in particular. It would probably apply to most of the million or so francophones outside Quebec. Some attitudes would be shared by many francophone Quebeckers. This is not a time when there are wide divisions on foreign policy among those Canadians, liberal or conservative, eastern or western, anglophone or francophone, who think in terms of a federal Canada. The wide division is between those who think of Quebec and Canada as destined to have separate existences in the community of states and those who do not. Even among separatists, however, there are those who think of hostile separation and those, probably a majority, who assume some kind of special relationship with Canada—and presumably also some sharing in special relationships with the United States. In the meantime Quebec has its own form of nationalism that is not identified with Canadian nationalism, although an indeterminate proportion of voting Quebeckers would not consider their own nationalism and that of Canada incompatible and would prefer, with varying degrees of skepticism, to share also in a Canadian nationalism that was reasonably bilingual and bicultural. The attitude of the Quebec nationalist to English Canadians on the grounds of their "economic domination," "arrogance," and "neglect of French Canada" is remarkably similar to the attitude of English-Canadian nationalists toward the United States. The Quebec nationalist tends to be contemptuous of the English Canadian's nationalism and minimizes his identity, and the English-Canadian nationalist is frustrated because the Quebec nationalist will not make common cause.

Paradoxically, however, one may argue that there is in 1974 less confrontation and more separation, and perhaps that is cause and effect. Economic rather than constitutional issues are now dominant; and there is, for the time being at least, less sense of crisis, although the relationship between economic and constitutional issues is by no means disregarded. Issues such as the energy crisis tend to emphasize the importance to Quebeckers of a healthy national economy, a fact reflected in the support given the Bourassa government in the provincial election of 1973. Emphasis is now on the cultural identity of Quebec, the flowering of which raises few questions affecting Canadian-American relations. The intelligentsia of Quebec live just about as separate and independent an existence as they would in their own state. Other Canadians are adjusting to this fact of life and, inspired to some extent by the Quebec example, have been making rapid strides in the creation of a more indigenous culture of their own. An unprecedented surge of drama, cinema, and literature, based on the experience of Newfoundland or Toronto or the Yukon rather than a mythical Canada or a revamped Surrey or Illinois, has in the past year or so given the Anglo-Canadians more self-confidence; the works are less preoccupied with the theme of survival from the Yankees and therefore less boring. Quebec nationalism is becoming less French, more native, and therefore more self-confident, less petty, and more serene. It has rediscovered its rich sense of humour and has ceased to reject its own language, American French or *joual*. This is healthy except that *joual* is so little comprehensible even to bilingual Anglo-Canadians, let alone Frenchmen or Americans, that it does in some ways isolate Quebec from all its neighbours. It is a private joke, like Switzerdietsch. The neighbours, however, have some reason to hope that Canadian culture, of both communities, will grow more rewarding and less obnoxious.

Attitudes in Quebec toward the United States vary considerably. Quebeckers accept their North American destiny. Although dedication to the preservation of a French-language culture is basic, France is of declining importance. Resentment of Parisian snobbery is an emotional element in Quebec nationalism. The English Canadians and the French rather than the Americans and the British are the butts of the Montreal chansonniers. The standard of living and much of the way of life of the Quebeckers are North American, and they are more willing than English Canadians to acknowledge this fact because they have less fear of their identity. Members of the large middle class of Quebec who drive their big cars off to Miami as do other North Americans have a pretty relaxed view of the United States. On the left wing of the separatist movement, the antipathy to the United States is expressed in the conventional language of Guevarists, but it is directed with even more bitterness against Anglo-Canadian capitalists. On the conservative wing are less revolutionary leaders, some of whom see in the United States a counterweight to English Canada. Proposals for an economic union or free-trade agreement with the United States have been put forward.[15] For some it may be a flirtation intended to prod and irritate an arrogant and neglectful spouse. The provincial Liberal government has frequently stated its opposition to the Canadian nationalists who would deny American investment, although in its anxiety to protect the Quebec economy it is nervous about American as well as Ontario domination. This Quebec view is identifiable with the view of other less favoured provinces, but suspicion of Ontario does not make them all avid continentalists. They are less confident than the Ontario industrialists of their ability to compete internationally. There is probably less anti-Americanism in Quebec than elsewhere in Canada, but there is less identification with the United States.

Except from a radical minority, Quebec nationalists have not felt much warmth or encouragement from Americans. The tendency in the United States to identify Quebec nationalism with the Front d'Liberation du Québec (FLQ) and Cuban mischief is a gross oversimplification that discourages the moderate Quebec independentists from a dialogue with the southern neighbours with whom they have to live whether federated or not. From the point of view of other Canadians, it is less mischievous than would be the rousing of American sentimentalism about an oppressed minority. Although anti-American Canadian nationalists dearly love to see CIA plots in Quebec, there has been no convincing evidence of any official or unofficial

[15] See Rodrigue Tremblay, *Indépendence et marché commun, Québec-Etats-Unis* (Montréal: Editions du jour, 1970).

American dispositions to play with separatists. Franco-Americans of New England seem even less disposed than Franco-Ontarians or Acadians to favour the Parti Québécois. Fear in Washington of a Quebec Cuba would presumably, if a crisis arose, lead any American administration to support a Canadian federal position. The Quebec situation, however, is so volatile that one does not know in what form confrontation might present itself. It may well not present itself at all. Canada may just go on in its well-known preference for evolution rather than revolution but evolve itself into something that does not look much like the Canada of today. The relationship of Canada and Quebec to the United States is bound to be a factor in the calculations or negotiations about Quebec's position vis-à-vis the rest of Canada, a unifying or a divisive issue among Canadians and Canadiens. The evolution is not likely to be placid, and given the very large American interests in Quebec and in Canada as a whole, the United States government and Americans in general may find it harder to maintain a totally neutral position. If their relations with Ottawa become nasty, as they may, temptations could be less resistible. Even not very well founded suspicions among English Canadians that American official or private interests were playing the separatist game could increase tension. (There is more suspicion at present of their playing with Alberta.)

A factor of importance to the continental relationship is that the strong Quebec stand on its social, economic, and cultural powers is being matched or supported by other provinces. There is a historic Ontario-Quebec axis vis-à-vis Ottawa or the western provinces. These forces cut across the idea of an Anglo-French confrontation, and they provide the possibility of accommodating Quebec quasi independence in a quasi-federal structure. As suggested above, the conventional view that the federal-provincial division of powers weakens Canadian resistance to the forces of continentalism depends on how one looks at it. The finding of a formula for a relatively independent and reasonably contented Quebec in a loose federation would strengthen the Canadian position. Canadian resistance to continental suction has been weakened by a lack of confidence in the future of the country as an entity. Part of this has been the association Canadian nationalists have tended to make between a strong Canada, national unity, and the affirmation of the federal power. This position is no longer tenable. Among other things, the Quebec nationalist has forced the Canadian nationalist to an agonizing reappraisal of the nature of Canada's political virtue. Some of the latter's more dogmatic assumptions about the management of the Canadian–United States relationship may be shaken up in the process.

THE NEW FACTOR: RESOURCES AND POPULATION

We seem to be on the verge of conceptual changes, both in the facts governing the relationship and in attitudes, requiring rapid adjustments of policy. They are related to altered attitudes in the world at large to growth and to the new Malthusianism. Typical of the impact is the shift within one year, 1973, of the nationalist Canadian complaint that the United States imposes unfair restrictions on imports of energy resources (see Greenwood's essay in this volume) and agricultural produce from Canada to the demand that Americans be prevented from draining Canada of the materials that its citizens need to maintain the standard of living to which they have an independent right. At the same time, the American grievances have shifted from Canadian advantage in the balance of trade to Canadian reluctance to sell energy resources. Policymakers find it difficult to see the long-term interest clearly as their attitudes to buying and selling fluctuate. Only dimly foreseen at present are the implications for traditional attitudes to population as well as resources.[16] The extremely unequal distribution of population on the continent has always been a worry to Canada, but it has not been a serious source of friction between the two countries while there was relatively free movement across the border. United States doubts about an increase of its own population have been apparent for some time and for understandable reasons. The new factor is that Canada, of all countries, is having second thoughts about an increasing population because of compulsive urbanization, endemic unemployment, and the ecology factor. To citizens of a crowded world, including Americans, such an attitude must seem inexcusable. The Canadian attitude is getting to be something like that of the Swiss, a nervous desire to protect a way of life and standard of living against too many people who want to share in it. Canadians had nourished for so long the myth of victimization that they were slow to realize that a mere 22 million people have a very good thing going for them.

What could provide, therefore, an important domestic political factor is the emergence of the United States in the past few years as the largest source of immigration to Canada.[17] The irritation about draft dodgers is, it is to be hoped, over. Ill feeling has been roused

[16] The Canadian percentage of the total population of North America (north of the Rio Grande) is rising rapidly. At the beginning of the century it was 6.6 percent. In the decade of the sixties it rose from 9.2 percent to 9.6 percent.

[17] Immigrants in 1972 from four largest sources: United States—22,618; United Kingdom—18,161; Portugal—8,737; Hong Kong—6,297. According to the 1973 annual report of the visa office of the US Department of State, Canadian immigration to the United States has declined steadily from 40,013 in 1965 to 7,278 in 1973.

among some Canadians by the fact that it is easier for an American to immigrate to Canada than for a Canadian to get into the United States and take employment. Canadian nationalists, however, are not unhappy with the latter provision. One may foresee a surge of Americans from their crowded and polluted cities toward the Canadian "wilderness." The idea that Canada is a land of wide open spaces for settlement is contradicted by the fact that Canadians themselves are leaving the land to crowd the cities, and that is where the immigrants go as well. This romantic motivation for moving north may be less important than a practical reason for moving to a country where fuel is more plentiful. The irritation over the Canadian permissiveness in admitting American "delinquents" may be replaced by anger over the solid Americans Canada will begin to keep out.

Americans have many advantages as immigrants, along with one disadvantage. They are the immigrants least disposed to realize that Canada is a country unlike the one they have left. They are often benevolent missionaries who want to bring Canada up to date in their image. Already their well-intentioned desire to "modernize" Canadian universities has inspired resentment of some political consequence. Some of them want to turn Canada into their own idea of anti-America. Either way old Canada would be engulfed. English Canada was, of course, a creation of American refugees, but 300 years of separate history has created a state dedicated to something more positive than simple opposition to American institutions. Waves of immigrants, including American immigrants, have been absorbed over two centuries. The Americans continue to supply a special kind of zeal that the more relaxed native Canadians appreciate and tolerate—up to a point. The present 22 million, by no means all of whom are native born, could be swamped. Persistent unemployment and new attitudes to population growth indicate a trend in Canada to more restricted immigration. Pressures of illegal immigration and the painful readjustment it is forcing in attitudes to population are creating one of the major political issues of the day.

Immigration to Canada from the United States has to be considered alongside the powerful thrust all over the world of peoples moving from regions of lesser to higher development, from the Mediterranean to northern Europe, from Latin America to the United States, from Asia and the Caribbean into Canada. Because of its relative security and ratio of people to resources, Canada is probably the world's most vulnerable country. Until very recently it has been one of the easiest to enter. Over the past decade racial distinctions have been eliminated from Canadian immigration laws. There are grounds for selection based on skill, education, or family ties, but no country or region is given preference over another. When Canadians removed all racial discrimination from immigration regulations, they thought in terms of adding new categories to the flow. They thought of equitable admission rather than equitable exclusion. If, as seems likely, they move increasingly to control the total flow, Britons, Frenchmen, or Americans have to be kept out or deported on the same basis as more exotic peoples. The only white country from which immigration is increasing is the United States. (Black Americans have shown less disposition than white Americans to cross the border.)

Neither Americans nor Canadians are used to harsh frontier controls. A spokesman from the US Department of State recently suggested that Canadians be exempted from the Western Hemisphere restrictions. Barbara Watson, administrator of the Bureau of Security and Consular Affairs, said adverse reaction had been "particularly marked in Canada which, because of our traditionally open border, has long felt itself to have a special relationship with the U.S." [18] Reciprocal preferences would presumably be expected. That sounds reasonable enough, but Canadians would have to examine the implications. Would they be moving toward the most continentalist of all conceptions—a free flow of people, a continental labour market? Not necessarily, but trends of that kind are incremental.

When it comes to keeping out Americans, Canadian popular attitudes are likely to be ambivalent. Hardship cases will make the headlines, and members of Parliament and congressmen will cry out. At this point one can only note the storm warnings. The tendency of American corporations to run their Canadian branches as regional plants is complicated by the barriers to the transfer of personnel. Opposition in Canada to the importation of American professors and plant managers suggests that many Canadians would not be unhappy in theory to frustrate in this way the continentalization of their economy. On both sides, however, there have been assumptions about personal mobility that would be challenged by the imposition of stiffer border controls of all kinds and the erection of the kinds of barriers that all North Americans associate with the more restrictive society of the Europe they rejected—and at a time when, in Western Europe, border restrictions are being eased. Neither federal nor provincial governments in Canada have been persuaded as yet to enact special legislation on the employment of Americans, but a climate of opinion has been created that has modified the personnel policies of universities and corporations. The tide, for the moment at least, is against continentalism in people.

[18] *Globe and Mail* (Toronto), 29 March 1973.

It is also against continentalism in land. Strong pressures are building up on provincial governments to prevent or restrict the purchase of Canadian land by foreigners, with a special eye on Americans buying up farms in Saskatchewan, resort country in British Columbia and Nova Scotia, as well as the already well-populated lake country in Ontario. This emerged as a major subject of concern when the provincial premiers met in Charlottetown in August 1973. As in the provincial talks about the control of resources and outside investment, there is also in the land question an ambivalence about whether foreigners are people in another country or another province.

The forces of continentalism are like powerful forces of nature. The pressure of American capital and American hunger for resources are phenomena of which Canadian politicians are well aware. In the earlier years Canadian lands were filled up with American settlers pushing west and north with little regard for ill-defined frontiers, and Canada had a hard time establishing its sovereignty in some areas. For the past half century Americans have been enjoying their own prosperity, and Canada has been making itself viable with more assimilable, or docile, immigrants from overseas. American immigrants are likely to compete directly with Canadians for jobs, whereas the West Indians and Portuguese and the Pakistanis and Greeks will do the support jobs native Canadians are spurning. The population of the continent, however, is still very unequally distributed, and Americans have a historic tendency to press toward frontiers. Canadians have traditionally thought they would like to have a larger share of the continent's population, but they have to cope with an increase in the work force from their own citizenry, which is larger in absolute terms than that of Britain or Germany.[19]

ALLIANCE AND PARTNERSHIP

Shifting attitudes toward the United States role in the world have, in recent years, inevitably altered Canadian attitudes toward the relationship. *Partnership* is a word less used now. The Canadian disposition seems to be toward more independence in foreign policy, and the shift of emphasis from strategic to economic issues fixes attention on areas where there is more conflict. The concept of partnership flourished during the war and postwar decades when the need to stand shoulder to shoulder against a clearly perceived threat from abroad was regarded as the basic national interest. That threat has grown more ambiguous.

[19] See *UN Statistical Yearbook, 1972* (New York: Statistical Office of the UN, 1973), pp. 95-96.

Some of this change, however, is more apparent than real. It is of significance that Canadians and Americans both seem to think that the foreign policies of the Trudeau government are more nationalist and independentist than those of its predecessors, although a strong case can be made that the United States was in fact defied more stubbornly by the St. Laurent–Pearson policies of the fifties. On the continental front, for example, the United States was pressed into collaboration on the St. Lawrence Seaway because the Canadian government decided to go it alone. In world affairs the St. Laurent government took advantage of its considerable leverage to oblige Washington to accept Article 2 of the North Atlantic Treaty and to oppose the United States over Korea with more courage than was required to recognize Peking in 1970 when the US no longer cared. A difference may be that there is now less confidence in Ottawa, and probably in Washington also, that the benevolence of an ally or a priority accorded to the common interest will prevail over a perceived national interest. Even those Canadians who concede that *quiet diplomacy* paid off among people who respected each other in the heyday of the NATO spirit speculate now as to whether the goodwill of allies is a commodity to be counted on. Has that gone with the cold war?

That priority once accorded to the alliance spirit was less in a continental than an Atlantic context. The broader trans-Atlantic spirit has soured even more certainly than the North American partnership. As a result, a bilateral partnership of sorts, wanted or unwanted, may be thrust upon North Americans by the exclusiveness of the West Europeans. It would be wrong, furthermore, to take for granted that Canadians as a whole and in the middle of the night have abandoned their reliance on North America as their bastion in a volatile world. Attitudes of the fifties have been abandoned. Canadians have learned that American military power can be employed in disastrous ways and is beyond their control, that there are almost insuperable strategic and logistic obstacles to the simple military collaboration they thought they once agreed to, but nevertheless most of them would rather have the United States stay as strong as the devils they do not know. NORAD was renewed in 1973, although for only a few years, without very much discussion. Unless and until overseas challenges look more menacing, or the cost escalates dramatically, NORAD is likely to look more like one of many sensible structures for handling transborder problems than the political commitment to common causes here and abroad that it appeared to be a decade or more ago. It may be all the more soundly based for being regarded as a practical mechanism and enduring convenience rather than as a gesture of solidarity dependent on shifting calculations of a threat.

It should be noted also that the new Canadian nationalism is a bourgeois as much as a left-wing phenomenon. The greater emphasis on the national interest paradoxically provides as strong an argument for being nice to the Americans as for standing up to them. That Canada's essential interests are economic and depend on US policies is a proposition widely taken for granted. Many tough Canadian nationalists, therefore, advocate Canadian foreign policies designed not necessarily to please Washington but to avoid irritating it and thereby risking something they regard as important, like the auto pact. They put the Canadian interest ahead not only of internationalism but also of mere anti-Americanism. Their nationalism is based on a vested interest in the Canadian economy and polity rather than concern for the image of Canada in world councils or support of the US as bastion of the "free world."

The divergences of the past few years have sharpened conflict, but they have also been a learning, and a sobering, experience. The crunch revealed how much each country had become dependent on the other. Canadians learned by standing firm against Mr. Connally that the American government would not or could not be as ruthless as they had feared. Having a better appreciation of their own strength and the areas of American dependence, they are more likely to seek agreements on the basis of mutual and balancing interest than by the enervating plea of special vulnerability. The energy crisis has been stark enough to cut through a lot of bluster and illusion. Among the things Canadians have learned is that they are not powerless to control their own resources even if these are owned by Americans. While Canada may at the same time be involved in an international network of corporations, governments, and institutions that restricts its range of choice, it is less so than most other middle powers.

Just as Mr. Connally and his associates retreated as it became clear that drastic measures for Canadians were double-edged, so too those Canadians who wanted to hold the Americans ransom for Canada's resources realized when the chips were being counted that there were two sides in that game. Using Ontario's plentiful hydroelectric power as a counter, for example, was rejected by the authorities of the Ontario Hydro-Electric Power Commission who pointed to their dependence on supplies of cheap coal from Pennsylvania. Diverting western oil entirely to eastern Canada was risky as the pipeline goes through the northern United States. Most important of all perhaps was a realization, when a showdown could be contemplated, that although Canadian energy resources were not the solution to America's problem, cutting them off with no regard for a neighbour's distress was not an act to be undertaken glibly. Aside from the danger of retaliation, there was a rediscovery under stress of the truth that the weaker power in the dyad is better off in the long run when the doctrine of mutual consideration is maintained.

At the same time, however, the Canadian government was driven in the course of a few months to take drastic measures in the direction of self-sufficiency that were heretofore politically impossible. Preserving and strengthening the Canadian advantage in resources is likely to be the endeavour of any Canadian government. A straw in the wind is Ontario Premier Davis's prediction at the end of 1973 that the greater availability of energy in Ontario will give a great advantage to the heartland of Canadian industry in the continental context. The continental spirit of give-and-take may be preserved in an era of hard bargaining, but the trend is against continental solutions. It may well be toward a more expedient approach to policymaking. In an interview of 1 January 1974, Donald Macdonald, minister of energy, mines and resources, said, when asked whether the Mackenzie pipeline was not "the spearhead toward continentalism," that "This is very much argued between two poles, the continental energy policy on the one hand and no truck nor trade with the Yankees on the other. Of course the reality does not exist at either pole. The best Canadian position exists in the middle, that is to be able to assess at any one time what is in our best interest in terms of sales and energy to the United States." [20]

The United States, considering its enormous strength, has been a remarkably good neighbour over two centuries. A question Canadians seriously ask themselves is whether this will continue to be the case if for the first time the Canadian standard of living becomes a reason for envy. That may depend on whether or not Canadians can keep their heads in such circumstances.

[20] *Globe and Mail* (Toronto), 1 January 1974.

PUBLIC OPINION ON UNITED STATES–CANADIAN RELATIONS

John H. Sigler and Dennis Goresky

Primary attention has been paid in much of the writing on public attitudes on foreign affairs to opinions about official interstate relations and foreign policy. One of the merits of the transnational politics paradigm is that it calls attention to the possibility that intersocietal relations may condition or influence the climate as well as the agenda of interstate relations. For the public opinion analyst, the paradigm invites attention to the relative degree of importance assigned by publics to intersocietal as contrasted to interstate relations and how changes in attitudes toward one sector may influence the climate in which relations in the other sector are conducted.

In this article we propose to examine public opinion polls in Canada and the United States to discern any patterns or trends in public attitudes toward intersocietal as well as interstate relations between the two countries, and the possible interaction of the two sets of attitudes. Our principal source materials are the Canadian Institute of Public Opinion (CIPO) polls for the years 1959 to 1973. The asymmetry in attention levels between the two countries about each other's affairs and their relations has often been noted, but it may be particularly dramatic at the level of mass publics. While questions about the United States per se or relations of the United States with Canada are extremely common in the CIPO polls, there are few questions about Canada in the American Institute of Public Opinion (AIPO) polls. The only poll that deals particularly with Canada (AIPO 840, December 1971) was commissioned by the Canadian

John H. Sigler and Dennis Goresky are members of the Department of Political Science at Carleton University in Ottawa.

embassy in Washington, and it is the one on which we principally rely for comparison with Canadian responses.[1]

As users of the commercial polls are aware, there are a number of serious drawbacks in the use of these data. Most important is the failure to repeat a question over time, thereby seriously limiting our ability to measure trends in opinion. The changes in wording and shifts in issue areas covered suggest the highly topical nature of the polls, mirroring salient public events whose own patterning has a random quality that seriously challenges the statistically minded social scientist. Contextual ambiguities are always a serious liability in survey research, and we are conscious of the problem of the interviewer structuring the response by the way in which the question is posed. In dealing with mass public samples, we have little indication of how strongly opinions are held. The Canadian Gallup organization uses "area probability" samples which provide reasonably accurate estimates of national opinion but are considerably less reliable in subsamples of opinion by region or social background. The data on these subsamples must be used with considerable caution as we are unable to project the results to larger populations with a known statistical margin of error. Our aim in this article is not prediction, as in electoral analysis, or hypothesis testing through inferential statistics. Here we are attempting to use the few traces we have to help discipline our speculation about shifting public attention on some salient issues in Canadian-American relations.

GENERAL STATE OF CANADIAN-AMERICAN RELATIONS

In the last fifteen years a number of questions pertaining to the general state of Canadian-American relations have been asked in the Canadian polls. Although the wording of these questions has varied, we have found a number with certain similarities. Questions about the general state of relations, often related to a change of government in Ottawa or Washington, were asked in 1963, 1965, 1969, and 1970. The question asked the respondent is whether or not he believes relations between the two countries are becoming better or worse. The responses from the national samples are reported in table 1. In this

[1] We wish to express our gratitude to the Social Science Data Archive at Carleton University, the Canadian Institute of Public Opinion, and the American Institute of Public Opinion for making available much of the data used in this study. Wherever available, we have used the data cards for our own secondary analysis. Where cards were not available, we relied on press releases from the Canadian Institute of Public Opinion and summaries of open-ended responses available in the Carleton archive. The responsibility for errors in tabulation and analysis remains entirely our own.

TABLE 1. STATE OF CANADIAN-US RELATIONS (in percentages)

	CIPO 305 1963	CIPO 315 1965	CIPO 335 1969	CIPO 343 1970
Better	31	33	48	38
Worse	5	8	24	26
Same & Don't Know	64	59	28	36
Coefficient of imbalance	+.081	+.083	+.115	+.046

and subsequent tables, we have computed a coefficient of imbalance [2] that permits us to represent in a single index number the relationship between favorable, unfavorable, and neutral or "don't know" responses. Otherwise, the reader is quickly lost in a morass of percentage comparisons by categories of response and respondent.

While a majority of Canadian respondents throughout the period believed that relations were improving or remaining the same, the late sixties indicated a growing perception of worsening relations, even though a plurality of Canadians sampled still believed that relations were improving. When Americans were asked this question, following the 10 percent surcharge imposition by the Nixon administration in August 1971 (AIPO 840, December 1971), 30 percent thought relations were improving and 32 percent thought they were worsening (imbalance coefficient −.006); for the university educated, 28 percent thought they were improving while 46 percent thought they were worsening (imbalance coefficient −.113). "Economic strain" was most often identified by American respondents as the principal contributing cause of worsening relations.

In the same 1971 poll, American respondents, using a Stapel scalometer test, continued to give a high affect rating to Canada with 93 percent having a favorable image of Canada compared to 94 percent favorable the last time this was asked in 1968.[3]

[2] The coefficient of imbalance, often used in content analysis, was devised by Irving L. Janis and Raymond Fadner, "The Coefficient of Imbalance," in Harold D. Lasswell et al., *Language of Politics* (Cambridge, Mass.: M.I.T. Press, 1965), pp. 153-71, in order to measure bias in communications. The formula is: $C_f = (f^2 - fu)/rt$, where $f > u$; and $C_u = (fu - u^2)/rt$, where $f < u$. In the formula, f refers to favourable units of content, u refers to unfavourable units of content, r to relevant units of content, and t to total units of content. For standardized data presented in percentage terms, we have treated r as 100 and squared it, making the divisor in all instances 10,000. By this device, the effect of "don't knows" is taken into account; the more "don't knows," the closer the coefficient toward zero. Simple ratios obscure the importance of "don't knows."

[3] George H. Gallup, *The Gallup Poll: Public Opinion, 1935-71*, vol. 3: *1959-1971* (New York: Random House, 1972), p. 2104. The Stapel scalometer test consists of ten boxes, numbered from +5 to −5. The person being tested is given a card showing the ten boxes and is told that the top box represents the highest degree of liking, and the lowest box, the lowest degree. He is then asked how far up the scale or how far down the scale he would place each nation.

American images of Canada were more favorable than for other countries evaluated at the same time: Great Britain (90 percent), Brazil (66 percent), the Soviet Union (30 percent), and the People's Republic of China (12 percent). In comparing the reponses on Great Britain and Canada, one finds that 65 percent of American respondents checked "highly favorable" with respect to Canada but only 44 percent used this category in evaluating Great Britain.

In October 1968, Canadians were asked to name characteristics of Americans. Positive adjectives were listed with considerably greater frequency by Canadians than by British respondents polled in the same period. The above questions attempt to measure relative degree of social distance between populations. Somewhat different results may be expected when the question suggests interstate relations. In June 1965 (CIPO 312) Canadians were asked "Which country is our best friend?" A majority of Canadians (58 percent) named the United States, followed by the United Kingdom (24 percent), and France (3 percent). In Quebec France was named more often (9 percent) than the UK (6 percent), but Quebeckers far exceeded the other regions in naming the United States first (70 percent). In Ontario 50 percent named the US while 35 percent named the United Kingdom. The same question asked in the United States and the United Kingdom in the same time period showed that 58 percent of Americans named the United Kingdom with Canada in second place (10 percent). From the foregoing, we find tentative evidence for the view that the United States and Canadian populations are more mutually responsive to each other than to others; but when interstate relations are introduced, power and prestige rankings influence judgments with the UK replacing Canada in American esteem, while the United States continues to hold a preeminent place in Canadian estimation. One of the more interesting findings in the American study is that a plurality of Americans (43 percent) believed that Canada did not have an independent foreign policy, but when asked which nation Canada must follow, the most frequent response was the United Kingdom (26 percent) followed by the United States (19 percent). Obviously, the symbolic ties to the monarchy rather than the realities of international politics continue to influence American views of Canada. The university-educated American, however, was slightly more likely to name the United States.

Questions about whether Canadian respect for the United States had increased or decreased over the previous year were asked in 1960, 1963, 1967, and 1972. The results as reported in table 2 do not indicate any trend over time but do suggest the impact on opinion of government leaders and specific policies. There is a strong hint here that

TABLE 2. RESPECT FOR THE UNITED STATES IN CANADIAN OPINION
(in percentages)

	CIPO 285 1960	CIPO 305 1963	CIPO 323 1967	CIPO 351 1972
Increase	20	54	16	8
Decrease	36	21	47	19
Same	28	18	23	68
No opinion	16	7	14	5
Coefficient of imbalance	−.058	+.178	−.146	−.021

a major shift toward a more favorable opinion occurred in the Kennedy years and shifted sharply by 1967 in the opposite direction.

An examination of the open-ended responses to the question asked in 1969 and 1970 in Canada on the state of relations between the two countries provides some indication of the salient issues. In 1969 (CIPO 335), of those who perceived the two countries growing closer together (48 percent), 32 percent thought it was because of increased economic ties, 19 percent cited travel, while 14 percent cited cooperation among leaders, and 9 percent, defence. Of those who saw the two countries drifting apart (24 percent), 27 percent emphasized Canada's independent foreign policy, 25 percent the war in Vietnam, and 14 percent the United States taking Canada for granted. In 1970 economic questions topped the list of salient issues for those who saw the countries as coming together (38 percent) as well as those who saw the countries as growing apart (26 percent). Among those who saw the countries growing closer together (38 percent), 50 percent cited increasing economic ties, and 26 percent travel and geography. Among those who saw the two countries as growing further apart (26 percent), 37 percent cited United States control of industry and natural resources while 18 percent cited dislike of US policies in Vietnam and domestic unrest in the United States, and 17 percent attributed the differences to growing Canadian nationalism. In comparing these responses with those in 1969 and the general trend earlier, we can discern the growing importance of economic questions, although more people see this as a reason for growing closer together than further apart in both years. However, no conclusions can be drawn from these responses as to Canadian opinion on the desirability of coming closer together or drawing farther apart. Those who see the two countries growing closer together because of increased economic ties may easily deplore this trend while those who see the countries drawing further apart may oppose this trend.

A careful examination of the list does suggest that intersocietal relations (economic ties and travel) were perceived as more salient than interstate relations (leaders and defence) in understanding the closer integration of the two countries. Disagreement appeared to center on interstate relations in 1969 (independent Canadian foreign policy and the war in Vietnam), but intersocietal relations (US control of the Canadian economy) clearly dominated the issues in disagreement in 1970. One hypothesis frequently discussed in Canada is that hostility toward United States policy in Vietnam became the basis for hostility toward the American economic presence in Canada. While this may account for the anti-American positions of some Canadians, our reading of the above responses would be that only 6 percent of the Canadian population sampled saw Vietnam as the salient issue in 1969 and only 5 percent in 1970. The dramatic shift in loss of respect toward the United States generally which occurred in Canada between 1963 and 1967 may also be consonant with the Vietnam opposition hypothesis, but other factors, including reactions to growing US cultural influence in Canada, perceptions of domestic unrest in the United States, dislike of American leaders and American foreign policy in other areas than Vietnam, and the growth of Canadian nationalist feeling based largely on domestic preoccupations, would also need to be examined. A number of Canadian writers have focused on American economic penetration of Canada as the principal issue in Canadian-American relations. A recent empirical study by Tai, Peterson, and Gurr demonstrates that anti-Americanism in Canada (measured by anti-American actions and statements), as in many Afro-Asian countries, is more strongly correlated with American economic presence than with domestic economic stress or domestic social stress. Given the extensive American economic presence in Canada, and Canadian sensitivity to it, the above authors conclude that it is surprising that Canadian hostility toward the United States has not been even stronger.[4] Given this argument, we propose to look first for evidence in the public opinion polls of trends or patterns in attitudes toward the American economic presence in Canada.

FOREIGN INVESTMENT

Ownership and control of much of Canadian natural resources and manufacturing enterprise—over 80 percent in a number of industries (see Gilpin's essay in this volume)—by American interests gave rise initially to Walter Gordon's Royal Commission on Canada's Economic Prospects in 1957,[5] the Watkins report in 1968,[6] the Wahn

[4] Chong-Soo Tai, Erick J. Peterson, and Ted Robert Gurr, "Internal Versus External Sources of Anti-Americanism: Two Comparative Studlies," *Journal of Conflict Resolution* 17 (September 1973) : 455-88.
[5] Canada, *Royal Commission on Canada's Economic Prospects* (Ottawa: Queen's Printer, 1957) ; also referred to as the Gordon report.
[6] Canada, Task Force on the Structure of Canadian Industry, *Foreign Ownership and the Structure of Canadian Industry* (Ottawa: Queen's Printer, 1968) ; also referred to as the Watkins report.

report in 1970,[7] and the Gray report in 1972.[8] During this time period
public controversy also developed. Though the Gray report purports
to show a steady increase in nonresident control,[9] table 3 suggests
stability since at least the beginning of the 1960s. Any shift in
Canadian opinion in our time period probably could not be interpreted as a reaction to growing American control per se, but more to
the increased volume of US investment as well as increased attention
to the issue stimulated by the political elite.

To investigate public response to this debate over US investment
in Canada, we examined the polls for questions bearing on this problem. We have followed the practice of attempting to distinguish between cognitive (knowledge), affective (feelings), and active (policy)
components of attitudinal orientations. Unfortunately, we have few
questions on the Canadian side dealing with the cognitive aspect of
United States investment in Canada. A repeated affective-oriented
question assumes or supplies knowledge to the respondent and then
asks for an attitudinal response. Whether the respondent was aware
of the factual aspects remains problematical. The question asked was:
"As you know, a lot of Canada's development has been financed by
US money. Do you think this was a good thing for Canada, or not
a good thing?" The repeated policy question was: "Do you think
there is enough US capital in Canada now, or would you like to see
more US capital invested in this country?" Again, we do not know the
respondent's factual knowledge. Responses to these questions are
summarized by region in tables 4 and 5.

A modest downward shift in the evaluation of US capital occurred between 1959 and 1967, the last time this question was asked.
A majority of Canadians in all regions believed that the importation
of US capital was a good thing, outnumbering critics by a margin of
two to one in all regions but the Prairies. No trend can really be
discerned in a limited data set of only three time points. Particularly
positive evaluation of US capital's contribution to Canadian development came from the Atlantic provinces and Ontario.

A similar question asked in different national polls in 1969, 1970,
1971, and 1972, and analyzed by Murray and Kubota, permits us to
extend the time line somewhat further.[10] This question asked whether
United States ownership of Canadian companies was a good thing for

[7] Canada, House of Commons, Standing Committee on External Affairs and
National Defence, *Report No. 33*, 28th Parl., 2d sess., 1969-70; also referred to as
the Wahn report.
[8] Canada, Gray Task Force, *Foreign Direct Investment in Canada* (Ottawa:
Information Canada, 1972); also referred to as the Gray report.
[9] Ibid., pp. 17, 21.
[10] J. Alex Murray and A. Kubota, "What Canadians Think of U.S. Investment,"
The International Review, 12 February 1973, pp. 35-41.

TABLE 3. FLOW OF INVESTMENT CAPITAL, US-CANADA 1961-70 (in millions of dollars and percentages)

Year	Total US Direct Foreign Investment [a]	US Direct Foreign Investment in Canada [a]	Percent of US Total in Canada	Total Canadian Direct Foreign Investment [b]	Canadian Direct Foreign Investment in US [b]	Percent of Canadian Total in US	Percent US Control Capital in Canadian Industries [b]	Percent US Control Capital in Mfg., Mining, Petroleum [b]
1961	34,684	11,804	34.0	2,596	1,724	66.4	26	51
1962	37,226	12,133	32.6	2,784	1,786	64.2	27	51
1963	40,686	13,044	32.1	3,082	1,922	62.4	27	52
1964	44,386	13,796	31.1	3,272	1,967	60.1	27	51
1965	49,474	15,319	31.0	3,469	2,041	58.8	27	50
1966	54,562	16,840	30.9	3,711	2,100	56.6	27	51
1967	59,267	18,069	30.5	4,030	2,190	54.3	28	51
1968	64,983	19,535	30.1	4,617	2,540	55.0	—	—
1969	71,016	21,127	29.7	5,040	2,760	54.8	—	—
1970	78,090	22,901	29.2	—	—	—	—	—

[a] The source for these columns was the *Statistical Abstract of the United States* which defines direct foreign investments as "private enterprises in one country controlled by investors in another country or in the management of which foreign investors have an important voice."

[b] The source for these columns was Statistics Canada, *Canadian International Investment Position, 1926-1967* (December 1971).

TABLE 4.   ATTITUDE TOWARD US CAPITAL IN CANADA NATIONALLY AND BY REGION

Question: As you know a lot of Canada's development has been financed by US money. Do you think this is a good thing, or not a good thing?

	1959 CIPO 275					1963 CIPO 303					1967 CIPO 323				
	N	PER-CENT GOOD	PER-CENT NOT GOOD	DON'T KNOW	COEFFICIENT OF IMBALANCE	N	PER-CENT GOOD	PER-CENT NOT GOOD	DON'T KNOW	COEFFICIENT OF IMBALANCE	N	PER-CENT GOOD	PER-CENT NOT GOOD	DON'T KNOW	COEFFICIENT OF IMBALANCE
Canada	(657)	61	19	20	+.256	(709)	55	29	16	+.143	(603)	59	28	13	+.183
Atlantic	(59)	81	17	2	+.518	(70)	66	18	16	+.317	(63)	57	27	16	+.171
Quebec	(181)	46	14	40	+.147	(194)	50	25	24	+.125	(161)	54	29	17	+.135
Ontario	(243)	66	20	14	+.304	(250)	58	30	11	+.162	(220)	64	24	12	+.256
Prairies	(111)	65	25	10	+.26	(126)	50	33	17	+.085	(104)	60	35	5	+.150
British Columbia	(63)	67	25	8	+.281	(69)	59	33	7	+.153	(55)	56	26	18	+.168

TABLE 5. SUFFICIENCY OF US CAPITAL IN CANADA NATIONALLY
Question: Do you think there is enough US capital in Canada now,

	N	PER-CENT MORE	PER-CENT ENOUGH	PER-CENT DON'T KNOW	COEFFI-CIENT OF IMBALANCE
1961 CIPO 286					
Canada	(726)	33	52	15	−.099
Atlantic	(71)	47	44	9	−.014
Quebec	(221)	36	39	25	−.012
Ontario	(245)	26	60	14	−.204
Prairies	(119)	30	63	6	−.208
British Columbia	(70)	34	57	9	−.131

	N	PER-CENT MORE	PER-CENT ENOUGH	PER-CENT DON'T KNOW	COEFFI-CIENT OF IMBALANCE
1967 CIPO 323					
Canada	(699)	24	61	15	−.226
Atlantic	(65)	29	57	14	−.16
Quebec	(185)	18	62	20	−.273
Ontario	(244)	26	59	15	−.195
Prairies	(122)	26	56	17	−.168
British Columbia	(63)	19	70	11	−.357

	N	PER-CENT MORE	PER-CENT ENOUGH	PER-CENT DON'T KNOW	COEFFI-CIENT OF IMBALANCE
1972 CIPO 351					
Canada	(721)	22	67	11	−.302
Atlantic	(64)	22	61	17	−.238
Quebec	(206)	31	58	11	−.157
Ontario	(259)	18	72	10	−.389
Prairies	(121)	17	72	11	−.396
British Columbia	(71)	21	65	14	−.286

AND BY REGION
and would you like to see more US capital invested in this country?

		1963 CIPO 305			
	N	PER-CENT MORE	PER-CENT ENOUGH	PER-CENT DON'T KNOW	COEFFI-CIENT OF IMBALANCE
Canda	(705)	33	46	21	—.060
Atlantic	(71)	42	30	28	—.054
Quebec	(189)	29	39	32	—.039
Ontario	(254)	31	51	18	—.102
Prairies	(122)	33	52	15	—.099
British Columbia	(69)	42	48	10	—.029

		1970 CIPO 343			
	N	PER-CENT MORE	PER-CENT ENOUGH	PER-CENT DON'T KNOW	COEFFI-CIENT OF IMBALANCE
Canada	(720)	25	62	13	—.230
Atlantic	(66)	38	53	9	—.079
Quebec	(202)	33	48	19	—.073
Ontario	(260)	18	70	12	—.364
Prairies	(121)	21	68	11	—.320
British Columbia	(71)	24	65	11	—.267

Canada. The shift in wording has important implications in structuring responses, and we would expect greater negativity than in the Gallup question. Trends are, however, what interest us most. In recomputing the Murray and Kubota data with the coefficient of imbalance, we find that Canadian national opinion remained slightly favorable to this question in 1969 (.04) with a steady shift toward increasing negativity (−.01 in 1970, −.02 in 1971, and −.04 in 1972). Even in this more critical form for the question, Canadian opinion remains substantially balanced on the merits of US investment. A trend toward negativity is apparent, but the questions are too ambiguous for us to make any further judgments as to the compelling reasons for the answers to the questions. It is not clear whether the respondent believes that US capital was never useful or that it was useful in the past but is now less beneficial to Canadians. In a poll of provincial legislators, Stevenson permitted clarification of responses and found that a number of respondents had answered the question in the affirmative but indicated a shift in their judgment if they were evaluating present and future rather than the overall record from the past.[11] To clarify this point, we cross-tabulated responses to the question about the evaluation of United States capital with the judgment about its sufficiency in the 1967 poll, and we found that somewhat over half of the respondents who evaluated US capital favorably believed that there was then enough in Canada.

On the policy question of the sufficiency of United States capital in Canada, we have five time points and can more readily examine trends. The overall belief that there is enough US capital in Canada is reflected in the increase from 52 percent of the population sampled in 1961 to 67 percent in 1972, with only a modest dip in the overall trend in 1963. Only in the Atlantic region in 1961 and 1963 did opinion favoring more US capital exceed the belief in sufficiency. Centennial year (1967) was marked by a sharp upward movement, especially in Quebec, in the belief that there was enough United States capital in Canada and a decided drop in the opinion that more was needed.

Although there is a policy component in the question relating to the sufficiency of US capital in Canada, it scarcely provides any guidance to the policymaker as to regulation. The governmental arguments center less on the volume of capital flows than on their nature and how they may be regulated or reduced in terms of the relative proportion of US control of key Canadian-based industries. A com-

[11] Garth Stevenson, "Foreign Direct Investment and the Provinces: A Study of Elite Attitudes," Carleton University, Department of Political Science, 1973. (Mimeographed.)

mon approach in other countries to this problem has been to provide for 51 percent indigenous ownership, and this proposal has been advanced in Canada as well. The question asked in September 1970 (CIPO 343) was: "Some experts are suggesting that Canada should buy back majority control, say 51 percent of US companies in Canada even though it might mean a big reduction in our standard of living. Would you approve or not?" [12] Response to this question by region, party preference, education, and occupation are summarized in table 6. While a plurality of Canadian opinion on this question was in favor of the 51 percent idea, opinions were more divided on this than the other general questions on United States capital. Some class divisions of opinion are suggested in the response to this question, with a plurality in the professional and business occupations opposed but a plurality in sales-clerical, labor, and farm occupations in favor. Regional opinion was also divided, with a plurality favoring the proposal in all regions except the Atlantic, where a plurality opposed the proposal. Opinion in British Columbia was more sharply divided on this point than was opinion in Quebec, Ontario, or the Prairies. A majority of Liberal and New Democratic party followers favored the move as did a plurality of Progressive Conservative party followers.

Another survey conducted in the fall of 1971 showed that Ontarians alone would be willing to accept a lower standard of living in exchange for economic independence.[13] There was only a 2.7 percent difference between positive and negative replies for the country as a whole.

Another policy question in this area in January 1972 (CIPO 351) asked respondents if they approved of the government's plan, developed from the Gray report, for an agency to screen new United States capital investment in Canada. This proposal received substantial support from all sectors of the Canadian sample surveyed, although it was much criticized by economic nationalists for not going far enough in dealing with a much larger problem. The proposal received strongest support regionally in British Columbia. Again, Liberal party followers occupied a middle ground between New Democratic party (NDP) followers who were overwhelmingly in favor and Progressive Conservative party followers who were less so.

Six months later, in July 1972 (CIPO 354), three months before the federal elections, the public was asked a more general question about approval of the policies that the government was following on

---

[12] The use of *expert* in the opening phrase may be expected to prejudice opinion to be on the side of the experts. *Big* reduction may also be expected to prejudice responses, although the two terms work in contrary directions.

[13] J. Alex Murray and Mary C. Gerace, "Canadian Attitudes toward the US Presence," *Public Opinion Quarterly* 36 (Fall 1972) : 396.

TABLE 6. PUBLIC ATTITUDES ON POLICY RE UNITED STATES CAPITAL

September 1970
(CIPO 343): 51 Percent Canadian Ownership

	N	PER-CENT AP-PROVE	PER-CENT DISAP-PROVE	PER-CENT UNDE-CIDED AND QUALI-FIED	COEFFI-CIENT OF IM-BALANCE
Canada	(720)	47	32	21	.071
Atlantic	(66)	36	44	20	—.035
Quebec	(202)	47	29	24	.065
Ontario	(260)	49	30	21	.931
Prairies	(121)	49	30	21	.931
British Columbia	(71)	44	40	16	.018
Liberal	(223)	51	33	16	.092
Progressive Cons.	(144)	47	36	17	.052
New Democratic	(75)	56	23	21	.185
Public	(221)	42	27	31	.060
Secondary	(379)	49	34	17	.074
University	(83)	47	39	14	.038
Professional	(44)	34	46	20	—.055
Business	(97)	34	38	18	—.015
Sales and Clerical	(88)	41	27	32	.057
Labour	(299)	38	22	40	.061
Farm	(49)	31	22	47	.028

July 1972
(CIPO 354): Approve Government policy on US Control

	N	PER-CENT AP-PROVE	PER-CENT DISAP-PROVE	PER-CENT UNDE-CIDED	COEFFI-CIENT OF IM-BALANCE
Canada	(722)	34	40	26	—.024
Atlantic	(66)	26	42	32	—.067
Quebec	(205)	33	30	37	.019
Ontario	(258)	42	36	22	.025
Prairies	(121)	29	51	20	—.112
British Columbia	(71)	24	58	18	—.197
Liberal	(217)	55	25	19	.165
Progressive Cons.	(144)	26	49	24	—.113
New Democratic	(63)	12	71	16	—.419
Public	(185)	31	32	37	—.003
Secondary	(388)	34	41	26	—.028
University	(98)	42	46	12	—.018
Professional	(56)	38	48	14	—.048
Business	(73)	37	38	25	—.004
Sales and Clerical	(116)	41	45	14	—.018
Labour	(289)	33	38	29	—.019
Farm	(57)	32	47	21	—.075

BY REGION, PARTY, EDUCATION, AND OCCUPATION

January 1972
(CIPO 351): Screen US Capital

	N	PER-CENT GOOD IDEA	PER-CENT NOT GOOD IDEA	PER-CENT UNDE-CIDED	COEFFI-CIENT OF IM-BALANCE
Canada	(721)	69	15	16	.373
Atlantic	(64)	66	16	19	.330
Quebec	(206)	68	16	17	.354
Ontario	(259)	67	14	19	.355
Prairies	(121)	71	20	9	.362
British Columbia	(72)	80	10	10	.560
Liberal	(198)	73	16	11	.416
Progressive Cons.	(128)	70	14	16	.392
New Democratic	(90)	79	11	10	.537
Public	(160)	55	20	24	.193
Secondary	(399)	69	15	15	.373
University	(105)	84	11	5	.613
Professional	(58)	69	19	12	.345
Business	(71)	65	24	11	.267
Sales and Clerical	(96)	68	23	9	.318
Labour	(275)	69	21	10	.331
Farm	(52)	73	19	8	.394

US control of Canadian industry and natural resources. A critical public mood emerged. Only 34 percent nationally approved the government's policies, and 40 percent disapproved. When asked to clarify their opposition, only 10 percent of the opponents argued that they thought the government was going too far in this area. About half of the opponents argued in terms of dislike of American domination of Canada, objecting in particular to profits going out of the country.

The July 1972 (CIPO 354) poll and the general trends suggest a growing critical attitude toward US capital in Canada. The difficulty comes in assigning a priority to the saliency of this issue among other issues of public concern. In September 1972 (CIPO 355), the month just prior to the election, Canadians were asked to name the most important problem facing the country. Less than 3 percent gave American domination or control as their response; the problem of inflation and unemployment dominated the responses. This was down from the 8 percent that had named the American penetration problem in 1970 and was similar to the 3 percent that named it for the first time when this question was posed in 1966. The reduced saliency of this issue may explain why the question of American influence, considered by many to be a leading contender as the major campaign issue in 1972, was scarcely mentioned even by the NDP. In the poll data analyzed by Murray, Canadian national opinion focused very heavily on unemployment (46 percent) and inflation (30 percent), with a low 3.2 percent of the population (again somewhat higher in Ontario and the Prairies) citing Canadian-American relations as the most important issue facing Canada.[14]

On the American side, the only question in AIPO 840 dealing with US capital investment asked what percentage of United States annual foreign investment went to Canada. For the whole population, the modal response was 9 percent, with elite opinion most often answering 17 percent, considerably below the actual figures that ranged from 34 percent in 1961 down to 29 percent in 1970. On this question, as many others, the relative asymmetry in Canadian and American awareness of the other appears to be a central problem in the conduct of relations between the two countries.

TRADE

The exchange of goods between the two countries does show a significant change during the decade of the sixties, particularly after the automobile and automotive products agreements in 1965 provid-

[14] J. Alex Murray, "An Analysis of Public Attitudes on the Question of US Investment in Canada," University of Windsor, International Business Research Unit, 1973. (Mimeographed.)

ing a variety of duty-free trade in new automobiles and parts between the two countries. The composition of Canadian trade to the United States changed markedly with the automobile agreement, and manufactured items (largely automotive) made up half of total Canadian trade to the United States (table 7) by the end of the decade.

TABLE 7. US-CANADIAN TRADE, 1961-70

	Total Trade * in Millions of US Dollars	Percent Total Canadian Foreign Trade	Percent Total US Foreign Trade	Percent Manufac- tured Items Canadian Export to US	Manufac- tured Items Without Auto to US
1961	7,079.8	59.9	19.4	14	14
1962	7,534.6	62.2	19.7	15	15
1963	7,766.7	60.3	19.7	16	15
1964	8,921.0	59.4	19.9	20	19
1965	10,266.0	62.1	21.4	23	19
1966	12,390.4	64.1	22.9	32	21
1967	13,224.7	67.4	24.5	41	24
1968	16,907.1	68.6	25.2	45	24
1969	19,342.6	70.2	26.4	50	26
1970	19,901.2	66.4	24.3	49	26

SOURCE: International Monetary Fund, *Direction of Trade.*
* US and Canadian statistics do not agree due to different accounting procedures. Arrangements were made between the two statistical series in 1973 to agree on common procedures. The Canadian figures are used here.

Survey items on trade, unlike those on capital investment, are not repeated over time but are directed to specific topical issues. The 10 percent import surcharge imposed by President Nixon in August 1971 generated a number of items in both the Canadian and American polls at approximately the same point in time—November 1971. When asked if they had heard of Nixon's new economic policies on CIPO 350, 42 percent of Canadian respondents said they had not. Among the remaining 58 percent of the sample, 10 percent thought they would have a beneficial effect on Canadian economic life, 9 percent were undecided, 18 percent thought they would make no difference, and the remaining 63 percent (36.5 percent of that total) thought they would be harmful to Canada. In the US poll, respondents were informed that the United States had placed a 10 percent surcharge on goods imported from abroad and were then asked if the policy was more likely to affect Canada than others. In the American sample, 34 percent thought the tax would affect Canada more than others, 46 percent said no, and 20 percent were undecided. Residents of New England, the Rocky Mountain states, and the Pacific Coast were more likely to see the policy as adversely affecting Canada.

Only 26 percent of the US population sampled could identify any Canadian products purchased in large quantities in the United States. Automobiles and heavy machinery were most often cited, although the university educated were more likely to select natural resource or wood products first. Businessmen were the most likely to give greatest weight to the automotive trade.

As noted earlier, the context and wording of a question will have important effects on the responses. In Canada, the questions about US-Canadian trade relations were placed in the context of the 10 percent surcharge. Those who heard of the surcharge (58 percent of the sample) were then asked:

> Some people believe that as a result of these policies Canada's export business to the US will drop sharply. If this happens, which of these statements comes closest to the course which you think Canada should take?
>
> A. Remain as a Canadian nation and work to develop trade in other countries even though this could take many years and we might face a serious depression? [60 percent]
>
> B. Join the US even though this would mean losing Canadian independence? [5 percent]
>
> C. Enter into some form of economic union, or common market, with the US even though this might mean that most of our job opportunities in manufacturing might move to the US? [18 percent]
>
> D. None or can't say. [17 percent]

Only in Quebec was there a plurality (43 percent) that favored option A, with 12 percent for option B and 17 percent for the economic union. Among party followers, a NDP–Liberal–Progressive Conservative spectrum appears with 68 percent of NDP followers, 65 percent of Liberal followers, and 50 percent of Progressive Conservative followers favoring option A; 0 percent of NDP, 5 percent of Liberals, and 10 percent of Progressive Conservatives favoring B; and 14 percent of NDP, 21 percent of Liberals, and 25 percent of Conservatives aligned with option C. Among occupational categories, farmers were most divided on this question, with 46 percent favoring option A, 10 percent option B, and 36 percent option C. The poll nevertheless suggests residual Canadian public support for Secretary of State for External Affairs Mitchell Sharp's declared policy of working toward greater independence from the United States in preference to maintaining present policies or working for closer integration with the United States.

Americans in 1971 were asked if they favored the elimination of tariffs between the United States and Canada, with 48 percent in favor and 37 percent opposed. University-educated persons favored the elimination of tariffs by a ratio of more than two to one. A similar question about free trade in Canada asked in 1963 (CIPO 303) showed 50 percent in favor, 32 percent opposed, and 18 percent with no opinion. Ontario was evenly divided with 40 percent in favor and 40 percent opposed. The question was repeated in 1968 (CIPO 327) with an even more favorable evaluation: 56 percent in favor, 27 percent opposed, and 17 percent with no opinion. The question has been a continuing one on the agenda of economists and other analysts in Canada and the United States.[15]

By mid-1973, the energy crisis became a common topic in the mass media in Canada and the United States. A large natural gas sale to the United States was the subject of a Canadian query in November 1970 (CIPO 344). At that time, only about half (52 percent) of the Canadians sampled had heard anything about the sale, and only 23 percent in Quebec. In Ontario and the western provinces, the figure was 65 percent. Asked if they approved of the sale, 55 percent of those who were aware of it approved, 26 percent disapproved. Opinion in British Columbia was most divided with 40 percent approving, 30 percent disapproving, and 30 percent undecided. Approval was at its highest in Quebec and the Maritimes. Business and professional persons were most pleased with the sale, although a majority in all occupational categories favored the sale. Among party followers, only the NDP opposed the sale, with Progressive Conservatives most in favor and the Liberals in the middle.

In March 1973 (CIPO 358) Canadians were asked: "The US is currently facing a shortage of energy resources such as heating oil and gas. Do you think that, in view of this, the Canadian government should nationalize our energy resources such as oil and gas—that is, even operate them, or do you think that private enterprise should still control them as at present?" In the national sample, 48 percent favored nationalization and 36 percent favored continuing control by private enterprise. NDP and university graduates most favored the nationalization option—69 percent of NDP followers and 59 percent of university educated. The upper income group in the country was the most evenly divided of the categories examined, with 45 percent favoring and 39 percent opposed. Nevertheless, substantial support for the policy was found in the context of the question posed which

---

[15] Sperry Lea, *A Canada-US Free Trade Arrangement* (Montreal: Canadian-American Committee, 1963); Ronald J. Wonnacott and Paul Wonnacott, *Free Trade Between the United States and Canada: The Potential Economic Effects* (Cambridge, Mass.: Harvard University Press, 1967); and Peyton V. Lyon, "Canada-US Free Trade (CUFTA) and Canadian Independence," Carleton University, School of International Affairs, 1973 (Mimeographed).

related United States needs to Canadian resources, perhaps the most sensitive form for nationalist consensus in Canada.

OTHER QUESTIONS RELATED TO ECONOMICS

In the category of general affect tied largely to economic relations, two recent questions in the Canadian polls are relevant. In March 1972 (CIPO 352) the Canadian sample was asked a question whose tone may be indicative of the changed mood in Canadian-American relations: "Some people think that US attitudes toward this country indicate that they think of us as a partner; others disagree and say that the US thinks of us as a colony. What is your opinion?" Respondents differed widely on this provocative question. Of the national sample, 37 percent answered "partner" and 34 percent "colony"; 29 percent fell in the undecided and "don't know" category. Regional differences show that a plurality of Quebec opinion is most likely to answer "partner" (44 percent), followed by the Maritimes (37 percent). In Ontario and the Prairies, opinion was equally divided between "partner" and "colony" (35 percent), while in British Columbia a plurality answered "colony" (37 percent). Among party followers, Liberals were most likely to answer "partner" with a plurality at 44 percent, the Progressive Conservatives equally divided (36 percent), and the NDP answering "colony" (45 percent). A plurality of businessmen answered "partner" (39 percent), while a plurality of professionals (38 percent) and farmers (40 percent) answered "colony." The university educated were equally divided, while secondary and primary school graduates showed pluralities for "partner." The young (18-20) were most likely among all age cohorts to answer "colony" (54 percent).

The second question asked in April 1963 (CIPO 302) and repeated in July 1972 (CIPO 354) asked about the general issue of dependence on the United States: "Do you think dependence on the US is a good thing for Canada, or not a good thing?" The national sample in 1972 responded as follows: 34 percent "good," 53 percent "bad," 13 percent "don't know," with a coefficient of imbalance of −.101. The 1963 national sample had responded: 48 percent "good," 44 percent "bad," 8 percent "don't know," with a coefficient of imbalance of .019. In all regions but Quebec, a majority in 1972 thought such dependence a bad thing. In Quebec only a plurality answered in this manner (42 percent). Among party followers, the NDP showed a 21 percent to 75 percent split, the Liberals a 38 percent to 52 percent split, and the Progressive Conservatives a 40 percent to 49 percent split. The university educated were most likely to judge such dependence as a bad thing (66 percent) and primary educated least likely to do so (43 percent). Professionals were most likely to see dependence as bad (77 percent) and farmers least likely (51 percent).

AMERICAN CULTURAL INFLUENCE

While we can discern a trend toward a more critical evaluation of the American economic presence in Canada over time, particularly among the highly educated and the professionals, a more dramatic shift is found in reactions to the impact of American culture. Geographical and cultural proximity, reinforced by the tremendous disparity in market size and productive capacity, have meant that Canada has been flooded with the products of American mass media—books, films, magazines, radio, and television. In 1961 (CIPO 291) and again in 1966 (CIPO 318), Canadians were asked, "Do you think the Canadian way of life is, or is not being too much influenced by the United States?" [16] Responses are summarized in table 8.

Only Quebeckers, professionals, and the university educated were inclined in 1961 to react against American cultural penetration, but by 1966 all regions but the Atlantic, all occupational groups except the professionals, all educational categories, and all political parties had shifted toward this view. The 1961 question came during the early euphoria of the Kennedy years, and it may be that the subsequent reaction was to the tarnished image of the United States marked by urban violence, student unrest, and political assassination. Quebec opinion changed little, suggesting a less volatile reaction to these events in the United States.

The Canadian government demonstrated concern about American cultural influence well before its more recent concern with American economic influence. The Royal Commission on National Development in the Arts, Letters, and Sciences (1949-51) was given the task of investigating the ways in which the United States was influencing Canadian cultural development. The National Film Board, the Canadian Broadcasting Corporation, the Canada Council, and the National Research Council of Canada all have a responsibility of emphasizing Canadian content in the development and promotion of Canadian culture. The Royal Commission on Publications (1961) recommended discriminatory measures in terms of advertising and postage rates on American publications in order to ensure the survival of Canadian publications. The Canadian Radio-Television Commission requires Canadian television stations to provide at least 60 percent Canadian

[16] Even in this context, Canadians were most apt in 1961 to cite American control of Canadian industry as the reason for their concern. In adding the open-ended responses, however, we find 54 percent of the responses can be related to cultural matters while 42 percent are related to economic issues. *Way of life* therefore contains both cultural and economic dimensions.

TABLE 8. CANADIAN OPINION OF UNITED STATES INFLUENCE ON WAY OF LIFE

Question: Do you think the Canadian way of life is, or is not being too much influenced by the United States?

	CIPO 291				
	N	TOO MUCH	NOT TOO MUCH	NO OPIN- ION	COEFFICIENT OF IM- BALANCE
Canada	(665)	39	49	13	.049
Atlantic	(56)	21	64	14	.2752
Quebec	(188)	46	24	30	—.101
Ontario	(241)	37	57	5	.114
Prairies	(110)	30	65	6	.228
British Columbia	(70)	49	50	1	.005
Professional	(46)	54	39	7	—.081
Business	(71)	49	47	4	—.010
Sales and Clerical	(102)	44	45	11	.005
Labour	(268)	35	48	17	.062
Farm	(94)	35	54	11	.103
Public	(274)	32	47	21	.071
Secondary	(321)	40	53	7	.069
University	(76)	51	43	5	—.041
Liberal	(197)	42	55	14	.009
Progressive Cons.	(189)	36	55	39	.105
NDP	(22)	50	50		0

	CIPO 318				
	N	TOO MUCH	NOT TOO MUCH	NO OPIN- ION	COEFFICIENT OF IM- BALANCE
Canada	(696)	53	36	11	—.09
Atlantic	(66)	30	59	11	.171
Quebec	(191)	56	31	14	—.14
Ontario	(251)	52	38	10	—.073
Prairies	(122)	61	31	8	—.183
British Columbia	(66)	61	27	12	—.207
Professional	(37)	46	51	3	.026
Business	(65)	59	35	6	—.142
Sales and Clerical	(85)	52	39	9	—.068
Labour	(332)	53	36	11	—.090
Farm	(62)	58	29	13	—.168
Public	(240)	50	33	17	—.085
Secondary	(335)	53	39	8	—.074
University	(121)	64	32	3	—.205
Liberal	(217)	48	42	11	—.029
Progressive Cons.	(146)	53	33	14	—.106
NDP	(101)	64	28	8	—.230

TABLE 8 (continued)

	N	US TV Influence CIPO 339			
	N	TOO MUCH	NOT TOO MUCH	NO OPIN- ION	COEFFICIENT OF IM- BALANCE
Canada	(476)	48	41	11	—.034
Atlantic	(55)	38	46	16	.037
Quebec	(57)	33	58	9	.145
Ontario	(214)	52	38	10	—.073
Prairies	(90)	47	38	16	—.042
British Columbia	(60)	58	35	7	—.133
Professional	(47)	66	28	6	—.251
Business	(62)	48	39	13	—.043
Sales and Clerical	(65)	45	48	8	.014
Labour	(194)	46	42	12	—.018
Farm	(37)	39	43	19	.017
Public	(114)	40	41	19	.004
Secondary	(249)	47	43	10	—.019
University	(77)	66	30	4	—.238
Liberal	(143)	53	39	8	—.055
Progressive Cons.	(79)	42	47	11	.024
NDP	(61)	59	26	15	—.195

content in their programming. The closeness of the border and the spread of cable television permit Canadians to watch American television directly. CIPO 341 (May 1970) indicated that 60 percent of the Canadian population received American television directly, and with the subsequent spread of cable television, the percentage today is certainly higher. American influence on Canadian way of life was specifically tied to the influence of American television in a question asked in January 1970 (CIPO 339). Responses to this question are also summarized in table 8.

Quebeckers appear the least likely to identify American television as a primary instrument of cultural penetration. The reasons are obvious in examining exposure. On the same poll, nine out of ten non-Quebeckers reported watching American television, while only three in ten Quebeckers did. The language barrier showed up dramatically in blocking this particular avenue of influence. For the other categories, we find an expected elite-mass difference in opinion. The university educated, professionals, and businessmen were most likely to resent the influence of American television, while the mass audience from the less educated and lower status occupations tended to divide about equally on the question of excessive influence on Canadian culture. On the same poll, those who watch both Canadian and American television (71 percent of respondents) were asked which was better. Half replied the US programs were better, 30 percent said there was little difference, and only 15 percent found Canadian programs better. Of those who thought that American television was influencing the Canadian way of life excessively, more than half thought US programs were better. With Quebec opinion excluded, there is strong support for the argument that anglophone Canada finds American television a prime ingredient in American culutral domination.[17]

In January 1971, Canadians were asked if they were concerned that textbooks would now be published in the United States as a result of recent sales of Canadian publishing houses to American companies. This question revealed particular sensitivities. Thirty-five percent of the Canadian sample said they were very concerned, 28 percent were mildly concerned, while only 26 percent expressed no concern. In the open-ended replies, respondents expressed fear of an American bias in the textbooks as well as generalized resentment of American control. The textbook influence appeared considerably more sensitive

---

[17] Domination is used here in the sense of a psychological relationship that depends less on the intention of the dominator than the awareness of the dominator's presence and perception of weakness by the dominated. High attention and a perception of relative inferiority of Canadian television provide the basic ingredients for a relationship of domination.

than the presence of American professors in Canadian universities, a topic much debated by the 1970s, particularly in Ontario universities. Nearly half of the Canadian population sampled in May 1971 (CIPO 347) said the presence of American professors did not matter, while 36 percent said there were too many, and 15 percent were undecided. The younger (54 percent of 18-29 age group) and the university educated (60 percent) were more likely to say the presence of American professors was not a source of concern. Because these groups were previously the ones most likely to support Canadian nationalism, we concluded that whatever else may constitute the basic ingredient of Canadian nationalist feeling, it cannot be equated simply with anti-Americanism.

AMERICAN ROLE IN WORLD AFFAIRS

While specific problems in Canadian-American relations are our principal focus, these problems should be set against the general context of international politics as it has changed over the past decade. In reviewing the polls, our general impression is that questions about Canadian-American relations have come more to the fore in the past decade as East-West issues have fallen more into the background. We would expect East-West détente to result in reduced cohesion between alliance members as shared security needs appear less urgent.

Attitudes toward the conduct of the Vietnam War may have played a particularly important role in conceptions of the general tarnishing of the United States image among populations of its NATO allies. In examining the responses to questions about the Vietnam War asked over time since 1965, we find the prevalent view of a highly critical Canadian public somewhat exaggerated. When first asked in July 1965 whether it approved or disapproved the US intervention in Vietnam (and the Dominican Republic), 44 percent of the Canadian sample approved of US actions, 33 percent disapproved, and 33 percent were undecided. A majority (51 percent) of university-educated persons in Canada approved of the United States actions and only 25 percent disapproved. Rosenberg, Verba, and Converse also show greater support of government policy among university graduates than others in American attitudes toward the Vietnam War.[18] On the other hand, those in the American samples who went on to receive graduate degrees (master's and doctoral) were decidedly more dovish than less well educated compatriots on the war.

Although Canadian opinion in the initial stages was more critical of intervention than was the American public, Canadian opinion

[18] Milton J. Rosenberg, Sidney Verba, and Philip E. Converse, *Vietnam and the Silent Majority* (New York: Harper and Row, 1970), p. 58.

lagged behind the consistently critical attitudes of mass publics in the United Kingdom, France, Sweden, or Brazil, where the Gallup organization asked the same question at different points in time (table 9).

TABLE 9. WORLD OPINION ON THE WAR IN VIETNAM IN 1966 ACCORDING TO GALLUP POLLS (in percentages) *

	The US Should Withdraw Its Troops	The US Should Carry On As At Present	The US Should Increase Attacks	No Opinion
Canada	31	18	27	24
United States	18	18	55	9
Great Britain	42	17	16	25
West Germany	51	19	15	15
Australia	21	43	24	12
France	68	8	5	19

* Columns add to 100 percent across.

By 1967, US opinion showed a sharp increase (from 18 percent in 1966 to 32 percent in 1967) in the number of people who wanted troops withdrawn, matching 31 percent of Canadians who favored withdrawal at this time. Opinion in favor of withdrawal steadily increased in both countries after 1966, with Canadian opinion in favor of withdrawal lagging somewhat behind American opinion from 1968 on. A comparison of the most recent poll (November 1971, CIPO 350) with American Gallup data (1971) on whether the war was a mistake shows the following: Canada—51 percent said it was a mistake, 27 percent said it was not a mistake, and 22 percent was undecided; United States—61 percent said it was a mistake, 28 percent said it was not a mistake, and 11 percent was undecided.

Over time Atlantic Canadians were consistently more supportive of US actions and favored escalation over withdrawal. Quebeckers were consistently opposed to all areas of American intervention in the early years, but opinions in British Columbia and Ontario had become the most negative by 1971 (table 10). Given the strong hostility in France to American policy in Vietnam (table 9), one may speculate to what degree the hostile Quebec opinion was linked to the reliance by francophone Quebec media on French news services, particularly Agence France-Presse (AFP), for foreign news while anglophone media in Canada rely on the American news services.[19]

The negative Quebec opinion can also be related to the general isolationist orientation of Quebec opinion demonstrated in two world wars. When asked whether Canada should remain in NATO (1968, CIPO 332), Quebec opinion lagged considerably behind the rest of Canada.

[19] Joseph Scanlon, "Canada Sees the World through U.S. Eyes: One Case Study in Cultural Domination," Carleton University, School of Journalism, 1973. (Mimeographed.)

TABLE 10. CANADIAN VIEWS OF VIETNAM BY REGION (in percentages)

	CIPO 325 1967 Just from what you have heard or read which of these statements comes closest to the way you feel about the war in Vietnam? The US should:				CIPO 340 1970 Would your opinions of the US go up if the US withdraws all its troops from Vietnam in the next few months?			CIPO 350 1971 In view of the developments since the US entered the fighting in Vietnam, do you think the US made a mistake in sending troops to Vietnam?		
	WITH-DRAW	CARRY ON	IN-CREASE FIGHT-ING	CAN'T SAY	UP	DOWN	NO CHANGE	YES	NO	UNDE-CIDED
National	41	16	23	20	42	16	42	51	27	22
Atlantic	25	12	39	25	35	33	33	40	36	24
Quebec	53	15	15	18	43	7	50	48	26	26
Ontario	40	14	25	20	42	19	39	53	26	21
Prairies	38	21	25	17	45	14	41	47	31	22
British Columbia	46	18	22	14	47	17	36	68	18	14

One cannot easily differentiate between the two mass populations in the United States and Canada on the basis of attitudes toward the Vietnam War. Subnational groups (blacks in the US, the Quebeckers in Canada, women in both the US and Canada) were consistently the most opposed to the war. To be critical of American involvement in Vietnam may indicate opposition to the policies of the United States government, but considering the large majorities in the United States who were similarly critical, it is difficult to argue that this in itself can be construed as being anti-American.

The Vietnam War did lead to one specific transnational problem in Canadian-American relations—the American draft evaders and military deserters who sought political refuge in Canada. The few Americans in AIPO 840 who expressed negative attitudes to Canada were most likely to cite Canadian acceptance of American draft evaders as the principal reason for their dislike. To discover how general this opinion might be, American respondents were also asked whether Canada should accept American draft evaders. Somewhat surprisingly, a majority of Americans thought Canada should accept draft evaders. The same question asked in Canada in 1968 (CIPO 332) provoked the opposite view with a majority of Canadians (51 percent) saying Canada should not accept American draft evaders. Public attitudes in this instance worked in contrary directions to their own government's position on this issue and would have acted to moderate an interstate disagreement rather than exacerbate it.

The winding down of the Vietnam War coincided with widespread disillusionment in Canada over the assumed personal involvement of the American president in the Watergate scandal.[20] When Canadians were asked in September 1973 (CIPO 361) how much confidence they had in the ability of the United States to deal wisely with present world problems, a marked downward shift in opinion from the year before became evident. In September 1972 (CIPO 355), 41 percent of Canadians sampled said they had confidence in American ability while a year later the figure dropped to 28 percent. A reasonable surmise would be that Watergate had more than offset whatever beneficial effects on Canadian public opinion the Vietnam settlement may have caused. Quebec confidence in American leadership was lower (20 percent) than that of the rest of Canada (31 percent). In spite of this very low vote of confidence (not unlike American judgments of how well President Nixon was doing in his job), a majority of Canadians still expressed in this same poll a favorable judgment

---

[20] In the summer of 1973, 89 percent of Canadians versus 96 percent of Americans had heard or read of Watergate; 55 percent versus 45 percent, respectively, believed President Nixon knew in advance of the bugging (CIPO 360).

of the United States (64 percent) with the favorable opinion of French-speaking Canadians (67 percent) exceeding that of English-speaking Canadians (62 percent).

CANADIAN NATIONALISM

External and internal factors, both cultural and economic in nature, appear to operate in a complex manner in the recent increase of Canadian nationalist feeling. A careful analysis of the nationalist phenomenon would require more focused data than that available from the Canadian Gallup polls. The previous analysis suggests that nationalist feeling among many English-speaking Canadians is closely tied to a negative reaction to American cultural and economic penetration of Canada. The groups that gave the most positive evaluation of Canadian nationalism in a poll conducted in November 1972 (CIPO 344) were the same groups that had the most negative view of American cultural and economic penetration: residents of Ontario, NDP followers, professionals and businessmen, and the university educated.[21] Considerably less support for Canadian nationalist feeling is found among residents of Quebec and the Atlantic region. There may be a lingering suspicion in these areas that preoccupation with the United States, whether judged positively or negatively, detracts attention from the needs, both symbolic and material, of the less privileged areas of Canada. The reaffirmation in the 1960s of a vibrant, self-assertive Quebec culture may have been the stimulus from which Canadians as a whole began to explore and expand their own unique multinational identity based more on national development and purpose than on reaction to their southern neighbor.[22]

---

[21] Respondents were asked simply if they regarded Canadian nationalism as a "good thing." Positive reactions were as follows: Atlantic—40 percent; Quebec—47 percent; Prairies and British Columbia—58 percent; Ontario—72 percent; professionals—65 percent; NDP followers—69 percent; Liberal followers—62 percent; and Progressive Conservative followers—58 percent.

[22] Persons who view their own nation and their own lives in a favorable light tend to see other nations in the same manner, and those who are pessimistic about their own lives and their own nations are pessimistic about others as well (see William A. Scott, "Psychological and Social Correlates of International Images," in Herbert Kelman, ed., *International Behavior* [New York: Holt, Rinehart, and Winston, 1965], pp. 87-89). Consistently throughout this decade we found that Quebeckers were much more likely than other Canadians to see relations between the English and the French in Canada to be improving. From this we infer a growing self-confidence and optimism in Quebec culture, identity, and outlook. This interpretation is of course at variance with much that is written on Quebec separatism. In the polls we examined, only a minority of Quebeckers favored separation from the rest of Canada. Even on the question of the likelihood of separation, only 25 percent of Quebeckers (1973) thought separation likely in the next five years.

CONCLUSIONS

What trends and patterns in public opinion do we discern in the data reported here?

1. Economic relations, particularly American investment in Canada and control of substantial sectors of the Canadian economy, are perceived by the public as the most important issues in Canadian-American relations. Canadians believe that past US investment has been beneficial to Canada but that further investment is not needed. There is widespread support for government regulation of United States investment but a divided opinion on the means for achieving this regulation were it to imply some reduction in the Canadian standard of living.

2. Although cultural issues are less frequently mentioned than economic issues as major problems in Canadian-American relations, substantial support can be found particularly among the elite for government policies of regulating the flow of American cultural imports and supporting Canadian cultural development.

3. Current Canadian nationalism at the mass level appears to be a complex mixture of growing Canadian consciousness and attention to internal problems as well as a reaction to American economic and cultural penetration.

4. Interstate political issues appear to play a far less salient role in terms of attention and attitudes in recent Canadian-American relations, although Canadian government criticism of the conduct of the Vietnam War was shared by substantial sectors of the Canadian populace.

5. Public moods in English-speaking Canada toward the United States are strongly affected by the drama of national politics in the United States. The Camelot to Watergate decade has left its traces on Canadian confidence in American leadership.

6. While a trend toward increased resentment of American economic and cultural penetration can be identified, we find no evidence to support the view of rampant anti-Americanism in the Canadian mass public. Canadians continue to feel closer to the United States than any other country, and esteem, while diminished, remains high.

7. Substantial regional, occupational, and educational differences can be found in Canada toward issues in Canadian-American relations. The Atlantic region is marked by substantial sympathy for the United States and is less critical of American cultural and economic penetration. Quebec opinion appears more insulated from the effects of American penetration. Quebeckers are less apt than others to express any views on this range of issues and less likely

to be concerned about United States economic influence. Their
resentment of the impact of the American way of life on Canadians
is not linked to direct penetration through such media as television
but may be linked to the notion that excessive attention to the
United States detracts English-speaking Canadians from Canadian, and specifically Quebec, problems. Anti-American orientations generally seem to find less support east of Ottawa in the older
established cultures of Quebec and the Atlantic. Ontario respondents, while most appreciative of the benefits of American investment in the past, manifest the most consistent position of opposition to American cultural and economic penetration and the most
support for Canadian nationalism.

The Canadian elite, in educational and occupational terms,
appear more concerned by American cultural and economic penetration than the rest of the public and are more supportive of current governmental practice in regulating the flow of American
capital, trade, and ideas. The mass shares less of the elite concern
with cultural penetration but will respond more enthusiastically
than the elite to more stringent measures of economic regulation,
including 51 percent Canadian ownership and nationalization of
energy resources.

8. NDP followers are clearly the most nationalist in their orientation
    on all issues in Canadian-American relations. The Progressive
    Conservative followers are the most sharply divided, possibly re-
    flecting the regional differences in party strength between Ontario
    and the Atlantic region. The Progressive Conservative followers
    occupied the middle ground on the American question in the early
    sixties during the leadership of Prime Minister Diefenbaker, who
    often adopted a critical posture toward the United States and a
    defense of the monarchy. Liberal followers have occupied the
    middle ground since the middle sixties, largely reflecting their own
    regional electoral strength in Quebec. On this, as many other ques-
    tions in Canadian politics, it is primarily Quebec opinion that
    influences the agenda and establishes constraints on federal gov-
    ernment policy.

9. The American public has a high regard for Canada but little
    knowledge of Canada or the impact of the United States on Can-
    ada. The paucity of interest and attention in the United States
    may be one of the most serious asymmetries in Canadian-American
    relations.

The Canadian government appears to have been slow in reacting
to growing unfavorable public opinion about increasing private US
investment and control of the Canadian economy. Substantial support

can be found for efforts at regulation of US investment, even nation-alization in such sensitive areas as petroleum which is preponderantly controlled by American multinational corporations. Federal govern-ment hesitation in these areas may be explained by the greater salience of questions of employment and prices, the fear that interference with capital or trade flows may jeopardize Canadian prosperity, and dif-ferences in provincial government interests.

Canadian government initiative in this area appears severely restricted by the dependence of the country's economy on trade with the United States, a dependence that was further extended by the Canadian government in initiating the free-trade area in automotive products in the mid-sixties. Free trade in general, which appears to be supported by public opinion in both countries, may be beneficial to Canada as a whole, but those regions with a substantial indigenous Canadian industry and capital, notably Ontario and British Columbia, may find themselves relatively disadvantaged and lose their present privileged position. In this sense, we find some support for the argu-ment that Canadian nationalism, directed in the general public pri-marily at American economic penetration, finds its greatest support among the more privileged in Canada, whether defined in regional (Ontario), educational (university educated), or occupational terms (professionals and businessmen). It can be argued that a dispropor-tionate number of the attentive public that is aware of the issues involved and active in the political process is found in these same categories.

For Canada, transnational relations with the United States are a critical ingredient in the politics of the country as a whole, operating largely through political culture and domestic political processes more than in interstate relations directly. Increased attention to the United States through media penetration and increased involvement through heavy investment and trade have raised major questions for Canadian identity and independence. A healthy concern with Canadian prob-lems and Canadian identity built on the unique character of this multi-ethnic society appears to be emerging as Canadians divert some of the excessive attention of recent years to the United States and the American presence.

PART III

ISSUE AREAS

CAPITAL MOVEMENTS AND GOVERNMENT CONTROL

Gerald Wright and Maureen Appel Molot

Canadian anxiety about increasing involvement with the American economy is partly based on a deeply rooted conviction that economic dependence necessarily brings political dependence in its wake. That conviction was at the bottom of the Canadian rejection of proposals of reciprocity with the United States in the general elections of 1891 and 1911. It has also been explicitly recognized as an underlying rationale of Canadian policy toward the United States in the Department of External Affairs's recent paper on Canadian-American relations.[1]

In the early 1960s, the capital movements linkage joining Canada and the United States suddenly became the object of a government's bid for control. Our intention is to illustrate the dynamic whereby one particular variety of economic dependence was translated into political consequences and to evaluate the outcome.

THE CAPITAL LINKAGE

The American share of foreign long-term capital investment in Canada has long been greater than that of other countries, and by the late 1950s more private American capital was invested in Canada than in any other country. The return flow of Canadian capital was a mere fraction of this amount, but it represented the greatest proportion of Canadian funds sent abroad. For our purposes, the most salient components of the linkage constructed by these capital transactions were United States direct investment in Canada and movements of equities and long-term debt.

Gerald Wright is with the Donner Canadian Foundation in Toronto, and Maureen Appel Molot is a member of the Department of Political Science at Carleton University in Ottawa.
[1] Mitchell Sharp, "Canada-US Relations: Options for the Future," *International Perspectives* (bimonthly publication of the Department of External Affairs), special issue (Autumn 1972).

Over half the flow of capital from the United States to Canada in the 1950-63 period was in the form of direct investment. These funds were used to finance capital formation, to buy existing Canadian-owned assets, or to provide working capital. The fundamental attractions of the Canadian economy were its market opportunities and its resources. American companies wishing to expand their operations abroad were able to move into a market that was close at hand, politically stable, and exhibited cultural characteristics broadly similar to those with which the companies were familiar. Moreover, the discovery of large supplies of natural resources in Canada, such as the oil reserves of the Province of Alberta, expanded the range of profitable opportunities for investment.

The second major component of the capital linkage was portfolio transactions in Canadian and foreign securities. These included transactions in outstanding securities and, more importantly, the flotation of new issues by Canadian borrowers in the New York capital market. In the early 1960s, Canadians accounted for almost half of the new issue borrowing in New York by foreigners. Many of the Canadian borrowers had established close ties with US underwriters, and enjoyed good reputations among lenders. Canada was one of the safest possible locations for American funds, and this explained why United States insurance companies, trust companies, pension and endowment funds—institutions that had to place a special premium on the security of their investments—had been major purchasers of Canadian securities.

Canadian borrowers' requirements were much too large and lumpy for the domestic resources that could be committed to them. Canadian savings could actually have financed a larger portion of net capital formation than the then prevailing figure of 60 percent, but a considerable amount was invested abroad, mostly in New York. There, for example, Canadian investors were able to purchase the glamor stocks of fast growing companies, choose from a much greater diversity of investments, and move in and out more easily because of the depth of the market.

The existence of the capital linkage created several important structural limitations on the freedom of action of the Canadian government in seeking to attain national goals. Direct investment, of course, carried with it the influence of US head offices and, indirectly, the influence of the American government on these head offices.[2] Further, the distinguishing characteristic of an integrated market

_____

[2] For a discussion of the potential for conflict arising from this head-office influence, see Isaiah A. Litvak and Christopher J. Maule, "Canadian-US Corporate Interface and Transnational Relations," in this volume.

was that capital movements were highly responsive to interest rate differences between countries. Depending on the circumstances, these movements could be supportive or subversive of a government's monetary, fiscal, and debt management policies.[3] The linkage thus helped determine the parameters of Canadian freedom of action. As we will see, it could also affect the outcome when the two governments collided over policy goals.

THE CLASH OF OBJECTIVES

The major force that transformed the capital linkage into a subject of bilateral controversy was the United States administration's perception of a serious payments problem. Americans were exporting immense quantities of capital, which increased the dollar *overhang*, the outstanding dollar balances that the government was pledged to redeem for gold. Some foreign central banks, as well as individual purchasers, were forcing the United States to make good on this pledge, and the picture of a continuously dwindling American gold supply was causing mounting anxiety at home and abroad.

By deciding to make the reduction of the deficit on capital account its central policy thrust, the Kennedy administration appeared to disregard the United States's evident comparative advantage as an exporter of capital. This policy decision could have been shown to be counterproductive over the long term, for the capital investment already in place was a source of interest and dividend payments, and provided important export markets, all of which bolstered the current account. However, the pressing task confronting US decision makers was to alter the psychology of world financial markets. They had to be able to show an immediate statistical improvement in the payments balance to restore international confidence in the American dollar.

The extent to which the United States government formulated a specific goal of improving the bilateral balance with Canada, and indeed the extent to which US policymakers possessed a clear perception of the capital linkage, are still matters of debate.[4] Statements

---

[3] For an empirical analysis of the impact of capital flows on national policy, see Richard E. Caves and Grant L. Reuber, "International Capital Markets and Canadian Economic Policy under Flexible and Fixed Exchange Rates, 1951-1970," in Federal Reserve Bank of Boston, *Canadian–United States Financial Relationships* (proceedings of a conference held in September 1971), pp. 9-36.

[4] The view that the Interest Equalization Tax was inadvertently applied to Canada can be found in Walter Gordon, *A Choice for Canada* (Toronto: McClelland and Stewart, 1966), p. 72. A contrary view is taken in Gerald Wright, "Persuasive Influence: The Case of the Interest Equalization Tax," in W. Andrew Axline, James Hyndman, Peyton Lyon, and Maureen Molot, eds., *Continental Community? Independence and Integration in North America* (Toronto: McClelland and Stewart, 1974).

made by Secretary of the Treasury Douglas Dillon and Undersecretary Robert Roosa in 1963 did indicate explicitly that Canadian borrowings, which had been unprecedentedly high in the early part of that year, should be significantly moderated, though not entirely halted. By 1968, the kernel of the United States problem was clearly understood to be the payments deficits with West European countries. Yet a natural predilection for uniformity, the difficulty of justifying special treatment for one country to European allies and to the Congress, and the possibility that an exempted country could leak American funds abroad—all militated against special status for capital transactions with Canada.

Furthermore, the willingness of United States officials to treat Canada differently from other countries could hardly have been enhanced by the noticeable upsurge of Canadian nationalism, which appeared to have gained a temporary foothold in the new government of Lester Pearson. In June of 1963, Minister of Finance Walter Gordon made an abortive effort to limit the degree of American control of Canadian enterprise. His first budget proposed a tax of 30 percent on foreign take-overs of Canadian-owned companies and introduced a differentiation in the rate of withholding tax on dividends, favoring the shareholders of companies that had at least 25 percent of their shares in Canadian hands. An immediate downturn on Canadian stock exchanges and an angry deputation to the minister from the Montreal Stock Exchange, complaining of the budget's effect on foreign providers of capital, caused the take-over tax to be jettisoned. Later, the withholding tax changes were also considerably diluted. Mr. Gordon's biographer has reported that this action was due to complaints received from Canadian businessmen and the US Department of State.[5]

Mr. Gordon's measures were avowedly formulated in such a manner as to leave unhindered the inflow of debt capital from US financial institutions. Canada had consistently been running a large current account deficit with the United States.[6] For the Canadian monetary authorities, therefore, the capital inflow was the means on which they relied to pay for most of their current deficit. For Canadian provincial, municipal, and corporate borrowers, too, the link was important. It represented access to a market with unparalleled depth and efficiency, on which they depended to meet a substantial portion of their

---

[5] Denis Smith, *Gentle Patriot: A Political Biography of Walter Gordon* (Edmonton: Hurtig Publishers, 1973), p. 197.

[6] According to Canadian statistics, the deficit was $1,092 million in 1962 (Dominion Bureau of Statistics, *The Canadian Balance of International Payments, A Compendium of Statistics From 1946 to 1965* [Ottawa: Queen's Printer, 1967], pp. 20-21).

capital needs, and to which no alternative source of funds was then available.

In the 1960s, the financial requirements of the provincial governments began to increase enormously. Over the decade the total provincial government debt doubled, from $10 billion to $20 billion. Massive social expenditures were undertaken to expand the role of government assistance from that of an emergency palliative to that of a provider of universal security. Highway construction, university building, and the expansion of hydroelectric power utilities all made heavy financial demands. In particular, Quebec's need for capital reflected political aspirations that if unsatisfied could have had seriously disintegrative effects on the Canadian federation.

A possible rupture of the capital linkage, therefore, threatened consequences of much greater immediacy for Canada than for the United States. The adjustment process promised to be lengthy and difficult for Canadians and their government. At the same time, the particular interests dependent on foreign capital possessed the political means of strengthening the Canadian government's resolve to preserve the flow of American investment. In a different sense, dependence on this flow had become a conventional wisdom of the Canadian business community. American capital had, after all, developed natural resources, brought in new technologies, created employment opportunities, and opened up new markets.

CANADA AND THE AMERICAN CAPITAL RESTRICTIONS

The Interest Equalization Tax

The Interest Equalization Tax, the first serious measure taken by the United States government to stem the capital outflow, was made public on 18 July 1963. This tax was intended to add 1 percent to the cost of all long-term borrowing by foreigners in the United States, and to increase the price of purchases of foreign equities by 15 percent. The Canadian financial community reacted in considerable panic. A loss to the exchange reserves of about $110 million was, in large measure, due to the actions of corporate treasurers of US subsidiaries. Fearing that the Canadian government's response to the new tax would be to devalue the dollar, they transferred available cash reserves back to their head offices. At the same time, heavy selling on the stock exchanges reflected another possibility—that the Canadian authorities might seek to overcome the new disincentive for US capital export to Canada by encouraging a rise in interest rates, and that this would renew the economic recession of the preceding period.

A Canadian delegation led by Louis Rasminsky, governor of the Bank of Canada, left at once for Washington to meet with an American group, headed by Secretary Dillon. The Canadian officials tried to convince their American counterparts that Canada's capital drawings were going to pay for its large current deficit with the United States. In overall terms, transactions with Canada were actually contributing strength to the American balance. Yet if the flow of US capital were to be cut off, the Canadian government would have had to take immediate action to reduce the current deficit. This would have been bound to hurt United States exports to Canada, and thereby negate any improvement in the overall US balance.[7]

The spreading financial panic in Canada had already convinced the authors of the tax to exempt new Canadian issues. However, they wanted an understanding that Canadians would not overborrow, and so they asked that borrowing in their market be controlled.[8] When the Canadian negotiators protested that the constitutional position of their government was too weak to enable it successfully to regulate the foreign borrowing of provincial governments, American officials settled, instead, for a Canadian commitment not to let the prevailing level of monetary reserves be exceeded.

While the commitment was to be interpreted with some flexibility, Canada's reserve levels were from then on subject to constant American surveillance. In response to an American request to help "dress up" the year-end balance, for example, the Canadian authorities called a temporary halt, at the end of 1964, to provincial borrowing in New York. This move was repeated, and extended to all Canadian borrowing, for a period at the end of 1965.

[7] Bank of Canada Governor Louis Rasminsky summarized the Canadian position on a number of occasions, for example, in the Bank's 1964 annual report: "Canada has a large current account deficit with the United States which exceeds our imports of capital from that country. When all of Canada's borrowings and other imports of capital from the United States have been used to pay for our net imports of American goods and services, there remains a balance owing to the United States. This is paid for out of our net earnings from trade with other countries, out of the proceeds of our current gold production, and out of our capital imports from other countries. If the United States took steps to cut its exports of capital to Canada sharply below the level needed to finance the deficit which remained after we had used all the non-American sources of finance referred to, we would be faced with a severe loss of reserves and with the inevitable need to cut our current account deficit. Since the whole of this deficit is with the United States and about 70 percent of our imports come from that country, the impact of whatever steps we took would necessarily fall very largely on the United States, and that country would not have succeeded in improving its payments position" (Bank of Canada, *Annual Report of the Governor To The Minister of Finance for The Year 1964* [Ottawa, 1965], p. 8).

[8] Interviews with Canadian negotiators, 3 September 1971 and 11 January 1972.

The 1965 Guidelines

In February 1965, the United States administration made another attempt to restrict capital outflow by promulgating guidelines to regulate the foreign operations of industrial corporations, banks, and other financial institutions. The administration tightened these guidelines considerably in December 1965. Canada was exempted from a Federal Reserve Board restriction on capital outflow, because of the American officials' unwillingness to incur a repetition of the 1963 crisis,[9] but only after the Canadian authorities had agreed to lower the reserves ceiling by a further $100 million.

Canada was, however, made subject to the direct investment guideline, which in practice meant that the 1966 investment inflow from US corporations would have to be cut back from the 1965 level. Direct investment was defined to include earnings retained by a foreign subsidiary as well as the parent's new transfers of capital abroad. This was particularly threatening to Canada, where undistributed earnings from US direct investment in manufacturing had been a much larger source of capital expansion than fresh flows of United States funds.

By means of the guideline, the American government was forcibly enlisting companies with Canadian operations in the pursuit of a national economic policy objective. These companies were enjoined to make a greater contribution to the US payments balance by increasing exports, repatriating foreign earnings, and raising investment funds abroad. Worksheets were issued to them for quarterly reports of capital movements. The personal responsibility of corporation presidents for their companies' performance was stressed. The adjective *voluntary*, which officially described the guideline, was interpreted with a grain of salt, for it was widely believed that the withdrawal of government purchasing orders and other similar, informal sanctions would follow from noncompliance.

The Canadian government's initial reaction was typically anodyne, but a growing wave of protest over the guideline's implied interference with Canadian business behavior, combined with official concern about its potential effect on employment, forced more aggressive representations to Washington. In consequence, in March of 1966, the United States–Canadian Committee on Trade and Economic Affairs issued a communiqué stating that the US government did not expect American subsidiaries in Canada to make the considerable repatriation of funds seemingly required by a literal interpretation of the guideline.[10] The degree to which transactions with Canada remained

---

[9] Interview with US official, 5 April 1972.
[10] The communiqué is reprinted in Canada, House of Commons, *Debates*, 9 March 1966, p. 2348.

restricted was left, quite deliberately, shrouded in ambiguity. Once again, however, the American authorities had had to recognize that the dimensions of the American stake in the Canadian economy made it a special case. The conviction of at least some of the officials on both sides was that the spending programs of subsidiaries in Canada were so integrally connected with those of the parent companies that strict application of the direct investment guideline would have been practically inconceivable.[11]

A major reason that United States officials did not want to give Canada a more definitive exemption was their abiding suspicion that US funds were, in effect, being leaked by banks, insurance companies, and possibly by multinational industrial corporations to the lucrative Eurodollar market. The Canadian authorities attempted to allay these suspicions by requesting, in February of 1965, that all chartered banks conduct their foreign currency operations in such a way that the net position of their head offices and Canadian branches vis-à-vis residents of the United States not be reduced below the position that existed at the end of 1964. A long unannounced policy of discouraging foreign borrowing in Canada was made explicit in March of 1966, when the minister of finance requested Canadian investors not to purchase "offshore" securities of US corporations (or their non-Canadian subsidiaries). Even before that request, Canadian underwriters, in apparent deference to the US government's concern, were refusing to make Eurodollar bond issues available to potential Canadian purchasers.[12]

The 1968 Guidelines

A worsening payments problem, compounded by the Vietnam War and British devaluation in November of 1967, induced the Johnson administration to intensify its remedial efforts at the beginning of 1968. Canada preserved its privileged access to the US capital market but was made subject to a mandatory limit on direct investment, in several respects more stringent than that of 1965. Again, the finance minister tried to soothe public apprehensions, but this time he was even less successful than in 1965. This further flouting of Canada's economic interdependence with the United States triggered a crisis of confidence which other international and domestic difficulties had prepared. Hedging of Canadian dollar positions markedly increased during January, much of it, in the opinion of Canadian authorities, traceable to US-controlled subsidiaries. The evidence of economic weakness was self-generating, as speculators pushed the value of the

[11] Interviews with Canadian and US officials, 20 October 1971 and 5 April 1972.
[12] *Globe and Mail* (Toronto), 18 February 1966.

Canadian dollar to the lower limit of its permitted fluctuation. In January, the Canadian reserves lost about $350 million.

Canadian officials urgently requested the United States treasury secretary to emphasize that executives of subsidiaries in Canada should not transfer abnormal quantities of funds to their parent companies. This was done by means of a statement on 21 January, but to little effect. The subsidiaries appeared to be moving their funds ahead of expected retaliatory action by the Canadian government. In February, Mr. Pearson and his ministers did indeed give serious consideration to floating the dollar, but were apparently dissuaded from this by Mr. Rasminsky's warning that the United States government would retaliate by revoking the exemption from the Interest Equalization Tax.[13] The crisis did, however, precipitate another series of intense bilateral negotiations.

Again, as in 1963, it was the disarray of the Canadian financial community that swayed the American authorities. The run on the Canadian dollar appeared particularly dangerous because the administration's bill to remove the gold backing from the US currency was before Congress at the time.[14] This was intended to strengthen international confidence in the dollar by freeing all United States reserves for its defence. A Canadian devaluation, by seeming to worsen prospects for the US balance of payments, would have undoubtedly caused an immediate increase in the gold outflow, thus damaging the prospects of the bill.

A blanket exemption from the guidelines program was agreed upon, but not before American officials attempted unsuccessfully to fix a firm constraint on Canada, in the form of an undertaking to keep its foreign exchange surplus with third countries undiminished.[15] A more practical concession, which was extracted from the Canadian negotiators, was agreement to shift Canada's US dollar holdings into a form in which these would not be shown as a liquid claim on the United States. Secondly, the Canadians undertook to mount a more comprehensive effort to block the pass-through by issuing their own guidelines governing the holding of foreign currency claims on residents of countries other than the United States and Canada. The price of exemption was, in essence, the extension of the United States regulations to include its partner in the capital linkage.

The cross-border capital flow continued throughout this period. While President Johnson's direct investment guidelines did affect the spending programs of US-controlled subsidiaries, there was no obvious

[13] Smith, p. 341.
[14] Interview with US official, 6 April 1972.
[15] Interview with Canadian official, 20 October 1971.

sign of stress for the Canadian economy. Canada's surplus on bilateral portfolio transactions in Canadian securities nearly doubled
between 1963 and 1968 (see diagram 1). There was a considerable
movement of short-term capital in favor of the United States, but the
US basic balance with Canada deteriorated steadily until 1971.

Canadians showed much greater hesitancy to borrow abroad, partly
because of their government's requests to underwriters to keep borrowing at home, and partly because of uncertainty over future United
States actions.[16] Econometric analysis has demonstrated that the
sensitivity of Canadian borrowing to US long-term interest rates
declined in this period.[17] Thus, the degree of capital market integration was somewhat reduced, probably due to the repeated governmental interventions.

On the other hand, the moral suasion that kept borrowers at home
also contributed to the broadening and deepening of the Canadian
capital market, whereby it could absorb a much larger volume of new
issues. Fortuitously, large concentrations of investment capital were
now also available in Europe. Ontario and Consolidated-Bathurst
Limited both floated loans with West German banks in 1968. The
federal government sold its own bonds in Italy and Germany at this
time and suggested the same course to other provincial governments,
which followed suit.[18] The level of bilateral portfolio transactions in
Canadian securities abruptly declined for a period after 1969 (see
diagram 1). This lessened the importance of the New York market,
though it was still to be required for floating major provincial issues
and assuring the financing of future large-scale resource developments, like the Mackenzie pipeline or the James Bay power project.

THE POLITICAL OUTCOME

Policy Coordination

We have seen that between 1963 and 1968 the Canadian government deliberately made a number of policy choices that were supportive of the American payments objective. Moreover, two concrete
commitments were fixed on Canada: the reserves ceiling in 1963, and
an undertaking in 1968 to make a more comprehensive effort to
prevent pass-throughs.

The price Canada paid for the maintenance of reasonably free
access to the American capital market from 1963 to 1968 was the

---

[16] Even after the announcement of the Canadian exemption from the Interest
Equalization Tax, for example, borrowers did not feel free to return to the New
York market until the first half of 1964.

[17] Caves and Reuber, pp. 28-29.

[18] Interview with Canadian official, 3 April 1972.

retention of a ceiling on monetary reserves. The ceiling was initially set at $2.7 billion (US), later lowered to $2.6 billion in return for exemption from the 1965 Federal Reserve Board guideline, and reduced again in May 1966 to $2.55 billion. Its effect was that Canada's surplus in transactions with third countries had to be used in support of the United States balance.

Though the ceiling was sometimes breached, there appears little doubt that it had an inhibiting effect on Canadian monetary policy. By mid-1965 the Canadian economy had recovered from an earlier recession, and its productive capacity was at the point of being fully utilized. Yet the Bank of Canada continued to permit unusually large increases in the money supply, apparently to moderate the interest rate differential between Canada and the United States and thereby to control the inflow of American funds. Domestic considerations, such as the need to dampen rampant inflation, were subordinated to an external constraint—the need to stay within the reserves limit.[19]

In 1967, Canadian officials began to make serious efforts to get the ceiling on reserves lifted, arguing, in their customary way, that the United States would not want, for its own good, to feed inflationary forces on the North American continent. The Canadian agreement to shift US dollar holdings into a less liquid form of securities lessened the Americans' need for the ceiling, and it was relaxed in December 1968. The Americans referred to the new understanding as a "redefinition" of the 1963 agreement, whereby Canada could now accumulate reserves but not by means of borrowings in the United States. As the widening spread between long-term interest rates in the two countries showed, the Canadians considered they had won a total abrogation of the reserves agreement.

The Canadian guidelines of 1968, the quid pro quo for exemption from President Johnson's mandatory program, were promulgated in stages, after being shown to the joint Balance of Payments Committee. The guidelines for chartered banks had the effect that an increase in lending in countries other than the United States or Canada had to be compensated by an increase in deposits from these countries. Foreign currency claims on residents of third countries held by nonbank financial institutions (e.g., investment companies, insurance

[19] In his annual reports of 1965, 1966, and 1967, Bank of Canada Governor Louis Rasminsky referred to the influence of the reserves accord on Canadian monetary policy. In his 1965 report the governor stated: "The fact . . . that monetary policy did have to take account of important external factors, including the reserve agreement with the United States, provides a clear reminder of one of its important characteristics, namely its influence on international capital flows which may in certain circumstances be a limitation on its use" (Bank of Canada, *Annual Report of the Governor to The Minister of Finance For The Year 1965* [Ottawa, 1966], p. 6).

companies, pension funds) were not to rise above a specified level unless accompanied by an equal increase in foreign currency liabilities to third country residents, or unless the rise could be accounted to net earnings of foreign branches or subsidiaries. The guidelines for non-financial corporations requested general restrictions on capital transfers abroad, especially to continental Europe; an exception was made for investments "expected to bring large and early benefits to Canada's trade and payments position." [20]

The Canadian restrictions did not precisely replicate the American programs. Canadian institutions were unaffected in their control of retained earnings, and no measure comparable to the Interest Equalization Tax was instituted to induce individuals to keep their funds at home. Yet taken together with the March exemption from virtually all US restrictions, the 1968 Canadian guidelines established a form of a continental common market for capital. Funds could flow freely between the countries but movements between Canada and overseas were restricted in much the same way as movements between the United States and overseas. As the US government altered its directives after 1968, the Canadian regulations were amended to remain parallel with these, until, in early 1974, both governments simultaneously lifted their controls.

Flows of investment capital from Canada to third countries had not, in the past, been very large. Yet at least in the eyes of the US administration, Canadian banks had developed the expertise that made imminent the assumption of a major role in the Eurodollar market. Both banks and other financial institutions were rendered unable to exploit fully the opportunities afforded by this market, or by the newly developing Japanese growth funds. Similarly, some Canadian manufacturers were probably prevented from making initial investments abroad.

Institutional Links

The only new institutional link established as a result of the 1963-68 events was the joint Balance of Payments Committee. Both sides had been convinced of the need for better communications by the turmoil following announcement of the Interest Equalization Tax. The committee was set up in September 1963 to facilitate more continuous consultations about the impact of each government's policies on the bilateral balance. Representation at the meetings, which could be held several times a year, varied with the issues discussed, but it

[20] "Statement by the Minister of Trade and Commerce dated September 19, 1968, announcing guidelines for Canadian incorporated companies, other than financial institutions," contained in Bank of Canada, *Annual Report of the Governor to The Minister of Finance for The Year 1968* (Ottawa, 1968), p. 72.

always included the Department of Finance, the Department of Trade and Commerce, and the Bank of Canada, on the Canadian side, and the Treasury Department, the Federal Reserve Board, the Department of Commerce, and the Council of Economic Advisers, on the American side.

The personal relationships forged in committee sessions carried over into the frequent informal contacts of officials. It was customary that after the formal sessions Treasury Department and Federal Reserve officials, on the American side, and Department of Finance and Bank of Canada officials, on the Canadian side, would hold private meetings. It was at these meetings that the most sensitive issues of Canadian reserve levels and forward market positions were raised.[21] Officials of both the US Department of Commerce and the Canadian Department of Trade and Commerce were deliberately excluded. These officials could have disrupted an attempt to build common ground between the two sides on the basis of a shared interest in international monetary stability because their perspective on international payments issues would have been colored by a primary interest in national trade balances.[22]

The committee thus possessed the makings of a significant transgovernmental coalition or possibly of an influence base, but it was never really effective in either respect. The members did make a joint effort to get their governments to apply fiscal restraint in the mid-sixties, but they were positioned too far below the top policymaking level to command serious attention on either side.[23] On occasion, the United States representatives suggested the possibility of a single integrated balance-of-payments presentation for both countries, dangling the carrot that this cosmetic alteration might make it easier to justify special treatment for Canada.[24] Yet the Canadians were too wary of any mechanism that implied a degree of policy coordination to be attracted to this. In addition, the sense of shared interest that was promoted by common professional backgrounds, perspectives, and tasks was held in check by disagreements over the Canadian pass-through and forward market dealings.[25]

[21] Forward market dealings could have served the Canadian authorities as a means of escaping the constraint of the reserves limit.

[22] Interviews with Canadian and US members of the committee, 4 July 1969 and 6 April 1972.

[23] Interview with US member of the committee, 5 April 1972.

[24] Interview with Canadian member of the committee, 20 October 1971.

[25] For a more detailed discussion of formal and informal Canadian-US consultation during this period as well as some discussion of the reasons behind Canadian reluctance to participate in highly institutionalized mechanisms of joint policy coordination, see Maureen Appel Molot, "The Role of Institutions in Canada–United States Relations: The Case of North American Financial Ties," in Axline et al.

Elite Attitudes

The 1963-68 episode made more explicit the Canadian financial community's commitment to the free flow of capital between Canada and the United States. This was first evidenced by the protest of the influential Canadian-American Committee against both the Gordon budget and the US Interest Equalization Tax of 1963.[26] The succeeding experience of unexpected announcements of capital restrictions, of intergovernmental understandings kept disconcertingly vague, and of governmental interventions in private decisions of business strategy was an unpleasant novelty as far as operators in the continental capital market were concerned. It lessened the confidence with which private dealings could be undertaken and, by enforcing inefficiency in the allocation of capital resources, appeared, in particular, to weaken Canada's economic structure.

This attitude compounded the Canadian financial community's consciousness of dependence on the US economy, and of vulnerability to its problems. The indelible impression that the primary thrust of the American programs left on private actors' minds determined their cooperativeness or recalcitrance when called upon by either government, even when the US administration tried hastily to qualify the effect of its measures on Canada. At the same time, Canadian concessions, in return for exemptions, further articulated Canadian dependence. Nervousness over the possible termination of Canadian access to the American capital market was compounded by different interpretations of the reserves agreement which were making the rounds.[27] A common view was that the monetary authorities were powerless to tackle the inflationary spiral because of the reserves ceiling.[28]

The distemper of the business community helped shape the reactions of Canadian policymakers. There was no doubt that Canada had received a hard buffeting from the American payments measures. One of Mr. Rasminsky's constant themes in the 1960s was that "A situation in which Canada needs to import a great deal of capital from a country which is trying to restrict the export of capital is inherently unsatisfactory, and there is no easy or satisfactory way of dealing with it." [29]

---

[26] Canadian-American Committee, *Recent Canadian and US Government Actions Affecting US Investment in Canada* (Washington: National Planning Association; and Montreal: Private Planning Association of Canada, 1964).

[27] Interview with Canadian official, 20 October 1971.

[28] A prominent businessman who reinforced this impression by his public utterances was W. E. McLaughlin, chairman of the Royal Bank, which is Canada's largest chartered bank.

[29] Bank of Canada, *Annual Report of the Governor to The Minister of Finance For The Year 1965*, p. 10.

The governor's annual reports indicated that the reserves agreement was increasingly felt to be a constraint on monetary policy.[30] Moreover, the Canadian quid pro quo for exemption from the mandatory guidelines of 1968 gave a very high degree of definition to the integration of the economies. Several senior officials have testified that the experience raised the issue of political independence for them in very stark terms. There was a sense of having, almost unwittingly, become locked into US economic policy decisions. This was sharpened by journalists and politicians who leveled scathing criticisms at the practice of Canadian negotiators going "cap in hand" to Washington to ask for concessions whenever a new United States program was announced.

A purposive effort to moderate the intensity of the capital linkage was, therefore, gradually set in motion. The goal of extrication from a possibly dangerous dependence was one motivation behind the government's drive to improve its bilateral trade balance by, for example, increasing auto production in Canada. That goal was reflected even more directly in the interest in exploiting new sources of capital, foreign and domestic.

THE GOVERNMENTS' PERFORMANCE

How did the existence of the capital linkage afford Canadian and American governments instruments for grappling with each other? How successful were they, in turn, in getting the cooperation of the individuals and institutions composing the linkage—corporation executives, institutional lenders, private and public borrowers, investment dealers, and banks?

The actual, and anticipated, reactions of financial markets to the successive American programs decisively influenced the way the two governments dealt with each other during this episode. In the first place, the possibly contagious effect of a Canadian financial crisis helped Canadian negotiators persuade the American officials not to go through with their policy of restricting capital outflow to Canada. The Americans were made to realize that they, too, had an interest in the preservation of the capital linkage.

United States officials were unable to calm the Canadian markets because of a more pressing need to maximize the psychological impact of their policies, by promulgating these in the form of highly publicized, declaratory injunctions. In such circumstances, it was almost impossible to communicate what was the probable intention of US policymakers—that transactions with Canada were to be restricted but not altogether abandoned. The announcement of the US programs

[30] See footnote 19 above.

had the effect of stressing Canadian vulnerability in the face of a policy offensive that appeared to be far too cumbersome and unyielding to discriminate between its victims.

American officials then substituted for their original intention an attempt to tie Canadian policy more firmly to their own by forcing a substantial degree of policy coordination. Such sporadic evidences of an antagonistic Canadian purpose as the Gordon budget had cast doubt on the linkage partner's reliability. The concern of the US administration was evidenced by Undersecretary of State George Ball, when he implied that participation in the intracontinental flow of capital imposed certain ground rules on the respective governments that could not be broken with impunity.[31] If the administration could not bring about a contraction in the capital outflow resulting from the linkage, it was evidently bound to make more explicit the political obligations of the linkage partner.

The need to calm panicky securities and foreign exchange markets also served to lever the Canadian government into assuming these obligations as the cost of exemptions. The concern that Canada might have to experience the full brunt of the United States programs provided a continuing motivation for the Canadian authorities to stay within the reserves ceiling. This was reinforced by occasional rumblings from Congress that, whether or not seriously intended, were sufficiently loud to make credible US negotiators' harping on the possibility that the exemptions might be nullified when these came up for legislative review. By repeatedly indicating their concern, provincial governments and corporate borrowers also kept up the pressure on the Canadian government to help keep their access to the New York market.

The official Canadian response to American actions was one of deliberate mildness. Ministers and officials avoided recourse to such abstractions as Canadian sovereignty, which they could have claimed was in danger, and appeared bent, instead, on blurring any public perception of a clash of states' wills. They found their bargaining advantage in the interdependence of the two national economies, on the basis of which they repeatedly argued that the health of the Canadian economy represented an important US interest. At the same time, the Canadian negotiators showed themselves quite adept at containing United States pressures for a greater degree of policy coordination in the form of more tightly defined, more easily inspected undertakings.

The compact size and close interconnections of the business and

---

[31] George W. Ball, "Interdependence: The Basis of US-Canada Relations," address to the American Assembly, Arden House, New York, 25 April 1964.

government communities in Canada allowed the Canadian government to use relatively informal techniques for influencing other participants in the capital linkage and permitted a much more sensitive response to changing circumstances. Unlike the United States administration, the Canadian authorities could transmit the spirit of their intentions by the nuances of their fairly continual communication with corporate actors and large-scale borrowers. Above all, transnational actors on the Canadian side shared their government's concern for the maintenance of access to American capital.

The deputy minister of finance needed only the telephone to effect the postponement of provincial bond offerings on the New York market. Though he lacked any legal or constitutional control over the provincial authorities, they were accustomed to defer to the knowledge and expertise of the federal government in respect of borrowing abroad.[32] When an unruly Quebec cabinet minister, Eric Kierans, suggested that being cut off from American capital would be preferable to the concessions required by the Americans for exemption, the governor of the Bank of Canada was able to get him reprimanded by his premier for antagonizing the United States government.[33]

Similarly, the chartered banks were more amenable to plugging the pass-through of funds to Europe because of their intimate relationship with the Bank of Canada. This both ensured that their operations were under official surveillance and gave them confidence that their competitors were having to play by the same rules. They were also most anxious to preserve their profitable New York agency business that was under attack by United States bankers.

CONCLUSION

In 1963, the straightforward and mutually satisfying congruency of perceptions of interest, by governments and transnational actors of both countries, was cracked. The effect of the transnational actors' behavior on governmental performance was to ensure that the capital linkage remained more or less intact in the succeeding five years. By the same token, the transnational actors helped to realize the linkage's potential for political constraint on the junior partner. However, the forced adjustments in the behavior of both private and official actors had the paradoxical effect of creating a greater Canadian self-reliance by decreasing the perceived value and the dimensions of the bilateral capital flow. In a narrow issue area, and over a period of fairly short duration, therefore, economic interdependence generated both political force and counterforce.

[32] Interviews with Ontario officials, 17 September 1973 and 15 January 1974.
[33] Interview with Canadian official, 11 January 1972.

DIAGRAM 1. CANADA'S RELIANCE ON THE US CAPITAL MARKET:
NET PORTFOLIO TRANSACTIONS IN CANADIAN SECURITIES BETWEEN
CANADA AND THE UNITED STATES, 1962-1971

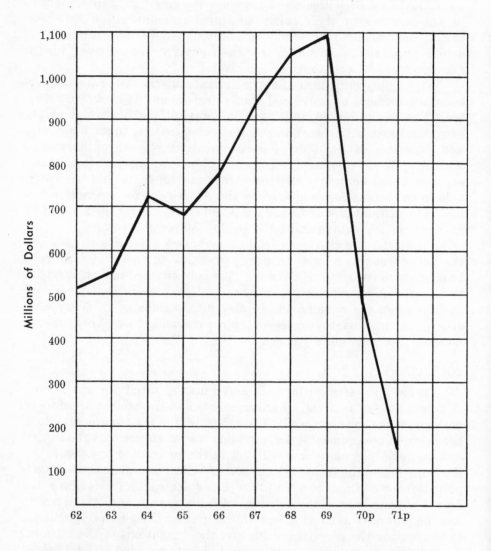

SOURCES: Dominion Bureau of Statistics, *The Canadian Balance of International Payments: A Compendium of Statistics From 1946 to 1965* (Ottawa: Queen's Printer, 1967), pp. 20-21; and Statistics Canada, *The Canadian Balance of International Payments, 1971* (Ottawa: Information Canada, 1973), p. 39.

p=preliminary figures

CANADIAN–AMERICAN TRADE IN ENERGY RESOURCES

Ted Greenwood

As events since October 1973 have again underscored, security of supply and price of energy resources have enormous strategic and economic implications for any industrialized country. Nevertheless, trade in energy resources between Canada and the United States has not always been closely managed by the central governments that are responsible for national security and economic development. In fact, the energy trade involves a wide variety of actors that continually seek transnational contacts and alliances of opportunity to further their own self-interest almost as if the national border did not exist.

In Canada this trade has become an important part of the national economy. For many years after the discovery of significant oil and gas reserves in Canada, the strong government commitment to the development of the fledgling industry led to a commonality of interest between Ottawa, industry, and the producing provinces. Ottawa was sometimes content to let others take the lead in this development but frequently became an active promoter itself. To the extent that this development required exports to the United States, Ottawa sought to provide the opportunities. More recently Ottawa has often seemed merely to react to or struggle against the initiatives and preferences of the provinces and private industry.

In the United States, where the economic impact is less, Canadian-American energy trade has tended to be buried in the press of more visible public issues unless world events or the urging of interested parties brings it to the fore. Now that all matters pertaining to energy, both domestic and international, have become politicized in both countries, the degree of central government involvement in and management of energy policy is rising. While the independence of transnational (and perhaps even transgovernmental) actors in the Canadian-American context will probably decrease as a result, the importance of transnational interactions will almost certainly remain

Ted Greenwood is assistant professor of political science at the Massachusetts Institute of Technology. Research for this article was made possible by support from the University Consortium for World Order Studies.

high. In Canada, moreover, the importance of transnational actors in domestic disputes over energy policy is likely to increase.

Since the very existence of trade in energy resources is dependent on the active participation of the oil, gas, and electrical industry (including public utilities, regulated pipeline companies, multinational oil companies, independent entrepreneurs, and multifirm consortia formed to accomplish a particular purpose), these firms have traditionally been the most important transnational actors. They provide technical and managerial talent, organize the supply and marketing networks, and mobilize capital. In carrying out these functions, individual firms must deal with other firms, regulatory bodies, states and provinces, and the federal government on both sides of the border. More often than not in recent years, the transnational interactions have been initiated by American firms seeking access to Canadian resources or the advantages of Canadian industrial incentives and by Canadian firms seeking access to American markets and American capital. But prior to the completion of the Trans-Mountain and Interprovincial oil pipelines, much of Canada bought its oil from the United States. The Ontario Hydro-Electric Power Commission still buys coal from mines in Appalachia, and the oil and gas industry of Montana is attracting an increasing amount of capital and skilled labor from Alberta.[1]

North American geography, disparate patterns of economic development, the uneven distribution of natural resources, and, particularly in Canada, problems arising from the constitutional allocation of authority over these resources have led to wide variations in regional interests within each country. Each region has a unique stake in the bilateral trade in energy. A producing region like Alberta seeks high prices while consuming regions like Ontario and the American Midwest prefer low prices and must compete for supplies. While regions do pursue their desired ends through the conduit of their own federal governments, they also engage in direct cross-border contact, both with other governments and with industry. Such contacts provide leverage to influence their central governments, create faits accomplis, or, in the case of some provinces, occasionally serve almost as instruments of an independent foreign policy.

Subunits of the federal governments exert their primary influence on energy policy and energy trade by participating in the debates and consensus-building process within each government. There are exceptions, however. Since there is frequent cross-border contact between subunits that share similar functional responsibilities and

---

[1] "Montana Attracting Oilmen from Alberta," *Globe and Mail* (Toronto), 16 November 1973, p. B5.

since central control over the bureaucracy is difficult to maintain, there is ample opportunity to form alliances across the border in support of particular policy preferences. Federal regulatory agencies also play a transgovernmental role if they are sufficiently independent of political decision makers to pursue their own policy or when, on a particular issue of bilateral importance, interested firms exert political pressure on such agencies. Since they have the legal responsibility to issue permits and licenses, regulatory boards hear presentations from both sides of the border and frequently have veto power over the establishment of new trading patterns.

The environmental interest groups form another set of transnational actors that have become increasingly important in recent years. These groups can influence bilateral relations directly through contacts and alliances with like-minded groups across the border and by coordinating political lobbying on both sides. But actions taken only in one country or the other can also have indirect influence, such as encouraging industry to site new plants across the border rather than at home where environmental constraints may be more stringent.

The primary focus of this article is on the impact of these transnational and transgovernmental actors on the conduct of bilateral relations between Canada and the United States in the energy field. However, because of its important implications for the future of these relations, some attention is also given to the impact of these actors on questions of sovereignty and regional development in Canada. Finally, the question of benefits and the projected future of transnational relations in the area of energy is addressed.

THE CONDUCT OF BILATERAL RELATIONS

Since there have been few barriers to inhibit the initiation of transnational contacts whenever mutual benefit is anticipated, the bilateral relations between Canada and the United States in the energy area have been influenced in a major way by such contacts. Unless governments create artificial barriers, an Alberta oil man has no less reason to look for markets to the south than to the east, and a Maritime province premier has no particular incentive to seek development capital in Toronto rather than New York. Many such contacts exist with little or no attention from Ottawa or Washington. This is not only because the governments cannot be concerned with all issues at all times, but also because they are frequently content to leave the provinces, states, or the private sector in control. Often, however, what begins as a transaction between noncentral actors eventually receives publicity and government attention. In such cases the policy options of government may be so severely constrained that it can merely ratify existing situations. Transnational actors may even have veto power over particular aspects of national policies. In attempting to exert their own authority, Ottawa and Washington almost inevitably find themselves confronted by transnational coalitions trying to influence the policy outcome. The great influence of such coalitions is frequently demonstrated by the nature of the outcome of controversial issues. Of course, the governments themselves also join cross-border coalitions and use them as instruments of their own policy.

There are many instances of transnational activity that flourish without significant attention from the central governments. The best example is probably the trade of electric power between utilities in several provinces and their American neighbors. By exchanging surplus electricity on a seasonal or even a daily basis, operating costs are reduced and help is available in the event of equipment failure and during routine maintenance of facilities. Although regulatory boards must issue licenses under which these exchanges take place, the arrangement was begun and is maintained on the initiative of the utilities, states, and provinces involved. For many years this trade not only provided mutual benefits but also was in rough balance and involved only a small percentage of either country's electrical capacity (less than 4 percent in the case of Canada [2]). During that time it received relatively little attention from federal politicians or senior civil servants.

An example of a totally independent transnational contact is the establishment of alliances and working arrangements between Canadian and American environmental groups. Maine residents opposed to the Pittston Company's plan to build a refinery at Eastport received information and assistance from Canadian scientists at the nearby federal biological station in St. Andrews, New Brunswick. Canadian and American environmentalists were certainly in contact over the Trans-Alaska pipeline issue. Canadian groups even made a presentation during the American court proceedings.

Sometimes transnational activity continues unhampered for many years and then, either because of a change in political environment or a gradual change in the activity itself, it rapidly becomes a matter for government attention. For example, for many years prior to 1970 the National Energy Board of Canada readily granted permits for the export of gas so long as the price was right. Price was the central issue in the 1967 refusal to permit Westcoast Transmission Company, Limited, to increase its exports.[3] When a better price was accepted

---

[2] Canada, Department of Energy, Mines and Resources, *An Energy Policy for Canada Phase 1*, vol. 2 (Ottawa: Information Canada, 1973), p. 290.

[3] Anthony Westell, "Westcoast Refused Permission to Export Gas at FPC Price," *Globe and Mail* (Toronto), 23 December 1967.

by the Federal Power Commission, the relevant American regulatory agency, the license was granted.[4] In 1970, however, the combination of applications for record levels of exports and a growing concern for Canada's own long-term supply resulted in the Board's paring the requests.[5] Moreover, because of increasing politicization of the gas export issue, the Canadian cabinet's review of the Board's recommendations was more deliberate than in the past.[6] The following year, citing a deficiency in Canada's long-term supply, the Board denied all applications.[7] Because of the American shortage of electric-generating capacity and a Canadian surplus, the rough balance of electricity trade has been swinging toward net Canadian exports. In 1972 the export was 7,932 million kilowatt hours.[8] Export of electricity is now a political issue in Canada. Questions have been raised about the export aspects of Quebec's James Bay development project,[9] and environmentalists unsuccessfully asked the National Energy Board to refuse the Ontario Hydro-Electric Power Commission's request to increase its exports on the grounds that it would greatly increase air pollution in Ontario.[10]

Questions about oil and gas sales have been recurrent issues in the bilateral relations between Ottawa and Washington. During the 1950s and 1960s the major concerns revolved around market penetration and protection. Canadian producers of oil and gas sought access

[4] Michael Gillan, "US-Canada Compromise Clinches Westcoast Deal," *Globe and Mail* (Toronto), 17 February 1968.

[5] See Canada, National Energy Board, *Report to the Governor in Council in the Matter of the Applications under the National Energy Board Act of Alberta and Southern Gas Co. Ltd., Alberta Natural Gas Company, Canadian-Montana Pipe Line Co., Consolidated Natural Gas Ltd., Consolidated Pipe Line Co., Trans-Canada Pipe Lines Ltd. and Westcoast Transmission Co. Ltd.* (Ottawa: National Energy Board, August 1970).

[6] Ronald Anderson and Nicholas Latter, "Four of Five Gas Permits Sought Receive Export Licence Approval," *Globe and Mail* (Toronto), 30 September 1970, and "Sale of Natural Gas to United States," *International Canada* 1 (September 1970) : 184-85.

[7] See Canada, National Energy Board, *Reasons for Decision in the Matter of the Applications under the National Energy Board Act of Alberta and Southern Gas Co. Ltd., Alberta Natural Gas Co., Canadian-Montana Pipe Line Company, Consolidated Natural Gas Ltd., Consolidated Pipe Lines Co. and Trans-Canada Pipe Lines Ltd.* (Ottawa: National Energy Board, November 1971).

[8] Canada, Department of Energy, Mines and Resources, *An Energy Policy for Canada Phase 1: Summary of Analysis* (Ottawa: Information Canada, 1973), p. 3.

[9] Boyce Richardson, *James Bay: The Plot to Drown the North Woods* (Toronto: Clark, Irwin and Co., 1972), pp. 150-53.

[10] "Ontario Hydro Asks Boost of One-Third in U.S. Power Sales," *Globe and Mail* (Toronto), 23 October 1973, p. 1; "Hydro Admits Pollution Potential at Hearing on Export Increases," *Globe and Mail* (Toronto), 24 October 1973, p. 8; and Terrance Wills, "Ottawa Facing a Test on Energy Export to U.S.," *Globe and Mail* (Toronto), 22 November 1973, p. 5.

to nearby American markets while the American industry sought either government protection from competition in the case of independent oil producers or the use of Canadian resources as a means of expanding their own operations in the case of many gas pipeline companies and multinational oil companies. Industry and individual entrepreneurs took the initiative during this period, putting together coalitions and rival coalitions to build and finance major Canadian pipeline projects. Since potential backers considered these proposals to be financially viable only if they included sales to the large American market, the coalitions were necessarily transnational. Governments were able to exert some leverage: rival coalitions could be manipulated to achieve government ends as they were when Minister of Trade and Commerce C. D. Howe molded the Trans-Canada pipeline project by forcing the amalgamation of two separate and rival groups.[11] But the latitude for government control was severely circumscribed. At various times throughout the frustrating years in which the Canadian government sought to create a viable, all-Canadian gas pipeline from Alberta to Quebec, the Federal Power Commission, American gas transmission companies, and the Canadian subsidiary of Gulf Oil Company all exerted enormous influence over the project's future.[12] When financing and scheduling problems left TransCanada PipeLines Ltd. no choice but to offer temporary majority ownership to American interests, the Canadian government was not happy but saw no other option, given its commitment to private ownership and rapid completion of the line.[13] Nevertheless, this transfer of ownership provided fuel for the stormy pipeline debate in 1956 and helped bring about the subsequent defeat of the Liberal government in 1957. The threat and reality of oil import quotas have always been a means by which the American government could restrain the importation of foreign oil and thereby protect American independent producers. But at least in part by nurturing allies within the American bureaucracy, Ottawa, Alberta, and the multinational companies, acting in this case in concert, repeatedly gained special exclusion for Canada. Even after the imposition of voluntary limitations in 1968, pressures from Canadian exporters and, more importantly, the shortages of oil at American refineries along the pipeline from Canada continually resulted in imports beyond the agreed level.

For reasons having little to do with Canadian-American relations, the official government positions on oil and gas trade gradually

---

[11] William Kilbourn, *Pipeline* (Toronto: Clark, Irwin and Co., 1970), pp. ix-xiii and 42-44.
[12] Ibid., chapters 5, 6, 7, 8.
[13] Ibid., pp. 93-97.

became exactly reversed. Shortages of domestic oil and gas in the United States and rising world oil prices have caused an increased American demand for Canadian crude and calls by both American legislators and administration officials for a continental energy policy (the latter albeit with decreasing frequency). At the same time the combination of declining conventional reserves, disappointing results in frontier exploration, and rising Canadian nationalism has led to a Canadian rethinking of long-term strategy for oil and gas exports. In the short term Ottawa has taken measures to prevent both American shortages and price escalation from spreading to Canada. Exports have been curtailed, and by means of an adjustable export charge and a subsidy in the east, the price of crude in Canada has been decoupled from the price in the United States.

The oil-producing provinces and the oil industry strongly object to these federal controls. They prefer free access to the American market, if only as a means of forcing up domestic prices. Industry really has little recourse in Ottawa except to argue its case that higher prices are required if new and more expensive reserves are to be found and developed. Consequently, the oil companies tend to rely on the goodwill of the provinces as the latter undertake their own political battles with Ottawa. Alberta takes a view compatible with that of the oil industry since successive governments have seen the industry's health as essential to the well-being and economic growth of the province. The present Progressive Conservative government has acted to tie its royalty receipts to the price of oil, to take them in oil rather than in cash, and to form an oil-marketing board as a means of recovering the ability to set prices.[14] Nevertheless, it has also guaranteed that industry would benefit handsomely from a rise in prices. The New Democratic government of Saskatchewan also acted to recapture price control from Ottawa, seeking to freeze the wholesale price and thereby reserve all the economic rent for itself.[15] The extent to which these provinces will be successful in extending their influence in these areas is still unclear at this writing. The independence and therefore the transnational importance of the industry will be weakened whatever the outcome of the federal-provincial disputes.

Beyond the short-term questions of oil and gas exports, other energy-related matters have not, as yet, attracted the same political attention, permitting greater independence on the part of the transnational actors. In the future allocation of Arctic gas, for example,

[14] Thomas Kennedy, "Alberta Sets Up Petroleum Marketing Body," *Globe and Mail* (Toronto), 7 December 1973, p. B1.
[15] "New Saskatchewan Tax Plan Proposed Oil Profit Controls," *Globe and Mail* (Toronto), 11 December 1973, p. B5.

industry has already taken preemptory action that may constrain
Canadian government options. The need for large amounts of capital
for northern exploration and the desire of American gas companies to
assure themselves of future supplies have led to the early commitment
of approximately 30 trillion cubic feet of Canadian Arctic gas to
American buyers or their Canadian intermediaries.[16] This commitment will fuel the inevitable criticism by Canadian nationalists that
building a gas pipeline down the Mackenzie River valley will guarantee the wholesale export of Canadian resources to the United States.
Indeed, it will also exert strong pressure on the National Energy
Board and the cabinet when the decision is ultimately made whether
and how much Arctic gas to export.

Even when American projects impinge on Canadian interests, the
initiative in opposing them is not always taken by Ottawa. When the
Seattle Municipal Light and Power System decided to exercise an
option of many years' standing to raise the level of Ross Dam on the
Skagit River and flood about 5,000 acres of the Canadian valley upstream, it was the outcry of the local environmentalists that forced
the matter to the attention of the two central governments. Similarly,
local interests were the first to raise alarms about the dangers of a
tanker route through Canadian waters to the proposed refinery at
Eastport, Maine.

In matters relating to regional development the provinces have
considerable independence. In the past few years, for example, two
American-controlled oil companies have made commitments to build
new refining capacity of 680,000 barrels per day in the Maritime
provinces. Some of these refineries have been subsidized by the provinces,[17] and they are still looking for more.[18] The provinces expect that
the availability of deepwater ports and subsidies together with the
relative lack of public opposition will provide sufficient inducement.
Unless oil becomes available as a result of exploration on the continental shelf, these refineries will have to rely on imported crude. Moreover, their primary markets are expected to be the American East
Coast, where a refinery shortage exists, and Europe. This arrangement by which refineries in Canada use foreign crude to produce
refined products for export is likely to create problems for Canada

---

[16] Thomas Kennedy, "Millions Paid for Gas Not Yet Found," *Globe and Mail*
(Toronto), 1 September 1973, p. B2.

[17] John O'Brien, "Premier Indicates Firm Refinery Commitments," *Halifax
Chronicle-Herald*, 7 February 1973; and Lyndon Watkins, "Newfoundland, N.S.
Put Up $143.5 Million in Loans for Oil Refineries," *Globe and Mail* (Toronto),
2 August 1973, p. B5.

[18] Lyndon Watkins, "N.S. Premier Confirms Refinery Talks with Middle East,"
Globe and Mail (Toronto), 27 April 1973, p. B1; and "Dock, Refinery Urged at
N.B. Thermal Plant," *Globe and Mail* (Toronto), 12 October 1973, p. B4.

in future years if government export restrictions remain. The new refineries will almost certainly seek to be treated differently from refineries using domestic crude, but, despite support for this proposition from Premier Hatfield of New Brunswick,[19] Ottawa will probably find it politically difficult to do so. Despite this potential for future conflict, Ottawa is not trying to inhibit the expansion of Maritime refining capacity: its growth is an important component of Maritime development strategy, and the politics of regional disparities in Canada require Ottawa's cooperation. In fact, Ottawa is paying for the construction of the dock facilities for use by the refineries in Newfoundland.[20]

Environmentalists have offered relatively little resistance to these new refineries in the Maritimes. When the Newfoundland fishermen heard about the dispute over supertankers in the Bay of Fundy, they did begin to question the future of the fishing industry in Placentia Bay, at the head of which two new refineries will be located,[21] but the opposition has been far weaker than the recent outcries over refinery siting in the United States. Canadians who do oppose these refineries on environmental grounds can expect no support from their American colleagues. American environmentalists are partially responsible for driving such oil refineries out of the United States and into Canada.

In the case of Quebec, Ottawa's apparent reluctance to interfere with any plan to which the nonseparatist provincial government is strongly committed continues to guarantee its autonomy. In September 1973, for example, after reopening the possibility of extending the crude oil pipeline to Montreal, federal Minister of Energy, Mines and Resources Donald Macdonald was quick to reassure Quebec that this would not jeopardize its hopes of building a supertanker port on the lower St. Lawrence River.[22] Similarly, although the federal government has provided financial support to the Indians and Eskimos who are engaged in a legal battle against the James Bay hydroelectric project, it has remained relatively quiet about the project's faults despite substantial environmental risks and economic uncertainties.[23]

There have been occasions in the past when domestic actors on both sides have exerted transnational influence by exercising veto power over government policy on energy matters. The Province of

[19] "Forsees Fight," *Globe and Mail* (Toronto), 30 November 1973, p. B2.
[20] Lyndon Watkins, "Newfoundland, N.S. Put Up $143.5 Million in Loans for Oil Refineries," *Globe and Mail* (Toronto), 2 August 1973, p. B5.
[21] Bren Walsh, "Fishermen Have Doubts About Route of Tankers," *Globe and Mail* (Toronto), 12 May 1973, p. 8.
[22] "Projects Compatible," *Globe and Mail* (Toronto), 15 September 1973, p. 2.
[23] For a critical evaluation of the James Bay project, see Richardson.

Alberta's conservation board refused to permit the export of gas in 1951 and thereby delayed the initiation of pipeline construction for export.[24] Once Alberta's permission was granted, the Federal Power Commission delayed the construction of the Westcoast Transmission Company pipeline by refusing to grant import permits.[25] In 1955 efforts to finance TransCanada PipeLines Ltd. fell through when the Bank of Canada tied its support to government control and Gulf Oil Canada Limited refused to sell to a government-controlled firm.[26] In the case of the negotiations over the Columbia River power projects, British Columbia's participation and constitutional authority over natural resources permitted it to influence materially the final outcome.[27]

An important means by which transnational and transgovernmental actors try to influence the policy of central governments is by the formation of alliances. Such alliances can be made with several specific purposes in mind. An actor can seek allies across the border in an attempt to change the policy of its own government. In 1953 during Ottawa's early promotion of the Trans-Canada pipeline, the city of Toronto and Consumers' Gas Company, both of which wanted a gas supply before the pipeline would be in operation, allied with the Tennessee Gas Transmission Company in an effort to bring American gas into Ontario near Niagara Falls, a plan that was thought to be a serious impediment to Trans-Canada.[28] In another instance the state of New York, because of its interest in the electric power aspects of the St. Lawrence Seaway, supported the efforts of Ottawa and the White House to win congressional approval of American participation in building the Seaway.[29] Alliances can also be made with the purpose of influencing the other government. In the state of Maine's efforts to safeguard its Canadian oil supplies during the Arab oil boycott, Maine sought assistance from New Brunswick and the Midwest refineries gained support from the Canadian oil producers and the producing provinces.[30] At other times both governments must be con-

---

[24] Kilbourn, pp. 17-19.

[25] Ibid., p. 21.

[26] Ibid., chapter 6.

[27] For a discussion of these negotiations, see Donald Waterfield, *Continental Waterboy: The Columbia River Controversy* (Toronto: Clark, Irwin and Co., 1970).

[28] Kilbourn, pp. 38-42 and passim.

[29] On the history of the St. Lawrence Seaway, see William R. Willoughby, *The St. Lawrence Seaway: A Study in Politics and Diplomacy* (Madison, Wis.: The University of Wisconsin Press, 1961).

[30] "May Have Right to Cut Oil Flow to Montreal, Maine Leader Says," *Globe and Mail* (Toronto), 18 December 1973, p. 3; "Maritimes' Oil Outlook Worsens Following Embargo Information," *Globe and Mail* (Toronto), 21 December 1973, p. B2; Terrance Wills, "National Energy Board Eases Controls, Will Permit Oil to Flow to Maine Mills," *Globe and Mail* (Toronto), 22 December 1973, p. 10; and "Production Cut," *Globe and Mail* (Toronto), 1 December 1973, p. B1.

vinced together of the wisdom and feasibility of a particular project. Just as a large consortium of American and Canadian companies was assembled to create the Trans-Canada pipeline in the 1950s, another one, the Canadian Arctic Gas Study Ltd., has been put together in recent years to mobilize support in both capitals for the proposed Mackenzie River valley gas pipeline. On the other hand, an alliance like that developing between the New England states and the Maritime provinces (and particularly Maine and New Brunswick) can cut across issue areas and encompass a wide range of contacts and matters of mutual interest.[31] This particular alliance includes tourism, environment, and forestry as well as energy matters, such as electricity sharing and the distribution of refined oil.

The Trans-Alaska pipeline (TAP) debate provides an interesting example of a potential cross-border coalition that was never formed. American environmentalists opposed the pipeline because of the risk to the environment within the state of Alaska and managed to delay it for years through court action. In general they preferred a pipeline through the Mackenzie River valley as a safer alternative. Senators and congressmen from the Midwest also preferred the Mackenzie route primarily because it would bring Alaskan oil to their area. The major oil companies favored the Alaska route because it could be built faster than the alternative, because they had invested a great deal of money and effort in it, and because it obviated the necessity of dealing with native rights and domestic control issues in Canada. Moreover, as Canadian oil and gas export policy appeared to become more nationalistic over the years that TAP was in abeyance, the willingness to permit Canada to have potential control over the Alaska supply line decreased. The Nixon administration gave its strong support to TAP as did Senator Henry Jackson (Democrat from the state of Washington), who, through his chairmanship of the Senate Committee on Interior and Insular Affairs, was able to exert great influence on the matter.

In Canada there was almost universal opposition to TAP because of the fear that the tanker route from Valdez to the refineries on the American West Coast would result in major damage to the British Columbia coastline. Of primary concern was the plan to route tankers through the Juan de Fuca Strait to bring Alaskan crude to four refineries in northwestern Washington. Although the tidal currents in the area are such that the Canadian islands and shoreline would be very vulnerable to an oil spill, the route itself could be entirely within American waters. Canada, therefore, had no authority to prevent its

[31] "N.B., Maine Sign Agreement," *Globe and Mail* (Toronto), 29 June 1973, p. B2.

use. During much of the critical period of the TAP debate in the United States, the implications of the Mackenzie route were unclear in Canada, and not until late in 1972 were extensive studies of the matter completed. Although most government officials did not take irrevocable positions on the subject, preferences did develop. The Department of Energy, Mines and Resources tended to share the oil industry's hope that a Mackenzie oil pipeline would provide a means to bring south oil that may be found in the Canadian Arctic. In fact, as ongoing exploration in the Mackenzie River delta failed to reveal large quantities of oil, it became increasingly likely that whatever was found would be exploited only if a pipeline built for another purpose were readily available. On the other hand it was realized that an oil pipeline down the Mackenzie would mean a delay in building the proposed gas pipeline. They could not be built at the same time.[32] Canadian environmentalists were in a dilemma. Most of them liked the Mackenzie route little better than TAP, seeing insufficient benefit to Canada to balance the risk to its northern environment. The federal minister of the environment did, however, prefer the Mackenzie route.[33] The Department of Finance was generally opposed because of the potentially adverse economic impact. The Department of Indian Affairs and Northern Development that has jurisdiction over the area was split, reflecting its internal divisions between development-oriented and conservation-oriented sections. Canadian nationalists, including important elements of the New Democratic party on which the Liberals were relying to stay in power, saw a Mackenzie oil pipeline as a step toward continental integration of energy resources and therefore did not favor it.

The official position of the Canadian government on the Mackenzie River valley route was that a request for a permit would be welcomed.[34] Even though the major oil companies as early as 1971 told the ministers of the Departments of Energy, Mines and Resources and of Indian Affairs and Northern Development that they had no intention of making an application to build the Mackenzie pipeline, the government did little to promote the project. It refused to enter into negotiations with the United States, thereby creating the impression that it was not really interested in the Mackenzie route.[35] Although

---

[32] "Canada Feels Oil Pipeline Would Delay Gas Line," *Globe and Mail* (Toronto), 7 July 1973, p. B2.

[33] Peter Ward, "Alaska Oil Pipeline Could Cost Canada $850,000 a Day," *Toronto Telegram*, 21 January 1971.

[34] Bogdan Kipling, "Why Ottawa is Pushing for the Mackenzie Valley Route," *Financial Times* (Montreal), 1 May 1972.

[35] "State Department Says Canada Barred Oil Pipeline Talks," *New York Times*, 24 July 1973, p. 13; Ross H. Munro, "Reluctance of Ottawa to Discuss Pipeline Reason for Alaska Route, U.S. Official Says," *Globe and Mail* (Toronto), 24

the National Energy Board's authority to rule on pipeline proposals prevented formal cabinet endorsement unless and until the Board had accepted an actual application, much could have been done informally. There was no lack of potential American allies, including environmentalists, much of the press, and the midwestern legislators. Nonetheless, the Canadian government made no attempt to form alliances. This may be explained in part by its reluctance to interfere in a decision before the American Congress and in part by its continuing hope that either Congress or the courts would stop TAP or at least delay it until the advantages of the Mackenzie route were fully appreciated.[36] More important, however, was the lack of consensus within the government that prevented decisive action.

Ottawa did have a fallback that it kept in reserve. It offered to supply the Washington refineries with Canadian crude and thereby obviate the necessity for tankers to enter the Juan de Fuca Strait. If this idea had been suggested early in the debate, coupled with official rejection of the Mackenzie route, it may have been accepted by the administration as a means of undermining TAP opponents (although that is by no means certain). By the time the suggestion was in fact made, shortly before the crucial congressional votes, it was too late. Since the administration no longer felt on the defensive over TAP, it had no incentive to accept the offer. Moreover, it was clear that a guaranteed supply to Washington, which could readily receive oil by tanker, would eventually lead to a cutback in the supply to the Midwest, where Canadian crude is badly needed.[37] For this reason both the midwestern legislators and the administration strongly opposed the plan.[38] Canada's potential allies therefore became its opponents when the fallback proposal was made.

Ottawa was in the enviable position of being able to pursue its objective of protecting the coastline either by joining the proponents of the Mackenzie River valley pipeline or by abandoning them and seeking a deal with the pro-TAP faction. However, in the absence of a clear decision either for or against the Mackenzie route, both opportunities were foregone. Both the Mackenzie oil pipeline and the possibility of eliminating the risk to the coastline were lost.

Several years ago, before it became clear that Canada would not find enough frontier gas and oil to become a major supplier of Ameri-

July 1973, p. 1; and Iain Hunter, "Sharp Admits Canada Rebuffed U.S. in Mackenzie Pipeline Talk Offers," *Ottawa Journal*, 24 July 1973.

[36] George Russell, "Prospects Felt Good," *Globe and Mail* (Toronto), 12 May 1972.

[37] Ross H. Munro, "Oil Guarantee Plan Against U.S. Interests," *Globe and Mail* (Toronto), 1 August 1973, p. B2.

[38] Ross H. Munro, "U.S. Rejects Deal for Overland Delivery of Oil," *Globe and Mail* (Toronto), 19 September 1973, p. B2.

can needs, the future seemed to hold a greater potential for conflict over energy policy than it does at present.[39] With the disappointing results of drilling in the north and on the Atlantic shelf, no informed observer still expects that Canadian energy resources can be a major remedy for the United States energy shortage. Americans realize they must look elsewhere to supplement their own supplies. Canada's contribution must be rather small. With this lowering of expectations came an associated reduction in the risks of serious conflict. The low-key manner in which the administration expressed its opposition to Canada's export controls and export tax[40] is probably indicative of American willingness to accept rather stoically the growing Canadian reluctance to send its energy resources south.

There are, nevertheless, bound to be recurrent disagreements in the future over transportation methods for Arctic oil and gas, Canadian sales of oil and gas (and possibly electricity and uranium), environmental issues related to energy-resource mining, transformation, transportation, and use, and the effects on the bilateral trade balance of high oil and gas prices. The proposal of El Paso Natural Gas Company to build a trans-Alaska gas pipeline and liquefaction plant and to bring north slope gas to the United States by tanker will be in direct competition with the Mackenzie valley gas pipeline. Those American regions relying heavily on Canadian imports will be unhappy about cutbacks that may come as a result of increased Canadian demand for Canadian energy resources. The Midwest refineries, for example, can probably expect a decreased supply of Canadian crude when the pipeline to Montreal is built. Failure to renew some of the short-term electricity sales contracts or to permit exportation of all the Arctic gas in which American pipeline companies have already invested would certainly lead to substantial animosity if alternative sources are unavailable. On the other hand, the decrease of direct electricity sales by Canadian utilities to American firms should make it easier to repatriate electricity than it has sometimes been in the past. Electric power utilities, unlike most firms, have the ability to build substitute electric-generating capacity. The same is not true in the case of gas exports, since much of Alberta's supply is committed to individual American firms.[41]

---

[39] For a different view of the potential for conflict over energy resources, see Richard Rohmer, *Ultimatum* (Toronto: Clark, Irwin and Co., 1973).

[40] Ross H. Munro, "Washington Shows No Surprise," *Globe and Mail* (Toronto), 6 September 1973, p. B1; Ross H. Munro, "U.S. Angry with Ottawa for Increase in Oil Price," *Globe and Mail* (Toronto), 15 September 1973, p. 1; and Ross H. Munro, "U.S. Not Surprised by Higher Tax," *Globe and Mail* (Toronto), 3 November 1973, p. 3.

[41] I am indebted to Larratt T. Higgins for alerting me to the distinction between sales to individual firms and sales to utilities and for emphasizing its importance.

Since Canada is the supplier of oil, gas, and electricity, there is little the United States can do directly either to increase Canadian exports or to prevent their reduction. One option in an emergency situation may be to retaliate by cutting off the export of coal to Ontario or the flow of oil through the American section of the Inter-provincial or Portland-to-Montreal pipelines. Such suggestions were heard during the winter of 1973-74,[12] but not from administration spokesmen. In the longer term, if the supply of crude to the mid-western refineries is reduced, taxing the throughput of the American section of the line may not be out of the question, especially if Canada taxes American gas that flows through a future Mackenzie gas line. It seems more likely, however, that the United States may try to create political linkages between energy and other issues, an approach to bilateral relations that Canada has traditionally opposed. It is clear that while the transnational contacts of industry will in many respects exacerbate disagreements in this area, the strong desire for long-term market stability should encourage at least the large firms to try to moderate potentially disruptive political tensions.

Various institutional frameworks can be envisaged for dealing with bilateral energy matters. These could range from joint manage-ment of North American resources or international jurisdiction mod-eled after the International Joint Commission's jurisdiction over boundary waters to institutionalized dispute settlement and joint planning or regular or ad hoc consultations at the political level. Implementation of either of the first two options would require much stronger commitments to close cooperation on energy matters and to mutually acceptable basic principles than seems likely to exist on either side in the foreseeable future. Because of the highly political nature of the issues involved, even institutionalized dispute settle-ment and joint planning will be possible only if the process is con-trolled and overseen by high-level officials on both sides.

REGIONAL DEVELOPMENT AND SOVEREIGNTY IN CANADA

As with most areas of bilateral relations, a flow of energy re-sources that is of relatively minor importance to the United States takes on huge proportions in Canada. About half of Canada's annual production of two trillion cubic feet of gas and of its daily produc-tion of two million barrels of oil is exported to the United States where it supplies 5 percent to 6 percent of total consumption. The United States would willingly take more. At current rates of extrac-

[12] "May Have Right to Cut Oil Flow to Montreal, Maine Leader Says," *Globe and Mail* (Toronto), 18 December 1973, p. 3.

tion, Canada's proven reserves, excluding frontier areas and the tar sands, would be exhausted in about 25 years in the case of gas and in about 13 years in the case of oil. Oil reserves have actually been decreasing in recent years.[13] The large commitment of resources to the United States and the strong pressures from Alberta and industry, much of which is American controlled, to develop rapidly both northern gas and the Athabaska tar sands and to commit much of this new output to the American market are issues that help to fire the regional divisions over economic disparities and the ideological divisions over national sovereignty that exist in Canada.

For all their disagreements over taxes and royalties, Alberta and the major oil companies have continually shared a desire to extend their penetration of the American market and to receive higher prices for their oil and gas. This puts them in direct opposition to Ontario, the major Canadian consumer, which seeks low prices and a secure supply for the future. The proximity and size of the American midwestern and Pacific Coast markets provide compelling economic reasons for a predominantly north-south rather than east-west flow. Alberta's early opposition to the all-Canadian gas pipeline to Ontario reflected this preference, and the years of difficulty in financing it verify the basic economic sense of Alberta's case, at least at that time. But the strong protectionist tendencies in the United States restricted the degree of penetration into the American market. The Canadian industry grew by means of a variety of subsidies, including federal aid in financing the Trans-Canada gas pipeline and the national oil policy that prohibited the sale of cheaper imported crude west of the Ottawa River valley. For many years prices were kept stable by government regulation in the case of gas and by a worldwide surplus in the case of oil.

The situation has changed radically in recent years. The growing gas shortage in the United States caused Canadian gas, sold on long-term contracts, to be priced under its true market value. Alberta has been trying hard to exploit American scarcities to force up both domestic and export prices. While Americans are willing to pay more, Ontario has been complaining bitterly, and Ottawa has been drawn unwillingly into the middle of a difficult and divisive interprovincial fight. The price of Canadian crude oil generally followed world prices upward after the Teheran agreement of 1971 until the Canadian government imposed price controls and a variable export tax in September 1973. Since these price increases had provided substantial financial benefits to the producing provinces as well as the oil industry, it

---

[13] Canada, Department of Energy, Mines and Resources, *An Energy Policy for Canada, Phase 1*, vol. 1 (Ottawa: Information Canada, 1973), p. 81.

is not surprising that the federal government's actions have greatly angered Alberta and Saskatchewan.

Despite the belated offer to return the revenue from the export tax to the producing provinces,[44] there is still a natural dispute over which level of government should control the distribution of the economic rent resulting from the increased market price of oil. Moreover, it is widely feared that suppressing industry's profit may retard or reverse the recent boom in new exploration and impede the development of the tar sands. To the producing provinces, the domestic controls on oil and gas prices appear to be subsidies for the industrialized areas of central Canada at their expense. They would rather maximize their returns from what is, after all, a nonrenewable and rapidly depleting resource and prepare for their own future by attracting industry west with the offer of cheap energy. Ontario's pleas that Alberta should put the national interest first and accept a lower price for sales in Canada is viewed from the west as rather self-serving and devoid of economic sense. At least as important as these economic issues, however, is the provinces' claim that Ottawa is interfering with their constitutionally guaranteed prerogative to control their natural resources, an authority that they see as one of the keys to their future development.

Regional disparities play just as important a role in the approach of the eastern provinces to some aspects of domestic energy policy and energy exports to the United States. The Maritime provinces have always been the poor relations of the Canadian confederation and have continually sought to catch up with the rest of the country. With the strong support and encouragement of the federal Department of Regional Economic Expansion, the Maritimes are becoming increasingly committed to taking advantage of their deepwater ports and their geographic location between the industrial centers of Europe and North America. By exploiting modern transportation technology, they hope to make their area into a major gateway to North America and a center for both bulk industry and secondary manufacturing.[45] The refineries located on the Strait of Canso, Nova Scotia, at Comeby-Chance, Newfoundland, and one that may be built at Lorneville, New Brunswick, all of which have ports with excellent deepwater harbors, are seen as the seeds for the growth of world-scale industry. Their economic viability depends, at least for some years, on the

---

[44] "Alberta Gets Tax Revenue," *Globe and Mail* (Toronto), 29 November 1973, p. 12; and "Federal Oil Export Tax Share Set for Energy Role," *Globe and Mail* (Toronto), 14 December 1973, p. B2.

[45] See the staff paper prepared by the Department of Regional Economic Expansion, *Atlantic Region: Economic Circumstances and Opportunities* (Ottawa: Department of Regional Economic Expansion, April 1973), pp. 28-32, 48-50, 54-55.

export of refined products to Europe and the United States.

The Province of Quebec has its own similar plans to develop a deepwater port in the lower St. Lawrence River and build on the already substantial refining, petrochemical, and manufacturing industries of the Montreal area. For both Quebec and the Maritimes the ultimate prize is increased tax revenues, more jobs, and full participation in the industrialized, high technology world economy. While the recent rises in the price of imported oil certainly dampened the spirits of the supporters of these bold schemes, the effect may be transitory. The discovery of commercial quantities of oil on the Atlantic shelf would provide an enormous impetus.

The availability of abundant electric power is also important to the industrialization of these areas. Quebec's James Bay project, the lower Churchill River project in Labrador, and the plans of New Brunswick to build both a nuclear power plant and a large fossil plant must all be seen in this light. As with the refineries, much of the electricity generated by these facilities will be exported to the United States, at least initially. Cooperation—for temporary export, for capital import, or even for increased integration of the local economies with the United States—is not seen by the eastern provinces as a sellout of Canadian sovereignty but as both necessary and welcome assistance in improving the standard of living of the areas.

Canadian economic nationalists, especially in industrial but energy-poor Ontario, see the willingness to export Canada's resources to the United States as the height of folly. Exporting energy and minerals and importing manufactured goods from the United States has the net effect, they argue, of exporting jobs. The oil and gas industry—in extraction, transportation, and refining—is very capital-intensive and provides rather few Canadian jobs for the investment. Moreover, since the ownership of the resources and refineries is in American hands, much of the financial benefits leave the country through dividends to American shareholders and the conduit of the multinational oil companies. Much better to develop slowly, assuring Canadian ownership and responding to domestic demand. The rush to build the Mackenzie gas pipeline is seen as a means of assuring that Canadian Arctic gas is sold to the United States, of causing major labor dislocation while construction is in progress, and of either contributing to Canadian inflation if a large amount of capital is imported or depriving other sectors of the economy of investment funds if Canadian capital is used. The major beneficiary would be the United States. If Canada's cheap gas were not being exported in large quantities, it is claimed, Arctic reserves would not be needed in the domestic market for decades. The same arguments apply equally to the development of the Athabaska tar sands.

Regardless of the validity of either the continentalist or the nationalist point of view, this ideological split in Canada is politically significant, and the almost total control of Canadian refineries and oil and gas reserves by multinational oil companies exacerbates it enormously. The companies seek to reap the economic benefits that arise from marketing and planning on a continental scale and from developing and selling resources in the short term rather than leaving them in the ground for the future. Extensive exploration in the north makes no sense unless means are provided to bring out the oil and gas discovered, and the sooner the better. If this can be done only by committing large amounts of new reserves to the American market, the companies see no disadvantage to that. They see no reason to sacrifice economic benefit for the sake of xenophobic nationalism.

In large measure the multinational oil companies, both American based and European based, come under attack in Canada because they are vertically integrated networks that maximize their corporate interest on a world scale. The companies claim that a very large percentage of profits stays in Canada in the form of royalties, taxes, reinvestment, and dividends to Canadian shareholders, but that does not take account of outflows that result from transfer pricing between different parts of the corporate entity. Imperial Oil, a subsidiary of Exxon, can buy Venezuelan oil from Exxon and use Exxon tankers to transport it, both at artificially high prices; Great Canadian Oil Sands Limited or Gulf Oil Canada can sell to their American parent companies at less than market value. If they do, the reported financial position of the companies will not indicate that the Canadian subsidiaries are subsidizing the parent companies. It is clear that decisions taken at the head office are determined by interests different from those of Canada or the Canadian subsidiary. Even before the 1973 Middle East war, for example, some oil companies began diverting to their American markets refined products from their Caribbean refineries that had traditionally supplied eastern Canada.[46] Nevertheless, during the period of American oil import quotas the multinational companies served Canada's interest by helping to secure the overland exemption.

The very existence and scale of operation of the American-owned oil companies raises questions for Canada about its own sovereignty and control of its domestic and international affairs. The problems are not qualitatively different from those raised in other areas of the economy that are dominated by Americans, but the strategic importance of energy resources, the uncertainties of the world supply net-

[46] Ross Henderson, "Ottawa Juggles Supplies as U.S. Diverts Fuel Oil," *Globe and Mail* (Toronto), 20 September 1973, p. 1.

works, escalating world prices, and the attention and emotion generated by American cries of an energy crisis have heightened the importance of the sovereignty issue in Canada. The policy decisions of the Trudeau government in the energy area seem increasingly to reflect a nationalist perspective. While that may in part reflect the pivotal role of the New Democratic party from 1972 to 1974, it also results from a willingness to rethink energy strategy in terms of the long-term Canadian benefit. The federal government's decision to create a national petroleum company,[47] British Columbia's establishment of the British Columbia Petroleum Corporation,[48] and Saskatchewan's efforts to control prices and move into the exploration business—all seem to suggest a trend toward a decrease in the influence of the multinationals.

CONCLUSION

How are the benefits of the Canadian-American trade in energy resources distributed and how do transnational interactions influence this distribution? The answer varies from case to case and from issue to issue and depends in part on one's position on the issues raised by the Canadian nationalists. It may be argued in the case of the Maritime refineries that because of the enthusiasm with which the provinces endorsed the projects, they offered unnecessarily advantageous terms to the Shaheen Natural Resources Company. In the cases of the tar sands development and the Mackenzie gas pipeline, the ease of establishing strong transnational advocates helped both to begin before potentially competing projects could get organized. Canadian and American nationalists will consider this head start a detriment to both countries. Those Canadians interested in economic efficiency, continental sharing, and development will consider it a great benefit for Canada, and those Americans whose major concern is finding new energy sources rapidly will consider it a great benefit to the United States. In the case of the electricity-sharing programs of neighboring electric utilities, the benefits are clearly mutual.

Those in both countries who take the continentalist viewpoint would probably say that the benefits derived by each country from the present cooperation are about equal. Canada gets jobs, tax revenues, regional development, assistance in developing its resources, and other improvements to its standard of living. American investors receive

---

[47] Terrance Belford, "Fuel Policy: Freeze Extended to Spring, Oil Self-Sufficiency Pledged," *Globe and Mail* (Toronto), 7 December 1973, p. 1.

[48] "B.C. Plans Near-Doubling of Price of Natural Gas," *Globe and Mail* (Toronto), 13 October 1972, p. 1.

a fair return on their capital and the United States obtains needed energy resources. Ignoring the political boundary permits economies of scale that would otherwise be impossible. Without the sale of American coal to Ontario, the cost of electric power would be higher there. Without the exports to the United States, the Canadian oil and gas industries could not have grown as fast or as efficiently. According to this view, increased interaction across the border is mutually beneficial, government interference is undesirable, and transnational transactions, to the extent that they foster greater cooperation, are welcome.

Canadian nationalists, on the other hand, see much of the cross-border trade as the selling out of Canada to the United States. To show that the United States gains and Canada loses, they point to the profits of American companies flowing out of the country, the importation of American pollution with each refinery built for the export market, American control of Canadian resources, and the prospect of importing American shortages and high energy prices. The overwhelming presence of American interests in the oil and gas industries detracts from Canadian sovereignty. The American multinationals should be shackled as much as possible; more control is needed from Ottawa to assure that Canadian resources are used for the benefit of Canadians; the Canadian energy market should be decoupled from the American.

In the United States the importance of nationalism to energy policy is taken for granted and has always exerted a strong influence. The view that dependence on oil imports weakened national security and endangered the health of the domestic oil industry contributed significantly to the policy of protectionism. While nationalists, like everyone else, are eager to obtain Canadian resources during the current period of shortage and consider them more secure than imports from most other countries, they are unwilling to rely permanently on Canadian goodwill for needed energy supplies.

These widely differing perceptions of benefits are not easily reconcilable. They depend not only on different ideologies but also on different discount rates, the assessments of the value of current benefits compared to future benefits. The discount rate of industry is high: current profits are worth much more than future profits. Resources must therefore be extracted and sold quickly. Arctic gas should come south and the tar sands be developed sooner rather than later. Environmental costs are small because they are borne primarily in the future. But to the nationalists as to the environmentalists, discount rates are low. What happens in the future is very important. The quality of life of future generations, the preservation of Canadian or American independence, and, particularly in Canada, the guarantee that future generations will be able to benefit from nonrenewable resources are central considerations.

The trend of recent years seems to point to less rather than greater cooperation on energy matters and decreasing potency of transnational interactions. Energy questions have become highly visible and politicized in both countries and are likely to remain so for many years. Central governments will become more deeply involved in making decisions and managing cross-border interactions. The trend in Canada, where the initiative can lie in this instance, seems to be toward greater independence from the United States. Whatever one thinks of the economics of the new method of oil pricing and the export tax or the propriety of how this policy was initiated, it seems to point clearly in the direction of decoupling. The same tendency is evident in the United States. To the extent that American government and industry perceive bilateral relations with Canada to be uncooperative and unpredictable, they will be unwilling to rely on Canadian sources or Canadian goodwill for their energy supply. Already in discussions of the relative merits of a Mackenzie gas pipeline versus the El Paso scheme to transport liquefied natural gas from the south coast of Alaska, the security advantages of an all-American route are playing a prominent role.[49] President Nixon's call for the United States to become self-sufficient in energy resources does not appear to make any exception for Canada.

In large measure the choices seem to be economic versus political advantage. Increasing ties and encouraging relatively free flow of transnational interactions would probably yield, as they have in the past, significant economic benefits for both sides (disproportionate benefits for the United States, the Canadian nationalists would say). Constraining those interactions and decoupling the energy policies of the two countries would serve the cause of nationalist sentiment and possibly security of supply on both sides. The choices in the two capitals are likely to be based primarily on the course of domestic politics in each country and on the prevailing sense of the larger arena of world energy markets and world politics.

[49] Ross H. Munro, " 'Canadian Chauvinism' Seen Improving Chances of U.S. Tanker Plan," *Globe and Mail* (Toronto), 2 October 1973, p. B1; "Mackenzie Gas Line Hopes Wane as El Paso Seeks to Block Plan," *Globe and Mail* (Toronto), 3 November 1973, p. B2; and Thomas Kennedy, "Brokers Appear to be Losing Enthusiasm for Mackenzie Line," *Globe and Mail* (Toronto), 30 November 1973, p. B1.

CANADIAN–UNITED STATES CORPORATE INTERFACE AND TRANSNATIONAL RELATIONS

Isaiah A. Litvak and Christopher J. Maule

Transnational relations involving parent companies of United States multinational enterprises with subsidiaries in Canada have begun to interest not only the social scientist but also the politician and businessman. What is the effect of such transnational relations on the economic resources and performance of each country? What political means are used to influence corporate behaviour? What is the effect of the constitutional system on such transnational relations? What are the ways in which the countries reacted to resolve certain related interstate conflicts?

Each of these issues arises from the emergence of the multinational enterprise. Contemporary business transactions often have no single geopolitical base, and these interactions accentuate the costs and the benefits that flow across national borders in complex patterns involving concerns and interests of several nations. The complexity of these patterns is heightened by the form and behaviour of the multinational enterprise.

In the first part of the essay, the nature of the parent-subsidiary relationship is highlighted to show the organizational and decision-making attributes that allow the parent and subsidiary to act as a transnational organization promoting increased interaction between corporate and governmental systems. In the second part of the essay, the corporate decision-making framework is applied to those areas that give rise to transnational processes with implications drawn for Canadian–United States relations.

Isaiah A. Litvak is a professor of economics and international affairs at Carleton University in Ottawa, and Christopher J. Maule is an associate professor of economics and international affairs at Carleton University. The authors thank Annette Baker Fox, Douglas Klassen, Joseph Nye, and Maureen Appel Molot for their helpful comments on an earlier draft of this essay.

CORPORATE DECISION MAKING

The design of corporate strategies and the organizational structures are among the key areas of decision making in business organizations.[1] In the case of firms that have established foreign affiliates,
these areas are of prime concern to the senior corporate officers. The
foreign subsidiaries are usually viewed as appendages of the national
corporate headquarters organization, necessitating a degree of transnational planning, control, and direction to ensure that they perform
and behave in accordance with the corporate goals of the (national)
firm.

Complex problems of suboptimization arise and are always present in multinational enterprises. Suboptimization results from conflicting pressures emanating from parent company and host country.
For example, cost considerations may suggest that inputs of a subsidiary company should be made through imports. However, this
procedure may conflict with the host country's desire to promote local
industry for which financial assistance may be available. The parent
company is thus faced with deciding in what country to locate or
expand its operations, which is tantamount to having to discriminate
between its various foreign subsidiaries. It is for this reason that
management of multinational enterprises argue that the functions of
planning, coordination, and control must reside at the center to prevent management of the subsidiaries from pursuing strategies [2] and
responding to governmental pressures in a way that would tend to
suboptimize the corporate goals of the firm.

One method of obviating parent-subsidiary management conflicts
is to divide the strategy function between the headquarters firm and
its overseas subsidiaries along predetermined lines. The degree to
which the headquarters organization of the multinational enterprise
can control the commercial pursuits and behaviour of its overseas
affiliates is partially determined by the structural (power) relationship between them.[3]

To comprehend the nature of corporate power and the manner in
which it is exercised is fundamental to understanding the many concerns expressed by national governments about the transnational
processes that involve the commercial behaviour and performance of
multinational enterprises. One major concern arises from the fact

[1] E. Raymond Corey and Steven H. Star, "Organization Strategy" (Harvard
School of Business Administration, Division of Research), p. vii.
[2] Strategy in this context may be viewed as "the determination of the basic goals
and objectives of an enterprise, and the adoption of courses of action and the allocation of resources for carrying out these goals." See Alfred D. Chandler, *Strategy
and Structure* (Cambridge, Mass.: M.I.T. Press, 1962), p. 13.
[3] Chandler, p. 13.

that the corporate strategy of the multinational enterprise may run counter to the economic, political, and sociocultural goals of particular nation states, and thus may constitute a threat to their sovereignty. Some national governments, including Canada's, see themselves behaving as observers of foreign-managed corporate activities in their own country over which their central policy organs exercise little control. In fact, there are times when host governments perceive themselves as being constituent parts of the multinational enterprise system as opposed to the enterprise being a constituent part of the nation state.

The ability of the subsidiary to develop its own strategy and structure is largely determined by the grants of authority delegated to it by its parent company. Grants of authority limit the ability of the subsidiary to make decisions, qualitative and quantitative, in such areas as market development, financing, determining the source of inputs, research and development, product design activities, promoting market research, exporting, appointing and promoting executive and professional personnel, pricing, advertising and sales promotion, and public relations. All Canadian subsidiaries operate under grants of authority whether spelled out in formal terms or effected through informal channels.[4]

The variables that affect grants of authority and control relationships between parent and subsidiary include the following: size, age, profitability, productivity, and product diversity of the subsidiary; size of the parent and ratio of size of parent to the subsidiary; nature of product and production process; and the degree to which the subsidiary is a part of the international network of operations of the parent company, including the extent to which the parent enjoys economies of scale from such operations. However, while the variables are many, there appear to be two critical elements that affect the scope for business activity on the part of the Canadian subsidiary, namely, the corporate strategy of the firm and the organization of production within the firm.[5]

ISSUE AREAS

In the US parent–Canadian subsidiary system, decisions are made with respect to four major types of activity that flow across the

[4] See Isaiah A. Litvak and Christopher J. Maule, "Branch Plant Entrepreneurship," *The Business Quarterly* 37 (Spring 1972) : 45-53.
[5] For further discussion see Isaiah A. Litvak and Christopher J. Maule, "Marketing and Good Corporate Behavior: The Case of the U.S. Subsidiary," in D. N. Thompson and D. S. R. Leighton, eds., *Canadian Marketing: Problems and Prospects* (Toronto: Wiley Publishers, 1973), pp. 73-81.

border.[6] They are, first, the flow of funds, such as equity capital, loans, dividends, interest, royalties, fees, head office expenses, and the payment for intracompany exports and imports; second, the flow of goods, such as the export or import of raw materials, components, and final products in the case of the primary and secondary sectors of the economy; third, the flow of persons, both management and labour; and, fourth, the flow of information, such as information with respect to the managerial functions of research, production, finance, and marketing.

In terms of the exchange of goods and services, the pricing of the flows is an intracompany decision that permits the corporate management some discretion in establishing transfer prices.[7] It is this discretionary power of the corporate system that can come into conflict with the governmental systems, both Canadian and US. For example, pricing will affect the balance of payments and tax revenues of the two countries, the latter being a concern in a federal state not only to the central government but also to provincial or state and municipal governments.

These flows will reflect corporate decisions made about the location of research, production, and marketing facilities of the companies, about which part of the enterprise is going to serve which markets, and about where the entrepreneurial impetus for the enterprise will lie and thus what distribution of skills is required in different parts of the enterprise. All these characteristics of the decisions can affect national objectives in the two countries, for example, exports, regional economic policy, and the development of highly skilled manpower.

The flows also concern the activities of professional associations and the structure of trade unions. In the case of industrial relations, a company may be dealing with unrelated unions or related ones, as in the automobile industry, where United States parent and Canadian subsidiary must negotiate with different branches of the same union, the United Automobile Workers (UAW).[8] The union as well as the company thus becomes a vehicle for transmitting conditions in one

---

[6] These are similar to the four types of global interactions suggested by Joseph S. Nye and Robert O. Keohane, "Transnational Relations and World Politics: An Introduction," *International Organization* 25 (Summer 1971): 332.

[7] See J. S. Shulman, "Transfer Pricing in the Multinational Film," *European Business* 20 (January 1969): 46-54.

[8] See John Crispo, *International Unionism—A Study in Canadian-American Relations* (Toronto: McGraw-Hill, 1967); Isaiah A. Litvak and Christopher J. Maule, "U.S. Domination of Canadian Labour," *Columbia Journal of World Business* 7 (May-June 1972): 57-63; and *Globe and Mail* (Toronto), 18 September 1973, p. 1. See also Cox and Jamieson in this volume.

country to the other, as in the case of bargaining by Canadian workers for wage parity with the United States.

A basic model for analysing Canadian–United States conflicts identifies four actors—the United States and Canadian federal governments, the parent company in the United States, and its subsidiary company in Canada—and the relationships between them (see figure 1). This model can be made more complex in a number of ways, such as through the addition of provincial or state and local governments and of trade unions. Reference to these additional actors is made in the subsequent analysis.

Six components in the system of relationships can be identified, five of which involve transnational processes, in that at least one of the actors is not a government.[9] Relationships 1, 4, and 5 are clearly transnational. Numbers 2 and 3 refer to government-company relationships in their respective countries and have transnational implications in that they can be used to channel effects into the other country through the parent-subsidiary relationship. Number 6 is an interstate, government-to-government relationship and is of relevance in that it is used to handle some of the issues that arise due to the other five interactions. The content and significance of these interactions are now examined in terms of the conflicts that arise between corporate decisions and governmental decisions or policies.

Four ways in which conflict originates are as follows: from essentially corporate-initiated policies, from US government-initiated policies that are transmitted through the parent to the subsidiary in Canada, from Canadian government initiatives and transmission through the subsidiary to the US, and from joint initiatives by the two governments that affect the relationship between parent and subsidiary. None of these conflicts are necessarily independent of each other. For example, in the case of corporate-initiated policies, they all take place within a legal framework establshed by government.

Corporate-Initiated Policies

The parent company makes decisions as to the organization of production within the corporate system, establishing where each item will be produced, where research will be undertaken, where financing will be done, where the subsidiary will be allowed to export, where the entrepreneurial drive will originate, what transfer prices and final product prices will be set, where cutbacks in production will occur in times of recession, and what information will be disclosed by the subsidiary. In sum, the whole range of functional areas within the cor-

[9] See Nye and Keohane, p. 334.

FIGURE 1. PRINCIPAL COMPONENTS OF THE TRANSNATIONAL SYSTEM
INVOLVING GOVERNMENTS AND CORPORATIONS IN CANADA AND THE
UNITED STATES

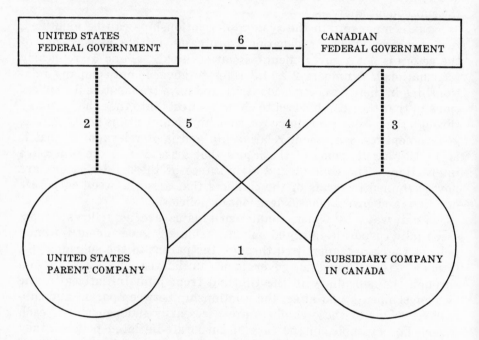

Numbers 1, 4, and 5 (indicated by a straight line) are transnational relations.

Number 6 (indicated by a broken line) is interstate relations.

Numbers 2 and 3 (indicated by a dotted line) are intrastate relations with transnational implications.

porate system are subject to numerous decisions emanating from the parent company. These decisions have to be made, and assuming that they are made in the best interests of the corporation, they will at times come into conflict with Canadian national objectives established by the federal government, and thus give rise to conflicts that are identified as being of United States origin. From an economic point of view, the decisions may reflect the approximate underlying conditions of comparative advantage, but this is no answer to the student of international relations. If interests in Canada perceive these conflicts to exist and to have a US dimension, then there exists a problem for relationships between the two countries.

Our earlier case studies provide examples of some of these issues.[10] The lack of research activity in the subsidiary operations[11] conflicts with the Canadian government's objective of promoting a research and development capability in Canada as espoused by the Canadian Department of Industry, Trade and Commerce. It has further important implications in the area of educational policy. The aims of postsecondary education include the production of a distribution of skills in the labour force with emphasis on highly skilled and qualified manpower. To the extent that these skills are not in demand because of the ownership characteristics of the manufacturing sector of the economy, then a problem exists or is perceived to exist. This problem might be inconsequential if it were not for the fact that a high proportion of Canadian industry is US owned and controlled, and this is particularly the case for growth and research-intensive industries such as automobiles, aircraft, chemicals, and electronics. Issues of research capability and educational opportunities have become politicized in Canada as a result of the investigations and reports of the Senate Special Committee on Science Policy, entitled *Science Policy For Canada*.[12]

Lack of research in the subsidiary is often reflected in a lack of entrepreneurship in the subsidiary. This tends to vary with the organization of production. In the case of the *miniature replica effect*, the output of the parent company is duplicated by the subsidiary, which at the extreme becomes a mere assembly operation for parts imported from the parent in the United States.[13] The opportunities for the

[10] Isaiah A. Litvak, Christopher J. Maule, and R. D. Robinson, *Dual Loyalty: Canadian-U.S. Business Arrangements* (Toronto: McGraw-Hill, 1971).

[11] Ibid., pp. 57, 69, 130; and P. L. Bourgault, *Innovation and the Structure of Canadian Industry* (Ottawa: Information Canada, 1972).

[12] Canada, Senate, Special Committee on Science Policy, *Science Policy for Canada*, vol. 1 (1970), vol. 2 (1972), vol. 3 (1973).

[13] See H. E. English, *Industrial Structure in Canada's International Competitive Position* (Montreal: Canadian-American Committee, 1964); and Litvak, Maule, and Robinson, *Dual Loyalty*, pp. 53-60.

exercise of entrepreneurial drive by the Canadian management of the subsidiary are minimal in this instance. Where the subsidiary is in a vertically integrated relationship with the parent company, buying components from the parent, making other components, and reselling the output to another subsidiary or elsewhere, then some exercise of entrepreneurship may be undertaken with respect to the manufacture of components. This occurs with Garrett Manufacturing, Limited (Canada), which builds aircraft components for sale to other parts of the Garrett Corporation in the United States and to third parties.[14] Finally, there is the specialization of production format, which is a variation of the foregoing, whereby the subsidiary is detailed to produce a particular item in the corporation's product range for sale worldwide, with responsibility for the product from research through to marketing resting with the subsidiary. Imperial Oil Limited experiences this with certain products and is notable for a degree of entrepreneurial autonomy in some areas.[15]

The specialization format may seem to apply to the automobile industry, since the Canadian-US automotive agreement has led to certain plants in Canada being allocated the production of certain types of cars. However, this does not lead to any entrepreneurial autonomy in the Canadian plants for two reasons. First, although the Canadian plants often specialize in the production of a certain model, the same model is usually produced in one or more plants in the United States; so the Canadian plant is not unique. Second, the technology of automobile production is such that it can be concentrated in one place, which is almost always near the parent company, and is then modified and transmitted to different plants that produce different models in the product range.

The way in which foreign investment has undermined the entrepreneurial drive of Canadians has been highlighted by Professor Kari Levitt, who points to past Canadian tariff policies leading to foreign investment in Canada. She suggests that the problem with the tariff was that it did not result in a Canadian bourgeoisie becoming entrepreneurs and stimulating growth of Canadian industries but created a bourgeoisie satisfied with managing a branch-plant economy.[16] It is now recognized that this deficiency, which is often attributed to past Canadian policies,[17] is one that needs to be overcome if Canadian-

[14] Litvak, Maule, and Robinson, *Dual Loyalty*, pp. 75-86.

[15] Ibid., pp. 112-24.

[16] See Kari Levitt, *Silent Surrender: The Multinational Corporation in Canada* (Toronto: Macmillan of Canada, 1970).

[17] This position was taken in: Canada, Task Force on the Structure of Canadian Industry, *Foreign Ownership and the Structure of Canadian Industry* (Ottawa: Queen's Printer, 1968); also referred to as the Watkins report because Melville H. Watkins headed the task force.

owned and controlled enterprises are to be born and are to flourish. This position is reflected in the objectives of the Canada Development Corporation, in the Program for the Advancement of Industrial Technology of the Department of Industry, Trade and Commerce, and in its policies to promote Canadian firms.[18]

These examples of the commercial behaviour of the parent giving rise to concern and response by the Canadian government have not led to major political incidents comparable to that involving the Mercantile Bank and the First National City Bank of New York,[19] but they are examples of forces described by Professor H. G. Johnson as the *new mercantilism*.[20] Governments are seeking ways to protect or promote their industrial capability, and in the absence of tariff barriers, they are resorting to programmes of special support and subsidy for their native industry at the expense of imports or in order to promote exports. An example of this in Canada, although not involving a United States company, was the US reaction to the subsidies given to the Michelin Tire Company to locate in Nova Scotia.[21] On 10 February 1973 the United States government applied a 6.6 percent surcharge on Michelin tire imports in reaction to a $50 million loan from the Province of Nova Scotia and a large grant from the federal Department of Regional Economic Expansion to Michelin to locate in Nova Scotia. (Most of its tires were to be exported to the American market.) The United States government claimed that the countervailing duty was to offset a "bounty or grant" to the exports which could be interpreted as unfair competition under General Agreement on Tariffs and Trade (GATT) rules. A further example of the new mercantilism is the continuing discussion by the Canadian government of an industrial strategy for Canada. The point is that corporate policies lead to government reaction which in turn leads to further corporate and government reaction in other countries. The era of the new mercantilism may only be in its infancy, but if allowed to flourish, its ramifications for international relations, including Canadian–United States, will be considerable.

Other types of corporate-initiated policies that have brought forth

---

[18] See *Annual Report of the Department of Industry, Trade and Commerce,* 1 April 1971 to 31 March 1972 (Ottawa, 1973).

[19] For further details, see David Leyton-Brown's essay in this volume; and John Fayerweather, "The Mercantile Bank Affair," *Columbia Journal of World Business* 6 (November-December 1971) : 41-50.

[20] "Mercantilism: Past, Present and Future," paper presented at the Canterbury Annual Meeting of the British Association for the Advancement of Science, 20 August 1973.

[21] See *Journal of Commerce,* 1 March 1973; and John Holmes's essay in this volume. Also see the *New York Times,* 6 January 1973; *Wall Street Journal,* 8 January 1973; and *International Canada,* January 1973, pp. 10-12.

a Canadian response are the constraints imposed on many subsidiaries preventing them from exporting to third countries. This is especially true of companies that have a regional form of organization. The Canadian government response can be found in its establishment of a screening agency for foreign take-overs, one criterion for which would be the extent to which the subsidiary would promote exports from Canada.[22]

Considerable concern has been expressed in Canada over the way in which the parent company cuts back production in time of recession. The claim is often made that where an option exists, and this depends on the organization of production, the subsidiary's output is reduced and labour laid off first in the Canadian subsidiary and only later in related plants in the United States. This becomes an extremely sensitive domestic political issue concerning unemployment among Canadian workers which is traced to US corporate sources. An example of this behaviour can be found in the plant shutdowns in the automobile industry in the Windsor, Ontario, area in 1972.[23] Not only does this issue involve the two governments but also relations between the locals of the unions involved, which view themselves as playing a zero-sum game. Current discussions concerning the need for multinational collective bargaining are in part a response to this concern about employment.

The issue of transfer pricing usually results from the parent company's attempt to minimize its tax payments to the governmental authorities. In such instances, negotiations may take place between the Canadian Department of National Revenue and the US Internal Revenue Service, illustrating the role of lower-level central government bureaucracies, both of which are faced with transfer-pricing problems.[24]

Switching funds between parent and subsidiary is another corporate activity that creates problems for the functioning of Canadian monetary and exchange rate policy. Under a system of flexible exchange rates, the immediacy of the effects on exchange reserves is less important; but even with flexible exchange rates, the central government will intervene in the market to prevent violent fluctuations that

[22] Canada, House of Commons, *Bill C-132, Foreign Investment Review Act*, submitted by the Minister of Industry, Trade and Commerce, 1st reading 24 January 1973 (enacted December 1973).

[23] We would like to thank Professor A. Murray of the University of Windsor for bringing this point to our attention. For an interesting case study involving one company, Auto Specialties Ltd., see *Windsor Star*, 17 January, 28 April, 9 and 10 June 1972.

[24] Litvak, Maule, and Robinson, *Dual Loyalty*, p. 132.

may undermine trade, and thus corporate activity cannot be ignored. The foreign exchange crisis of January 1968, when Canada had a fixed exchange rate, involved the speculative activity of US companies with Canadian subsidiaries,[25] and was only ameliorated after negotiations had taken place between representatives of the United States and Canadian governments at both political and bureaucratic levels.[26] An interesting aspect of this crisis was that it resulted from the corporate system's response to US government policies which in turn led to a Canadian reaction at the governmental level.

Corporate pricing policies have given rise to charges of price discrimination by firms against Canadian purchasers of farm machinery. In 1967, it was noted that Ford tractors manufactured in the United Kingdom were being sold in Canada at substantially higher prices than in the UK.[27] The differential could not be explained away in terms of transportation and distribution costs but was due to higher profits earned on the tractors sold in Canada. The ability to sustain this differential was due to an artificial separation of the British and Canadian markets; the Ford Motor Company made its UK dealers sign an agreement not to sell their products for export from the UK.

This example is slightly more involved as it brings in Ford's British subsidiary as well. Ultimately, however, the situation is similar to those examined earlier. The parent company of Ford in the United States initiates a policy of price discrimination that is transmitted through its UK subsidiary to its dealerships in Canada. Canadian combines (antitrust) authorities attempted to deal with this situation but appear to have received little assistance from either US or UK authorities, who felt they experienced few ill effects from the incident. The United Kingdom has no legislation dealing with pricing behaviour that discriminates between domestic and export prices, although concern may be expressed about lost export earnings. US affiliates, even if they wanted to act, argue that the pricing behaviour originates in another national jurisdiction, and the Canadian government finds itself impotent to affect behaviour in the UK. It is probable that government cooperation on such issues is not likely to take place until a number of countries find themselves subjected to similar

[25] See Louis Rasminsky (then governor of the Bank of Canada), "Monetary Policy and the Defence of the Canadian Dollar," speech given to the Canadian Club of Victoria, 17 October 1968, p. 8.

[26] See Maureen Appel Molot, *The Role of Institutions in Canada-U.S. Relations: The Case of North American Financial Ties*, Carleton University School of International Affairs Occasional Papers, no. 24, November 1972.

[27] Royal Commission on Farm Machinery, *Special Report on Prices* (Ottawa: Queen's Printer, 1969) pp. 61-90.

problems concerning multinational enterprises on which general agreement can be reached or issues traded.[28]

US Government-Initiated Policies

Relationship number 2 in figure 1 refers to policies initiated by the US government that apply to the parent company, but with the intent of influencing its subsidiary's operations by getting the parent to implement certain commercial policies in the subsidiary. A number of actions fall into this category, including antitrust policy, balance-of-payments policy, freedom-to-export rules, and Domestic International Sales Corporation (DISC) legislation.

In the antitrust field, United States policies have led to cases where a US company was prevented from acquiring a Canadian company, e.g., the proposed take-over of Labatt Breweries by the Jos. Schlitz Brewing Company. In other US court decisions, the ownership composition of Canadian corporations has been altered, as in the case of Alcan Aluminum Limited and Canadian Industries Limited. This action led to joint Canadian-US ministerial statements and to notification agreements in the event of future extraterritorial application of United States laws to firms in Canada.[29] The introduction of amendments to the Canadian Combines Investigation Act in November 1973, which block the application of foreign court judgments to firms in Canada, indicates that the Canadian government feels that something stronger than a notification agreement is needed in this area.[30]

A more sensitive political issue has arisen where United States laws and policies have prevented the export of goods from subsidiary operations in Canada, because of the US Trading With The Enemy Act and related export control regulations that apply to United States companies. Similar sensitivity has been shown when US balance-of-payments policies have influenced the flow of funds between parent and subsidiary, either by restricting the outflow of funds to the subsidiary or by encouraging the repatriation of earnings or the repayment of loans from the subsidiary to the parent.[31]

---

[28] The conflict between the Swiss-based company, Hoffmann-LaRoche, and the UK government concerning the pricing of Librium and Valium is a further example of one government requiring the assistance of another. See UK Monopolies Commission, *A Report on the Supply of Chlordiazepoxide and Diazepam* (London: Her Majesty's Stationery Office, 11 April 1973).

[29] See Isaiah A. Litvak and Christopher J. Maule, "Extraterritoriality and Conflict Resolution," *Journal of Conflict Resolution* 13 (September 1969): 305-19.

[30] See Canada, House of Commons, *Bill C-227*, Amendments to the Canadian Combines Investigation Act, 1st reading 5 November 1973, sections 31.5, 31.6, and 32.1.

[31] Litvak, Maule, and Robinson, *Dual Loyalty*, p. 57.

In these three instances there is an obvious potential conflict with Canadian national objectives. Freedom-to-export and balance-of-payments policies may conflict with Canadian policies, and US anti-trust policies may conflict with the structure of industry desired by the Canadian government. The actual effects of the antitrust and freedom-to-export policies have probably been minimal to date, although there may be an iceberg effect in that the parent and subsidiary may refrain from exporting because of the known attitude of US authorities. In these circumstances, it is not the known cases that count but rather the general restraint exercised because of the existence of the policies.

All these activities have become sensitive political issues in Canada because of the obvious linkage of subsidiary commercial behaviour with government policies in the United States. Official Canadian government reports, by commenting on them, have also served to focus attention on this issue of extraterritoriality.[32] The other side of the coin is seldom stressed, namely that certain extra-territorial US policies may redound to the benefit of Canada. For example, the United States has tended to provide leadership in the promotion of automobile safety standards, drug testing, and environmental protection. The standards that have been applied to US manufacturers have often been applied to their subsidiaries in Canada even when Canadian laws do not require them.

An evolving area of concern is that posed by US legislation on pollution. It may well be that its effect will be to encourage the location abroad of certain activities that present a high environmental hazard and a low labour content, such as oil refining. Refineries have already been located in the Canadian Atlantic provinces, attracted there, it is true, by provincial authorities.[33] As with many of the other issues mentioned above, the Canadian authorities are free to prevent this locational pattern. However, Canadian constitutional arrangements present certain difficulties. Provincial governments in the depressed regions of Canada are loath to turn away any industrial activity because of the economic stimulus it provides. The formulation of any federal policy toward foreign investment in Canada has been severely constrained by the attitudes, largely favourable to foreign

[32] See Watkins report, pp. 310-46; Canada, House of Commons, Standing Committee on External Affairs and National Defence, *Report No. 33*, 28th Parl., 2d sess., 1969-70; and Gray Task Force, *Foreign Direct Investment in Canada* (Ottawa: Information Canada, 1972), pp. 253-90. See also the essay by David Leyton-Brown in this volume.

[33] For example, refineries have been located by Shaheen Natural Resources of New York and Gulf Oil in Newfoundland and by Texaco and Imperial Oil in Nova Scotia.

investment, of the individual provinces, which have the right to attract industrial activity. In fact, competition between provinces for foreign investment often results in substantial benefits from the investment being lost to the country as the result of the provincial governments offering tax concessions to the foreign investors.

The new mercantilism of government support for industry has its strong supporters in the United States as well as in Canada and elsewhere. Manifestations of it can be found in the DISC policy of the US government, which offers tax incentives for export development located in the US.[34] The implementation of DISC may not substantially affect Canadian industry, but its existence serves to increase the tension between the two countries.

Canadian Government-Initiated Policies

Relationship number 3 in figure 1 refers to attempts by the Canadian government to influence the subsidiary operations in Canada. These attempts are positive as well as negative and include trying to induce existing US subsidiaries in Canada to expand their operations, to increase their technological and innovative capability, and to locate in certain areas of the country with the assistance of regional economic incentives. As noted above, provincial governments provide incentives as well through such measures as tax relief and subsidies.

The restraining influence of the Canadian government is exercised most obviously through its establishment of a foreign take-over screening agency, which can be viewed as a way of restricting or controlling the opportunities for United States and other foreign companies to acquire subsidiary operations, to establish new operations, or to expand existing operations into unrelated fields in Canada. The criteria for assessing a potential foreign take-over reflect some of the issues concerning US direct investment about which Canadians are sensitive. However, the Foreign Investment Review Act (Bill C-132) is only the most recent in a series of policies produced largely on an ad hoc basis over time.

Canadian foreign investment policies have been discussed in detail elsewhere and can only be summarized here.[35] Essentially, they identify certain sectors of the Canadian economy as key sectors that should remain Canadian by some means, such as a limitation of for-

---

[34] See John Holmes in this volume. See also *Journal of Commerce*, 3 August 1973, and 11 May 1973.

[35] See Department of Industry, Trade and Commerce, Foreign Investment Division, Office of Economics, *Selected Readings in Laws and Regulations Affecting Foreign Investment in Canada*, March 1972, plus amendments nos. 1, 2, 3. A discussion of these policies can be found in *Dual Loyalty*, pp. 36-47.

eign ownership, Canadian content requirements in the mass media, the assurance of some Canadian presence in certain industries, and special assistance to Canadian-owned firms. In addition, the Income Tax Act contains special provisions relating to Canadian-owned and foreign-owned firms; the new Canada Corporations Act [36] requires a majority of Canadians on the boards of directors of federally incorporated companies; the Department of Industry, Trade and Commerce issues voluntary guidelines for good corporate behaviour by Canadian subsidiaries of foreign companies; [37] and the Canada Development Corporation has been established with the objective of helping to "develop and maintain strong Canadian-controlled and Canadian-managed corporations in the private sector." [38]

The purpose of these policies initiated by the Canadian government is to influence the performance of foreign subsidiaries either by regulating performance directly or by establishing ownership conditions in order to influence performance. The provisions of the Income Tax Act and the Canada Development Corporation have less direct impact on subsidiary operations but are intended to be complementary policies by promoting the development of Canadian-owned industry.

Relationship number 3 (figure 1) aims at influencing the subsidiary in Canada but has transnational implications in that what happens to the subsidiary is likely to affect its relationship with the parent company in the United States. Outstanding examples of these policies that led to political issues between the two governments occurred in the Mercantile Bank affair and with respect to *Time* and *Reader's Digest*.[39] One reason these cases became highly politicized was the influence that certain American business interests could muster within the US government, combined with the willingness of that government to act on behalf of such firms. In addition, there was strong American objection to the introduction of retroactive legislation that would adversely affect the two periodicals. The United States government often appears to act resolutely in instances that if carried out by the Canadian government could provide examples for other countries to follow, i.e., may lead to a domino effect which would

[36] See Canada, House of Commons, *Bill C-213, An Act Respecting Canadian Business Corporations*, 1st reading 18 July 1973.

[37] See "Some Guiding Principles of Good Corporate Behavior for Subsidiaries in Canada of Foreign Companies," in Department of Industry, Trade and Commerce, *Foreign-Owned Subsidiaries in Canada* (Ottawa: Queen's Printer, 1967), pp. 40-41.

[38] Canada, House of Commons, *An Act to Establish the Canada Development Corporation*, 1st reading 25 January 1971 (passed 9 June 1971), section 2.

[39] See John Fayerweather, pp. 41-50; and Isaiah A. Litvak and Christopher J. Maule, *Canadian Cultural Sovereignty: The "Time–Reader's Digest" Case Study* (New York: Praeger, 1974). For further discussion see article by David Leyton-Brown in this volume.

result in retroactive action against US companies elsewhere. In the case of *Time* and *Reader's Digest,* Canadian sensitivity was increased because of the sociocultural and political dimensions of the issues involved.

Jointly Initiated Policies

The US-Canadian automotive agreement and the defense production sharing agreement are examples of two agreements [40] made at the interstate level (relationship number 6 in figure 1) but that affect the parent-subsidiary relationship (number 1). The outcome and implications of these agreements for two companies, Ford Motor Company of Canada, Limited, and Garrett Manufacturing, Limited, have been examined elsewhere.[41] For the purposes of the present essay, the main observation to make is that the performance of the companies under the agreements has been such that one government or the other has wanted to renegotiate the arrangement because the outcome has not been as anticipated or has been felt to be harmful.

The foregoing relationships, numbers 1, 2, and 3, are fairly familiar, although when aggregated they present a formidable array of transnational actions undertaken by governments or firms. The other two relationships, numbers 4 and 5, are less obvious, and number 5 probably has little if any content. That is to say, it is unlikely that the United States government, except perhaps through its officials in Canada, will interact with the subsidiary company. It has no need to because of relationship number 2, interaction with parent company, and number 6, interstate politics. Even the example of US courts requiring the surrender of documents from a subsidiary, which is banned by law in Ontario and Quebec,[42] is primarily a case of approaching the parent company to recover documents from its subsidiary.

Relationship number 4 is more pervasive and is of growing importance. It refers to contacts made between the Canadian government and the parent company in the United States. This takes place in a number of different ways. The Trade Commissioner Service of the Department of Industry, Trade and Commerce provides one level of contact with US companies which may or may not be parent companies at the time of contact. More relevant examples are the dis-

---

[40] Litvak, Maule, and Robinson, *Dual Loyalty,* pp. 195-225.

[41] Ibid., pp. 61-86. See articles in this volume by Roger Swanson and David Leyton-Brown.

[42] See *The Business Records Protection Act, Revised Statutes of Ontario,* 1960, ch. 44 (Queen's Printer); and *The Business Concerns Records Act, Revised Statutes of Quebec,* 1964, ch. 278 (Queen's Printer).

cussions held by federal and provincial bureaucrats with United States companies in order to induce them to invest in Canada, to expand, or do something new in the case of firms with existing subsidiaries in Canada. This activity may be undertaken in conjunction with relationship number 3, where the Canadian government provides incentives through its regional policies or research and development policies to encourage firms to invest in Canada. Examples of these activities include the negotiations leading up to the location of International Business Machines (IBM) Corporation in Quebec, the expansion of Control Data Corporation in Ontario, and the location of Lockheed Petroleum Services in British Columbia. IBM, Control Data Corporation, and Lockheed Petroleum Services all received financial assistance from the Canadian government.[43]

The defense area is illustrative of another procedure, namely the offset agreement or bargained reciprocity. In instances where the Canadian government purchases large items of military equipment from United States firms, such as aircraft, offset agreements are negotiated between Canadian government officials and United States firms to ensure that a certain amount of production is located in Canada. A similar example can be found in the civil aviation field when Air Canada purchases US aircraft. In this case, Air Canada, being a crown corporation, has to clear the offset agreement with the Canadian government before closing the deal.

A further example of this linkage is the 30 percent equity interest in Texas Gulf Sulphur, a United States company with operations in Canada, acquired by the Canada Development Corporation which is financed by the Canadian government. This action represents a form of Canadian nationalization of a US company, both the parent company in the United States and its subsidiary in Canada.

In sum, relationship number 4 is illustrative of some of the ways in which the Canadian government attempts to implement an industrial policy using the public purse and its bargaining strength. The significance of this relationship is that it promotes bilateral trade resulting from reciprocal negotiations rather than open market transactions, and it encourages countries to establish nontariff barriers to trade.

The basic model used to analyze the six relationships discussed above can be modified in a number of ways. More explicit recognition

---

[43] Among the numerous examples of provincial governments seeking US investment are speeches made to the business community in New York by Premier Bourassa of Quebec and ex-premier Smallwood of Newfoundland extolling the advantages of locating industry in these provinces. In addition, the Province of Saskatchewan negotiated with the state of New Mexico to support its potash industry. See Holsti-Levy article in this volume for this case.

can be given to the role of provincial and state governments and to the inclusion of trade union activities, and the case of Canadian parent companies with subsidiaries in the United States can be introduced together with the case of US subsidiaries in Canada that in turn have subsidiaries in third countries.

Taking the case of Canadian parent companies, in 1969 Canadian direct investment abroad totaled $5,040,000,000, of which 54.8 percent was located in the US. However, 30 percent of the total was investment made by US-controlled corporations in Canada.[44] The oft quoted remark that Canadians per capita invest more heavily in the United States than Americans do in Canada has to be modified by details of the real origin of the investment.

Take the following instance of Canadian investment in the United States. Maclean-Hunter in Canada has in recent years expanded its American operations, which may explain the change in this company's attitude toward the activities of *Time* and *Reader's Digest* in Canada. During the hearings before the Royal Commission on Publications,[45] Maclean-Hunter argued against the two American periodicals being given special tax treatment in Canada. However, Maclean-Hunter reversed this position in its submission to the Special Senate Committee on the Mass Media in 1970.[46] Fear of retaliation against its operations in the United States may have led to this change of heart. Or consider the state of New York's advertising campaign, "It pays to locate in New York State," and the state's offer of financial incentives to attract Canadian firms (especially from Ontario) to locate there. State officials have published a brochure listing the Canadian firms that have responded to their campaign. Across the border in Ontario, the issue of financial subsidies to firms to locate in that province has given rise to a political issue because a number of large US companies have been the recipients of these subsidies. Thus at the provincial or state level, the public purse has been used to persuade foreign enterprises to locate abroad.

A more complex example of Canadian foreign investment is that of the Ford Motor Company of Canada, which itself has subsidiaries in South Africa, Australia, New Zealand, and Singapore (and Rhodesia from 1960 to 1967). This organizational setup reflects the system of imperial tariff preferences that gave an advantage to firms operating within the British Empire. However, since 1965 the group director of the Canadian Overseas Group has been responsible to an

---

[44] Statistics Canada, *Canada's International Investment Position* (Ottawa: Information Canada, 1971), pp. 69, 79.

[45] Canada, *Hearings before Royal Commission on Publications*, 1957.

[46] Canada, Senate, *Hearings before the Senate Committee on Mass Media*, vol. 1, 1970, p. 159.

executive vice-president of Ford-US in charge of overseas operations.[47] The relationship of the Canadian Overseas Group to Ford-Canada has merely been as a financial pass-through. However, the relationship is sufficient to involve the Canadian government in cases where the United States applies its foreign trade regulations through such subsidiaries in third countries.

The fourth example is still more complex. In 1971 the government of Guyana nationalized the Demerara Bauxite Company, a wholly owned subsidiary of Alcan.[48] While Alcan is about 50 percent Canadian owned and has its head office in Montreal, it had American antecedents and not until the 1950s did a US antitrust court decision separate the ownership of Alcan from that of Alcoa (Aluminum Company of America). Moreover, it is well known that Alcoa used Alcan prior to 1940 to gain proxy membership in the international aluminum cartel based in Europe. It is not surprising, therefore, that the Guyanese government perceived Alcan as one of the North American multinational corporations in the aluminum industry, and felt that Alcan was being subjected to pressure by corporations such as Alcoa, Reynolds, and Kaiser not to give in to the demands of the Guyanese. These companies were concerned that nationalization would provide a demonstration effect in the Caribbean where they had interests, such as in Surinam and Jamaica, as well as in other parts of the world.

The Guyanese believed the United States government to have a direct interest in the outcome of the negotiations for nationalization since the US companies were insured by the federal government under the Overseas Private Investment Corporation (OPIC). Moreover, the involvement of Mr. Arthur Goldberg, counsel for Reynolds Aluminum, in the compensation negotiations was seen as involving an emissary from the US government because of his earlier official positions. In fact, the Guyanese saw the US government as being more involved in the negotiations than was the Canadian government, which at the time was trying to develop its own policy toward foreign investment in Canada. Prime Minister Burnham described the role of the Canadian government during the negotiations as "impeccable," a comment reflecting the hands-off attitude taken. The significance of this example is that in the aluminum industry, certain companies are identified by bauxite-producing countries as North American companies with little or no recognition given to the Canadian aspects of Alcan. The US government is known to be active on behalf of its corporations with overseas investments and it is assumed that they act on behalf of

[47] Litvak, Maule, and Robinson, *Dual Loyalty*, chapter 5.
[48] The remarks in this section are extracted from research currently being undertaken by the authors.

Alcan as well. The absence of a stated policy by the Canadian government toward outward investment serves to substantiate this view and is likely to lead to future issues in Canadian-US relations.

CONFLICT RESOLUTION

The resolution of conflicts arising from the parent-subsidiary relationship shown in figure 1 has taken a number of different forms, including unilateral action by each government and bilateral governmental action involving interstate negotiations. Those policies of the Canadian and United States governments identified as the new mercantilism are examples of unilateral actions. Bilateral negotiations have taken place over balance-of-payments, freedom-to-export, and antitrust issues, at times leading to concessions or early-warning agreements, over special arrangements for industry sectors such as the automobile industry, and over special concessions granted to firms such as the Michelin Tire Company.[49]

Conflicts are also resolved within the corporation between the management of the parent and that of the subsidiary. As with transfer-pricing procedures, the form and nature of such conflict resolution is difficult to determine. However, it is clear from discussions with the management of Canadian subsidiaries that at times they will argue against parent company directives that are viewed as not being in the best interests of Canada. Sometimes this reaction may be due to a concern for Canada and sometimes to a belief that the image of the subsidiary and its associated commercial performance will be harmed by the action required by the parent company. Where Canadians manage the subsidiary they frequently display a personality whose loyalty is split between the US-controlled corporate system and Canada.[50]

In the context of Canadian-US interstate relations, the multinational enterprise has increased the importance of politico-economic bargaining across multiple issue areas involving governmental and nongovernmental actors. Professor Stanley Hoffmann took note that "the competition between states takes place on several chess boards in addition to the traditional military and diplomatic ones: for instance, the chess boards of world trade, of world finance, of aid and technical assistance, of space research and exploration, of military technology,

[49] Litvak, Maule, and Robinson, *Dual Loyalty*, pp. 36-48, and note 21 above.
[50] The ability to resolve conflicts within Canada is also constrained by federal-provincial relationships where provincial governments are anxious to promote industrial activity at almost any price. In the case of Quebec, little distinction is made between English-Canadian capital and that from the United States. In fact, at times there seems to be a preference for the US variety.

and the chess board of what has been called 'informal penetration.' " [51]
It is our belief that the preeminent presence of the US multinational
enterprise in Canada has increased the subtle and complex linkages
between these chess boards for both players. For example, although
the US government is host to the headquarters organization of the
multinational enterprise, and has the legal authority and power to
affect certain commercial activities of US multinational enterprises,
it may choose not to do so for political and/or economic reasons
because of its relations with Canada. This has been evident in the
concessions by the United States in the areas of freedom-to-export,
antitrust, balance-of-payments, automotive, and defence-sharing
agreements. Implicit in any bilateral consultative agreement is the
giving up of some freedom of action by both parties.

Our case studies have shown that the presence of the multinational enterprise promotes the interdependence of political and
economic issue areas between Canada and the United States. Offset
agreements are becoming an important consideration in the negotiations between the two governments, limiting their scope in some areas,
while expanding it in others. It appears obvious that the US multinational enterprise has increased the potential costs of applying certain actions by one nation against another if both are constituents of
the same corporate system. This phenomenon will make the multinational enterprise an increasingly important ally or opponent in
interstate politics—depending on whether the national interests of the
governments involved coincide or conflict with those of the corporation. Consideration of cases involving Canadian companies with subsidiaries in the United States and elsewhere reinforces this view.
Thus, the multinational enterprise may be seen as a constraint on a
nation's autonomy, which applies to both parent and host governments. In short, the multinational enterprise as a transnational actor
presents nations with a revised set of payoffs in their interactions
with one another.

---

[51] Stanley Hoffmann, "International Organization and the International System,"
International Organization 24 (Summer 1970) : 401.

THE MULTINATIONAL ENTERPRISE AND CONFLICT IN CANADIAN–AMERICAN RELATIONS

David Leyton-Brown

Multinational private enterprise is perhaps the most prominent transnational organization active in world politics today. Increasing attention has been paid to the challenge to state sovereignty posed by multinational enterprise, either as an autonomous actor or as an instrument in interstate conflict.[1] This question is of particular relevance to Canadian-American relations, because of the central role of foreign-owned (and especially American-owned) firms in the Canadian economy.[2] This essay assesses the impact on the host Canadian government of the 27 identifiable cases of politicized conflict that have been generated in Canada by the activities of United States-owned multinational enterprise from 1945 through 1971, and which are publicly known to have occurred.[3]

Each case of conflict presented here is a politicized dispute that the Canadian government or some provincial government is a party to, that concerns some specific actual or proposed action by one or more United States-owned multinational enterprise, and that comes to a definite and recognizable conclusion.[4] Multinational enterprise is

David Leyton-Brown is a member of the Department of Political Science at Carleton University in Ottawa.
[1] A comprehensive model of transnational relationships involving governments and corporations in Canada and the United States is presented elsewhere in this volume by Isaiah A. Litvak and Christopher J. Maule.
[2] Canada, Gray Task Force, *Foreign Direct Investment in Canada* (Ottawa: Information Canada, 1972), pp. 17-18; also referred to as the Gray report.
[3] A systematic treatment of these cases can be found in my "Governments of Developed Countries as Hosts to Multinational Enterprise: The Canadian, British, and French Policy Experience" (Ph.D. dissertation, Harvard University, 1973), pp. 91-116.
[4] Elsewhere in this volume Joseph S. Nye examines cases of interstate conflict involving the governments of Canada and the United States. His boundary conditions of incompatibility of objectives and an initially unfulfilled intergovernmental request give rise to a somewhat different universe of cases, even where multinational enterprise is involved. His magazine tax, auto pact, and Arctic pollution zone cases are essentially similar to the *Time–Reader's Digest*, auto pact, and

involved in every case, either as a participant in a dispute with the Canadian (host) government, or as an instrument of policy, or as the subject of an interstate dispute. Instances have occurred where conflict has developed between the United States government and American-owned multinational enterprise, but such cases are not discussed because the focus here is on the experience of the host government.

The criterion of politicization is very important. Countless instances of conflict that never came to public attention may well have occurred, and any in-house government evaluation of its policies would have to take them into account. However, it is only the cases that are politicized, and come to public awareness, that shape public opinion and thereby influence the relations between states and the making of public policy. It is true that these politicized cases may represent only the tip of an iceberg, and that the nature and outcomes of nonpoliticized cases may be very different. Nevertheless, this essay concerns the entire tip of the iceberg, in which the criterion of public knowledge of the events and public concern with the outcome is satisfied.

The cases can be separated according to initiation of the conflict by the parent United States government, by multinational enterprise, or by the host Canadian government. The United States government can seek to make use of American-owned multinational enterprise as an instrument to advance its interests and achieve its policy goals, and when the resulting corporate actions run counter to Canadian government interests and policies, conflict can ensue. By this criterion, the United States government is understood to have initiated each case involving export controls over American-owned subsidiaries in Canada by its initial prohibiting action, and subsequent Canadian requests for exemption constitute response rather than initiation.[5] Alternatively, a multinational enterprise can engage in action to promote its corporate interests and policies, and this action may contradict host government desires. Finally, the Canadian government itself may seek to alter the behavior of American-owned subsidiaries, or to use American-owned multinational enterprise as an instrument to achieve its own policy goals, and this could produce conflict with either the multinational enterprise or the United States government. Though

Humble Oil cases discussed here. However, his treatment of a series of interactions as a single conflict if the same major objectives were pursued throughout results in two cases, extraterritorial control of corporations and US balance-of-payments guidelines, that in this essay are treated as issue areas, each comprising several distinct cases.

[5] Thus initiation of conflict corresponds more closely to Nye's first government action than to his first interstate request (see his table 6).

it is sometimes difficult to determine where in a long chain of interactions the initiation of conflict occurs, for analytic purposes initiation in each case will be considered to rest with the party to the dispute that provided the initial impetus to trigger, for its benefit, the
specific actual or proposed action by one or more multinational
enterprises.

The two principal indices by which all of the cases of conflict are
compared are the intensity of conflict and the value of the solution as
perceived by the Canadian government. The index of intensity of conflict is not impressionistic but is composed of a measure of the level
of attention given to the case within the Canadian government and a
measure of the extent of bargaining activity by the various parties
to the conflict. The measure of the level of attention is based on the
presumption that the greater the perceived importance of a problem,
the higher the authority of the decision maker who will handle it. The
measure of the extent of actions is based on the presumption that
a wider range of influencing measures indicates the expenditure of
greater political resources, and a greater perception of the seriousness
of the conflict. The resulting scale of conflict is divided into low,
moderate, high, and very high intensity.[6]

In addition, each case is discussed as to the value of the solution
to the Canadian government. Value of solution relates to the perception by officials of the host government of the immediate, short-run
outcome of the case as favorable, unfavorable, or approximately neutral, and not to any objective economic or other calculation of the

---

[6] The indices used here are based upon coding categories developed by Joseph S.
Nye and Robert O. Keohane. The level of attention is coded as 1 if the highest
known substantive decision-making action occurred at the bureaucratic level, and
as 2 if such action was at the cabinet or prime ministerial level. The extent of
action by multinational enterprise in its relations with the Canadian government
is coded from 0 to 5 according to the number of different actions undertaken, including (a) procedural discussions, (b) discussions involving known threats of
positive or negative sanctions, (c) enlisting domestic support, (d) enlisting
foreign support, and (e) carrying out threats or promises. The extent of
action by the Canadian government in its relations with multinational enterprise
is similarly coded from 0 to 5 according to the number of different actions undertaken, including (a) private discussions, (b) generation of public support (tactical
politicization), (c) new legislation or regulations, (d) border policy action (prevention or restriction of corporate entry), and (e) internal policy action (expro-
priation or requirements for corporate behavior). The extent of action by the
Canadian and United States governments in interstate relations are each coded
from 0 to 5 according to the number of different actions undertaken, including (a)
private discussions, (b) publicized discussions to generate political support
(tactical politicization), (c) known attempts to link settlement of the case to
another issue, (d) explicit international agreement, (e) formal diplomatic protest,
and (f) diplomatic rupture. The five resulting code values are added to produce
the index of intensity of conflict. The intensity scale is separated into low (1-6),
moderate (7-9), high (10-12), and very high (13-22).

appropriateness of the government perception and policy goals.[7] The determination of the value of solution makes possible the analysis of gains and denials achieved by the Canadian government. If the outcome is considered favorable when the triggering action is taken, such a case constitutes a gain for the Canadian government; but if the outcome is considered favorable when the triggering action is prevented from occurring, such a case constitutes a denial. Similarly, the cases with an unfavorable value of solution would be unsuccessful gains when action of which the Canadian government approved failed to occur, and unsuccessful denials when action occurred against the wishes of the Canadian government. Note that neither the value of solution nor the concept of gains and denials implies that the Canadian government has won or lost. Value of solution connotes Canadian government satisfaction with the outcome and does not preclude equal or greater satisfaction for some other party to the conflict. Such variable-sum situations of joint benefit are discussed below.

A brief capsulized listing of the 27 identifiable cases of conflict generated by United States multinational enterprise in Canada are presented in the chronological order in which they rose to public attention (see table 1).

1. *Ontario documents.* In 1950 the United States Department of Justice sought in United States courts to obtain documents from American-owned pulp and paper companies in Canada. The Canadian government protested, and the Ontario government passed its Business Records Protection Act prohibiting the forced removal of corporate records from Ontario. The documents were not produced.[8]

2. *Alcoa.* In 1950 a United States court ordered the Aluminum Company of America (Alcoa) to divest itself of its interests in the Aluminum Company of Canada, despite the resentment of Canadian government officials at the intrusion of United States law into Canadian industrial organization. The change of ownership occurred.[9]

3. *Canadian Industries Limited (CIL).* In 1951 a United States court forced the termination of the joint ownership of CIL by Du Pont and Imperial Chemical Industries Limited. Du Pont divested itself of its Canadian holdings despite Canadian government resentment of the intrusion of United States law into Canadian industrial organization.[10]

---

[7] Here again Nye's definitions elsewhere in this volume differ from mine. He focuses not on satisfaction with the outcome but on whether the outcome is closer to one or the other government's initial objectives.

[8] Kingman Brewster, Jr., *Antitrust and American Business Abroad* (New York: McGraw-Hill, 1958), p. 49.

[9] Kingman Brewster, Jr., *Law and United States Business in Canada* (Montreal: Canadian-American Committee, 1960), pp. 16-17.

[10] Ibid.

TABLE 1. CHRONOLOGICAL FREQUENCY OF CANADIAN CONFLICT CASES

Number of Cases	Year Case Arose
2	1950
1	1951
1	1957
1	1958
4	1959
5	1965
4	1966
2	1968
1	1969
1	1970
5	1971

4. *Ford trucks.* In December 1957 a Canadian trader charged that the Ford Motor Company of Canada refused to ship trucks to the People's Republic of China because of the United States Trading With The Enemy Act. A joint Canadian-American probe resulted in the Diefenbaker-Eisenhower agreement of 1958, which provided a means of consultation in cases involving export controls, leading to the possibility of exemption. Whether or not a genuine order was received, the sale did not take place.[11]

5. *Rayonier, Inc.* In 1958 China negotiated for the purchase of pulp and paper from the Canadian subsidiary of Rayonier. Under the consultative mechanism of the Diefenbaker-Eisenhower agreement, the Canadian government sought and received an exemption from US export controls. Despite the exemption the sale did not occur, perhaps because of the outbreak of hostilities in the Formosa Strait.[12]

6. *Alcan-China.* In January 1959 it was reported in Parliament that Alcan Aluminum had refused a possible sale to China. Alcan claimed that United States legal factors were not involved, and the Diefenbaker-Eisenhower consultative mechanism was not utilized. Nevertheless, members of the Canadian government attributed the refusal to fear of legal reaction against United States nationals on the board of the parent holding company.[13]

7. *Fairbanks-Morse.* In 1959 the Canadian subsidiary of Fairbanks-Morse Company was reconditioning locomotives owned by Canadian National Railways for sale to China. The Canadian government pressed strenuously and successfully for exemption from United

---

[11] Canada, House of Commons, *Debates*, 18 December 1957, p. 2514, and 11 July 1958, p. 2142. See also Brewster, *Law and Business*, pp. 24-26; and Isaiah A. Litvak, Christopher J. Maule, and R. D. Robinson, *Dual Loyalty: Canadian-U.S. Business Arrangements* (Toronto: McGraw-Hill, 1971), pp. 24, 42-43.

[12] Brewster, *Law and Business*, p. 25.

[13] Canada, House of Commons, *Debates*, 23 January 1959.

States export controls. Despite the exemption, the sale did not take place.[14]

8. *Radio patents pool.* In 1959 a United States court, on the grounds of illegal restraint on United States exports, forced the termination of a patents pool participated in by Canadian subsidiaries of General Electric, Westinghouse, and Philips and designed to protect manufacture in Canada. This pool had previously been investigated to the satisfaction of Canadian anticombines authorities. During the prosecution of the case, the Fulton-Rogers agreement of 1959 was negotiated and announced, providing for prior consultation on antitrust problems.[15]

9. *Peat moss.* Later in 1959 a joint sales agency of all the major peat moss producers in western Canada (largely American owned) was charged in the United States with restraint on competitive importation and distribution. Through the consultative procedures of the Fulton-Rogers agreement, Canadian authorities voiced no objection to the complaint but expressed their views on the remedy.[16]

10. *Auto pact.* On 16 January 1965 the Canada–United States automotive agreement was signed, providing for duty-free trade by manufacturers in new automobiles and automobile parts between Canada and the United States. The pact, designed to provide economies of scale to Canadian automobile production and to rationalize the continental automobile industry, was agreed to by the United States government to avoid unilateral changes in the Canadian tariff structure. The four American automobile companies participated in the negotiations, and attached formal letters of undertaking to the agreement.[17]

11. *1965 guidelines.* In February 1965 the United States government instituted a program of voluntary guidelines for American corporations regarding their reinvestment and other practices in order to decrease the capital outflow from the United States. Canada was largely exempted from the initial guidelines, but was included in December 1965. To quiet rising criticism that the United States government was dictating the reinvestment, dividend, purchasing, and financial policies of Canadian corporations, the minister of industry, trade and commerce issued, on 31 March 1966, "Some Guiding Principles of Good Corporate Behavior for Subsidiaries in Canada of Foreign Companies." [18]

[14] Brewster, *Law and Business*, pp. 25-26.
[15] Ibid., pp. 17-18, 21-22. See also J. N. Behrman, *National Interests and the Multinational Enterprise* (Englewood Cliffs, N.J.: Prentice-Hall, 1970), p. 118.
[16] Brewster, *Law and Business*, pp. 19-20.
[17] Litvak, Maule, and Robinson.
[18] See the essay in this volume by Gerald Wright and Maureen Appel Molot. See also David Godfrey and Melvin Watkins, eds., *Gordon to Watkins to You* (Toronto: New Press, 1970), p. 51.

12. *Time–Reader's Digest.* The 1965 budget of the Canadian government introduced a measure recommended in 1960 by the Royal Commission on Publications to remove income tax deductions for the cost of advertising directed at the Canadian market and placed in a newspaper or periodical more than 25 percent owned by non-Canadians. Extensive pressures by *Time* and *Reader's Digest,* and by the United States government, led to the exemption of those two magazines from the provisions of the budget as passed.[19]

13. *Cuba flour.* In 1965 the Canadian government concluded a wheat sale with the Soviet Union, involving the shipment of flour to Cuba. The United States government ordered American-owned milling companies not to fill the order, and the Canadian government was unable to persuade them to do so. Canadian-owned companies were finally found to make the sales.[20]

14. *Vietnam drugs.* In 1965 Canadian Quakers sought to send medical supplies to aid war victims in both North and South Vietnam. Canadian subsidiaries of United States drug firms refused to fill the orders, and the Quakers finally found a Canadian-owned supplier.[21]

15. *Schlitz-Labatt.* In 1966 a United States court prevented the Joseph Schlitz Brewing Company from acquiring John Labatt, Limited, a Canadian brewery.[22]

16. *Standard Oil-Potash.* In 1966 a United States court prevented Standard Oil (New Jersey) from acquiring the Potash Company of America, a producer of potash in both Canada and the United States, because Jersey's Canadian subsidiary, Imperial Oil Ltd., had made rich potash discoveries of its own and was a potential competitor in the United States market.[23]

17. *Wage parity.* In 1966, despite the Canadian government's anti-inflationary urgings of voluntary limits on wage increases, the major automobile companies and the United Automobile Workers negotiated a wage settlement providing for progression to wage parity for Canadian and American automobile workers.

18. *Mercantile Bank.* In October 1966 the Canadian government introduced amendments to the Bank Act restricting non-Canadian holdings in chartered banks. The legislation applied only to the Mercantile Bank, a small Dutch-owned bank, which had been acquired in

[19] Peter C. Newman, *The Distemper of Our Times* (Toronto: McClelland and Stewart, 1968), pp. 225-26. See also Walter L. Gordon, *A Choice for Canada* (Toronto: McClelland and Stewart, 1966), p. 97.

[20] Behrman, p. 113. See also Malcolm Levin and Christine Sylvester, *Foreign Ownership* (Don Mills, Ont.: Paperjacks, General Publishing Co., 1972), pp. 85-86.

[21] Levin and Sylvester, p. 86.

[22] Jerrold G. Van Cise, "Antitrust Guides to Foreign Acquisitions," *Harvard Business Review,* November-December 1972, p. 83.

[23] Litvak, Maule, and Robinson, pp. 121-22.

1963 by the First National City Bank of New York (Citibank) despite warnings from Canadian officials that the Canadian government would act retroactively to limit foreign holdings in Canadian banks and limit Mercantile's growth. Citibank sought an exemption from the legislation, but despite intense corporate and United States government pressures, including an exchange of diplomatic notes, received only a five-year exemption. Mercantile has been issuing new shares to Canadian residents to bring Canadian ownership up to the specified levels.[21]

19. *1968 guidelines.* On 1 January 1968 the United States balance-of-payments guidelines were made mandatory. Though the guidelines were directed mainly at investment in Western Europe, corporate repatriation of capital put serious pressure on the Canadian dollar. In March Canada was granted an exemption from the regulations in exchange for a commitment to institute controls to prevent Canada from being used as a *pass-through* for United States capital and to convert $1 billion of Canadian foreign exchange reserves into non-liquid United States Treasury securities.[25]

20. *Humble Oil.* In 1968 the *Manhattan* made its exploratory voyage through the Northwest Passage. Subsequently the United States government objected to the Canadian declaration of a 100-mile pollution-free zone in the Arctic, but Humble Oil extended recognition of Canadian jurisdiction. After being informed by the Canadian government that it would not be permitted to ship oil without recognizing Canadian authority over the pollution-free zone, Humble signed letters of compliance accepting Canadian pollution regulations and coast guard cutter escorts, though no more voyages have been made.[26]

21. *Royal Securities.* In May 1969 Royal Securities Corporation of Montreal, a large Canadian investment dealer, was acquired by the American brokerage firm, Merrill Lynch, Pierce, Fenner & Smith, Inc. This case is set apart from the many other foreign take-overs of Canadian enterprises by the sensitive sector occupied by the firm, and by the expressions of official government disapproval yet impotence to stop the sale.[27]

22. *Denison Mines.* In March 1970 Prime Minister Trudeau intervened in Parliament, ostensibly under the authority of the Ca-

---

[21] Newman, pp. 419-22, 517-18.

[25] See the essay in this volume by Wright and Molot. See also Godfrey and Watkins, pp. 54-57; Behrman, pp. 90-91; and Gray report, p. 286.

[26] I am indebted to Joseph S. Nye for my initial understanding of this case.

[27] Canada, Library of Parliament, Research Branch, "Laws and Regulations Preventing Undue United States Influence on Canadian Financial Institutions, Transportation, Communications, and Energy Industries," Ottawa, 2 March 1970, p. 8.

nadian Atomic Energy Control Act, to block the sale of a controlling
interest in Denison Mines Ltd., Canada's largest uranium producer,
to an American company. New regulations were announced to restrict
foreign ownership in Canada's uranium industry.[28]

23. *Home Oil.* In 1971 the Canadian government forbade the sale
of Home Oil Company, Ltd., Canada's largest independent oil producer, to an American-owned company, and promised money would
be available to make Canadian offers equally attractive.[29]

24. *McClelland and Stewart.* In 1971 the owner of McClelland
and Stewart Limited, a Canadian publishing company, sought to sell
his firm because of lack of working capital. Only American buyers
expressed interest. The Ontario government, to prevent a foreign
take-over, gave a $1 million loan to McClelland and Stewart to keep
it under domestic ownership.[30]

25. *August 1971.* On 15 August 1971 the United States government announced a new policy in its balance-of-payments program,
including a 10 percent surcharge on most categories of imports. The
surcharge applied to most imports of manufactured or processed goods
from Canada but not to most imports of unprocessed materials, which
threatened major dislocations in the pattern of interaffiliate trade.
Once again Canadian government officials appealed for an exemption,
but this time they were refused.

26. *Chrysler wage freeze.* On 15 August 1971 President Nixon
announced a 90-day freeze on wages, prices, and rents. Despite the
statement by the secretary of state for external affairs that the
Canadian government would not tolerate the importation of the freeze
into Canada, some American companies did extend the freeze to their
Canadian subsidiaries. Chrysler Canada, Ltd., informed its 1,365
supervisory and administrative employees that a 5 percent wage
increase they were due to receive in September would be deferred
while the freeze remained in effect.[31]

27. *Douglas wage freeze.* The 15 August 1971 90-day wage freeze
was announced in the United States while Douglas Aircraft Company
of Canada, the Canadian subsidiary of McDonnell-Douglas Corporation, was in the process of negotiating a new contract with 5,600 employees. Douglas informed the union that it would not make a wage
increase offer until the freeze was lifted in November, even though the
existing contract expired in September.[32]

---

[28] Levin and Sylvester, pp. 9-18. The regulations can be found in Canada,
House of Commons, *Debates*, 19 March 1970, pp. 5250-51.
[29] *Gazette* (Montreal), 16 June 1972, p. 25.
[30] Levin and Sylvester, pp. 22-24.
[31] Ibid., pp. 76-77.
[32] Ibid., p. 77.

A cursory examination of this brief chronology (see tables 1 and 2) indicates an important difference between the cases in the 1950s and those in the 1960s. A significant increase in the intensity of conflict and in the number of issue areas involved is noticeable in the 1960s. The nine cases that arose during the 1950s were all parent government initiated, and all involved the extraterritorial issues of export controls or antitrust. Six of the cases were of low intensity and three of high intensity. The eighteen cases that arose between 1965 and 1971 were initiated by all three parties, and involved, as well as export controls and antitrust, additional issue areas of balance-of-payments policy, labor relations, foreign take-overs, and host government initiatives. A greater proportion of these cases were of higher intensity—eight low, four moderate, two high, and four very high.

Among the total of 27 cases, four were of very high intensity, five of high intensity, four of moderate intensity, and fourteen of low intensity. The four cases of very high intensity were the 1968 guidelines, *Time–Reader's Digest*, Mercantile Bank, and the auto pact. One of these was of parent government initiation, one of multinational enterprise initiation, and two of host government initiation, which suggests that each party can exercise initiatives that have major consequences. Table 3, which contrasts intensity and initiation of conflict, suggests that Canadian government initiatives, which are in any event rare, are likely to generate considerable conflict. Alternatively, it could suggest that what may be frequent instances of Canadian government initiatives to affect the actions of multinational enterprise at low levels of conflict never come to public attention, and so do not appear in this study.

Twelve of the 27 cases had outcomes perceived as favorable by the Canadian government, while thirteen had outcomes perceived as unfavorable, and two as approximately neutral. Without differentiating the importance of cases, it is evident that in almost half of all cases the Canadian government has achieved an outcome it desired. Certainly the Canadian government has not been consistently disadvantaged.

Among the very high intensity cases, three were seen as favorable in outcome, and one as unfavorable. Of the high intensity cases, two had outcomes perceived as favorable and three as unfavorable. Of the moderate intensity cases, three were perceived as favorable in outcome and one as unfavorable. Among the cases of low intensity of conflict, four had outcomes perceived as favorable, eight as unfavorable, and two as approximately neutral. This seems to suggest that escalation of tension has been a productive tactic for the Canadian government, since the proportion of outcomes favorable to the Canadian government generally rose as the level of intensity of conflict rose. Of course, escalation of tension also raises the costs of an unfavorable outcome,

TABLE 2. CANADIAN CONFLICT CASES

Case	Intensity of Conflict	Value of Solution for Canadian Government	Initiation	Issue Area
1. Ontario documents	high	favorable	parent government	antitrust
2. Alcoa	low	unfavorable	parent government	antitrust
3. Canadian Industries	low	unfavorable	parent government	antitrust
4. Ford trucks	high	unfavorable	parent government	export controls
5. Rayonier	low	favorable	parent government	export controls
6. Alcan-China	low	unfavorable	parent government	export controls
7. Fairbanks-Morse	low	favorable	parent government	export controls
8. Radio patents pool	high	unfavorable	parent government	antitrust
9. Peat moss	low	favorable	parent government	antitrust
10. Auto pact	very high	favorable	host government	host government initiatives
11. 1965 guidelines	high	favorable	parent government	balance-of-payments policy
12. *Time-Reader's Digest*	very high	unfavorable	host government	host government initiatives
13. Cuba flour	moderate	unfavorable	parent government	export controls
14. Vietnam drugs	low	unfavorable	parent government	export controls
15. Schlitz-Labatt	low	neutral	parent government	antitrust
16. Standard Oil-Potash	low	neutral	parent government	antitrust
17. Wage parity	low	unfavorable	multinational enterprise	labor relations
18. Mercantile Bank	very high	favorable	multinational enterprise	foreign take-overs
19. 1968 guidelines	very high	favorable	parent government	balance-of-payments policy
20. Humble Oil	moderate	favorable	host government	host government initiatives
21. Royal Securities	low	unfavorable	multinational enterprise	foreign take-overs
22. Denison Mines	moderate	favorable	multinational enterprise	foreign take-overs
23. Home Oil	moderate	favorable	multinational enterprise	foreign take-overs
25. August 1971	low	favorable	parent government	balance-of-payments policy
26. Chrysler wage freeze	high	unfavorable	multinational enterprise	labor relations
27. Douglas wage freeze	low	unfavorable	multinational enterprise	labor relations
24. McClelland & Stewart	low	unfavorable	multinational enterprise	labor relations

TABLE 3. INTENSITY AND INITIATION OF CANADIAN CONFLICT CASES

Initiation of Conflict	Intensity of Conflict				
	LOW	MODERATE	HIGH	VERY HIGH	TOTAL
Parent government	9	1	5	1	16
Multinational enterprise	5	2	0	1	8
Host government	0	1	0	2	3
Total	14	4	5	4	27

and so entails considerable risk. The Canadian government has done proportionately better in those cases that mattered most to it, since the intensity of conflict represents the level of attention and the extent of influencing measures taken; thus a higher intensity of conflict would indicate a greater salience of the problem to the Canadian government.

Table 4 contrasts the intensity of conflict with the value of solution in the cases initiated by each of the parties. It appears that the Canadian government achieved the most satisfying balance of outcomes in the cases where it initiated the conflict, and did comparably well in the cases initiated by either the parent government or multinational enterprise.[33] In some cases of parent government initiation, both the Canadian and United States governments perceived favorable outcomes. In the 1965 guidelines and 1968 guidelines cases, the United States government succeeded in improving its balance-of-payments position, while the Canadian government succeeded in maintaining its level of capital inflow. In parent government-initiated cases involving the extraterritorial application of United States jurisdiction (export controls and antitrust), significant joint benefit is not evident. Variable-sum outcomes are not apparent in the cases initiated by multinational enterprise. In the four cases in which multinational enterprise succeeded in taking its desired action (wage parity, Chrysler wage freeze, Douglas wage freeze, and Royal Securities), the outcome was perceived as unfavorable by the Canadian government, though the intensity of conflict in each case was low. In the four cases in which multinational enterprise was prevented from taking its desired action (Mercantile Bank, Denison Mines, Home Oil, and McClelland and Stewart), the outcome was perceived as favorable by the Canadian government, and the intensity of conflict was generally higher.[34] Cases initiated by the host government also provide for the possibility of joint perception of benefits. The auto pact was

[33] In his article in this volume, Nye argues that outcomes tended to be closer to the objectives of the government that initiated the interstate request, but that this did not hold in such cases as those involving export controls. Remember that the criterion of initiation I use corresponds more closely to Nye's first government action than to his first interstate request (see footnote 5 above).

[34] One very high, two moderate, and one low.

TABLE 4. INTENSITY AND VALUE OF SOLUTION OF CANADIAN
CONFLICT CASES

Value of Solution	Intensity of Conflict				
	LOW	MODERATE	HIGH	VERY HIGH	TOTAL
A. Parent Government-Initiated Cases					
Favorable	3	0	2	1	6
Unfavorable	4	1	3	0	8
Neutral	2	0	0	0	2
Total	9	1	5	1	16
B. Multinational Enterprise-Initiated Cases					
Favorable	1	2	0	1	4
Unfavorable	4	0	0	0	4
Neutral	0	0	0	0	0
Total	5	2	0	1	8
C. Host Government-Initiated Cases					
Favorable	0	1	0	1	2
Unfavorable	0	0	0	1	1
Neutral	0	0	0	0	0
Total	0	1	0	2	3

viewed favorably by the Canadian and United States governments, and by the auto companies, though to different degrees. Though the dominant perception of the *Time–Reader's Digest* case in the Canadian government was of an unfavorable outcome, the Canadian government was split on the issue. The Humble Oil case was viewed as politically disadvantageous by the United States government, but it did provide economic gains for an American corporation and the possibility of additional oil for the American market.

Tactical politicization, a technique by the Canadian government to rally public support for its position, occurred in fourteen cases, nowhere more successfully than in the Mercantile Bank case. David Baldwin has pointed to the Canadian government's highly publicized rejection of the United States government protest note as a classic case of publicity as a bargaining tactic. "The subsequent uproar in the Canadian press and parliament demanded reassurances from the Prime Minister that the Government had no intention of 'giving in' or of 'retreating before American pressure.' This domestic hue and cry made it easier for the Canadian Government to convince Washington that it could not afford to compromise for fear of losing domestic political support." [55] Of the fourteen cases, eight had outcomes perceived as favorable by the Canadian government, and six had unfavorable outcomes. This distribution of outcomes (8-6-0) is slightly

---

[55] David Baldwin, "The Myths of the Special Relationship," in Stephen Clarkson, ed., *An Independent Foreign Policy For Canada?* (Toronto: McClelland and Stewart, 1968), p. 14.

more favorable to the Canadian government than the distribution of outcomes in all cases (12-13-2). This supports the earlier conclusion that escalation of tension is a productive tactic for the Canadian government.

This must be set against the fact that in two cases (Ford trucks and radio patents pool) the outcome involved international agreements intended to depoliticize similar cases of extraterritoriality of antitrust and export controls in the future. These agreements are shown to be successful by the low intensity of conflict in subsequent cases in the same issue areas. In only one such case (Cuba flour) did conflict reach the moderate level. In fact, since most of the identified cases in these issue areas occurred before or at about the same time as these agreements, it may be that the agreements have worked so well as to shield subsequent cases from public awareness. Since the nub of complaint in both these sorts of cases is sovereign sensitivity and popular resentment, "consultation to be effective must be private and confidential." [36] It is important to remember, though, that these agreements did not end the substance of conflict in such cases. They merely established mechanisms of consultation to keep conflict at low levels.

As was discussed above, the coding scheme adopted in this article permits the comparison of gains and denials. The Canadian government achieved gains in five cases where positive action occurred and the value of solution was favorable. In the peat moss case, the sales continued, and Canadian government proposals were included in the final legal judgment. In the 1965 guidelines and 1968 guidelines cases, capital inflow into Canada continued. The auto pact promised economic benefits in the form of redress of deficit in the sectoral balance of trade and expansion of production in Canada. The Humble Oil case gave political benefits to Canada through the recognition of its Arctic sovereignty by an American corporation.

The Canadian government also achieved seven denials. In the Denison Mines, Home Oil, McClelland and Stewart, and Mercantile Bank cases, foreign take-overs of sensitive Canadian enterprises were prevented. In the Ontario documents case, compliance with a foreign court order was prevented. In the Rayonier and Fairbanks-Morse cases, the Canadian government succeeded in preventing the application of United States export controls, even though the proposed sales did not in fact take place.

On the other side of the ledger, there were five unsuccessful gains in the cases where action the Canadian government favored did not take place. In the Ford trucks, Alcan-China, Cuba flour, and Vietnam

[36] Brewster, *Law and Business*, p. 27.

drugs cases, the proposed sales to proscribed Communist customers did not occur, and no exemption was given. In the August 1971 case, no exemption from the surcharge was given to Canada, and the pattern of interaffiliate trade was temporarily disrupted.

There were also eight unsuccessful denials in cases where action of which the Canadian government did not approve took place in any event. In the Canadian Industries Limited, Alcoa, and radio patents pool cases, United States courts effected a restructuring of Canadian industry. In the wage parity, Chrysler wage freeze, and Douglas wage freeze cases, multinational enterprise engaged in labor relations practices of which the Canadian government did not approve. In the Royal Securities case, there occurred a foreign take-over of which the government did not approve, but which it considered itself powerless under law to prevent. In the *Time–Reader's Digest* case, the Canadian government yielded to pressures to grant an exemption to *Time* and *Reader's Digest* though its budgetary measures had originally been aimed at precisely those magazines.

It is useful to compare the nature and outcome of conflict in cases in different issue areas. The 27 cases in this study fall into six different issue areas: export controls, antitrust, balance-of-payments policy, labor relations, foreign take-overs, and host government initiatives. Table 5 presents the patterns of intensity of conflict and of value of solution in each of these issue areas.

In the area of export controls, which is probably the most visible area of extraterritoriality, the number of cases has been relatively frequent, though occurring primarily in the earlier part of the period. The intensity of conflict has also been relatively low, which is largely due to the success of the Diefenbaker-Eisenhower agreement designed to lessen conflict in this area, which was concluded during the earliest and most intense case (Ford trucks). The agreement established procedures whereby an American subsidiary in Canada would ordinarily be exempted from export controls if the export in question is of significant benefit to the Canadian economy, and if the order could be filled in Canada only by a firm whose parent is subject to United States control.[37] Some have argued that because of the routinized procedures of consultation in this issue area, these cases do not properly constitute conflict.[38] Nevertheless, where such an interaction becomes politicized, public opinion requires that the Canadian government respond to the structural initiation of conflict by the United States government. The Canadian government considered the outcome unfavorable rather than favorable in twice as many of the cases

[37] Ibid., p. 26.
[38] I am indebted to Charles Stedman on this point.

TABLE 5. INTENSITY AND VALUE OF SOLUTION IN DIFFERENT ISSUE AREAS

	Issue Area					
	EXPORT CONTROLS	ANTITRUST	BALANCE-OF-PAYMENTS POLICY	LABOR RELATIONS	FOREIGN TAKE-OVERS	HOST GOVERNMENT INITIATIVES
Intensity of Conflict						
Low	4	5	0	3	2	0
Moderate	1	0	0	0	2	1
High	1	2	2	0	0	0
Very High	0	0	1	0	1	2
Total	6	7	3	3	5	3
Value of Solution						
Favorable	2	2	2	0	4	2
Unfavorable	4	3	1	3	1	1
Neutral	0	2	0	0	0	0
Total	6	7	3	3	5	3

in this area. Two cases constituted denials, and four were unsuccessful gains. The United States government, in this issue area, has been able to use multinational enterprise as an instrument to further its foreign policy goals, and to impose constraints on Canada that Canada would not willingly impose on itself. However, the foreign policy gains to the United States government were minimal. In the two most recent cases (Cuba flour and Vietnam drugs), alternate Canadian-owned suppliers filled the orders, while in the Rayonier and Fairbanks-Morse cases, exemptions to the controls were given. Even had the export controls been total in effect in every case, the effect on the proscribed Communist countries would have been minimal. It appears that the United States government was motivated more by the concern that its export controls should apply equally to all American nationals, regardless of whether they owned a subsidiary in Canada, than by expectations of major foreign policy effect. At this writing, a new case involving the proposed sale of 25 locomotives to Cuba by MLW-Worthington, a subsidiary of Studebaker-Worthington, threatens to terminate the Diefenbaker-Eisenhower agreement and lead to new Canadian legislation to block compliance with United States export controls.[39]

In the antitrust issue area, conflict has been primarily at a low intensity, and the balance of outcomes has been remarkably even. Canadian government objections have centered on the interference of outside authorities in matters within Canadian jurisdiction, and not on calculations of economic advantage or disadvantage. Only in the radio patents pool case were the latter sort of considerations important. These cases involved one gain (peat moss), one denial (Ontario documents), and three unsuccessful denials (Canadian Industries Limited, Alcoa, and radio patents pool). In this issue area there occurred an international agreement, the Fulton-Rogers agreement, designed to ameliorate tensions in this area in the future, but which promised no assurance that the outcomes of future cases would be favorable to the Canadian government.

Cases involving the extraterritorial application of United States law impair the image of multinational enterprise as a good corporate citizen in any country of operations. The importance of an alternate domestic supplier has been demonstrated in cases involving export controls. Conflict is likely to be more urgent when no alternate supplier is available, but the United States government is less likely to yield when an alternate supplier does exist. Countervailing power is also important for the host government in the antitrust area. A favorable outcome was achieved in the Ontario documents case through the

---

[39] *Globe and Mail* (Toronto), 6 March 1974, pp. 1-2.

application of countervailing domestic law. However, United States courts broke up the radio patents pool, despite the fact that it had been investigated and approved by Canadian legal authorities.

The intensity of conflict in the balance-of-payments policy issue area was higher than in most other issue areas, no doubt in reflection of the great economic importance of these cases. In the two cases of favorable outcomes (1965 guidelines and 1968 guidelines), which can be considered gains, the Canadian government achieved its policy goals of restoring monetary stability and maintaining capital inflow. The Canadian government considered these outcomes to be favorable, though critics have charged that Canada sacrificed its monetary independence in these cases.[40] The August 1971 case constituted an unsuccessful gain since Canada failed to get an exemption to the surcharge, and marked a decrease in policy coordination in this issue area between the two governments.

The labor relations issue area contains three cases of low intensity and outcomes perceived as unfavorable by the Canadian government, and which must all be considered unsuccessful denials. The Canadian government in these cases was demonstrably unable to prevent changes in the internal operations of established firms by its normal procedures. It is unlikely that this is the only area of continuing operations in which the Canadian government is displeased with corporate activity, but it does seem that this is the only such area in which conflicts become politicized.

In cases of conflict involving foreign take-overs, the Canadian government has been very successful in achieving its desired outcomes, even without a take-overs screening process. There are four denials (Mercantile Bank, Denison Mines, Home Oil, and McClelland and Stewart), but only one unsuccessful denial (Royal Securities). Of course there have been a great many foreign take-overs (100 in 1968 and 130 in 1969)[41] that did not rise to the level of politicized conflict, and Canadian successes in these sensitive cases must be understood within the broader context.

Cases involving host government initiatives involved more intense conflict than most other issue areas, but also involved a predominance of favorable over unfavorable outcomes. In the auto pact case, the Canadian government made use of the unique characteristics of foreign-owned multinational enterprise as an instrument of its policy to achieve impressive economic gains. In the Humble Oil case, foreign-owned multinational enterprise was used as a policy instru-

[40] Kari Levitt, *Silent Surrender: The Multinational Corporation in Canada* (Toronto: Macmillan of Canada, 1970), p. 13.
[41] Gray report, p. 478.

ment to achieve significant political gains on the question of Arctic sovereignty. In the *Time–Reader's Digest* case, the Canadian government failed in its attempt to dislodge those magazines from the Canadian market, and in fact the outcome left them in a stronger position than before because the incursion of other American competitors is prohibited.

Substantial interstate conflict between the Canadian and United States governments, in which at least one of the governments used means other than private discussions,[42] occurred in ten of the 27 cases: Ford trucks, Fairbanks-Morse, Ontario documents, radio patents pool, 1965 guidelines, 1968 guidelines, August 1971, Mercantile Bank, auto pact, and *Time–Reader's Digest*. All but one (Fairbanks-Morse) of these cases are of high or very high intensity. However, the value of solution for the Canadian government was favorable in six of the ten cases, and unfavorable in only four. Thus the balance of outcomes in these cases involving substantial interstate conflict is more favorable to the Canadian government than the balance in all cases, indicating that Canada's record of achievement in cases of interstate conflict has been far better than many critics have charged.

A lower level of interstate conflict, involving only private discussions, occurred in eight other cases: Rayonier, peat moss, Humble Oil, Cuba flour, Canadian Industries Limited, Alcoa, Schlitz-Labatt, and Standard Oil–Potash. In the Rayonier, peat moss, and Humble Oil cases, and possibly in Cuba flour, the private discussions could be considered to have had some substantive effect on the outcome, but not in the others. The remaining nine cases involved no direct interstate conflict.

In only two of the 27 cases was there an alliance between the United States government and multinational enterprise against the Canadian government. Those two cases were Mercantile Bank and *Time–Reader's Digest*. Both of those cases were of very high intensity, while one had a favorable value of solution for the Canadian government and the other unfavorable. In all the other cases, multinational enterprise has relied on its own resources, consisting mainly of economic performance benefits, or has been used as an instrument of United States government policy.

Nine of the 27 cases resulted in new Canadian legislation or regulations or in international agreements. The Ford trucks case and the radio patents pool case led to international agreements to depoliticize conflicts. In the Ontario documents case, legislation was enacted by the Ontario government to prevent the release of business records in Ontario to foreign courts. The 1965 guidelines case culminated in the

---

[42] See footnote 6 above.

issuance of guidelines of good corporate behavior for foreign subsidiaries in Canada. The 1968 guidelines case led to the institution of
controls to prevent Canada from being used by United States capital
as a pass-through to third countries. The Mercantile Bank case led
to amendments to the Bank Act, and the Denison Mines case resulted
in new regulations restricting foreign ownership in Canada's uranium
industry. The auto pact involved changes in Canadian tariff regulations as well as an international agreement. The *Time–Reader's
Digest* case ended with passage of the 1965 budget, though *Time* and
Reader's Digest were exempted from its provisions.

Coordination of policy between the Canadian and United States
governments increased in four cases and decreased in one. The Ford
trucks and radio patents pool cases led to international agreements
that established consultative mechanisms. The auto pact contained
provisions for regular consultation between the governments on matters related to the pact. The 1968 guidelines case resulted in coordination in the monetary policy areas, due to the Canadian pass-through
controls, and holdings of nonmarketable United States Treasury securities in the Canadian exchange reserves. Policy coordination in the
monetary policy area decreased in the August 1971 case.

Only in six cases was a deliberate effort made by one or more
parties to the conflict to link the settlement of the dispute to some
other issues.[43] In the three balance-of-payments policy cases (1965
guidelines, 1968 guidelines, and August 1971), Canadian negotiators
consistently linked the continued inflow of capital into Canada to
Canadian ability to purchase American exports.[44] In the Mercantile
Bank case, the United States government in a diplomatic note threatened retaliation against Canadian banking operations in the United
States, and United States banks threatened to withdraw clearing
facilities from Canadian banks.[45] In the *Time–Reader's Digest* case,
Walter Gordon claims the United States government linked the exemption of *Time* and *Reader's Digest* to possible review of oil import
quotas and passage of the auto pact.[46] Only in the auto pact case does
there appear to be a possibility of a linkage between a transnational
and a security issue, when it is purported that Lyndon Johnson might
have thrown additional support behind the pact because of his pleasure at Canada's entirely independent decision to send troops for
peacekeeping in Cyprus.[47]

---

[43] Elsewhere in this volume Nye discusses linkages in interstate conflict.
[44] Gray report, pp. 285-90.
[45] Newman, appendix K, pp. 517-18. See also Levitt, p. 6.
[46] Gordon, p. 97. See also A. F. W. Plumptre and Pauline Jewett in Clarkson.
pp. 47, 52.
[47] A. E. Safarian in Clarkson, p. 51.

Given the federal system of government in Canada, it is hardly surprising that provincial governments should have been active in these cases as well as the federal government. In two cases, Ontario documents and McClelland and Stewart, it was the Ontario government that took direct action. In the 1965 guidelines case, the acting minister of revenue in the Quebec government played a large role in raising the intensity of conflict and arousing public and official concern.

The Canadian government has been more successful in achieving its objectives in publicized cases through the exercise of policy action at its borders rather than internally. It has been able effectively to deny entry or to impose conditions on the entry of United States-owned multinational enterprise. It has been less able to influence the internal operations of American-owned subsidiaries. Influence on the behavior of subsidiaries in Canada by the United States government has given rise to conflict, and in the absence of alternative domestic suppliers or countervailing domestic law, the Canadian government has enjoyed little success in bringing about desired outcomes. Other cases involving the internal operations of multinational enterprise have dealt with labor relations, where Canadian government influence over the outcomes has been minimal.

The United States government has attempted to use multinational enterprise as a policy instrument a greater number of times, and in a greater number of ways, than has the Canadian government. The Canadian government has ordinarily been put in the position of responding to the initiatives of others rather than originating its own. This is consistent with the idea that in a relationship of asymmetrical interdependence, initiatives are more likely to travel from the larger party to the smaller. But Canadian initiatives, though less numerous, have not been less important. In all cases initiated by the parent government, the triggering activity concerned only one instance in a broader policy program, and the net effects have been very limited. A handful of sales to Communist countries were prevented, but the economies of those Communist countries were not seriously affected thereby. Antitrust actions in Canada had little visible effect on economic competition in the United States. The United States balance of payments was aided temporarily, but the problems were not ended and the "good citizenship" behavior of American enterprise in Canada was impaired. On the other hand, in the auto pact and Humble Oil cases, the Canadian government was able to achieve both immediate and long-term economic and political goals.

These cases of conflict have had considerable impact on the making of official Canadian government policy, and thus on the structure of Canadian-American relations. As mentioned earlier, nine of the

27 cases resulted in new Canadian legislation or regulations or in new international agreements. The resulting policies have worked in two different directions—increased Canadian-American coordination and consultation on the one hand, and increased Canadian autonomy on the other. Whether the outcomes of subsequent cases of conflict will be viewed as favorable or unfavorable by the Canadian government will depend in large part on which policy direction characterizes Canadian objectives at the time.

Such cases as Ontario documents have suggested to Canadian nationalists that the existence of countervailing domestic law can protect Canada from the extraterritorial outreach of American jurisdiction. However, the issue is not so clear-cut. The radio patents pool was dissolved by United States courts despite its acceptability under Canadian anticombines legislation. Possible Canadian legislation barring Canadian subsidiaries of United States parent corporations from compliance with United States export controls might only serve to confront corporate executives with a dilemma in which they would stand in violation of the law whatever their course of action. Past efforts to resolve this issue of extraterritoriality have resulted in the establishment of mechanisms of consultation that have lessened tension but failed to end the substance of conflict. Nevertheless, such mechanisms stand as significant illustrations of the closeness of Canadian-American relations in the period studied, and are not duplicated with other countries, such as France or the United Kingdom, where similar cases involving United States export controls or antitrust have occurred.

The Canadian government has considered the outcome favorable in approximately half of all cases, and in over half of the cases involving significant interstate conflict. The disparate cases studied here do not readily lend themselves to weighting, but they are clearly not identical in importance. If the intensity of conflict can be taken as a rough indicator of the importance of the case, the conclusion is clear. The proportion of outcomes viewed as favorable by the Canadian government rose as the intensity of conflict rose. The use of Canadian government perception of the outcome as favorable or unfavorable does not address the questions of whether government officials were correct in their perception of effects or were pursuing the "wrong" objectives. This study cannot assess whether the Canadian government is constrained by the context of foreign ownership to want too little. Nevertheless, on its own terms, the Canadian government has not been overwhelmed by the extraterritorial decision making associated with multinational enterprise and hah been satisfied with the outcome of a majority of the most important cases of conflict involving American multinational enterprise in Canada.

CANADIAN–AMERICAN RELATIONS: LAW OF THE SEA

Ann L. Hollick

The governments of Canada and the United States are playing very active roles in negotiations to define the law of the sea, which has been the subject of international conferences in 1958, 1960, and that beginning in December 1973. These provide the framework for a study of US-Canadian relations in the uses of the sea. Three perspectives may be adopted to understand the political processes involved in law of the sea relations: (1) the state-to-state model, (2) the bureaucratic politics approach, and (3) the transnational systems perspective.

With the passage of Canada's Arctic Waters Pollution Prevention Act and related legislation in 1970, law of the sea became highly politicized in both countries. In Ottawa the issue was cast as one of control over adjacent waters, whereas in Washington the issue was perceived as one of national security. The behavior of both governments in this controversy can be explained by conceiving of governments as *unitary actors*.

Within the Canadian government, law of the sea policy is formulated and implemented through a highly centralized foreign affairs bureaucracy. This is partly due to the continuing political salience of law of the sea, to the parliamentary system, to the small size of the Canadian bureaucracy, and to the preponderance of interests tending in a single direction. In contrast in the United States, bureaucratic politics, the diffusion of power, and conflicting interests result in a different kind of decision-making process for determining law of the sea policy.

The existence of a variety of private and governmental interests that are not easily reconcilable by the foreign policy organs of government provides an opportunity for transnational and transgovernmental relations to flourish. With the politicization and exacerbation

Ann L. Hollick is an assistant professor of American foreign policy and executive director of the Ocean Policy Project in the School of Advanced International Studies at The Johns Hopkins University.

of law of the sea relations in 1970, however, the role of transnational and transgovernmental phenomena diminished. As long as law of the sea remains politically salient in Canada, the decision-making process will remain centralized and high level, and transgovernmental interactions can be expected to languish.

LAW OF THE SEA ISSUES AND NATIONAL POLICIES

Before considering United States–Canadian relations in matters relating to the law of the sea from 1958 to 1970, it is useful to review the several issue areas that are encompassed within the negotiations. They are naval and commercial mobility, jurisdiction over the petroleum resources of the continental margin, marine science research, protection of the marine environment, fisheries, and the deep seabed regime. Canadian and United States interests and policies diverge on some of these questions and not on others. While there are periodic intergovernmental consultations, present policies appear to be formulated in response to domestic interests and to prevailing views in the United Nations Seabed Committee rather than through close Canadian-US cooperation.

The United States is a major maritime power with global interests. Whatever the prospects for détente, the US government places high priority on its deterrence strategy and on US naval mobility to carry out that strategy. Although the United States lacks an extensive commercial fleet operating under its flag, it is a major trading nation and is particularly dependent, at least for the next half decade, on increasing imports of petroleum. Naval mobility is perceived as necessary to protect shipping lanes, and to maintain order when threatened by local conflicts. The United States claims a three-mile territorial sea, and in the law of the sea negotiations of 1958 and 1960 as well as in the current negotiations, the government has sought international agreement on relatively narrow territorial sea limits. The present official position is that the United States will accept a twelve-mile territorial sea if freedom of transit through and over all international straits is guaranteed.

Canada has neither an extensive merchant fleet nor a large navy although it is a major trading nation. Canada cooperated closely with the United States at the 1958 and 1960 conferences in rallying support for agreement on narrow territorial seas. In 1970, however, Canada extended its own territorial sea to twelve miles and established pollution control zones and extensive fishing zones despite United States protests over this unilateral declaration. Canada has, furthermore, indicated its support for the regime of innocent passage in all straits thus covered by twelve-mile territorial seas, taking special pains to note that the Northwest Passage is not an international strait.[1] Since the 1958 and 1960 conferences, Canadian defense considerations have shifted from NATO concerns to those of continental defense. Now that technology has facilitated man's use of the Arctic, Canadian notions of defense have gone well beyond strictly military considerations.

The United States has substantial coastal as well as maritime interests—the fourth longest coastline in the world, 863,000 square nautical miles of continental margins,[2] and abundant offshore resources. Potential recoverable petroleum resources to a depth of 200 meters are estimated at 200 billion barrels of oil and 850 trillion cubic feet of natural gas.[3] With regard to extending jurisdiction over the petroleum resources of the continental margin, the United States has reversed its policy several times. In the 1945 Truman Proclamation, the United States laid claim to the resources of its continental shelf. Then in 1958 the Geneva Convention on the Continental Shelf established coastal state sovereignty over seabed resources to a depth of 200 meters or beyond that point to the depth admitting of exploitability. This remained official US policy until May 1970 when the United States announced support for a policy renouncing national claims to seabed resources beyond the 200-meter isobath and calling for the establishment, beyond this point, of an international regime to govern the exploitation of seabed resources. Behind this policy reversal was a bureaucratic struggle and the victory of strategic over resource interests. Since 1970, the United States position on the intermediate zone of coastal state authority has gradually reverted to favor greater coastal state authority in response to domestic and international pressures. In July 1973 the United States submitted a draft proposal for a coastal seabed economic area, of undetermined width, in which the coastal state would enjoy exclusive rights to seabed resources. Included in this proposal are five international features: no unjustifiable interference with other uses of the area, international pollution standards, guarantee of investments, compulsory settlement of disputes, and revenue sharing.

With the reorientation of Canadian foreign policy under Prime Minister Trudeau, the Canadian government has come increasingly to

---

[1] Canada, "Third United Nations Conference on the Law of the Sea," paper submitted by the government to the Standing Committee on External Affairs and National Defence, House of Commons, 2 November 1973.

[2] US Department of State, Office of the Geographer, *Limits in the Seas*, Series A, No. 46, 12 August 1972. The continental margin is the submerged prolongation of continents and includes the continental shelf, slope, and rise.

[3] Don E. Kash et al., "Energy Under the Oceans: A Technology Assessment of Outer Continental Shelf Oil and Gas Operations," National Science Foundation, September 1973.

view Canada as a coastal state having much in common with developing countries. Canada has an 11,000 mile coastline, the fifth longest
in the world, and up to 1.24 million square nautical miles of continental margin [4] amounting to around 40 percent of its land mass. Canada
has 9 percent of the world's potential offshore oil and/or gas basins
with resource potential presently estimated at 59.6 billion barrels of
recoverable oil and 457.2 trillion cubic feet of recoverable gas. On the
basis of the 1958 Geneva Convention on the Continental Shelf and the
North Sea litigation, Canada claims the whole of the continental margin including the continental shelf, slope, and rise. With regard to a
possible intermediate or economic zone, the Canadian position has
shifted from stressing the principle of "non-interference with the
freedom of the high seas, subject only to the strict requirements essential for effective exploitation," [5] to emphasizing a more comprehensive
bundle of coastal state "functional" jurisdictions in their offshore
zone.

Among the jurisdictions to be exercised in the as yet undefined
intermediate zone—and disputed between Canada and the US—are
marine science research and pollution control. Scientific communities
in Canada and the United States share similar levels of expertise and
interests in carrying out research unfettered by coastal state restrictions. In neither country, however, does the marine scientist have the
power to significantly influence national ocean policy. Nevertheless,
thanks to the support of similar policies by stronger actors in the
US maritime debate, United States policy has consistently favored
freedom of marine science research beyond the territorial sea with
prior notification to the coastal state, availability of research data, and
open publication. The Canadian response has been to point out that
much research is conducted for economic and military reasons, and
therefore the coastal state must have the right to control and, when
necessary, prohibit research activities by foreign nationals.

The other nonresource jurisdiction at issue between the Canadian
and United States governments is that of marine pollution—the setting of standards and enforcement thereof. This particularly intractable issue was raised in 1970 with the passage of the Canadian Arctic
Waters Pollution Prevention Act. Viewing it a serious threat to high
seas navigation, the United States strongly opposed this legislation
and evolved in response a policy of exclusive international standards
beyond the territorial sea, with coastal state enforcement powers
limited to the territorial sea and flag state enforcement of inter-

[4] Excluding Hudson Bay.
[5] Allan Gotlieb, Statement in First Committee, United Nations General Assembly, Press Release 77, 15 November 1967.

national standards. A further refinement of the US approach has been to allow for port state enforcement against violations of international pollution standards occurring beyond the territorial sea. Canada, on the other hand, has linked the concept of coastal state pollution jurisdiction to resource jurisdiction. Indeed, below the 60° latitude, pollution zones established in 1970 were those areas encompassed within what were designated as fisheries closing lines.[6] Within areas under coastal state economic jurisdiction, Canada supports the right of the coastal state to enact and enforce environmental protection standards over and above internationally agreed upon standards.

The area in which Canadian-American interests have been generally similar is that of fisheries. The species inhabiting offshore waters of both nations are some of the most valuable in the world. In the past decade, coastal fisheries have been seriously depleted by the distant water fleets of Japan and the Soviet Union, and strong domestic pressure has been building to extend national fishing jurisdiction. US and Canadian distant water fishing interests are presently limited to tuna fleets operating out of San Diego, California, and New Brunswick, respectively. Although fishing represents a small and declining portion of GNP in both countries (1 percent in Canada and less than a half of 1 percent in the US), the fishing interest exercises a large influence in state and provincial governments and ultimately in the federal governments due to the concentration of voting strength in several coastal regions.[7]

In response to similar problems, both Canada and the United States have suggested a species approach providing for separate management schemes for coastal, anadromous, and highly migratory species.[8] Coastal species would be managed exclusively by the coastal state which would determine quotas and would enjoy a preferential share of the catch. Anadromous species (spawning in fresh water) would be reserved exclusively to the country of origin. Highly migratory species would be exempt from coastal state jurisdiction. Here Canadian and American fisheries policies part company. While the United States maintains the species approach as an alternative to a resource zone, Canada has, in addition to unilaterally extending its exclusive fishing zones, attempted to reconcile a species approach to that of a 200-mile zone. In this new policy, Canada would permit

[6] In the Arctic areas above 60° latitude, uniform pollution zones of 100 miles were declared.

[7] In Canada, with a population of 22 million, 80,000 people were employed in fishing operations and another 16,000 in processing in 1972.

[8] Sedentary species are covered by the Convention on the Continental Shelf. See Anthony Scott's essay in this volume.

exclusive sovereign rights to fisheries within 200 miles of shore with preferential rights to fisheries beyond.[9]

US and Canadian policies toward an international seabed regime beyond the limits of national jurisdiction are presently influenced by the domestic supply and demand for constituent metals of the manganese nodules scattered about the deep seabed. These include nickel, copper, cobalt, and manganese. The United States is a net importer of each of these minerals. In 1972 the United States imported 98 percent of its manganese, 92 percent of its cobalt, 84 percent of its nickel, and 19 percent of its copper. These considerations have only recently begun to weigh heavily in the determination of US seabed policy, due to intragovernmental trade-offs of resource for strategic interests and to the absence until recently of a strong seabed mining constituency. In August 1970, the United States tabled a draft treaty [10] proposing international machinery empowered to issue leases for seabed mineral exploitation on a first-come-first-served basis. The draft treaty envisioned low royalties, work requirements, and other features designed to spur seabed mineral production. The revenue-sharing provisions of the treaty represented an effort to encourage acceptance of US naval policy on narrow offshore limits. Since 1970 strong industry opposition to the treaty has developed as investments in deep-sea mining have increased.[11] With resource scarcities taking on national importance, the Treasury Department has also raised objections to the 1970 treaty.[12] The outcome of these objections for United States seabed policy is to move it further from a discretionary seabed authority.

Canada ranks fifth in world mineral production and produces 41 percent of world nickel, 10 percent of world copper, and over 7 percent of world cobalt. Of the constituent metals of manganese nodules, Canada is a net importer of manganese only (valued at $5 million in 1972). Canadian policy has reflected the fact that Canada is the world's major producer and exporter of nickel and seeks protection against any substantial increase in supplies of nickel.[13] In the UN Seabed Committee, Canada initially proposed a licensing system that included production controls, marketing, and distribution

---

[9] Canada, "Third United Nations Conference on the Law of the Sea," paper submitted by the government to the Standing Committee on External Affairs and National Defence, House of Commons, 2 November 1973.

[10] UN Document A/AC.138/25; "US Draft of UN Convention on International Seabed Area," *International Legal Materials* 9 (1970) : 1046.

[11] See below, p. 777.

[12] *Sea Breezes* (Save Our Seas newsletter) 1 (November-December 1973).

[13] See below, p. 777.

mechanisms.[14] Since then Canada has sought an approach that would combine the Canadian with the enterprise system supported by a large number of developing nations. In this scheme Canada suggests a mix of licensing and direct exploration and exploitation by an international authority, when it acquires the requisite means. Thus while United States seabed policy is moving away from that of the majority of developing nations, that of Canada is moving closer.

LAW OF THE SEA RELATIONS: 1958 TO 1970

It is apparent from the foregoing that even within the past four years Canadian and United States law of the sea interests and policies have fluctuated. Transnational and transgovernmental relations in some areas are clearly affected by policy developments in other areas. The change in US-Canadian transgovernmental relations is even clearer over the period since 1958. Relations between US and Canadian officials in law of the sea were closest in 1950, were plagued by minor irritations after 1962, and became openly hostile in 1970. Since then there has been a gradual warming trend between the law of the sea bureaucracies but with no discernible effect, as yet, on reestablishing transnational ties. This is made problematic by Canada's decision to play an independent role in the international negotiations.

The Canadian and American delegations enjoyed close and cordial relations at both the 1958 and 1960 law of the sea conferences. In 1960 Canadian officials persuaded the United States government, which had favored a three-mile territorial sea, that a six-mile territorial sea with a six-mile contiguous zone would preserve US strategic interests. The two delegations worked closely, as did their home governments, to sell the six-plus-six formula to the participating nations. Despite a brief period of lobbying the proposal came remarkably close to success—failing by only one vote of the required two-thirds majority.

Canada, which had been pursuing the goal of a twelve-mile fishing zone since the mid-1950s,[15] continued its efforts to gain international support for the six-plus-six formula after the second con-

---

[14] UN Document A/AC.138/59 ("International Sea-bed Regime and Machinery Working Paper Submitted by the Delegation of Canada"), 24 August 1971.

[15] A. E. Gotlieb and C. M. Dalfen, "National Jurisdiction and International Responsibility: Canadian Approaches to International Law," address to First Annual Conference of the Canadian Council on International Law, 13 October 1972. (Mimeographed.)

ference. Although the United States had reverted to its original position of a three-mile territorial sea, it said it was willing to consider the findings of the global canvass.[16] By 1962, the Canadian, British, and Australian governments had the support of 44 nations for the six-plus-six formula provided that the United States and other major powers would agree.[17] But the US response was negative, reflecting no doubt the United States preference for a universally accepted agreement as well as the abiding Department of Defense concern about the dangers of an expanded territorial sea.

The Canadians then resorted to a unilateral solution of their fisheries problem.[18] In July 1964 Canada passed legislation creating a nine-mile fishing zone beyond the nation's three-mile territorial sea and empowered the government to draw straight baselines in place of the sinuosities of the coast as the starting point for measuring the breadth of the territorial sea and fishing zones.[19] The Department of State promptly protested Canada's extension of jurisdiction, but two years later the US Congress followed suit and passed legislation for a fishing zone of nine miles. US legislation did not provide for straight baselines,[20] and this issue became a cause of friction between the two governments.

During the 1966 negotiations between the legal divisions of the Canadian and United States foreign offices over the implementation of Canada's legislation, Canadian officials told their US counterparts that Canada was considering straight baselines that would make the Gulf of St. Lawrence and parts of Queen Charlotte Sound internal waters. US legal officials protested that some baselines exceeded those permitted by international law and moreover did not follow the general direction of the coast. To register United States concern, Undersecretary of State Rostow headed a team to Ottawa in October 1966 and President Johnson spoke directly to Prime Minister Pearson.

Then in 1967 the Canadian government announced the first series of straight baselines along the coast of Labrador and the southern and

---

[16] In Canadian eyes, however, the United States undermined the effort by striking bilateral fisheries agreements with countries such as Brazil and Mexico.

[17] Mitchell Sharp, Secretary of State for External Affairs, "Canada Extends Its Territorial Sea," statement to the House of Commons, 17 April 1970. (Mimeographed.)

[18] "We really are not prepared, in light of these developments, to accept the proposition that it is always desirable to proceed multilaterally instead of unilaterally." Ibid., p. 2.

[19] Canada, Laws, Statutes, etc., *Territorial Sea and Fishing Zones Act*, 1964, 13 Eliz. 2, ch. 22.

[20] *Fisheries Zone Contiguous to Territorial Sea of the United States Act, U.S. Code*, Supplement 2, Title 16 (1966).

eastern coasts of Newfoundland.[21] The Canadians were quick to point out the moderate nature of these claims and the the fact that the baselines did not close the Gulf of St. Lawrence. The baselines finally adopted by the Canadians were indeed more moderate than those initially proposed to US officials, allowing both sides a measure of success. The United States did, as it had warned, protest the baselines as inconsistent with international law.

Having once set out on the course of unilateral action and having witnessed US emulation of some aspects of that action in 1966, the Canadian government continued to extend offshore jurisdiction. In April 1969 the government announced its intention to draw further straight baselines along the east coast of Nova Scotia and the west coast of Vancouver Island and the Queen Charlotte Islands.[22] Canada also adopted the concept of fisheries closing lines to put several areas that were too extensive to be enclosed by straight baselines out of reach of foreign fishing without extending the territorial sea. These exclusive fishery zones upset the delicate US-Canadian agreement reached in 1967, according to which Canadian fishermen had preferential rights off the Canadian coast in recognition of the coastal state's special interest.

In 1970 when the fisheries closing lines were used for the first time (across the Gulf of St. Lawrence, the Bay of Fundy, Queen Charlotte Sound, and Dixon Entrance), they were adopted in conjunction with a series of measures aimed more or less directly at the United States.[23] The US-Canadian fishery agreement negotiated in February 1970 anticipated the events of that year. While it continued to provide for reciprocal fishing privileges, these extended to fewer stocks in fewer areas.[24] A separate but related development in March of 1970 was consideration of a Canadian bill (S-5) to provide statutory authority, above and beyond the 1958 Convention, to govern all aspects of oil and gas exploration and exploitation, including pollution prevention and control, on Canada's entire continental margin. The act was designed to tie in with other offshore mining legislation and to confirm Canada's wide shelf seabed resources position.

---

[21] Canada, Canada Privy Council, "Order Respecting Geographical Coordinates of Points from which Baselines may be determined Pursuant to the Territorial Sea and Fishing Zones Act," 26 October 1967, *Canada Gazette*, part 2, 8 November 1967.

[22] Those baselines went into effect in June 1969. *Canada Gazette*, 11 June 1969; Canada, Department of External Affairs, "Law of the Sea," Press Release No. 34, 4 June 1969.

[23] US Department of State, "Canadian Fisheries Closing Lines Legislation," Press Release No. 53, 12 March 1971.

[24] US Department of State, "Canada Drafts Agreement on Reciprocal Fishing Privileges," Press Release No. 47, 16 February 1970.

LAW OF THE SEA BECOMES HIGH POLITICS

Although amicable relations about the law of the sea between Canada and the United States suffered minor setbacks beginning with the 1964 Canadian Territorial Sea and Fishing Zones Act, the politicization of law of the sea relations occurred in 1969 and 1970. The dynamic of action and reaction during this period is difficult to capture given the number of overall pressures at work and the variety of issues at stake. Within Canada, the Trudeau foreign policy review was beginning. Deliberations in the UN Seabed Committee sustained a constant pressure on both countries to formulate positions on law of the sea. And finally, there were the direct confrontations—over fisheries jurisdiction, over Canada's newly extended territorial sea boundary, and over Canada's new claim to establish pollution safety zones in the Arctic and other areas.

With the 1969 voyage of the *Manhattan* through the Northwest Passage, Canadians perceived an explicit threat to their jurisdiction over their Arctic areas. While fisheries closing lines would obviously not protect that jurisdiction, establishing a twelve-mile territorial sea and closing the Barrow Strait and Prince of Wales Strait would.[25] In addition, a new type of authority was sought by establishing pollution prevention zones of up to 100 nautical miles from land above the 60° parallel of north latitude, and elsewhere to coincide with fisheries closing lines.[26]

The decisions regarding formulation and implementation of Canadian policy were handled in the office of the prime minister with legal counsel supplied by the Department of External Affairs. In meetings with the undersecretary of state and other United States officials, Canadian representatives referred to public pressure for immediate government action to protect the Arctic environment. The United States requested, in response, that Canada delay, forego, or submit such action to a multilateral conference. A unilateral claim, in the United States view, would stimulate others to similar actions and thereby damage prospects for international agreement safeguarding maritime mobility. For the Canadians the issue was fundamentally one of national sovereignty, and for the Americans it was one of national security.

The public exchange between the governments on Canada's pollution legislation showed the extreme importance that each attached to Canada's action. Taking issue with the "unilateral" nature of Can-

---

[25] Canada, *Bill C-203, Act to Amend Territorial Sea and Fishing Zones Act,* 1970, 18 & 19 Eliz. 2.
[26] J. A. Beesley, "Rights and Responsibilities of Arctic Coastal States: The Canadian View," *Journal of Maritime Law and Commerce* 3 (October 1971): 7.

ada's claim, the United States asserted that it "has long sought international solutions rather than national approaches to problems involving the high seas," and offered to litigate the issue in the International Court of Justice.[27] Canada's response was unequivocal. After stating that "Canada reserves to itself the same rights as the USA has asserted to determine for itself how best to protect its vital interests," the note went on to document all the US unilateral assertions of jurisdiction beyond the three-mile territorial sea. Included among these references were the Truman Proclamation of 1945, the US 1966 contiguous fishing zone, and nuclear testing on the high seas. Moreover, the note aired Canadian grievances over the fact that its "extensive and vigorous multilateral campaign" to secure agreement on a territorial sea breadth in the early 1960s "failed because the USA ultimately declined to participate." [28]

Asserting its "overriding right of self-defense" to protect its marine environment, the Canadian government rejected the notion of participating in any international conference on the Arctic that would deal with "questions falling wholly within Canadian domestic jurisdiction." Canada rejected "any suggestion that the Northwest Passage is . . . an international strait," and asserted that "Canada's sovereignty over the islands of the Arctic Archipelago is not, of course, an issue." More importantly, however, the Trudeau government placed reservations on Canada's acceptance of the compulsory jurisdiction of the International Court of Justice in "disputes arising out of or concerning jurisdiction or rights claimed or exercised by Canada in respect of the conservation, management or exploitation of the living resources of the sea, or in respect of the prevention or control of pollution or contamination of the marine environment in marine areas adjacent to the coast of Canada." [29]

Although the governmental interactions of 1970 were complex, the policy outcome was clear. The United States and Canada emerged from the year with law of the sea attitudes and policies pointing in different directions. All levels of the governments (including President Nixon and Prime Minister Trudeau [30]) had been involved in the

[27] US Department of State, Press Release No. 121, 15 April 1970; *New York Times*, 16 April 1970.

[28] Canada, House of Commons, "Summary of Canadian Note Handed to the United States Government on 16 April 1970," in *Debates, Official Report*, vol. 6, 28th Parl., 2d sess., 17 April 1970, pp. 6027ff.

[29] Text of reservation in R. St. J. MacDonald, "The New Canadian Declaration of Acceptance of the Compulsory Jurisdiction of the International Court of Justice," in *Canadian Yearbook of International Law*, vol. 8 (Vancouver: The Publications Centre, The University of British Columbia, 1970); p. 34; UN Document L/T/587/Rev. 1 (press release), 9 April 1970.

[30] John Best, "Nixon Was So Angry He Refused Trudeau's Call," *Globe and Mail* (Toronto), 25 August 1973, p. 7.

confrontation, and any retraction would thereafter prove difficult if not impossible. The landmarks of the policy divergence included, on the Canadian side, legislation on Arctic pollution, territorial sea, and fishing zones introduced in April 1970, and, on the US side, the president's policy statement of May 1970 and its subsequent elaboration in the August 1970 US Draft Treaty on the Seabed.

Faced with Canada's refusal to negotiate its claims to offshore jurisdiction bilaterally or regionally or to submit them to the International Court of Justice, the single arena remaining for a US-Canadian policy confrontation was the UN Seabed Committee. Within this forum, Canada's jurisdictional claim was simply a variation on coastal state extensions occurring elsewhere in the world. Indeed, Canadian actions were taken with the expectation that they might be sold to other UN members. Of all coastal state extensions, however, Canada's was the most alarming to the United States government and particularly to the navy.[31]

The extent to which the availability of the United Nations Seabed Committee as a negotiating forum has evoked or restrained Canadian-American disagreements over the law of the sea is ambiguous. Perhaps it stimulated the proliferation of national offshore claims. Certainly it served the United States as a court of last resort in 1970. In so doing, of course, the UN Seabed Committee contributed to linking fisheries, territorial sea, and straits issues with the deliberations about the ocean floor. Since 1967 negotiations relating to ocean issues had been handled on two separate tracks. While the UN Seabed Committee was heatedly debating the disposition of resources of the ocean floor, the maritime powers were quietly discussing with other nations the possibility of international agreement on the breadth of the territorial sea, straits, and fisheries. As in 1958 and 1960, the United States wanted universal agreement on the territorial sea breadth and was prepared by 1970 to support a twelve-mile territorial sea if freedom of transit through and over all international straits were guaranteed. To diffuse coastal state opposition, the United States had combined this proposal with a policy of preferential fishing rights for coastal states.

In response to the 1970 Canadian legislation and other coastal state claims, the United States on 23 May 1970 offered far-reaching resource and revenue concessions in exchange for navigational mobility. These called for the coastal state to renounce claims to seabed

---

[31] The Canadian legislation "provided that naval vessels and other ships owned by foreign governments may be exempted from the application of Canadian anti-pollution regulations, if the ships in question substantially met Canadian standards" (*Canadian Yearbook of International Law*, 1970, p. 34); UN Document L/T/587/Rev. 1 (press release), 9 April 1970.

resources beyond the depth of 200 meters, and for an international regime to govern seabed resource exploitation beyond this point.[32] The coastal state would have limited rights beyond the 200-meter depth contour to manage resource exploitation to the outer edge of the continental margin, and revenues from that area would be shared with the international community.[33]

An unintended effect of this US proposal was to contribute to pressure for combining all of the law of the sea issues in a single negotiating conference. In December 1970 the United Nations voted to convene a single conference on all law of the sea issues in 1973. The trade-offs would henceforth be between coastal and maritime interests across the range of ocean issues.

Since 1970 there have been modifications in both United States and Canadian policies on the law of the sea. In response to strong domestic as well as international pressure, the United States has upgraded the priority accorded to coastal fisheries and petroleum interests. And Canada, or at least its Ministry of Transport, has indicated interest in maintaining the principle of freedom of navigation to the greatest practical extent.[34] Additionally, in response to trends in the international negotiations, Canada has tried to accommodate its position to those favoring a 200-mile economic zone and has indicated a willingness to consider revenue sharing in areas beyond the zone. These shifts in policy since 1970 can be more fully explained by examining the processes leading to law of the sea decisions in both capitals.

DECISION-MAKING PROCESSES: OTTAWA AND WASHINGTON

While Canadian and American policies in present law of the sea negotiations reflect broad coastal and maritime interests of each country as well as the past decade of law of the sea relations, they also reflect the decision-making processes within each government. General characteristics of the processes have been similar on both sides of the border. A large number of agencies are involved in the policy process since law of the sea negotiations touch on a gamut of interests, from resource to national security considerations. Interagency groups were established to deal with law of the sea, and primary responsi-

---

[32] For the background to this decision, see Ann L. Hollick, "Seabeds Make Strange Politics," *Foreign Policy* 9 (Winter 1972-73): 148-70.

[33] Leigh S. Ratiner, "United States Ocean Policy," *Journal of Maritime Law and Commerce* 2 (January 1971): 249-59.

[34] Jean Marchand, Minister of Transport, before Standing Committee on External Affairs and National Defence, House of Commons, 29th Parl., 1st sess., Issue No. 26, 4 December 1973, p. 7.

bility for leadership or coordination of these diverse interests fell to the legal divisions in the foreign affairs departments of both governments.[35] Reports given to the top officials in each government have generally coincided with the sessions of the UN Seabed Committee, and the basic guidelines that were laid down two or three years ago provided the thrust of policy to 1974.

The differences in the decision-making processes are more interesting than the similarities and account to some extent for differing policy substance as well as style. Since 1970 law of the sea policy in the United States has been the product of intensive negotiations between opposing domestic and bureaucratic interests. Once agreed upon, portions of US policy are reopened or altered with utmost difficulty. Canadian policy, on the other hand, reflects the overwhelming preponderance of coastal interests, allowing the Canadian diplomat greater flexibility in adapting policy to coastal trends prevailing in the international negotiations.

The initial consolidation of United States bureaucratic machinery for ocean questions occurred in early 1970 as it became apparent that a wide variety of ocean issues would be handled within the single forum of the UN Seabed Committee. Three agencies, the Departments of State, Defense, and the Interior, were active in law of the sea and were represented on the US delegation to the UN Seabed Committee. Within these agencies, separate staffs for continental shelf and seabed issues, on the one hand, and for straits, territorial seas, and fisheries, on the other, were merged. A central policy body, the Inter-Agency Law of the Sea Task Force, was officially established in February 1970 under the chairmanship of John R. Stevenson, then legal adviser of the Department of State and head of the US delegation. The task force included representatives of all interested federal agencies and bureaus: The Departments of State, Defense, the Interior, Commerce, Treasury, Justice, Transportation, the National Security Council, the National Science Foundation, the Central Intelligence Agency, the Office of Management and Budget, the US Mission to the United Nations, and, more recently, the Environmental Protection Agency and the Council on Environmental Quality. Except for the Office of Management and Budget, each of the agencies has sent one or more representatives to the preparatory sessions of the United Nations Conference on the Law of the Sea.

Since 1932 Canada's Interdepartmental Committee on Territorial Waters has been the expert body handling maritime issues. Agency

---

[35] This is no longer the situation in the US Department of State, where in summer 1973 law of the sea was transferred to a special office attached to Undersecretary Rush and headed by John Norton Moore.

membership has fluctuated with government reorganization and depending upon the issue under consideration. With a change of cabinet committees under the 1970 Trudeau reorganization, the Interdepartmental Committee on Territorial Waters was reconstituted as the Interdepartmental Committee on Law of the Sea (ICLOS)—a title designed to reflect the scope of the Committee's concerns in the negotiations then underway at the UN. The legal adviser to the Department of External Affairs, J. Alan Beesley, served as chairman of ICLOS and head of the Canadian delegation to the UN Seabed Committee from 1969 through 1973. ICLOS includes among its members the Departments of External Affairs, National Defence, Energy, Mines and Resources, Environment, Industry, Trade and Commerce, Justice, Indian Affairs and Northern Development, and Transport, and the Ministry of State for Science and Technology. Few of the ICLOS member agencies have sent representatives to the UN Seabed Committee. Apart from the Department of External Affairs, only the Department of Energy, Mines and Resources has been consistently represented on the delegation since 1968 and the Department of the Environment since its creation in 1971. A representative from the Directorate of Sovereignty and Planning of the Department of National Defence attended a 1972 session of the UN Seabed Committee while another was detailed to the Department of External Affairs to serve as secretary to the Canadian delegation and to ICLOS.

The participation of United States government departments and the relative lack of it by Canadian government departments reflect different governmental systems and the relative strength of divergent domestic interests vis-à-vis each nation's foreign affairs office.[36] Each United States government agency has its own legal office from which representatives to the Inter-Agency Law of the Sea Task Force and to the US delegation are chosen, unlike Canadian departments that, with the exception of the Department of External Affairs, do not have legal divisions. Because the law of the sea negotiations are concerned with codification of international law, representatives of

[36] The small size of the Canadian delegations and their cohesiveness may be explained by what Mr. Beesley described as "Canadian theory and practice . . . that one of the functions of a foreign service is to represent the government and the country abroad, whether in bilateral negotiations or multilateral negotiations. When the subjects are technical, requiring special expertise, then other departments are either represented or, in some cases, lead the delegation. In every case, however, every member of the delegation is considered to represent the Canadian Government as a whole, and not merely his particular ministry. Thus, External Affairs officers are accustomed to reflect a composite governmental view rather than the position the External Affairs Department may have taken in the inter-departmental discussions leading to the development of the position." Letter to author from Ambassador J. Alan Beesley, Canadian Embassy, Vienna, Austria, 31 October 1973, p. 13.

United States government agencies with legal expertise are able to wield greater influence than their Canadian counterparts. They are able to participate directly in international negotiations as well as in drafting treaty articles.[37] The active involvement of legal offices of nonforeign affairs agencies in the United States has restricted the freedom of the legal adviser's office and the new law of the sea office (D/LOS) in the Department of State. Though it has acquired an increasingly important role since 1970, the Department of State has generally acted more as a compromiser of conflicting agency interests than as a director of the policy process. The difficulties of reconciling US interests accounts for the frequency of Inter-Agency Law of the Sea Task Force meetings—sometimes as often as once or twice a week.

In contrast, Canada's Interdepartmental Committee on Law of the Sea meets about six items a year, generally before and after negotiating sessions of the UN Seabed Committee. Except for the Department of External Affairs, agencies of the Canadian government must rely on the Department of Justice for legal counsel. In law of the sea matters, however, the Department of Justice has been primarily restricted to federal-provincial jurisdictional disputes and was not represented on the Canadian delegation until 1972. Efforts to absorb the Department of External Affairs's legal bureau into the Department of Justice operations have been strongly resisted.[38] The legal bureau has given the Department of External Affairs a commanding position among ICLOS agencies, and its Legal Operations Division [39] supplies the bulk of Canadian negotiating personnel. Unlike the Department of State's Office of the Legal Adviser and D/LOS, Canada's Bureau of Legal Affairs is staffed largely by foreign service officers with overseas experience. Rather than moving from private practice to government, Canadian legal officers are selected from career civil servants. An example of the coordinating role played by the relatively small group of legal and diplomatic experts in the legal bureau is the secondment of an official to the Department of the Environment to coordinate that agency's activities in fisheries and the marine environment.

In developing and negotiating national policy on law of the sea, Canadian and American civil servants differ in the latitude of their

[37] The Department of Defense has not been represented by its legal office since 1972, but it has continued to wield a unique form of influence based on strategic rather than legal expertise.

[38] Best, *Globe and Mail* (Toronto), 25 August 1973, p. 7.

[39] The legal bureau has two divisions, legal advisory and legal operations; the first is responsible for general expertise in international law and the second for presenting the Canadian case at international conferences. Within the Legal Operations Division, there are four sections, one of which is law of the sea.

discretion with respect to the elected officials of the state or provincial and federal governments. In both countries, reports to elected officials in the executive and legislative branches generally precede and follow sessions of the UN Seabed Committee. While the US civil servant may spend a substantial portion of his time testifying before the many interested congressional committees, his Canadian counterpart divides his efforts between cabinet committees, parliamentary committees, and on occasion provincial governments.

Canada's ICLOS reports through the secretary of state for external affairs to the Standing Committee on External Affairs and National Defence, and secondarily to the Cabinet Committee on the Environment. Due to the importance of law of the sea negotiations for a variety of interests and departments, the process of securing cabinet approval is not without its perils. As long as policy proposals reflect the prevailing views of the government, however, and as long as agreement is generated among the civil servants of the several departments or a preponderance thereof, the parliamentary system offers substantial latitude to the bureaucrat.

The operations of ICLOS exemplify the type of policy influence that the civil servant wields within the government. Unlike most elected officials, the Canadian civil servant becomes expert on a set of issues and has the time to devote to formulating and promoting policy proposals. In law of the sea matters, draft instructions are prepared within the Bureau of Legal Affairs and then go to the full ICLOS membership for amendment and approval. The draft instructions are next sent to the Standing Committee on External Affairs and National Defence where any problems that could not be resolved within ICLOS are ironed out between the ministers. Due perhaps to the smaller size of the Canadian government, the legal adviser may meet directly with cabinet committee ministers on bilateral as well as multilateral law of the sea negotiations. Once the committee has agreed to the instructions, full cabinet approval is a formality. Given the numerous responsibilities of cabinet ministers and the ability of Canadian law of the sea diplomats to satisfy the Parliament, if not all the agencies, the broad policy guidelines set out in March 1971 remained essentially unchanged to 1974. Those on pollution simply instruct the diplomats to protect coastal state interests. On a series of issues negotiated at the UN Conference on the Human Environment in Stockholm, the London Ocean Dumping Conference, the London Inter-Governmental Maritime Consultative Organization Conference, and the UN Seabed Committee, separate instructions have been given. Were there sharp disagreement between ICLOS members or if the chairman of ICLOS were unable to satisfy the few divergent interests that do arise, policy guidelines would no doubt be modified frequently and would be more detailed.

Perhaps most important in understanding the Canadian policy process in law of the sea is the national cohesion around coastal policy that was generated by the voyage of the *Manhattan* in 1969, the implicit denial of Canadian jurisdiction, and the resulting Canadian legislation in spring 1970. The Ministry of Transport, the Department of National Defence, and the Ministry of State for Science and Technology [40] have experienced difficulties in the past when their policy preferences have run counter to the coastal state orientation of Canada's law of the sea policy, and they have been reminded that the 1970 legislation was the only bill to receive the unanimous support of the Parliament. Only a major shift in the international situation toward maritime freedoms might influence the Canadian position, although even then Mr. Beesley has indicated Canadian readiness to resort to a multilateral conference of like-minded coastal states if the Law of the Sea Conference is not successful.[41]

In the United States the formal decision process for development of law of the sea policy has been within the National Security Council system. Prior to each session of the UN Seabed Committee, the Inter-Agency Law of the Sea Task Force prepares draft instructions that are then transmitted to the White House for approval. There difficulties have arisen in pushing the instructions through White House channels that are typically clogged with more pressing issues. As a result the instructions (in the form of National Security Decision Memoranda [NSDM]) have at times reached the US delegation several weeks after the start of a negotiating session. Delays have also been caused by disputes arising in 1970, 1972, and 1973 between the agencies comprising the task force. When this occurs, the dispute is taken to the undersecretary's committee where compromises are sought. If the agency disputants do not accept the compromise formulations, the dispute goes to the White House and perhaps to the president for a decision. As a result of these divergent domestic interests, even routine draft instructions which the Inter-Agency Law of the Sea Task Force forwards to the White House for approval reflect tenuous compromises between all agencies. The resulting National Security Decision Memoranda are necessarily quite specific on matters under contention. The active participation of many US agen-

---

[40] The Ministry of Transport has a major part in the Inter-Governmental Maritime Consultative Organization (IMCO) negotiations while the Ministry of State for Science and Technology has recently become an important participant.

[41] *Charlottetown Guardian*, 28 August 1973.

cies on the delegation assures that the instructions are not overstepped in the negotiating process.

Although the general American public is not as knowledgeable about law of the sea policies as is the Canadian public, certain American interests have followed the negotiations quite closely since 1970. In response to strong industry pressure, the relationship of these interests to the United States government was formalized in early 1972 with the creation of an Advisory Committee on the Law of the Sea. One member from each of its eight subcommittees—petroleum, hard minerals, international law and relations, marine science, fisheries, international finance and taxation, marine environment, and maritime industries—is represented on the United States delegation to the UN Seabed Committee. In addition to this formal watchdog role, law of the sea interest groups exert pressure in Congress. They also make their wishes felt directly on government officials who tend to move into and out of private walks of life more frequently than Canadian lawyers. While expertise on the technicalities of oceans policy bestowed a certain freedom on a small group of US officials up to 1970, the heightened activism of many private interests and public agencies gradually reduced their autonomy. The effect on policy has been a trend toward a more even balance between coastal state and maritime interests.

The diversity of United States interests and lines of influence makes the negotiation of a single national policy as difficult, if not *more* difficult, as negotiating the policy internationally. Because a position may be hammered out at the last minute, the United States finds it difficult to coordinate with or even give advance notice to other governments of policies it plans to support. A prime example of this problem in Canadian-American relations was the tabling of the US Draft Treaty on the Seabed Regime in August 1970. Bitterly fought within the US government, the draft treaty was pressed through an interagency controversy at the last moment and was forwarded to the Canadian government only three days before officially released. The Canadians were dismayed particularly with the provisions for international jurisdiction over the continental shelf beyond a depth of 200 meters and resented the lack of consultation before the draft treaty's presentation. The mode of presenting it to the Canadian government, as much as its content, did not enhance cooperative relations in law of the sea.

TRANSNATIONAL SYSTEMS

Despite the difficulties posed for intergovernmental cooperation by such last minute decision making, transnational as well as transgovernmental law of the sea relations between the United States and Canada might proceed unaffected. As in 1958 or 1960, Canada's Department of National Defence might consult with the United States Department of Defense on law of the sea matters of mutual concern. Or the mining companies and the relevant government departments on both sides of the border might harmonize their proposals on a regime for deep seabed mining. Such links, however, scarcely exist in today's negotiations. The full US and Canadian delegations meet bilaterally about once a year. These intergovernmental consultations increased in number before Canada passed its 1970 legislation, stopped for a period, and have since resumed. Representatives of the foreign offices have met with officials of other agencies in negotiating fisheries questions and at the Stockholm and Inter-Governmental Maritime Consultative Organization conferences. In law of the sea, the pattern of informal consultation has been between representatives of the maritime powers such as the US, the USSR, Japan, and certain European nations. For its part, the Canadian delegation maintains regular contact with Australia, Tanzania, Kenya, and a number of developing coastal nations. It is to these countries with substantial coastal interests that Canada has turned for support since 1970.

The records of the 1968 and 1969 meetings of the UN Seabed Committee show a now surprising degree of coordination and even cooperation between United States and Canadian delegates. Representatives of both countries to the Economic and Technical Subcommittee (the predecessor of Subcommittee I) shared with their British and Australian colleagues training in the disciplines of geology and geography. Within this highly politicized forum of legally trained delegates, a comfortable relationship developed—in the case of Canada and the United States between officials of the Department of Energy, Mines and Resources and of the Department of the Interior.[42] The major efforts of the delegates of Canada, the US, Britain, and Australia in 1968 and 1969 were directed toward injecting hard data into the subcommittee's discussions. To this end, speeches were orchestrated to raise the level of understanding of geological realities, the state of mining technology, alternative types of mining systems, the concerns and benefits of marine science, and the like.

The disappearance in 1970 of such coordinated efforts is traceable to a number of factors. Within the United Nations the stage of dis-

[42] Indeed, many technical provisions of the US draft treaty appear to be closely modeled on the Canadian system and can be traced to exchanges within the economic and technical working group. See, for instance, text of Statements of D. G. Crosby in the Economic and Technical Subcommittee of the UN Seabed Committee on 21 March 1969 and 13 March 1970.

cussion and exchange of technical information was superseded in 1970 by the stage of political bargaining and defining of trade-offs. At the same time, US-Canadian policies parted ways over Canadian offshore claims and the US counterproposal for renouncing claims to resources of the continental margin beyond the 200-meter isobath. Although the Department of the Interior had lost ground within the US government, Canada's Department of Energy, Mines and Resources played an increasing role in policy counsels. While Canada's global naval interests were being forced to contract their concerns from NATO defense to protection of sovereignty and domestic police functions, in some Canadian eyes "the Admirals had taken over" United States policy. With the military agency ascendant in the United States and the resource and environment agencies ascendant in Canada, earlier lines of informal communication quickly eroded.

The asymmetry in size and composition of the respective delegations accounts to some extent for the lack of transgovernmental interactions during meetings of the UN Seabed Committee. Few Canadian governmental agencies participate while US agency involvement is sizable and diversified.[43] Instead multinational, semi-institutionalized interest group contacts have developed during the law of the sea negotiating sessions. The earliest interest group to organize was the fishery experts who in effect set the pattern of weekly luncheon meetings for subsequent groups. Participants were selected on the basis of expertise, not country representation, and varied from week to week. The next group to be created after the "Fish Hook Luncheon Club" was the "Seabed Dredge and Drill Club" in 1972. Membership included petroleum and hard minerals geologists and engineers. Similar luncheon groups have been formed more recently for naval-military interests ("The Peacekeepers Group") and for marine science interests. The policy impact of these regularized transnational meetings is difficult to determine. Undoubtedly they provide a useful

[43] The only Canadian departments represented in 1968 and 1969 were the Departments of External Affairs, and of Energy, Mines and Resources. During the same years, US agency participation included the Departments of State, Defense, and the Interior. Since 1970, the only new agency regularly participating on the Canadian delegation has been the Department of the Environment, created in 1971. As noted above (p. 769) Department of National Defence participation has been limited primarily to detailing an officer to the law of the sea division of the legal bureau to serve as secretary to ICLOS and the UN Seabed Committee delegation. Although members of ICLOS, those departments with distant water interests have not participated in the negotiations: the Ministry of Transport, the Department of Industry, Trade and Commerce, and the Ministry of State for Science and Technology. The contrast with the sizable and diversified US agency participation is striking. Since 1970, new members of the United States delegation have come from the Departments of Commerce, Treasury, Transportation, the National Science Foundation, and the Environmental Protection Agency.

opportunity for delegates and private experts from as many as 30 countries to exchange views with at least a common basis of technical expertise. They do not, however, provide a forum for US-Canadian interest group exchanges. United States participation at these luncheon meetings has included private industry representatives who serve as advisers to the delegation. Private sector representatives have been absent from the Canadian delegation.

The absence of direct private interest participation in Canada and the concomitant reduction of transnational links can be traced to several factors. A paramount consideration is the politicization of law of the sea issues with the 1970 legislation. It would require herculean efforts for private interest groups to alter the momentum begun with Canada's 1970 legislation, and no compelling reason to do so is on the horizon. Canadian law of the sea interests do not all point in the same direction, but it has been the civil servants in the legal bureau of the Department of External Affairs—not the competition of interest groups—that have balanced the several considerations. These officials have maintained a cohesive coastal state policy that has in turn enhanced the ability of the Canadian delegation to play an important leadership role in the international negotiations.

While US private sector interests have pursued policy goals through representatives in a number of agencies (i.e., petroleum and hard minerals through the Department of the Interior and the Treasury Department, or science through the National Science Foundation and the Department of State's Coordinator of Ocean Affairs), interest group representations in Ottawa must be directed to the key Departments of External Affairs, the Environment, and Energy, Mines and Resources. Due in part to the nature of the Canadian economy, Canadian officials are able to keep private interests at arm's length. Foreign ownership of major industries is substantial, i.e., 99 percent of oil refinery capacity in 1969 or 85 percent of primary smelting.[44] As a result, the interest of a particular industry is rarely equated with the national interest. On the contrary, it is generally suspect. Whereas in the United States companies such as Exxon, Mobil, Texaco, and Shell may recieve a favorable hearing within several agencies of the government, their Canadian affiliates do not. The coincidence between the oil industry position on coastal state offshore jurisdiction and that of the Canadian government does not extend to the industry position on security of investment, compulsory settlement of disputes, and protection of the marine environment. Nationalism combined with the multinational connections of the oil industry leaves the Canadian civil

---

[44] Peter Newman, "Why Canada Wants Texas Gulf," *New York Times*, 5 August 1973.

servant free to formulate a national policy independent of industry interests.

Similarly, the Canadian government more closely regulates the activities of hard mineral mining industries than does the United States. Because the Department of Energy, Mines and Resources is concerned with the effect on Canadian mineral prices and employment levels, it does not wish to encourage unregulated seabed minerals exploitation. While the International Nickel Company (INCO) and other Canadian companies are as interested in nodule mining as American firms, they have been silent on the subject and have had little say in the determination of the Canadian position on the international seabed regime. INCO has invested $12 million in ocean mining technology but reportedly "with the intent of protecting its flanks by eventually marketing cheaper land-mined metal." [45] American firms, on the other hand, have entered the policy process in many ways. While Hughes's Summa Corporation is proceeding with its activities regardless of international deliberations, Deep Sea Ventures and Kennecott Copper have pressed for favorable legislation in both the Congress and the executive branch. Kennecott and Deep Sea Ventures are said to have invested about $20 million each and Summa Corporation in the vicinity of $100 million in ocean mining. The transnational interactions of the mining companies are reportedly extensive but cannot be documented. Apparently INCO has cooperated to a limited degree in pushing the ocean mining legislation, but relations with US companies are strained. [46]

The marine science interest in narrow boundaries can be disregarded in Canada, not because of foreign domination but simply because it is weak. Government officials find the scientific establishment to be unresponsive to overriding policy concerns and must, therefore, keep a wary eye on it. In one interesting case, transnational scientific relations with the United States evoked a transgovernmental Canadian response and ultimately an intergovernmental protest. Upon reading the November 1969 issue of *Geotimes*,[47] a senior official of the Department of Energy, Mines and Resources discovered that the *Glomar Challenger* operating under the Deep Sea Drilling Project would be conducting two drilling operations on Canada's continental margin, the most controversial one located 150 miles southeast of

[45] Barry Newman, "Mysterious Nodules at Bottom of Oceans May Yield a Treasure," *Wall Street Journal*, 21 September 1973, p. 1.

[46] According to the *Wall Street Journal*, a US corporate executive has described INCO as "the man who comes to the wife-swapping party without his wife."

[47] "Deep Sea Drilling Project Extended," p. 17.

Halifax and 140 miles southwest of Sable Island.[48] Upon further inquiry it was learned that the sites had been suggested by a Canadian scientist cooperating in the Joint Oceanographic Institutions Deep Earth Sampling Program (JOIDES). Not only was the off-Halifax site selected because of existence of oil related structures, but it had already been leased to the Shell Oil Company. On the basis of this information, a representative from Canada's Department of Energy, Mines and Resources made a statement to the UN Seabed Committee indicating that "a drilling programme would not be allowed to proceed on Canada's continental margin, whether it be with scientific or commercial intent, without assurance that adequate pollution control equipment and procedures were to be utilized." [49] In response to this speech and at the suggestion of the Department of Interior's representative on the US delegation to the UN Seabed Committee, the chief scientist of the Deep Sea Drilling Project in the National Science Foundation contacted the Canadian official. While those discussions were under way, and upon the advice of the Department of Energy, Mines and Resources, the Department of External Affairs made an official protest of the drilling to the Department of State through its ambassador in Washington.

Although the Canadian case for prohibiting the drilling rested overtly on the grounds of the *Glomar Challenger's* inability to handle blowouts, the underlying issue was that of sovereignty. Denying Canada's right to assert jurisdiction over an area as deep as 2,340 meters and over 100 miles from shore, the Department of State advised the National Science Foundation not to fill out the Canadian offshore drilling notices. The issue was ultimately resolved between officials of the Department of Energy, Mines and Resources and the National Science Foundation by a compromise in which it was agreed that the project would not drill off Halifax and the Canadian government would overlook the drilling off Newfoundland.[50] The lesson of that experience for Canadian scientists has been that they must not swim against the tide of government policy. They, like others with interests in the oceans, must have government sanction for their international dealings.

The fisheries policies of Canada and the United States are similar

---

[48] "Canada Apprehensive over US Program Seeking Ocean-Floor Drilling Sites," *Globe and Mail* (Toronto), 28 May 1970.

[49] Statement of D. G. Crosby in the Economic and Technical Subcommittee of the UN Seabed Committee, 13 March 1970, p. 6.

[50] The Deep Sea Drilling Project has since made it official policy to avoid structures that may contain gas pockets ("Deep Sea Project," *The Oil and Gas Journal*, 2 November 1970, pp. 120-22).

in many respects [51] due to comparable circumstances in both countries. The fisheries offshore both nations are some of the most valuable in the world; and until their depletion by distant fishing nations, the fisheries supported a sizable fishing community. Distant water fleets operate out of the United States and Canada, although the Canadian fleet is far smaller than that of the US. To provide for domestic interests in fisheries, both nations adopted the species approach within the UN Seabed Committee. In the evolution of the species approach in both countries, domestic factors played a significant role.

The United States fisheries policy in its final form reflects the direct influence of all segments of the nation's fishing industry. Thus, it has not evolved toward a zonal approach that would threaten US tuna fleets as well as naval interests. The Canadian species approach, though initially similar to that of the United States, has taken a somewhat different course recently. In 1973 government officials moved in the UN Seabed Committee to accommodate the species approach to the widely supported concept of a 200-mile economic zone.[52] With the government's adoption of fisheries closing lines extending Canada's fisheries jurisdiction, the highly vocal fishing industry issued a statement of support for the official negotiators.[53] Provincial fisheries ministers and industry have apparently continued to support the government in its effort to achieve recognition of resource jurisdiction at least to 200 miles if not out to the edge of the continental margin.[54] The delegation's move to support a 200-mile zone in the international negotiations has enhanced its reputation with developing coastal states.

[51] L. H. J. Legault, Statement to the Fourth Governor's Conservation Congress, 12-15 December 1971.

[52] UN General Assembly, *Draft Articles on Fisheries by Canada, India, Kenya and Sri Lanka*, A/AC.138/SC.II/L.38, 16 July 1973.

[53] "Whereas the Fisheries Council of Canada has felt in the past that the Government of Canada did not place sufficient emphasis on fisheries matters in the development and execution of international affairs policies; and Whereas to a large extent this shortcoming is now being corrected through extensions of fisheries jurisdiction; negotiation of bilateral fisheries agreements and development of principles of international law . . . and Whereas these activities have been accompanied as they proceeded, by an increasing *consultation with the Canadian fishing industry;* and Whereas an impressive team of international fisheries experts and negotiators . . . has been established in the Department of External Affairs. Therefore be it resolved that the Government of Canada be urged to keep this highly respected and qualified team together . . . in order that the necessary expertise and continuity may be maintained for the critical developments which lie ahead in international fisheries and international law of the sea." From a mimeographed sheet, entitled "Fisheries Council of Canada 1972 Annual Meeting Resolution No. 23, International Negotiations," which I received from the Canadian embassy.

[54] "Fisheries Minister Remains Optimistic About Industry," *Charlottetown Guardian*, 1 November 1973.

Unlike the international law of the sea negotiations, United States–Canadian transgovernmental relations take on a measure of importance in negotiations within regional fisheries organizations (such as the International Commission for Northwest Atlantic Fisheries). Allied against the distant water fishing nations, Canadian and American officials coordinate actions when appropriate. In both governments the negotiators include representatives of fisheries agencies as well as the foreign affairs departments.

The absence of a substantial number of transgovernmental interactions in US-Canadian law of the sea relations has several explanations. The concentration of decision-making power in Canada's foreign affairs department has been a major factor. The policy centralization was facilitated by the politicization of law of the sea issues in Canada in 1970. Moreover, Canadian policy vis-à-vis extending fishing jurisdictions, protecting the Arctic environment, and generally standing up to the United States has struck responsive chords within the Canadian public. In the case of those few domestic interests not satisfied with official policy, the Canadian context of growing nationalism precludes a resort by private or public officials to transnational relations with United States interests. Where a strong bureaucracy finds itself confronted with a substantial number of foreign-owned private interests, a judicious use of nationalist sentiment can ensure that policy formulation remains in the hands of the civil servants.

While United States and Canadian diplomatic officials continue to deal with each other as the third UN Conference on the Law of the Sea progresses, the future trend of transgovernmental relations in this area is unclear. The law of the sea policies of both countries have drawn closer since the divergence of 1970 and can be expected to come even nearer to each other during the conference. With national policies less sharply divided, transgovernmental links may be facilitated. The shifts in policies will occur in each government for different reasons. As Canada will no doubt continue to play a role in the conference as compromiser of divergent interests between the members, it will seek to conciliate major maritime interests. The United States government, on the other hand, is under strong pressure to conciliate its domestic coastal interests. Given the conflicting domestic interests in the United States, their reconciliation may require a decision taken in the White House. And in the present climate that decision is likely to favor resource considerations more than ever before. Thus while relations between the United States and Canadian delegations will not come full circle to approximate those of 1958 or 1960, international pressures on Canada and domestic pressures on the United States may be expected to bring policies closer. This in turn may lend itself to increased transnational interactions.

AN ANALYTICAL ASSESSMENT OF THE UNITED STATES–CANADIAN DEFENSE ISSUE AREA

Roger Frank Swanson

This article examines the United States–Canadian defense issue area from a transnational and transgovernmental perspective, and attempts to develop conceptually the transgovernmental dimension through empirical application.[1] The first part delineates those factors that encourage transnational and transgovernmental activity in the defense issue area. The second part considers *pure intergovernmental transactions,* referring to United States–Canadian dealings in which there is no transnational or transgovernmental activity. Because we know so little about how these dealings occur, this section examines pure intergovernmental transactions as a three-stage issue flow: *preprocess, process,* and *postprocess.* The third section identifies and examines the dynamics of *mixed transactions,* referring to intergovernmental flows having transnational or transgovernmental activity that does not essentially alter the outcomes of the flows. The fourth part identifies *transformative transactions,* referring to intergovernmental flows that become transnational or transgovernmental flows (or the reverse) through the involvement of new actors that significantly alter the outcomes of the flows. In summation, the fifth

Roger Frank Swanson is with the Center of Canadian Studies at the School of Advanced International Studies, The Johns Hopkins University, in Washington, D.C.

[1] I use the US-Canadian defense issue area to test my structural paradigm which is applicable to other bilateral and multilateral transborder interactions in all issue areas. This wider applicability does not mean that the defense issue area, and especially the "special" US-Canadian interaction, has an illustrative universality. Rather, the wider applicability lies in the analytical properties of the paradigm itself, which permits empirically grounded consideration of differences both between different issue areas and the activities of actor combinations within these areas. This paradigm, which is being developed and extended, is but one way of approaching what are conventionally regarded as diplomatic exchanges. It may be added that the case studies and examples used in this article have been intentionally selected to cover a maximum historical time span while drawing upon easily available primary and secondary sources.

section considers those factors militating against transnational and transgovernmental activity in the defense area.

This article concentrates on transgovernmental as opposed to transnational transactions, since the transgovernmental dimension has been most neglected in world polity analyses and appears to be rather more relevant to this issue area than is the transnational one. Although analyses of political organization incorporate the transgovernmental dimension in theory, they confine this dimension to the nonempirical use of a few examples, themselves often questionable because they are not grounded in the structural milieu in which they occur. This is not surprising. Because the units of analysis of transnational transactions are defined according to an actor's formal position, all an analyst has to do is identify nongovernmental actors involved in transborder dealings. For transgovernmental transactions, however, the analyst has to use a definition based not on position but on role. Not any subgovernmental transborder actor is by definition transgovernmental, but only those that act independently in international relations. Since it is often difficult to determine when an actor is acting independently in international relations, analysts are tempted to apply the position-based definition to transgovernmental transactions and inaccurately regard all subgovernmental transborder dealings and informal contacts as transgovernmental.[2]

Another point of clarification is also definitional in nature.[3] Those who define transgovernmental relations as transborder subgovernmental transactions not controlled or closely guided by the policies of cabinets or chief executives cannot identify their unit of analysis without first identifying what a government policy is at a given point. Notwithstanding advantages in such an approach, policy identification has limitations concerning its empirical application. These limitations stem from the level of generality in which executives so often formulate and articulate policy, the fact that so many functional US-

---

[2] To cite one example of a possibly confusing case, Washington State's director of civil defense and British Columbia's civil defense coordinator formally signed a "Letter of Understanding" on 23 October 1968 dealing with civil emergency planning. Their authority for so doing can be found in the *U. S. Office of Civil Defense Federal Civil Defense Guide* (Part G, chapter 2, appendix 1), in the *Canadian Emergency Measures Organization Bulletin* (B68-2, International Coordination 5/23/68), and bilaterally in an 8 August 1967 federal Exchange of Notes (18 UST 1795) which encourages and facilitates "cooperative emergency arrangements between adjacent jurisdictions on matters falling within the competence of such jurisdictions." This illustrates not a transgovernmental transaction but a sublevel intergovernmental transaction, because it is entirely integrated into the multileveled government processes of the two nations.

[3] However, in the interests of uniformity, Keohane and Nye's definitions in the "Introduction," with one major exception discussed in the third section, are used wherever possible.

Canadian dealings at the core of the relationship are processed entirely by lower-level action officers who receive no higher-level guidelines, and fluid shifts of bargaining positions and overall issue priorities.

An alternative way of identifying transgovernmental transactions is by looking at role deviation rather than at departures from government policy. The role in question is organizational in nature; indeed, it is less a role in a social-psychological sense than it is an operation or function in an organizational sense. I therefore define transgovernmental relations as those transborder dealings in which one or more governmental officials depart from the standard operating procedures (SOPs) of their organizations. Quite simply, they are organizationally unintegrated governmental points of contact across national boundaries. These SOPs, by which transgovernmental relations are identified, are not only relatively easy to isolate but also useful analytically.[4] For example, if one is interested in the effect of transgovernmental transactions on the erosion of overall governmental authority, analyses would seem to be more usefully directed at the SOPs and activities that constitute issue flows than at governmental policies. Moreover, the use of SOPs as a definitional base includes the significant possibility of chief executives themselves acting as transgovernmental actors.[5] In contrast, those who use cabinet and executive policies as a definitional base in identifying transgovernmental relations permit only lower-level bureaucracies to depart from these policies and hence be considered transgovernmental actors.

In considering alternative definitions, it is important to note that the ultimate criterion of the effectiveness of a theoretical approach is a researchable specificity rather than a heuristic inclusiveness. The

---

[4] According to my model, these SOPs consist of two dimensions: *statutory legitimacy*, which is written definitions of areas of responsibility and procedural rules of acceptable activity; and *operational legitimacy*, which is unwritten but consensurially defined areas of responsibility and procedures that are organizationally regarded as an acceptable extension of the written dimension. Taken together, they can be subsumed under the phrase *organizational mandate*. The operational salience of the organizational mandate is a function of the *decisional resources* (e.g., funding, number of personnel, degree of expertise) available to the actor. Transgovernmental transactions can therefore be defined as all transborder violations of a governmental actor's organizational mandate.

[5] For example, it is legitimate and useful to ask if Prime Minister Diefenbaker was not himself a transgovernmental actor during the 1957-58 establishment of NORAD. This question can be answered by looking not at the policies of the Diefenbaker government but at the SOPs of the Canadian parliamentary system. Thus, if the Canadian processing of the North Atlantic Treaty is taken as a representative model of Canadian SOPs in such matters, Diefenbaker could be considered a transgovernmental actor. See Jon B. McLin, *Canada's Changing Defense Policy 1957-1963* (Baltimore, Md.: The Johns Hopkins Press, 1967), pp. 38-49.

full potential of the world polity approach will be clear when it is used to address precisely the structural interrelationships among actors, their organizational milieus, and the concomitant SOPs through which issue flows are processed.[6] In short, those additional empirical possibilities that can be explained by certain revisions in definitions and their rigorous applications are worth the cost óf additional complexity.

FACTORS ENCOURAGING TRANSNATIONAL AND TRANSGOVERNMENTAL ACTIVITY

It may be hypothesized that there are five interrelated attributes of the defense issue area that encourage transnational and transgovernmental activity: (1) United States and Canadian procedural predilection for an informal defense relationship; (2) the relatively small number of actors involved; (3) the multiple roles of these actors; (4) the transborder professional identifications of these actors; and (5) the technological content of defense issues. The first factor is reflected rhetorically in a cautious juxtaposition of United States–Canadian similarities against the Canadian desire to maintain a separate national existence. Procedurally this is expressed in *special* as opposed to *comme les autres* decisional techniques. It is therefore not surprising that the United States–Canadian defense relationship is characterized by a marked absence of comprehensive joint agreements. Apart from the North Atlantic Treaty, there is no single formal agreement defining reciprocal strategic expectations and obligations. Indeed, the most definitive and comprehensive pledge of bilateral defense commitments remains that of the Roosevelt-King statements of 1938.[7] The August 1940 Ogdensburg Declaration, regarded as the genesis of the contemporary defense relationship, was not a declaration but a six-sentence, unsigned press release issued by King and Roosevelt. The April 1941 Hyde Park Agreement, generally

---

[6] *Structural* refers to the organizational environs (i.e., organizational mandates and their execution through organizational roles), and interconnections between these environs, within which the actors function. Indeed, the significance of the transborder activities of individuals, and the transborder movement of tangible items, is also organizationally grounded. The former involves the organizational roles these individuals are performing (e.g., corporate executive, government official, or trade union representative); the latter, the organizational context in which movements of these tangible items take place (e.g., oil, defense materials, or money).

[7] Even the 1817 Rush-Bagot "treaty," the rhetorical touchstone of the "undefended border," was not a treaty but an agreement implemented by a US-British exchange of notes, and subsequently confirmed by the US Senate. However, ratifications were not exchanged.

viewed as the economic counterpart of the Ogdensburg Declaration, was more specific in delineating its objectives but made no organizational provisions for its implementation. Even the North American Air Defense Command (NORAD) agreements (1958, 1968, 1973) have never defined specific United States and Canadian forces and facility level contributions, leaving these matters as an item of continuing negotiations. This informality, which is a response to the domestic exigencies of the United States and more especially of Canada, has permitted flexible reactions to both international and national vagaries. However, it has encouraged transnational and transgovernmental activity by leaving undefined and unsystematized the organizational roles of the defense actors and the scope of the defense relationship, whether in terms of crisis response, personnel and materiel commitments, or procedural and consultative matters.[8]

The second factor encouraging transnational and transgovernmental activity in the defense issue area is the relatively small number of actors involved. There are some 75 major defense actors in the United States and Canada who are professional experts in their respective fields, know one another personally, and meet in fairly regular sessions. This small transborder defense cluster expedites the resolution of defense issues along informal personalized lines.[9] The attitudinal impact of this small number of actors is manifested, as a United States official recently observed to me, in a profound transborder "sense of membership."

A third factor concerns the multiple roles of the actors in the defense cluster. For example, the joint US-Canadian Military Cooperation Committee (MCC) and the Regional Planning Group of NATO (RPG/NATO) have essentially identical membership and the same working teams and subcommittees. In addition, MCC normally meets in combined session immediately prior to the Permanent Joint Board on Defense (PJBD), a sequence that furthers the interactions

---

[8] A revealing example of this procedural informality occurred on 28 October 1946, when President Truman met with Prime Minister King in Washington to discuss joint defense. Immediately thereafter King recounted the meeting to Canadian Ambassador Designate Hume Wrong. Wrong sent a telegram summarizing the meeting to Lester Pearson, undersecretary of state for external affairs in Ottawa. In a conversation with US Ambassador Ray Atherton, Pearson recounted the Truman-King meeting in detail. Atherton then reported its content in a dispatch to J. Graham Parsons, assistant chief of the State Department's Division of Commonwealth Affairs, who recorded it in a top-secret memorandum. This memorandum served as the State Department's record of the Truman-King meeting, a record the department obtained from Canadian sources (Roger Frank Swanson, *Canadian-American Summit Diplomacy: 1923-1973* [Toronto: McCleland and Stewart, forthcoming]).

[9] This phenomenon is illustrated by the case studies and examples cited in this article.

of these two joint organizations. (PJBD is both civilian and military, whereas MCC and RPG/NATO are strictly military.) Members of the working teams of MCC and RPG/NATO also serve as military assistants to PJBD. The fact that membership on any of the joint US-Canadian defense organizations is part-time also encourages these multiple roles. Thus, officials of both the Canadian affairs offices of the Pentagon (Directorate for European and NATO Affairs) and the State Department (Office of Canadian Affairs) assist in the preparation of PJBD agendas and attend the meetings in addition to their regular functions. It is also important to note that these multiple roles are sequential for specific actors.[10] The import of these multiple roles as they encourage transnational and transgovernmental activity should not be underestimated.[11]

The fourth factor encouraging transnational and transgovernmental activity is the presence of transborder defense coalitions in which professional identifications tend to take precedence over national identifications within the dynamics of issue flows. In PJBD during World War II, an observer asserts that "divisions of opinion seldom occurred on strictly national grounds" but that generally "the cleavage was along service lines." [12] Another observer adds that "on one issue, Canadian and United States army officers might be found united in argument with Canadian and United States naval officers; or the service members of both nations might find themselves on the opposite side of a discussion from the civilian members." [13] These transborder coalitions continue today, notwithstanding the Canadian Armed Forces unification and the separation tendencies of the Nixon and Trudeau governments. Thus, the following transborder coalitions can be said to be relatively active: air-air, navy-maritime, army-land, Department of State–Department of External Affairs, Department of

[10] For example, Canadian General Maurice A. Pope, appointed to PJBD in 1941, remained on this body as he professionally advanced in the following sequence: assistant chief of the General Staff, vice chief of the General Staff, representative of the Cabinet War Committee in Washington and chairman of the Joint Staff, and the prime minister's military staff officer and military secretary to the War Committee.

[11] For example, one recent case involved a US military officer who was a member of one of the joint US-Canadian defense organizations. To help meet a US shortage of barbed wire needed for the protection of village-manned self-defense forces in Vietnam, the US officer, acting in his service rather than joint organizational capacity, telephoned his Canadian organizational counterpart about getting the wire from plentiful Canadian sources. The Canadian official then, acting in his service capacity, helped acquire the wire for the United States.

[12] H. L. Keenleyside, "The Canada-U.S. PJBD," *International Journal* 16 (Winter 1960-61) : 55.

[13] C. P. Stacey, "The Canadian-American PJBD: 1940-1945," *International Journal* 9 (Spring 1954) : 115.

Defense–Department of National Defence, defense production sharing, and research and development.[14]

The fifth factor concerns the technological content of defense
issues, which tends to decrease national barriers and increase specialized transborder collaboration. This goes quite beyond the US-
Canadian defense production sharing agreements to include a broader
economic-scientific relationship.[15] Seven facets can be discerned: supportive economic activity (e.g., World War II complementarity in
agriculture and taxation), collaboration in atomic energy, exchange
of defense-related scientific data, military standardization (e.g., sharing of materiels and parts), collaborative applied research, collaborative development, and collaboration in defense procurement. The significance of this technological content is evident in reviewing United
States–Canadian economic cooperation related to defense matters during World War II.[16] The rationale for this cooperation was twofold—

[14] To abstract a current example concerning a procurement issue, the Canadian
cabinet approved a Department of National Defence proposal to replace the aging
Argus with a long-range patrol aircraft for antisubmarine warfare. Given
cabinet concern with the replacement's multiple role capability, the three leading
candidates are an adapted version of the US Boeing 707, the US Lockheed P-3
ASW aircraft currently in service with the US Navy, and the more specialized
UK Nimrod, currently in service with the Royal Air Force. Canadian maritime
force officials agree with US naval officials that the Canadian purchase of the
P-3 would be mutually desirable for professional and budgetary reasons. Defense
Department officials responsible for the defense production sharing agreements
(DPSA) informally state to their Canadian counterparts the importance of
purchasing a US model, and in view of a cumulative US DPSA $500 million
deficit, they express reservations about DPSA's continuance should this not be
done. US Treasury officials strongly concur. After a cursory study requested by
the Department of Defense, systems analysts who are aware of Ottawa's concern
with the larger political and economic aspects arrive at neutral conclusions between the two US alternatives. Canadian officials of several departments then
decide to institute a fly-off between the alternative models, with strong indications
that the final decision will be determined by more than purely military rationales.

[15] Analyses of the production sharing agreements have failed to make the case
that the agreements are a discrete unit of analysis. These studies have not systematically considered the interrelationships between these agreements and the
other facets of the larger US-Canadian economic-scientific defense relationship.
Because the definitional boundaries are unspecified, it is never clear as to precisely
what we are dealing with (e.g., an issue area, the subcomponent of an issue area,
a sectoral phenomenon, or a crosscutting sectoral phenomenon). This lack of
definitional precision causes analytical distortions when these discussions consider
the agreements as an integrative process. Moreover, these analyses of the production sharing agreements are unduly restrictive in that even though they
acknowledge the origins of the agreements, they ignore the utility of the historical
dimension as a reference point for comparative measurement of integrative and
disintegrative processes.

[16] To implement the Roosevelt-King 1941 Hyde Park Agreement, a series of joint
committees were established during the war—Materiel Coordinating Committee,
Joint Economic Committee, Joint War Production Committee, Joint Agriculture
Committee, and Joint War Aid Committee. In addition, Canada joined two US-
UK combined boards—Combined Production and Resources Board, and Combined
Food Board.

to accelerate the acquisition of military materiels, and to alleviate the pressure on Canadian foreign exchange early in the war. The import of this cooperation did not escape Prime Minister King who observed that the Hyde Park Agreement "constitutes an acceptance of the economic interdependence of Canada and the U.S.," having a "permanent significance," and involving "nothing less than a common plan of the economic defense of the western hemisphere." [17] King's assessment was not hyperbolic, for World War II collaboration resulted in an unprecedented coordination of the US and Canadian economies, and in "the almost complete erasure of national boundaries for certain purposes." [18] This wartime collaborative environment encouraged transnational and transgovernmental activity. One author has noted that the "informal and direct methods used by the nondiplomatic missions raised certain issues concerning the control and synthesis of external policies." [19] Indeed, important agreements were sometimes "made quite informally, almost by word of mouth and outside the normal channels of diplomatic intercourse"; and even though the departmental representatives were "supposedly dealing only with matters of a technical nature," the fact remained that "some of the decisions taken bordered on high policy, especially in matters relating to war procurement and production." [20]

PURE INTERGOVERNMENTAL TRANSACTIONS AS A THREE-STAGE ISSUE FLOW

If a pure intergovernmental transaction refers to US-Canadian issue flows in which there is no transnational or transgovernmental activity, the question is what do such flows look like? It is analytically useful to regard such flows as a three-stage sequence of interactions occurring within each government and between the two governments. The *preprocess stage* consists of those activities and events that re-

[17] Canada, House of Commons, *Debates*, 28 April 1941, pp. 2288, 2289.
[18] Richardson Dougall, "Economic Cooperation With Canada: 1941-47," *Department of State Bulletin* 16 (22 June 1947): 1185. For example, the Combined Production and Resources Board recommended that a proposed war plant in Canada not be constructed because United States productive facilities were already sufficient for US and Canadian needs; the Combined Food Board reduced competitive bidding on foodstuffs that were shortage items; a 1942 US-Canadian agreement facilitated the transborder movement of agricultural labor and machinery; and according to a May 1942 US executive order, emergency purchases of war materiels could be imported without duty. Moreover, three major joint agreements were concluded regarding exemption of military construction from taxation. (Dougall, pp. 1186-89).
[19] H. Gordon Skilling, *Canadian Representation Abroad* (Toronto: Ryerson Press, 1945), p. 315.
[20] Skilling, p. 315.

quire a US-Canadian decision in the first place. Organizationally this stage involves only the activities within the government initiating the flow and ends when there is a formal transborder contact with officials of the second government. At this stage, officials of the initating government discuss what their government's position should be and what is negotiable (definition of conceptual parameters) while also deciding upon those channels through which the issue will be processed (definition of organizational parameters). The *process stage* begins when officials of the first government formally start negotiations with officials of the second government, and ends when the issue is perceived as being essentially resolved by the participating actors.[21] Organizationally, this process stage involves interactions within each government and transborder interactions between the two governments. At this stage the issue is resolved, but within the context of largely pre-established conceptual and organizational parameters. The *postprocess stage* consists of those activities taken to implement the resolution reached in the process stage. Organizationally it involves interactions within each government and transborder interactions, and consists of attempts to expedite the implementation of the issue resolution.

To illustrate what a pure intergovernmental issue flow, with its three-stage sequence, is like, an actual issue has been frozen and disaggregated—a US base closing in Canada in which the United States was the initiator of the issue. Because of severe budgetary pressures, the United States decided to execute worldwide personnel and base reductions involving 30 actions overseas and 300 in North America, of which only Base X in Canada was involved. The *preprocess stage* of this base-closing issue flow organizationally involved the following steps:

1. A middle-level official of the Plans and Policy Division of the Air Force (Department of Defense) informally notified a middle-level official in the Directorate for European and NATO Affairs (Office of the Assistant Secretary of Defense for International

---

[21] It should be noted that the definitional base has been shifted somewhat between determining the preprocess/process stage boundary and the process/postprocess stage boundary; the first is based on behavior whereas the second is based on perception. If the behaviorally oriented definition were used for consistency to determine the boundaries of both stages, this would shift the emphasis in analysis away from the significant questions about the differences between issue resolution and implementation as well as the concomitant differing utility of transgovernmental and transnational activity in the resolution and implementation phases. Although this alternative is still conceptually possible, at this point in my research using the behaviorally oriented definition for both cases would have few theoretical advantages, except perhaps in making it easier to identify the process/postprocess stage boundary. But since the perceptual defintion is also organizationally based, it has also proven empirically applicable.

Security Affairs) that the military was planning a cutback including US military personnel and Canadian civilian employees at Canadian Base X.

2. This second official consulted with an official of the Plans and Policy Directorate, Western Hemisphere (Joint Staff, Joint Chiefs of Staff, Department of Defense) and an official of the Office of Canadian Affairs (Bureau of European Affairs, Department of State) regarding the most appropriate means of consulting with the government of Canada.

This preprocess stage formally occurred entirely within the United States government. A general decision to close 330 bases catalyzed those US officials responsible for United States–Canadian defense relations. These officials discussed channels through which the issue would be processed, and coalitions within the United States government were formed in an attempt to decide what the United States position should be and what was negotiable concerning anticipated Canadian reactions. Organizationally the US actor expansion was noteworthy in this preprocess stage. The first step occurred entirely within two organizational units of the Department of Defense, while step two expanded to a third Department of Defense unit and included a unit in the Department of State.

The *process stage* of this issue flow organizationally involved the following steps.

1. A middle-level foreign service officer of the Office of Canadian Affairs approached the counsellor for political-military affairs in the Canadian embassy, outlining the overall issue and requesting at what level the Canadian would like to discuss it.

2. As a result, the minister of the Canadian embassy met with the following US officials: director, Directorate for European and NATO Affairs; director, Office of Canadian Affairs; chief, Plans and Policy Directorate; an official from the Office of the Assistant Secretary of Defense for Public Affairs; and an official of the Plans and Policy Division of the Air Force. The Canadan minister was briefed on US intentions, and the United States officials requested Canadian concurrence regarding press release policy. The minister of the Canadian Embassy requested time to discuss the issue with relevant Canadian officials, including local officials in the Base X area.

3. Internal Canadian government discussions followed, involving ministers of five Canadian government departments: National Defense, External Affairs, Transport, Supply and Services, and Manpower and Immigration. Local officials were also consulted.

4. The Canadian ambassador made requests regarding severance conditions for Base X Canadian personnel and met with US officials at the level of assistant secretary of defense for international security affairs.

5. The US officials reviewed the issue completely and received approval at the secretary of defense level to agree to certain of the Canadian requests. The United States position was returned through the assistant secretary of defense level.

6. After the Canadian ambassador consulted with his government, the counsellor of the embassy telephoned his government's concurrence in the press release policy and registered no objection to the US position.

This process stage involved both interactions within each government and transborder interactions between the two governments. Steps one and two consisted of the presentation of the United States position to the Canadian embassy (transborder). Again, the actor expansion was noteworthy, both organizationally and functionally. Step one involved a middle level of the Department of State and the Canadian counsellor, while step two involved the Canadian minister and high-level US officials representing four organizational units of the Department of Defense and one unit of the Department of State. Step three consisted of the Canadian formulation of its position and included very high-level discussions involving ministers of five government departments as well as local officials. Step four consisted of the Canadian presentation of its position to United States officials (transborder). Step five consisted of the US consideration and reply to the Canadian position (transborder). Step six involved the Canadian consideration of the United States position and resolution of the issue (transborder).

The *postprocess stage* of this issue flow organizationally involved the following step:

At Base X, the US base commander, nearest US consul general, local officials, and representatives of the five Canadian government departments began planning to alleviate economic problems and to investigate possible Canadian use of part of Base X facilities.

Hence, the postprocess stage involved United States and Canadian officials meeting to facilitate the implementation of the agreement reached in the process stage.

MIXED TRANSACTIONS: THE UTILITY OF TRANSNATIONAL AND TRANSGOVERNMENTAL ACTIVITY IN INTERGOVERNMENTAL FLOWS

Mixed transactions refer to intergovernmental flows having transnational or transgovernmental activity that does not essentially alter the outcome of the flows themselves. That is, those decisions involved in intergovernmental issue flows are not significantly affected by, or dependent upon, this transnational or transgovernmental activity.[22] Given the importance of holding the intergovernmental dimension as an analytical referent, I differ from the editors of this volume by expanding the definition of intergovernmental relations to include situations in which one actor is governmental and the other(s) transnational or transgovernmental. The alternative of defining such mixed transactions as transnational or transgovernmental would preclude their consideration as part of an intergovernmental flow, with attendant analytical constraints.

The advantages of holding an expanded intergovernmental category are threefold. It permits direct examination of (1) transnational and transgovernmental activity in governmental decision-making processes (i.e., especially the dynamics of transformative transactions as discussed in section four), (2) the decisional cost-benefits of this activity in these processes (i.e., the very utility of this activity in intergovernmental flows), and (3) the entire question of governmental erosion and control concerning this activity (i.e., the extent to which governmental decision-making processes mitigate for or against this activity in conjunction with the need for, and feasibility of, governmental control mechanisms). My use of this expanded

---

[22] To summarize and extend the concepts developed in this article, *pure transactions* are those transborder flows in which all the actors are of the same type. There are three categories: (1) pure intergovernmental, involving purely governmental actors acting in accordance with their organizational mandates (but including nongovernmental actors whose activities are entirely integrated into the organizational interfaces of the mandates of the governmental actors); (2) pure transnational, involving purely nongovernmental actors; and (3) pure transgovernmental, involving purely governmental actors acting outside their organizational mandates. *Mixed transactions* are those transborder flows involving more than one type of actor but in which the new actor(s) does not predominate. There are two categories. The first is intergovernmental, involving, in addition to predominate governmental actors acting within their mandates, transnational and/or transgovernmental actors. Thus, any flow involving governmental actors acting within their mandates at any point and at any level, regardless of salience, is considered a mixed intergovernmental flow. (It should be noted that any intergovernmental flow not termed *pure* refers to mixed intergovernmental flows.) The second category of mixed transactions is transnational/transgovernmental, involving a combination of transnational and transgovernmental actors, but without any governmental actors acting within their mandates at any point, at any level, and to any extent in that flow.

intergovernmental category is not without its costs, for it does not permit direct examination of the pure transnational, pure transgovernmental, or mixed transnational/transgovernmental categories.[23] However, these are limited categories, for there would seem to be relatively few transborder sequences of major import concerning loss of governmental control in which governmental actors would not formally attempt to monitor and control the activities in these sequences by interjecting themselves into the flows. This interjection would at least consist of formally notifying these actors of the relevance to their activities of the appropriate governmental parameters, if not legal frameworks. This notification would thus shift the pure transnational, pure transgovernmental, or mixed transnational/transgovernmental flows to the mixed intergovernmental category because the governmental actors become formally involved in the flows.[24]

The question at this point is, What is the utility of transnational and transgovernmental activity for those actors engaged in it? It can be hypothesized that its usefulness is dependent upon the stage in which it occurs in an intergovernmental flow. Three distinct types of this activity can be isolated. *Formulative* transnational or transgovernmental activity occurs in the preprocess stage when actors interject their position into another government's decision making before formal transborder contact is made. This interjection, which can create transborder coalitions, can be initiated by the actors themselves, or their participation can be invited by the actors of the other government. Such interjection enables actors to participate in another government's decision making before the procedures and positions of the latter government have coalesced. However, because the preprocess stage formally occurs entirely within a single government, it may be difficult for external actors to determine who is responsible for dealing with the issue. Moreover, it may be counterproductive for these external actors to become involved in the internal affairs of another government. *Resolutive* transnational or transgovernmental activity occurs in the process stage. Too late to define the conceptual and organizational framework of the issue flow, bureaucratic coalitions within each government line up with their transborder counterparts to maximize their positions and influence the outcome of the issue flow in a manner satisfactory to them. *Facilita-*

---

[23] For a definition of these three categories, see the preceding footnote.

[24] Even in those limited instances in which there is no formal governmental interjection in some form, examinations of pure transnational, pure transgovernmental, or mixed transnational/transgovernmental flows still require the use of mandated governmental activities as a definitional base against which the fact of organizational deviation can be verified as a prelude to categorization.

tive activity occurs too late to form transborder coalitions to influence issue outcomes. It is, however, still possible for transborder actors and coalitions to facilitate the implementation in a manner favorable to them. Both resolutive and facilitative activities are easier to undertake than formulative activities because the actors responsible for the issue are clearly delineated through transborder contacts which are themselves both legitimized and regularized through formal negotiating procedures. All three types of transnational and transgovernmental activity are particularly useful in that they enable actors to receive external support vis-à-vis internal bureaucratic coalitions.

An illustrative case of formulative transgovernmental activity occurred in the autumn of 1973, when the Canadian defence minister announced a five-year financing formula for Canadian defense expenditures. These budgetary arrangements prompted Canadian defense officials to decide to close three Pinetree radars in order to increase procurement flexibility in other areas. This decision was viewed as affecting United States defense interests.

1. In September United States defense officials held meetings with their Canadian counterparts in Ottawa. During one of these meetings, Canadian officials explained their intention and reasons for terminating the three radars. They then presented the US officials with the draft of a diplomatic note concerning the closings that they intended formally to submit to the US government. The Canadian officials requested that the United States officials (who would also process the formal note in Washington) read the draft note and discuss revisions with them before departing.

2. This first stage would then be followed by the Canadian government sending a formal diplomatic note to the United States government incorporating the suggestions of the US officials.

The utility of this formulative transgovernmental activity to both governments is significant. By inviting US officials to become involved in their preprocess stage internal discussions, Canadian officials, who initiated the flow, could test United States responsiveness to their position and absorb US reservations before formal negotiations began. The advantage to US officials consisted of their participation in the definition of the Canadian bargaining position and procedures before they had coalesced.

An illustration of resolutive activity occurred in January 1963 and deals with the Canadian acquisition of nuclear warheads which the United States and Canada had been formally discussing for some time.[25] Retiring as the Supreme Allied Commander Europe (SAC-EUR), General Lauris Norstad took his leave by visiting the NATO capitals.[26]

1. In Ottawa, Norstad first called on the governor general. Although Prime Minister Diefenbaker was in Ottawa he did not meet with the general. Associate Minister of National Defence Pierre Sevigny acted as the general's host.

2. During a press conference on 3 January 1963, Norstad asserted that contrary to the official Canadian government's position, Canada was committed to the acquisition of nuclear weapons within NATO, that the commitment had not been fulfilled, and that a prerequisite for both the emergency nuclear arms equipping of Canada's air division in NATO and the nuclear training of this division was a bilateral agreement with the United States.

Norstad was the first top-level NATO officer to take this position publicly. The impact of his press conference stemmed entirely from his NATO organizational role. His opinion of Canada's commitment therefore carried great weight in influencing Canadian opinion. And the fact that it was expressed on Canadian soil interjected it into the mainstream of the increasingly agitated Canadian public debate. This then tended to fortify the US position on the Canadian acquisition of nuclear weapons and armed those Canadians who opposed the government's policy. The general's action illustrates resolutive activity in that it constituted an attempt to influence the conclusion of the Canadian nuclear debate during the process stage in a manner satisfactory to the organization with which he was associated.

An illustration of facilitative transgovernmental activity occurred in June 1942.[27] US officials concerned about the Japanese threat to the Aleutian Islands held discussions with Canadian officials in which it was agreed that the Royal Canadian Air Force (RCAF)

[25] More specifically, this illustrates the transborder activity of a representative of an international organization that deviated from the SOPs followed among the international organization and national governments. However, space limitations preclude a discussion of the interesting question of Norstad's empirical, and hence analytical, status.

[26] This case study is abstracted from Peyton Lyon, "The Norstad Press Conference," in *Canadian Foreign Policy Since 1945*, ed. J. L. Granatstein (Toronto: The Copp Clark Publishing Co., 1970), pp. 111-14.

[27] This case study is abstracted from C. P. Stacey, p. 120. It illustrates transgovernmental activity that was encouraged by the joint organizational framework between the two nations in the defense area. In examining transnational and transgovernmental activity in this area, attention should be directed at all seven contemporary US-Canadian defense organizations, which are interesting because they are oriented toward formal political-military negotiation to a lesser extent than may be expected. Of the seven joint organizations, one is directly concerned

would provide immediate air reinforcements for Alaska. Although agreement was reached, the actual measures undertaken by the Canadian authorities were regarded as being insufficient by US officials.

1. To facilitate Canadian action on the US-Canadian agreement, Lieutenant-General Stanley D. Embick, the United States Army member of PJBD, telephoned Air Commodore F. V. Heakes, the RCAF member of the board. Embick, citing the formal joint war plan, requested that Heakes expedite matters to accelerate Canadian action.
2. Heakes agreed with Embick, interjected his request into the Canadian military decision-making process, and two RCAF squadrons were immediately ordered to move to Yakutat by the chief of the Canadian Air Staff.

Notwithstanding the fact that PJBD is an advisory body, this was an illustration of an executive action performed by a member of the board acting transgovernmentally. Indeed, although the issue had been resolved, further activity was deemed necessary in the postprocess stage to facilitate the implementation of the agreement.

TRANSFORMATIVE TRANSACTIONS

Given transnational and transgovernmental activity in intergovernmental flows (mixed transactions), can transnational or transgovernmental actors performing this activity predominate, and if so, what happens to the flows themselves? It is indeed possible that at some stage in an intergovernmental flow, governmental activity is absorbed or superseded by transnational or transgovernmental activity. The flow is therefore transformed from an intergovernmental one into a transnational one (*transnationalization*) or a transgovernmental one (*transgovernmentalization*). However, more important in the United States–Canadian defense issue area is the reverse variation—the transformation of a transnational or transgovernmental flow into an intergovernmental one (*intergovernmentalization*). All three forms are subsumed under the term *transformative transactions*, referring to flows in which new actors become involved and predominate in the sense that they significantly affect the decisions made in, and hence the outcomes of, the flows themselves. It must be emphasized that discussions of actor predominance refer both to replacing

with active strategic protection (NORAD); two perform planning-recommendatory functions (PJBD and MCC); one is concerned with the economics of defense (Senior Committee of DPSA); one with emergency planning (Civil Emergency Planning Committee); one with liaison (RPG/NATO); and one with cabinet-level consultation (Ministerial Committee on Joint Defense).

one actor with another and to the same actor starting out in one role and later switching to another role.

A case of intergovernmentalization occurred in 1943 with the Canadian decision to use its forces in the US campaign against the Japanese in the Aleutian Islands.[28] On 19 April General John deWitt (commanding general of US Western Defense Command) visited Major General G. R. Pearkes (Canadian G.O.C. Pacific Command) in Vancouver. They discussed the feasibility of a combined US-Canadian attack on the Japanese enclave at Kiska. Pearkes's report to his superiors did not mention possible Canadian participation.

1. On 8 May Major General Maurice Pope (chairman, Canadian Joint Staff Mission in Washington, Canadian member of PJBD, and liaison between the Canadian War Committee in Ottawa and the Combined Chiefs of Staff in Washington) discussed the matter with J. D. Hickerson (US Department of State officer and secretary of the US section of PJBD). Pope reported this conversation to Lieutenant General Stuart in Ottawa (chief of the Canadian General Staff), and on 12 May Stuart authorized Pope to discuss the project with General George Marshall (chief of staff, US Army). However, in his message to Pope, Stuart acknowledged that the minister of national defense (Ralston) had not yet been consulted in the matter.

2. Pope met with Marshall, and on 24 May learned that United States officers were pleased with the prospect of Canadian forces participating. Marshall also authorized deWitt to meet with Pearkes to establish plans and procedures.

3. The War Committee of the Canadian cabinet learned of the plans at this point. Prime Minister King was upset that his military officers had negotiated with their US counterparts before higher-level Canadian officials knew fully what was being proposed. On 28 May King and Ralston learned that Canadian forces were enroute. (There were eighteen officers going as observers.) King was distressed about this Canadian involvement occurring without his knowledge and without a request from the United States Joint Chiefs of Staff. He insisted that an invitation would have to come from either the president or the US secretary of war (Stimson).

4. In Washington Pope informed Hickerson that Canada wanted an invitation from the secretary of war to the minister of national defense. Pope then visited the US deputy chief of staff, notifying

---

[28] This case study is abstracted from James Eayrs, *The Art of the Possible* (Toronto: University of Toronto Press, 1961), pp. 82-85.

him of the request. A letter from Stimson to Ralston followed. After consideration in a 31 May Canadian meeting, it was approved in principle that Canadians would join United States forces, only a day before the invading force was dispatched.

This flow was initiated by transgovernmental actors acting independently of higher-level governmental authorities. King noted in his diary that he "objected strongly to our Chiefs of Staff and others of the High Command in Canada negotiating with corresponding numbers in the U.S. before the Minister had a full knowledge of what was proposed, the War Committee included, and most of all, myself as Prime Minister." However, the flow was transformed into an intergovernmental flow through a high-level authorization insisted upon by the prime minister himself. Again, to quote King: "It was finally agreed that the communication would have to come from either the President to myself, or Stimson to Ralston, to get matters on Ministerial level and out simply of the military level; indeed this whole thing has worked from the bottom up instead of from the top down. . . ." In short, the transgovernmental actors in the flow could not maintain their predominance because the final decision to proceed rested with higher-level governmental actors. Indeed, the actor risks involved in such transgovernmental activity are evident in King's assessment: "I would have insisted on a cancellation of the whole thing, were it not that . . . to have cut it off would have raised a serious situation regarding relations to U.S. and Canadian armies on the Pacific, and probably involve Stuart's resignation." [29] After the authorization of this transaction through the Stimson-Ralston correspondence, the transgovernmental actors themselves switched roles by becoming governmental actors in performing activities that now had been formally legitimized.

It should be noted that the implementation of King's requirement for a higher-level formal decision was not an easy request because it involved United States organizational SOPs. Given different SOPs on both higher and lower levels and involving civilian-military control as well as the jealousy with which the US organizational units guarded them from intrusion by other units, difficulties arose on the United States side. Pope is quoted as saying that when he told Hickerson the Canadian government wanted an invitation from the secretary to the minister to collaborate, Hickerson "laughingly told me to forget whatever Calvinistic tendencies there might be in my system and not to set out in an attempt to reform U.S. army procedure." [30] The US deputy chief of staff who finally approved the communication was at first

[29] Eayrs, p. 84.
[30] Eayrs, p. 84-85.

"hostile" but finally agreed that there was "no reason why Mr. Stimson should not address a general invitation to Mr. Ralston provided all details were settled through the military channel," adding that he did "not want this approach to Canada to go anywhere near the State Department." [31]

SUMMATION AND ASSESSMENT

In view of those factors encouraging transnational and transgovernmental activity in the defense issue area, one might conclude that even a casual projection would have to emphasize a continuing if not increasing transnational and transgovernmental content. However, such a conclusion would disregard the major factor militating against this activity. Of all the issue areas, that of defense involves matters of especially high national policy in conjunction with a government's insistence on maximum secrecy and maneuverability of action. In a more general sense, the extent to which transnational and transgovernmental activity is permitted by authoritative actors is dependent upon two facets of actor behavior—their tolerance level concerning this activity, and their decisional resources in monitoring and controlling it. This is essentially a question of the extent to which actors, at all organizational levels, attempt and are able to maintain a central role in making those decisions determining the outcome of a given issue. It can be speculated that most authoritative actors have a bias against unintegrated activity to the extent that it involves a loss of their decisional centrality.[32] However, they tend to utilize such activity themselves when they see it as being operationally effective, while simultaneously disavowing that it is unintegrated. And they may have a point, for while their organizational responsibilities are generally quite clearly defined, their operational roles are to a great extent self-determined and self-fulfilling. An actor's decisional resources in monitoring unintegrated activity are especially complex, for those capabilities enabling an actor to make a decision depend upon, inter alia, the extent to which he plays a central role within his organizational unit, and the extent to which his organizational unit plays a central role within the overall organization and sets of organizations.

---

[31] Eayrs, p. 85.

[32] In the defense issue area, this transgovernmental activity can involve the most basic constitutional considerations of the two governments—the parameters set by civilian control of the military. Transnational activity is also sensitive, but here there is a tradition of harnessing these actors. For example, the chairman of the 1917 Canadian War Mission to the US was Lloyd Harris, director of Massey-Harris. The prevelance of "dollar-a-year" men in the Canadian government defense production effort during World War II and the career patterns of many corporation executives are in keeping with this tradition.

The unknown factor regarding transnational and transgovernmental activity in all issue areas concerns shifts in overall organizational and governmental priorities. For example, defense matters in the United States have constituted the high priority item throughout the cold war, but current indications are that economic preoccupations have assumed the importance heretofore reserved for defense matters. Certainly such shifts are a major factor affecting transnational and transgovernmental activity, but how and to what extent we do not know. Indeed, we have not established the interrelationships between the priority level of an issue, the amount of activity within a government and between governments in conjunction with the priority level, and the degree of transnational and transgovernmental activity with respect to priority and amount. Nor have we examined in the context of transnational and transgovernmental relations the impact of shifts of governmental priorities on the dynamics of politicization (i.e., issues being raised from functional to political levels) and depoliticization. Nor have we rigorously considered the possibility that there may be entirely different decisional flows among the different issue areas, and within an issue area concerning the actor level at which an issue is processed.[33]

The assessment of decisional cost-benefits of transnational and transgovernmental activity is especially difficult. Suffice it to say that any assessment must take into account four considerations. Such assessments ultimately depend upon the referrent (i.e., is it being assessed from the standpoint of the United States, Canada, or the United States and Canada). Secondly, it must be acknowledged that the decisional motivations for pursuing congruent policies may be based on different if not contradictory interests, and that the cost-benefits accruing to both governments are not necessarily of the same type. Thirdly, caution must be exercised with respect to the superimposition of present preoccupations in evaluating past transactions. Finally, caution must be exercised concerning presuppositions that bargaining situations are inherently those in which one actor's gain is the other's loss.

An illustrative example of both the shift in issue priorities and the resultant assessment of cost-benefits concerns the United States–Canadian defense production sharing agreements.[34] Certainly the ad-

---

[33] I have found it useful to distinguish between two hierarchical categories of issues: *substantial issues*, those that require resolution at the level of the assistant secretary/assistant deputy minister or above on the part of at least one government, and *action issues*, those that are processed below this level.

[34] As background, Canadian curtailment of the CF-105 program suggested its future inability to develop major weapons systems independently, triggering concern about the viability of Canadian defense industry with all the domestic eco-

vantages Canada obtained in the 1959 agreement were noteworthy—
significant exemptions from the "Buy America Act" and regular US
customs duties. However, the 1959 arrangements were altered as
early as 1963 when it was agreed in principle that in the long run
there should be a general balance in the transborder defense trade. It
was this understanding that caused current difficulties given a cumulative United States $500 million deficit with Canada on the trans-
border defense trade. What appears to have happened is that the
United States assessment of the cost-benefits stemming from the
agreements have shifted as a result of an overall shift in United
States government priorities. That is, when United States priorities
shifted from strategic to economic, the US criterion of the agreements
became largely that of the effect on the balance of payments. Heretofore the United States was willing to endure what it saw as an increasing deficit with Canada due to such strategically important factors as
the maintenance of a Canadian defense industry in conjunction with
joint military collaboration and the acquisition of Canadian defense
materials for use in the Vietnam conflict. Hence, the US reexamina-
tion of the agreements resulted from the shift in overall governmental
priorities as between strategic and economic factors.

The Canadian assessment of the cost-benefits of the overall defense relationship includes to a very great extent political criteria in
terms of the United States impact on Canadian territorial and conceptual sovereignty. Indeed, the Canadian concern about the United
States impact, which is essentially attributable to bilateral isolation
and disparity, adds a major political dimension concerning the Canadian assessment of both United States defense activities in Canada
and the effect of Canada's involvement with the United States on
Canadian independence of external action. However, the case can
be made that the United States–Canadian defense relationship operates not in spite of different evaluative criteria but because of them.
That is, it may be because of these differing United States and Canadian perceptions of the defense links being formed, and the dissimilar United States and Canadian cost-benefits generated, that the
defense linkage is often possible in the first place. However, these
same differences may simultaneously limit its longevity as the international situation changes. If this speculation is substantiated, it

nomic ramifications. The US government was concerned about the viability of
Canadian defense industry in the overall strategic context of NORAD. However,
caution must be exercised in attributing decisional motivation to US and Canadian
officials, for it is tempting to oversimplify the dynamics of that period by juxta-
posing a purely Canadian economic preoccupation against a purely US strategic
one (e.g., US officials also perceived the agreements as having an economic
dimension in holding down US procurement costs).

would suggest that the United States–Canadian defense relationship is bilaterally dysfunctional. That is, it could be that what makes the defense relationship useful for both the United States and Canada (in enabling both nations, and especially Canada, to register and pursue their self-definition of national needs) results in a defense involvement that is bilaterally dysfunctional in the sense that differing decisional motivations and subsequent dissimilar benefits ensure fundamental United States and Canadian disagreement in the future.

The implications of this speculation for transnational and transgovernmental activity are important in analyses of the extent to which the US-Canadian defense relationship is an integrative process, especially in terms of its irreversibility. For example, this speculation might suggest that the linkages will not pass an irreversible point in terms of an integrative process, notwithstanding transnational and transgovernmental activity. On the contrary, it could be that the differing perceptions and subsequent cost-benefits ensure future disagreements that tend to arrest integrative dynamics precisely because these disagreements are grounded in the nature of the defense relationship itself.[35]

It may be added as a concluding note that the absence of descriptive propositions concerning the general nature and extent of transnational and transgovernmental transactions in the defense issue area does not stem from the absence of empirical data available on US-Canadian relations. Rather, it derives from the fact that the world polity perspective as heretofore developed has not provided adequate analytical tools for such descriptions, quite apart from explanation and prescription. In short, an examination of the US-Canadian defense issue area from a world polity perspective tells us less about substantive questions in this area than it does about those conceptual directions and empirical applications required if analysts are to explore meaningfully the dynamics of transborder governmental and nongovernmental interrelationships.

---

[35] This of course points to the need for rigorous empirical investigation of an organizational and governmental unit's disassociation possibilities and costs as the originally different but convergent forces furthering integration lessen. It may also be noted that the problem with any alliance is that as those congruent threat perceptions that create and sustain it diminish, the alliance becomes less cohesive. But if rather than congruent threat perceptions perpetuating an alliance, there are fundamentally different assumed payoffs, alliance cohesiveness is a priori subject to lesser-order disturbances than those that stem from a perceived diminuation of the external threat. Obviously this is not an either/or situation since all alliances involve both military and nonmilitary payoffs. However, the US-Canadian defense relationship, because of its bilateral isolation and disparity, might be especially characterized by a dichotomous payoff structure.

CANADIAN LABOR IN THE CONTINENTAL PERSPECTIVE

Robert W. Cox and Stuart M. Jamieson

The concept of a transnational system applies well to a study of labor in North America. For one thing, the chief characteristics of the labor market and of the institutions, procedures, and practices of labor relations are broadly similar in Canada and the United States as compared with other parts of the world.[1] Although such similarities are not alone sufficient to suggest a *system*, there is also a persistent structure of relationships and interactions in labor matters extending across the boundary between the two countries. American investment in Canada and the so-called international unions [2] are at the heart of this structure of relationships. Other segments of labor, whether organized in trade unions or unorganized, are connected with the heart of this transnational system through the continental flow of economic transactions.

Our aim in this article is to outline this transnational labor relations system, with particular reference to the way different segments of Canadian labor fit into it. The definition of a distinct Canadian identity and the issue of Canadian independence from American cultural and economic control have in recent years come to the fore in labor circles as among other groups in Canadian society. To depict Canadian labor within a continental system is not to deny these goals

Robert W. Cox is a professor in the Department of Political Science and the School of International Affairs at Columbia University, and Stuart M. Jamieson is a professor of economics at the University of British Columbia in Vancouver.

[1] Arthur M. Ross and Paul T. Hartman, *Changing Patterns of Industrial Conflict* (New York: Wiley, 1960), p. 5, considered that the industrial relations of the two countries constitute a single *system*.

[2] *International unions* (a concept peculiar to the North American continent) are trade unions with branches in both Canada and the United States. The membership and chief executives of these unions are overwhelmingly American, and their headquarters are entirely in the United States. Most are affiliated with the American Federation of Labor and the Congress of Industrial Organizations (AFL-CIO). Well over half of all union locals and almost two-thirds of all union members in Canada belong to international organizations.

of identity and independence; it could be an analytical prerequisite to a more realistic and effective strategy for affirming these goals.

The principal features that distinguish the position of labor in Canada and the United States from that in other comparably industrialized areas of Western Europe and the Pacific rim can be summarized briefly as follows:

1. A minority of less than one-third of the paid labor force is organized in unions, and only a slightly larger fraction has its conditions of work governed by collective bargaining. Concentrated as it is in the key sectors of the economy, however, the organized minority sets a pattern that influences conditions for the unorganized majority.

2. In the unionized sector, a bipartite relationship between unions and employers has been the predominant mode of resolving issues over wages and working conditions. Governmental intervention, i.e., in a tripartite relationship, has been minimal and is in general contrary to the dominant ideologies of both unions and management. Nor do unions play a very significant role in influencing government policy through planning or administrative agencies. Legislation and government intervention have been concerned primarily with maintaining an orderly framework and (by conciliation and mediation services) facilitating decisions through the bipartite relationship, rather than with influencing decisions in line with government policy goals.[3]

3. In the tradition established firmly by the American Federation of Labor in the late 1880s, there has been major emphasis on ensuring clear and exclusive jurisdiction of each union in a certain industry, trade, or plant (or groups of these), and elimination of *dual unionism*. This tradition has been enforced for more than three decades by the device of legal certification under American and Canadian legislation.

4. The basic power relations are at the level of the individual company or plant. However, plant-level contestants are often supported by the resources of headquarters, of corporate headquarters in management's case and of union headquarters in the union's case.

5. Most labor organizations pursue a policy of *business unionism*, oriented primarily toward the immediate material goals of their members, and the security, power, and prestige of the individual organizations themselves, rather than toward longer-run and broader objectives of social reform or radical change.

[3] Recent attempts to apply incomes policies represent a departure from this practice in the direction of tripartism. Unions in both countries continue to be suspicious of incomes policies.

6. The central federations are concerned mainly with political action, legislative lobbying, and foreign affairs, and have little authority or influence over their affiliated organizations in specifically trade union matters.

This, in brief, is the North American model of labor relations, pointing up the broad similarities between Canada and the United States. Of course, the Canadian scene also differs significantly from the American. Organized labor in Canada seems to have had far less political clout than does the American Federation of Labor–Congress of Industrial Organizations (AFL-CIO) in Washington, D. C., and most state legislatures. There is a higher degree of industrial concentration in Canada than in the United States, with one or a few large corporations exerting monopolistic or oligopolistic control over major fields of manufacturing or resource industries, finance, and other major sectors. By contrast, labor organization in Canada is more fragmented and divided than in the United States, so that to speak of a Canadian labor movement is an expression of hope rather than a reflection of reality. Organized labor in Canada comprises, essentially, large numbers of relatively small unions separated by great distances from one another across the country, and a few fairly large organizations confined for the most part to a few major industries in particular regions. The Canadian Labour Congress reflects this structure. It is a loose, decentralized federation of many geographically dispersed, small and medium-sized unions and a few large, geographically concentrated organizations.

Both capital and organized labor in Canada reflect the dependent nature of the Canadian economy and its colonial origins. Prior to World War I, most Canadian industry was financed and controlled by British interests. Since World War II, American capital has played an increasingly dominant role. Today the 4,000-odd branch plants or subsidiaries of American firms employ a large fraction, possibly a majority, of unionized Canadian workers. In the growth of trade unionism too, external influences have outweighed purely local initiative in Canada. During the nineteenth century, American, British, and European influences could be observed in the building of unions, and during the twentieth century American models and direct organizational activities have predominated in the growth of trade unions.[1]

Broadly generalizing, labor in Canada has been weaker in relation both to employers and to political leadership than is labor in the United States. And both employers and labor in Canada stand in a

---

[1] Harold A. Logan, Norman P. Ware, and Harold A. Innis, *Labour in Canadian-American Relations* (Toronto: Ryerson Press, 1937).

subordinate and dependent relationship to their counterparts in the US.[5] To document these propositions in detail, incorporating such nuances and exceptions as may be necessary, goes beyond the scope of this article.[6] Our purpose is rather to propose a framework of ideas that may help explain them. We offer this framework in the form of a paradigm of the power relations affecting labor. We hope the approach we suggest may be found useful, but wish to stress its preliminary character. To apply this framework empirically would require more extensive research than we have been able to do within the compass of this study.

THE STRUCTURE OF POWER RELATIONS: A PARADIGM

A transnational system implies a persistent structure of relationships extending across national boundaries. The term *structure* is used here in a fairly comprehensive way to include (1) formal organization, such as multinational corporations and international unions, (2) regular patterns of interaction of the relevant actors which are only partly through formal organizations, e.g., the processes of collective bargaining in an industry, and (3) relationships through the economy that juxtapose identifiable groups in a persistent way, e.g., where producers of one commodity supply users in another industry so that links of interdependency exist between them, or where the labor supply in one area is dependent upon one or a few employers. Being concerned with the structure of relationships affecting the whole labor force, we must consider the more than two-thirds who are not union members as well as those who are.

Three distinct currents of theory help us to define our framework. The first is the center-periphery model of dependency theorists, which has been applied both to economic relationships and to the broader set of political and cultural relationships.[7] Center-periphery theorists dis-

---

[5] Reactions against this dependency have occurred amongst workers, as in other population groups, through efforts to organize purely Canadian labor movements and numerous breakaways of Canadian local or regional branches demanding greater autonomy or independence from their American parent bodies. Both phenomena have been confined for the most part to particular regions or provinces, most notably Quebec and the west, especially British Columbia.

[6] There is a considerable literature on foreign investment in Canada referred to in other articles in this volume. On labor, see especially John Crispo, *International Unionism—A Study in Canadian-American Relations* (Toronto: McGraw-Hill, 1967) ; and Logan, Ware, and Innis, *Labour in Canadian-American Relations*.

[7] Among applications of the model to economics, see François Perroux, "Esquisse d'une théorie de l'économie dominante," *Economie appliquée*, no. 1 (jan-mars 1948) ; Gunnar Myrdal, *Economic Theory and Underdeveloped Regions* (New York: Harper and Row, 1957) ; Arghiri Emmanuel, *Unequal Exchange, A Study of the Imperialism of Trade* (New York: Monthly Review, 1972; originally published in French, Paris: Maspero, 1969) ; Samir Amin, *L'accumulation à l'échelle mondiale* (Paris: Ifan-Anthropos, 1970). As regards Canada, see Mel-

tinguish not only between national economies, some of which stand in a dependent or peripheral relationship to others, but also within countries between internal centers and internal peripheries linked in dependency relationships. The key to the transnational structure of dependency is the way the centers of two national economies are linked and the relationship of each with its internal periphery.

The second relevant current of theory is a model of labor market dualism developed recently by some American labor economists. They distinguish between a primary labor market with limited points of entry followed by career development within large organizations and a secondary labor market with multiple entry points to employment, virtually no career development, and considerable turnover. The purest case of the dual labor market has been Japan with its lifetime commitment labor force in big industry, flanked by the use of subcontracting and temporary workers; but the same essential structures have been found to exist in fact if not in ideology in other advanced industrial countries, including the United States.[8] In the primary labor market, employment is relatively stable, and skills are relatively high and are systematically developed. In the secondary labor market, skills are relatively low, and employment unstable. Those in the secondary labor market pay disproportionately the social costs of a downturn in the level of economic activity; they are the expendables who first experience unemployment and cushion the economic drop for the more fortunate ones in the primary labor market. In center-periphery terms, the secondary labor market is an internal periphery.

The third theoretical approach is through a typology of modes of social relations in production.[9] The types we use were developed for

ville H. Watkins, "A Staple Theory of Economic Growth," *The Canadian Journal of Economics and Political Science* 29 (May 1963): 144-58; and Kari Levitt, *Silent Surrender: The Multinational Corporation in Canada* (Toronto: Macmillan of Canada, 1970). Broader applications of the center-periphery approach to political and cultural linkages include Johan Galtung, "A Structural Theory of Imperialism," *Journal of Peace Research* 8, no. 2 (1971); F. H. Cardoso and Enzo Faletto, *Dependencia y desarollo en America Latina* (Mexico: Siglo veintiuno, 1969). Of special interest in connection with our study, since it deals with dependency relationships in the trade union field, is Jeffrey Harrod, *Trade Union Foreign Policy: The Case of British and American Unions in Jamaica* (Garden City, N.Y.: Doubleday, 1972).

[8] See Peter B. Doeringer and Michael J. Piore, *Internal Labor Markets and Manpower Analysis* (Lexington, Mass.: D. C. Heath, 1971); and Peter B. Doeringer, "Low Pay, Labor Market Dualism, and Industrial Relations Systems," Discussion Paper No. 271 of the Harvard Institute of Economic Research, 1973. (Mimeographed.)

[9] See Robert W. Cox, Jeffrey Harrod, et al., *Future Industrial Relations: An Interim Report* (Geneva: International Institute for Labour Studies, 1972). The concepts used in this report which is global in its scope were applied in more detail to North America by Mark Thompson in a publication by the Institute in the same series.

the purpose of classifying together workers in different countries whose power position in relation to production is essentially similar, and for studying trends in industrial relations over time and future probabilities from an analysis of the nature and dynamics of these modes and of their interrelationships.

As indicated above, the *bipartite* mode is preeminent in North America, in the sense that collective bargaining between employers and unions without state interference is widely regarded as the most legitimate form of decision making in labor matters. This is not, however, the majority's mode in North America; it is estimated that this mode covers only about 27 percent of workers. Bipartism's strength is in the major industries with a concentration of large corporations (such as steel or automobiles) and also in some industries characterized by a larger number of smaller employers where powerful unions effectively manage the labor market (e.g., in construction and road transport). A very substantial proportion of workers in some large organizations, both private and public, have their conditions determined through personnel management, in a kind of bureaucratized and impersonalized paternalism that can be called the *enterprise corporatist* mode. They account for about 20 percent of the North American labor force. *Tripartite* relationships, in which government is an active participant in influencing outcomes, have covered only a smaller number of workers, about 3 percent. These three modes together, totalling about 50 percent of the labor force, correspond roughly to the primary labor market, i.e., to the highest paid, highest skilled, most steadily employed, and most generally privileged part of the labor force.

The largest single mode in North America is the *enterprise labor market*, consisting largely of workers in smaller establishments, in commerce, and so forth—about 37 percent of the labor force in all. A small proportion of the total, about 4 percent, mostly migrants from rural areas, provide a pool of unskilled casual labor analogous to the marginal populations in less developed areas; these people are in a *primitive labor market* mode. The two last mentioned modes correspond roughly to the secondary labor market. In them are to be found most workers with a background of relative poverty and low education, the least favored ethnic groups, the most likely recipients of welfare. Unionization has made relatively little impact among them.[10]

---

[10] The remaining 9 percent are self-employed workers. Some, like consultants and professionals, exist in dependent relationship with the big organizations of the primary labor market. Others, such as small shopkeepers and small farmers, work in conditions more analogous to those of the secondary labor market.

These estimates, derived from the application of the classification by modes to available labor force and other relevant data, express the aggregates for North

The most institutionalized modes of social relations in production are those that characterize the primary labor markets of both Canada and the United States. Institutionalization permits the management of conflict; and conflict, where it occurs in these modes, is over the distribution of increments of income from production. Conflict does not touch the nature of the system, nor does it attack the basic structure of income distribution in the society. Unions—representing employees—and bureaucratized management have attained a state of symbiosis.

The secondary labor market modes lack institutionalization. Conflict in them is more anomic. It is tempting to revise the traditional definitions of social classes in such a way as to consider the employees of the primary labor market as co-opted into a broadened dominant majority class, now including a majority of the labor force. The line of distinction between exploiters and the most exploited would then fall between the primary and secondary labor markets. Objectively, there would be a good deal of justification for this because of the dependent and disadvantaged condition of the secondary labor market. Subjectively, however, in terms of consciousness, this revised definition of classes does not hold so well. Class consciousness is very little developed within the secondary labor market. Where consciousness of group solidarity against exploitation has arisen, it is most often associated with ethnicity rather than with social situation in relation to production. Whether or not such consciousness will grow amongst secondary labor market people is, nevertheless, one of the most interesting unresolved questions about the future dynamics of labor relations in North America. Were such consciousness to remain at the particularist level of ethnicity, it would seem more likely to lead toward facilitating opportunities for upward mobility into the primary labor market for some individual members of these groups rather than toward a broadening of class antagonisms.

The foregoing outlines similarities between Canada and the United States, distinguishing the center of each economy from its internal periphery. Overlaying these similarities is the dependent relationship linking the two national economies. The two specific aspects of this dependency most directly relevant for labor are the preponderance of direct American investment in Canadian industry and of international unions in labor organization. In both kinds of organi-

America. The proportions do not differ markedly between Canada and the United States, except that the tripartite mode is more important in Canada (6.2 percent compared with 2.9 percent in the US), the bipartite mode correspondingly less (reflecting a tradition of greater government involvement in industrial disputes), and the enterprise labor market is also larger (40 percent in Canada compared with 36.6 percent in the US).

zation the locus of decision making for Canadian affairs lies in the United States. Of course, many specific decisions are made in Canada. The important thing is, however, the ultimate control of policy in US headquarters. Decentralization may be regarded as a practical requirement for flexibility and efficiency in large organizations, but it is not inconsistent with central control of policy and fixing of goals.

The most important transnational linkages in labor organizations as in industrial management are between the centers of both economies. The geographical center in Canada of the continental transnational economy is located mostly in southern Ontario and to a lesser extent in the Montreal region of Quebec, and consists of a number of large manufacturing enterprises, largely but not exclusively United States controlled. They constitute a large part of the Canadian primary labor market. Integration reaches its highest degree in certain segments of the primary labor markets of both countries, as manifested, for instance, in virtual wage parity in the steel industry of the two countries [11] and in almost identical Canadian-American agreements in the automotive industry.

Also part of this most integrated segment of the transnational economy are a number of resource industries that are central in an economic though not in a geographic sense. These industries, such as mining and smelting, pulp and paper, and oil and gas drilling and refining, are located in a northern zone running through Quebec and Ontario and in Alberta and British Columbia. Workers in these industries are also organized mostly in international unions. Other components of the Canadian center are construction, longshoring, and road transport. In these industries the organizational linkage with the transnational economy is provided primarily by the international unions, while management is generally Canadian in small and medium-sized firms.

These close links with the transnational economy do not apply to the whole Canadian center. The center bifurcates into one part that is closely integrated into the continental transnational economy and another part that is more specifically national. The latter is predominantly the public sector, including the railways. So long as continentalism was the dominant policy concept of Canadian political economy, there was no contradiction between these two parts of the Canadian center. The emergence of nationalism has created tensions between them. At the same time, the public services have been the major growth area for trade unions during recent years. Now exclu-

[11] While the steel industry is largely Canadian owned and controlled, a large if not a major part of its output is sold directly to American-owned or controlled firms in Canada.

sively Canadian public sector unions with a militancy born of recent expansion challenge the hitherto dominant influence of the international unions within the Canadian Labour Congress (CLC).

This pressure from national unions within the CLC, reinforced by a broadening suspicion of external controls in the Canadian milieu, has strengthened tendencies toward greater autonomy for Canadian locals of some of the major international unions, such as the steelworkers and auto workers. Nevertheless, the workers in the transnationally most integrated part of the Canadian center are, among all Canadian workers, those who have benefitted most from the continental center-periphery structure.

The Canadian periphery can be defined in terms of a number of characteristics. The principal analytical category, already mentioned, is the secondary labor market. The secondary labor market is geographically dispersed, and has not as such become a site of conscious protest or demands. The peripheral consciousness is more usually associated with geography or language. The geographical periphery —the so-called middle Canada—is a belt running north of the main centers of population, from northern New Brunswick and Newfoundland, through north Quebec and Ontario, across the prairie region, and into British Columbia. Economic activity in this territory consists largely in natural resource industries, overwhelmingly American owned. In many parts of this area labor is well organized, again, mostly in international unions, and earnings are high; but with the exception of an elite of workers employed by large corporations, employment is relatively unstable and insecure. Some of the more depressed areas within this belt, e.g., in northern New Brunswick and Newfoundland, exemplify the full range of secondary labor market characteristics, including that of being a source of unskilled migrant workers.

The inferior economic status and lower level of employment opportunities of French-speaking Canadians underlie the political issues over federalism and Quebec separatism. It is consistent with other historical cases that consciousness of this economic disadvantage and the frustrations associated with it have become more acute at the same time as French-Canadian society and its educational institutions have become modernized and opportunities, at least for many French-speaking Canadians, enlarged.

The linguistic and geographical periphery overlap. The majority of the population in the middle Canada belt is French speaking (although this preponderance does not extend beyond central Canada to the west coast), and the nonfrancophones are largely of other backgrounds than Anglo-Saxon. Also to be included within the periphery are disadvantaged groups—the poor and the aged—and those, particularly among the intellectuals and the youth, who are most alienated from the ideology of continentalism.

Political culture differs between center and periphery. The center is moderate and reformist. Union members tend to divide their votes in roughly equal proportions between the Liberal, Progressive Conservative, and New Democratic (NDP) parties. The periphery is polarized: most of its population supports the traditional political parties, but there are some foci of radical protest as well.

The conservatism of the periphery is indicated by the substantially higher proportion of nonunion workers who vote for the Liberal party, and their lesser disposition to vote for the NDP, compared with union workers. As suggested, the categories of union and nonunion workers correspond roughly to primary and secondary labor market employment.[12]

The radicalism of the periphery is fragmented by geographic distance, ideological differences, and cultural divisions. Among its more visible manifestations have been: (1) left-wing nationalism and separatism in Quebec; (2) the right-wing Social Credit movement, which now draws most of its strength from the outlying regions of Quebec; (3) the long continued Communist leadership of such unions as the Mine, Mill and Smelter Workers in the middle Canada zone, as well as the United Fisherman and Allied Workers, the International Longshoremen and Warehousemen's Union, and (throughout the 1940s) the International Woodworkers in British Columbia; (4) several recent breakaways of local unions, especially in British Columbia, from internationals in such industries as mining and smelting, pulp and paper, and brewing and distilling; and (5) the success of the moderately socialist NDP in provincial elections in the western provinces of Manitoba, Saskatchewan, and British Columbia.

The center-periphery relationship is not something unilaterally imposed by the center upon an impotent and reluctant periphery. The essence of the relationship is that it is accepted by the periphery, usually through the agency of some elements in the periphery that perceive this to be in their interest and become the channels for the dependency relationship. Fragmentation of interests, low levels of consciousness, and an absence of political or labor movement cohesion

---

[12] The proportions for the 1972 federal election were as follows: union workers —Liberal, 34 percent; Conservative, 29 percent; NDP, 29 percent; and *nonunion* workers—Liberal, 44 percent; Conservative, 32 percent; NDP, 17 percent. The concept *workers* here excludes professional and white-collar workers. The source is figures released by the Gallup Poll of Canada in its survey of 20-21 October 1972 and reproduced in John W. Warnock, "A Socialist Alternative for Canada," Saskatchewan Waffle Movement, Regina, Saskatchewan, June 1973, p. 20. (Pamphlet.)

in the periphery are conditions that perpetuate dependency. By inference, a reversal of these conditions in the periphery could change or break the dependency relationship. British Columbia is in this sense exceptional in Canada. It is geographically far separate from the Canadian center and is highly specialized in a few resource-based industries. A higher proportion of these industries are, however, Canadian owned than in other Canadian provinces. British Columbia is also the most highly unionized and, on the average, highest wage province in the country. Quebec is the other province where, as we argue below, conditions may be emerging that could shatter the peripheral syndrome.

THE NORTH AMERICAN LABOR RELATIONS SYSTEM: SOME ISSUES

The paradigm sketched out above cannot, within the compass of this article, be applied at more than a few points. We look at three. The first concerns how the system functions as regards the trade unions—the nature of interactions and flows of influence in center-periphery relations of trade unions. The second point concerns how the system is confronting one major current issue of economic policy, that between economic nationalisms (both Canadian and American) and continental economic liberalism; we consider, specifically, how trade unions in Canada working through the transnational system are trying to cope with this issue. The third point examines the challenge to the system from developments within the labor movement in Quebec.

Center-Periphery Processes and Trade Unions

The degree of organizational autonomy of Canadian branches of international unions varies widely. At one extreme are a few old-line AFL craft unions, as in some building and printing trades, in which the US headquarters exert tight control in Canada over the election or appointment of union officers, collection and disbursement of union funds, the content and procedures of collective bargaining and strikes, and cooperation or conflict with other unions. At the other extreme are a few CIO industrial-type unions in Canada that have achieved such a high degree of autonomy from their parent American organizations that the relationship approaches that of a loose alliance between two sovereign bodies. Most international union branches in Canada fall between these two extremes.[13]

The attitude of other actors in the industrial relations scene has

---

[13] John Crispo, *International Unionism*, p. 67.

been an important factor in the emergence of the existing structures. Federal governments in Canada, particularly since World War II, have on balance shown a preference for international unionism as against independent Canadian organizations, particularly when the latter have been under left-wing leadership. Up to World War II Canadian employers in most cases were hostile to international unions, though if they had to choose, they preferred them to more militant or radical Canadian organizations. Since then employers in Canada, particularly the executives of larger corporations, have been predominantly favorable toward international unions. In part this is a by-product of the vastly expanded role of American direct investment in the Canadian economy since the war. American multinational corporations with branch plants and subsidiaries in Canada in most cases find it more convenient to deal with branches of the same unions, negotiating and administering similar agreements on both sides of the border.[14] In general, the international unions have had a moderating effect on industrial conflicts in Canada. Indeed, on numerous occasions local union leaders and members in Canada have accused their international officers of "selling out" and negotiating "sweetheart deals" with employers.

More recently, the movement for cultural and economic independence within the Canadian milieu has strengthened the demand for autonomy in trade unions. The CLC in May 1970 recommended to its American affiliates certain minimum standards of autonomy for their Canadian branches—a recommendation that has had little visible effect. A federal government Task Force on Labour Relations in a report presented to Parliament the same year made similar recommendations, and so did the House of Commons Standing Committee on Defence and External Affairs Respecting Canada–United States Relations.[15] Neither the federal nor provincial governments have, however, taken any specific action in furtherance of this objective.[16]

---

[14] Ibid., p. 224.

[15] Canada, Prime Minister's Task Force on Labour Relations, *Report* on "Canadian Industrial Relations," 1968; Canada, Standing Committee on Defence and External Affairs Respecting Canada-U.S. Relations, *Eleventh Annual Report*, 1970, pp. 33, 104-33, 107, 116, reproduced, in part, in "American-based Unions—the Wahn Report," in Abraham Rotstein and Gary Lax, *Independence—the Canadian Challenge* (Toronto: Committee for an Independent Canada, 1972), pp. 40-48.

[16] The only legislation that may be viewed as indicative to any degree is the Corporations and Labour Unions Returns Act (CALURA) which the Canadian Parliament passed in 1962. It requires foreign-based corporations and trade unions operating in Canada to furnish fairly detailed reports accounting for major receipts and expenditures in this country. The annual reports of CALURA disclosed for the first time a fact that critics of international unions had been alleging for many years and that their supporters had denied, namely, that these

Our paradigm suggests that fragmentation and rivalries in the periphery are conditions for maintaining center-periphery relationships. So long as these conditions prevail, rival Canadian trade union interests will seek alliance with United States centers of union power in order to influence the outcome of conflicts in Canada. This pattern can be formulated as a more general rule of pluralistic imperialism. Peripheral actors can influence outcomes in the periphery to the extent that they can find effective allies within the center. A further hypothesis is that politicization of an issue will tend to shift influence over the outcome of the issue away from the center toward the periphery. Thus, when Canadian unions perceive the US center of union power to be in opposition to their goals, they may seek the support of Canadian public opinion and the Canadian government by politicizing the issue.

There are various occasions when Canadian local unions rely on support from United States headquarters. Some involve cleavages between local or regional branches and the Canadian centers of international unions (a large proportion of which are in Ontario). Such branches often prefer to have American rather than Canadian business agents, international representatives, or higher officials intercede on their behalf. This preference on the part of the Canadian locals probably reflects a sense of relative weakness on the local scene, and the expectation that American agents will be less vulnerable to local pressures in representing their interests. US representatives tend to consider themselves as mediators on demand in the Canadian scene. They view with skepticism any expressed desires of Canadian locals for greater autonomy or independence from international headquarters and can argue with some conviction that they have functions in Canada because Canadians want them, not because they themselves want to be there.

American trade union support has also been crucial in interunion conflicts in Canada, such as arise over the representation of workers in particular industries. The CLC might be expected to resolve or moderate such issues, since its constitution gives it authority to settle jurisdictional disputes between its affiliates, and it can use the sanction of its power to affiliate or expel unions from the federation. In practice, however, international unions have often bypassed the CLC and sought direct support from their own American headquarters to

organizations in the aggregate have been receiving each year millions of dollars more in revenue from dues and other sources from their branches in Canada than they have expended in Canada. Donald McDonald, president of the CLC, and numerous Canadian representatives of international unions have repeatedly criticized CALURA reports on the ground that they do not give a full picture. See, for example, a Canadian press report in the *Sun* (Vancouver), 24 April 1973.

settle jurisdictional disputes. When the CLC has taken a stand, its action has sometimes been ineffective against branches of international unions that retain the support of their American headquarters. The Canadian locals of the Teamsters union, for example, survived and flourished after expulsion from the CLC and continued to raid the locals of a purely Canadian union, the Canadian Brotherhood of Railway Transport and Other General Workers. The Teamsters had the support not only of their own US headquarters but also of international building trades unions whose Canadian locals remained in affiliation with the CLC, and together they blocked the efforts of autonomous Canadian unions to gain a foothold in the construction industry in all provinces but Quebec. The threat of expulsion from the CLC has been more effective in deterring Canadian unions from raiding internationals, because they lack outside, i.e., American, support. The CLC also, in most cases, has refused to affiliate breakaway local or regional unions in Canada.

The consequences of CLC action have thus tended to support the status quo, and particularly the privileged position of the international unions in Canada. To be sure, on some questions, mainly of a foreign policy character, the CLC has taken positions independent of or sharply differing from those of the AFL-CIO. This has been the case in respect to the Vietnam War, trade with Cuba and China, participation in the International Labour Organization and the International Confederation of Free Trade Unions, Canada–United States trade policy, and support of a third party in domestic politics. In matters central to trade union organization and jurisdiction in Canada, however, the CLC's effective independence of US influences has been much more limited. The ambiguous position of the CLC between American dominance and aspirations for Canadian independence has reflected the general mood of Canadian opinion and has not differed markedly from the position of business or of the federal government. Independence has been more manifest on the more symbolic issues, those on which policies have the least immediate practical consequences, while the dependency pattern generally prevails where material interests are involved.

It remains to explore the hypothesis that politicization may tend to strengthen Canadian independence in trade union affairs and to undermine the dependency relationship. Cases of politicization are relatively few. One case arose after World War II in the shipping industry. The political context was the cold war, the impacts of which in Canada included the uncovering of a Soviet spy network implicating a number of Canadian Soviet sympathizers and the anti-Communist struggles for control within some of the international unions. These struggles were reflected in the congresses of the two

Canadian trade union federations, the Trades and Labour Congress (TLC) and the Canadian Congress of Labour (CCL), corresponding respectively to the AFL and the CIO. The specific case concerned the Canadian Seamen's Union (CSU), a Communist-led Canadian union that was at the time the most important Canadian affiliate of the TLC. The CSU president, Pat Sullivan, was also executive vice-president of the TLC. The rival union challenging the CSU's representation of Canadian seamen on the great lakes and eastern seaboard was the Seafarers' International Union (SIU), an international union supported by the AFL. A combination of pressures from the AFL, the shipping operators in eastern Canada, and the federal government worked in favor of the SIU. The TLC was forced to expel the CSU after the Canadian officers of fourteen international unions informed the TLC executive council that they would withdraw their organizations from the TLC if this were not done. The federal government as well as the government-owned Canadian National Steamships company violated Canadian labor legislation in refusing to certify the CSU in certain jurisdictions, and connived with certain international unions (the ones that had forced the TLC to expel the SIU) to circumvent other legislation. In violation of Canadian immigration laws, and by a somewhat clandestine arrangement with these organizations and their executives, an American labor organizer named Harold (Hal) Banks, who had a criminal record in the United States, was brought into the country to become Canadian director of the SIU. Banks and his organization, with the help of a number of "broad-shouldered boys" from the United States, as he described them, won a complete victory over the CSU by 1950, after a particularly ruthless and violent campaign.[17]

In a second case, politicization occurred on the initiative of a provincial government. This happened in 1959, when the International Woodworkers of America (IWA), supported by the CLC, attempted to organize loggers and pulpwood cutters in Newfoundland, most of whose output was sold to two large subsidiaries of multinational corporations that operated pulp and paper plants in the province. The premier of Newfoundland, Joey Smallwood, charged that the IWA campaign would be disastrous for the economy and employment in the province. Rebuffed by the federal government in his attempt to bring federal police reinforcements under provincial government command to the scene of the dispute, Smallwood—in violation of existing labor laws—had the IWA declared illegal in Newfoundland and then used his large majority in the provincial parlia-

[17] See Report of Industrial Inquiry Commission on the Disruption of Shipping on the Great Lakes, vol. 1: Report (Ottawa: Information Canada, 1963).

ment to enact new legislation establishing what amounted to a provincially sponsored company union—an action denounced by the CLC.[18] Once the IWA was routed from Newfoundland, Smallwood turned over his new union to the United Brotherhood of Carpenters and Joiners of America, thereby embarrassing the CLC, two of whose major affiliates were now in conflict in Newfoundland. Though the Carpenters were censured by a majority vote at the next CLC congress, they remained affiliated with the CLC and maintained their newly acquired position in Newfoundland. Politicization in this case, expertly but unscrupulously manipulated by the provincial premier, worked to reestablish the preexisting power relations in the pulp and paper industry. It worked to the advantage of the employers, and of one American-controlled international union prepared to profit from the situation, and to the detriment of the union that had sought to change the existing structure of labor relations in the woods of Newfoundland.

The third case was a sequel to the first. The SIU remedy to the purported menace of Communism proved to have ill consequences in the violence, illegality, and outright gangsterism with which Banks conducted his rule in the SIU, suppressing all internal opposition and raiding other unions. The anti-Communism that had obscured these proclivities in 1950 no longer had such myopic effects on opinion more than a decade later. Now, the CLC took the initiative by expelling the SIU and chartering a new organization, the Canadian Maritime Union (CMU), to take over jurisdiction of Canadian shipping from the SIU. This led to another series of violent conflicts in the shipping industry. The international executives of the SIU, the allied AFL-CIO Maritime Trades Department, and a majority of the AFL-CIO executive council supported Banks and his organization in this struggle. Finding that it had no effective influence directly with the AFL-CIO leadership, the CLC sought to involve the Canadian government. The AFL-CIO leaders backing the SIU could count on a compliant attitude on the part of the US government. There being no other force within the United States to oppose them, it seemed that only a confrontation between the governments might eventually induce the US government to pressure the American SIU backers to withdraw from Canada.

The Canadian government was at first unwilling. The CLC forced the government's hand by declaring a boycott against all ships carrying SIU crews. This was in retaliation against SIU attacks on Cana-

---

[18] This and the following case are described more fully in Stuart M. Jamieson, *Times of Trouble: Labour Unrest and Industrial Conflict in Canada 1900-66*, Task Force on Labour Relations, Study No. 22 (Ottawa: Information Canada, 1968).

dian ships carrying CMU crews. The CLC boycott could be made effective because it was supported by workers employed on shore installations of the St. Lawrence Seaway who were largely organized in the Canadian Brotherhood of Railway Transport and Other General Workers. This action, effectively paralyzing the seaway, brought about contact between Canadian and American governments at the highest level. The White House and the US Departments of State and Labor subsequently all exerted pressure on the SIU and AFL-CIO to withdraw support for Banks. The Canadian government, acting on the recommendation of a royal commission inquiry into the case, placed the SIU under trusteeship, pending the election of a new executive under proper democratic procedure.[19] Politicization in this case did achieve a result sought by Canadian unionists, but only after drastic measures (the boycott) had been employed to overcome the Canadian government's reluctance to become involved in a labor relations issue that had international implications.

Economic Nationalism Versus Continental Liberalism

The dual structures of foreign investment and international unions, which determine the dominant modes of labor relations in Canada, derive from and thrive within an open transnational economy. The foundations of this economy have recently been attacked by forces of economic nationalism in both the United States and Canada.

In Canada, nationalist critics have directed their fire mainly at the extent of foreign control over Canada's industry and resources. Some of their criticism spills over onto the international unions. The growth of this opinion has moved a seemingly reluctant Liberal government to initiate some measures to regulate future foreign investment. The issue places Canadian trade union leaders in a particular quandary. The most vocal of the economic nationalists have been the so-called Waffle group within the New Democratic party, the political party supported by the CLC and by many of the Canadian branches

---

[19] See Jamieson, *Times of Trouble;* Report of Industrial Inquiry Commission; and William J. Eaton, "The Battle of the Great Lakes," *The Reporter* (New York), 21 November 1963, pp. 38-40. The limitations of US government willingness to oppose American trade union interests in this case, and to support the Canadian position, were shown by the sequel. Banks was indicted in Canadian courts for various criminal offenses, and then let out on $25,000 bail while awaiting trial. He jumped bail and fled to the United States, where he was later discovered by a Toronto newspaper reporter to be residing on a yacht, owned by the International Longshoremen's Association, that was anchored in New York harbor. The US Department of State refused the Canadian government's request for extradition of Banks.

of international unions. The trade union elements, which provide the main organizational and financial support for the NDP, have opposed the Waffle within the party; indeed, union influence secured the exclusion of the Waffle from the Ontario provincial branch of the party in 1972. Trade union influence thus had a restraining effect on economic nationalism in the NDP.

In the United States, trade union elements have been foremost in charging the multinational corporations with "exporting jobs" by shifting production abroad. Union leaders have urged legislative and administrative measures to restrict American investment abroad. George Meany, president of the AFL-CIO, and several other influential American trade unionists have, in particular, expressed support for the Burke-Hartke bill, which calls for high tariffs and other measures of protection for US industry against competing imports, and for the Domestic International Sales Corporation Act (DISC), which provides tax advantages to American companies that produce for export in the United States rather than invest and produce in branch plants and subsidiaries abroad. Some important American unions and union leaders have not taken such an openly protectionist stand; some, indeed, envisage a policy of confronting multinational corporations through coordinated trade union action in countries where they operate rather than follow the protectionist route. Nevertheless, the American trade union movement must, in its aggregate, be accounted an important source of economic nationalism in the United States.

American trade union support for protectionist measures is, of course, an embarrassment to the CLC and to the leaders of Canadian locals of international unions. These measures present a special threat of plant shutdowns and layoffs in Canada in important sectors of manufacturing in which American capital is dominant. Canadian union representatives, egged on by Canadian government officials, have urged their international executives in the United States to withhold support for Burke-Hartke. The CLC has also urged the Canadian government to use all possible means of pressure and bargaining in Washington to oppose the bill. It is difficult to estimate what influence, if any, these Canadian pressures may have had on American union leaders and the United States Congress.

When the minister of labour in the Canadian federal government raised publicly the question of whether international unionism can effectively serve Canadian labor's interests now that the AFL-CIO has become avowedly protectionist, the president of the CLC responded "Don't interfere in our affairs." [20] American union leaders who have

---

[20] Canadian press report in *Sun* (Vancouver), 6 March 1973.

not taken a position favoring protectionist measures can claim that their Canadian affiliates require a more liberal stand on trade and investment, and argue that talk of withdrawal of major Canadian locals would at this time play into the hands of domestic protectionist forces.

How much real influence can Canadian membership of international unions have on an issue of such importance? The analysis of the Banks case suggests that Canadian trade union influence with the United States trade union movement does not amount to very much. It was only at the level of confrontation between the two governments that a solution acceptable to Canadian labor could be brought about. This was, however, a case in which there was little support within the US labor movement for the Canadian viewpoint. On an issue over which American trade union views are more divided, the potentiality of some marginal Canadian trade union influence retains at least some credibility—at least until the contrary is demonstrated. This is an issue that puts to the test those Canadian officials of international unions who contend that the best results for labor are to be had by working through the system.

Quebec Labor: Challenge to the System

Other forces in Canada contend that the system works to the detriment of Canadians. The most comprehensive challenge comes from Quebec. The milieu in which this challenge has arisen was shaped by French-Canadian nationalism. The roots of nationalism go back to the nineteenth century and were for long concerned exclusively with cultural identity and survival, inspired by a Catholic humanism unsympathetic to the morally and socially disruptive implications of industrialism. This nationalism for a time adapted, under the aegis of the provincial regime of Premier Maurice Duplessis during the post–World War II period, to a pattern of dependent capitalism in which Quebec offered relatively cheap French-Canadian labor, quiescent under the strong hand of an authoritarian government, for hire by American capital (and some other non-French-Canadian sources of capital) employing English-Canadian management. During the 1950s and 1960s nationalist feeling became increasingly aroused against this pattern of dependency. Nationalism became secularized, and labor protest fused with it. Both forces played an important role in the so-called Quiet Revolution of the 1960s, which brought about the secularization and democratization of education, a considerable enhancement in the scope and effectiveness of provincial government services, and articulation in economic terms of the goal for French Canadians to become masters in their own house—*maîtres chez nous*.

Through these developments that affected Quebec society as a whole, Quebec labor became radicalized. The erstwhile Syndicats

Catholiques, once a Church-controlled labor organization embracing an ideology of social peace, became during the 1950s increasingly secular, militant, radical, and political in orientation, with a growing minority favoring independence for Quebec. In 1960, this movement severed all formal ties with the Church and was renamed the Confédération des Syndicats Nationaux (CSN).[21] This is the only autonomous and purely Canadian labor movement that has managed to survive and grow over a period of several decades up to the present.

The CSN, through this evolution, became more militant and ideologically more radical than the other major segment of organized labor in Quebec, the Quebec Federation of Labour (FTQ), which groups the branches of American internationals and of English-Canadian unions in the province. A third major labor organization is the Quebec Federation of Teachers (CEQ), which is constituted separately under provincial law. Like the CNS, the CEQ has been animated by radical goals having political as well as trade union implications. The radicalization of labor caught up the leaders of the FTQ, who began to take their distance from the CLC and the headquarters of American internationals, and also gave birth to hopes for unity in Quebec's fragmented labor movement. In 1971, a Front Commun was formed between the CSN, FTQ, and CEQ behind the slogan *"briser le système."* This culminated in a massive confrontation with the provincial government, which was branded in union meetings and publications as a "tool of capitalist imperialism." The strike of more than 200,000 teachers and civil servants in April 1972 was by far the largest walkout in Canadian history and, relative to population, in North American history. It was preceded and followed by large demonstrations, widespread mob violence and illegality, violent attacks by police, and numerous arrests and convictions. The strike failed of its objective as the government would not accede to union demands, and the leaders of the three organizations were imprisoned for advising their members not to heed a back-to-work injunction.

These almost revolutionary events sharpened the ideological cleavages affecting labor in Quebec. They brought growing strain and conflict between the FTQ and the CLC as well as with inter-

[21] In English, the Confederation of National Trade Unions. The radical evolution in the CSN parallels what occurred in the Christian wing of the labor movement in France, where the Confédération Français Démocratique du Travail (CFDT) emerged as a militant organization without religious affiliation pursuing goals of participative socialism. The CFDT and the CSN are both members of the World Labor Confederation, the transformed Christian international trade union organization. Marcel Pépin, president of the CSN, is now president of the WLC. Donald McDonald, president of the CLC, is at the same time president of the International Confederation of Free Trade Unions.

national union headquarters in the United States. The FTQ has since assumed the powers of an autonomous trade union center, including the right to affiliate member unions (whereas it had been set up as an organization grouping unions affiliated by the CLC). Opposition to the CLC was such that when William Dodge, executive vice-president of the CLC, came to address the FTQ congress in Montreal late in 1973, he said he "felt like Golda Meir speaking to a meeting of Black September in Cairo." [22] The CSN was also affected when a minority segment of that movement seceded to follow a policy of *economisme* or business unionism. Meanwhile, the CEQ is considering how to discard its corporatist legal framework so that it could integrate into a broad-based trade union movement. Thus, the aim of a unified independent labor movement for Quebec is still very much alive, though it has not achieved organizational form. Obstacles to unity derive from past history and personal rivalries. Support for unity derives from what appears to be a rising level of class consciousness among Quebec workers and from some evidence of new structures emerging among the rank and file.

Committees to back strikers of whatever union affiliation have been set up in various parts of the province. They bring together local members of the FTQ, CSN, and CEQ. In some cases, strikers have rejected the services of American bargaining agents sent by the headquarters of their international unions and have improvised their own local representation. In one such case of a strike that lasted several months, a strikers' committee was set up to carry on the negotiation, each member of which was responsible for keeping in touch week by week with a group of ten or twelve strikers, so that the whole body of strikers could participate continuously throughout that long period in determining strategy and terms of settlement. The strikers were sustained by funds raised through local support committees from all union tendencies. [23]

Radicalization has been accompanied by politicization, which likewise has not yet taken any specific institutional forms but shows up in new emergent structures. The NDP, supported by the CLC, has never achieved any significant foothold in Quebec, and none of the labor organizations in the province have formally affiliated with a political party. A majority of trade union militants in Quebec, e.g., those who participate in union conventions, are probably supporters of the Parti Québécois, which has a platform of political independence for Quebec with a social democratic economic and social policy. Union

[22] *Le Devoir* (Montreal), 7 December 1973.
[23] Gilles Francoeur, "Une victoire de la base sur le syndicalisme d'affaire?," *Le Devoir* (Montreal), 18 January 1974.

leaders have not, however, wished to give formal endorsement to the Parti Québécois, whose predominantly technocratic leadership may have been out of tune with the mood of labor. The unions remain an unconventional political force outside of the political parties—a radical pressure on the left of the Parti Québécois.

The present state of Quebec opens considerable opportunities for such a force, since the parliamentary and party structures of the political system are not functioning so as to give full representation to important segments of Quebec society. The provincial elections of October 1973 gave an overwhelming majority of parliamentary seats to the Liberal party. The Parti Québécois became the official opposition, but with about 30 percent of the total vote (and over 38 percent of the French-speaking vote contrasted with 44 percent of the French-speaking vote for the Liberal party) it elected only a half dozen members. Prospects are that political action will shift to local levels, to school board and municipal elections, and that trade unions will play a prominent part along with some Parti Québécois members and, especially, with a revival of civic action groups. The Montreal municipal elections of 1974 will provide the first major opportunity for labor to take part in an extraparliamentary political front contesting established power in Quebec.

Judged by the conventional standards of the North American labor relations system, Quebec labor is a puzzle. The leaders seem to have become more radical than their members, and to have embarked upon unwise adventures leading to serious setbacks. By these standards the Front Commun was a colossal error in tactics which failed when a determined government broke the strike. By the same pattern of reasoning, the defeat of the Parti Québécois in the elections of October 1973 exposed the frailty of any political alternative likely to be more satisfactory to the union leaders.

The recent events in Quebec make more sense if they are not looked at from the perspectives of the established North American system but are instead viewed as its dialectical contradiction. The actions of the union leaders appear more rational as an effort to respond to, arouse, and channel social protest within the context of a profoundly changing society with a malfunctioning political system. Unions, in this perspective, are seen as the vanguard of a social movement seeking both economic and political goals—not, as in the rest of North America, as the institutional expression of their members' specific economic interests. Such leadership is bound to decide its priorities between the relatively privileged position of some members of international unions in Quebec and the secondary labor market status of the majority of French-Canadian workers. From this alternative perspective, the Front Commun is seen not as a material setback for the unions but as a drama sharpening the consciousness of conflict between an economic-political power elite, ultimately dependent upon American finance, and the workers of Quebec. Political action at the local level is seen as maintaining and developing this consciousness, while more specifically trade union issues at the workplaces broaden participation and support at the base and facilitate the severance of trade union links outside the province by rendering external support unnecessary. Local nationalism is an aid to mobilizing popular support, but has lost its older particularist character. Quebec's radical nationalism is now perceived as part of a broader set of antiestablishment and anti-imperialist struggles in other parts of the world. Contradicting the dependency pattern, allies are sought in the other peripheries, not in the center. A Montreal rally brought Caesar Chavez and Senora Allende to the same platform with the labor leaders of Quebec.[21] It would be premature to assess the long-term strength of these developments of which Quebec labor is a part, but to be understood they have to be seen as something structurally and ideologically in contradiction with the dominant North American system.

CONCLUSION

Our paradigm describes the transnational system of labor relations prevailing in North America—a system with a center-periphery structure that produces outputs beneficial to the participants in proportion to their centrality within it. This system is being challenged in a number of ways in Canada at present: by public sector employees advocating a national orientation within a CLC hitherto dominated by international unions; by economic nationalists mainly outside the trade unions who urge anything from increased controls over foreign investment to socialization of the Canadian economy, and who also want US-Canadian trade union links to be broken; by young workers contesting the present trade union leadership; and, above all, by the organizational, ideological, and political developments within Quebec labor.

These challenges take place in a Canadian milieu that gives increasing emphasis to aspirations of national identity and independence. However, those segments of society that have benefited relative to others from the continental system have not been eager to envisage the lower incomes for themselves that a drastic severance of the continental economy would likely imply.

---

[21] *Le Devoir* (Montreal), 3 December 1973.

We see a latent conflict within Canadian society between inward-directed policies, which are gaining in emotional commitment and legitimacy, and the immediate economic interests of particular groups having a special stake in the transnational system. This latent conflict is often intrapersonal: only at the extremes are Canadians polarized; in the broad middle range individuals continually define their position in relation to the transnational system by their actions. The conflict has become manifest in trade union circles, and the CLC is now in the heart of it. The coalition of trade union interests that brought together the former Trades and Labour Congress and Canadian Congress of Labour (paralleling and reflecting the merger of the AFL and CIO) to form the CLC is now far less stable than it was in the late 1950s. Possibly, given the range of conflictual issues besetting labor throughout Canada, the times are not propitious to renegotiate labor unity. Fragmentation is the alternative prospect. Were Quebec labor and the public sector unions to withdraw from the CLC, the international unions would be left more than ever dependent upon their American support. Insofar as this prospect can be avoided, and a new, more unified labor movement emerge in Canada over time, it seems likely that this unity will have to find its consensus in a strengthening of independence and a corresponding weakening of the transnational system.

FISHERIES, POLLUTION, AND CANADIAN–AMERICAN TRANSNATIONAL RELATIONS

Anthony Scott

In this essay I suggest a newcomer to the list of types of transnational relationships discussed in this volume. This is the relationship that arises from the use of a common-property natural environment. These relations are not new, of course, and have led to conflict and accommodations at various levels for centuries, as Innis's work on the cod fisheries testifies.[1] As world population grows and technology broadens, both demand and capacity to exploit these international common-property resources in ways that will harm other users have also increased. Yet international law has not been able to devise rights of tenure for international property as efficient as those for, say, agricultural land. This resulting lack of suitable concepts of ownership (or sovereignty) has, therefore, been one source of the loss of control by central governments that is frequently mentioned in the transnational relations literature.

The first section of this essay sets forth some economic definitions of common-property and public-good environmental resources, and suggests probable consequences of their existence for neighbouring nations. The second section deals with the general approach to Canadian environmental policies, and with the influences of trans-

Anthony Scott, from 1968 to 1972 a member of the Canadian section of the International Joint Commission, is a professor of economics at the University of British Columbia in Vancouver. An earlier version of this essay was written with Peter Gardner as coauthor. Much of the structure of the present essay stems from his reconnaissance of the whole subject and research into intergovernmental environmental organizations. However, he was not able to participate in the present version of the essay, which was revised into final form in the light of constructive comments received from Stuart M. Jamieson, Robert Keohane, Annette Baker Fox, Lloyd C. MacCallum, Keith Henry, Mark Zacher, David Bates, Parzival Copes, Peter Larkin, and others.

[1] For an exploration of the role of intergovernmental and nongovernmental organizations in this issue area, see Edward Miles, "Transnationalism in Space: Inner and Outer," *International Organization* 25 (Summer 1971): 602-25. See also Harold A. Innis, *The Cod Fisheries* (Toronto: Ryerson Press, 1940).

national relations on them. The third section returns to the problem of shared international resources, concentrating on the conditions for successful management of fisheries and water resources by international organizations.

ECONOMIC DEFINITIONS OF COMMON-PROPERTY AND PUBLIC-GOOD ENVIRONMENTAL RESOURCES

The existence of common property is of course the absence of private property, or at least of that control over and containment of the effects of production or consumption that is supposed to be typical of small-scale farm or manufacturing activity. There can also be common property between or among nations: environments within which the effects of activity in one country move uncontrolled and unabated. The terminology therefore runs as follows: Because it is in part common property, the environment becomes a medium for spillovers that, to the extent they affect neighbours, are regarded by them as *externalities* (i.e., external diseconomies or economies) in their domestic activities. Because the effect is external, or abroad, it is not taken into account when the originating firm is making decisions about the amount or character of its activity. If the externality is beneficial, there is usually very little heard about it. There is no payment to the originator, and no charge to the beneficiary. However, when the foreigner suffers rather than benefits from externalities (from transfrontier pollution for example), incentives exist to forge links that will bring some relief or accommodation. These may take the form not only of complaints and negotiations through familiar interstate channels but also of pressures and influences through existing or new transnational relationships. Eventually agreements and international organizations may emerge. These may reflect and indeed provide for direct representation of the actors whose transnational relationships were originally influential.

Fisheries can easily be fitted into this way of looking at environmental relations. Although they are not production or consumption activities in the sense mentioned above, the behaviour of nationals of one country can certainly cause spillovers that affect their neighbours. Among the list of activities are: investment—outlays that lead to the augmentation or protection of the migration or spawning of fish; abstention—preservation by refraining from catching fish that may move into other waters; depletion—catching fish that would otherwise or later be caught elsewhere; and congestion—crowding fishing grounds or using gears that damage or conflict with equipment used by other nations. The salmon fishery is an example of a resource that gains greatly in value from agreements or organizations to reduce the externalities that would be suffered by both nations, but most fish are migratory enough to inspire some joint action. On the high seas, of course, the fish are probably more mobile than the fishermen, unimpeded as they are by any property lines or frontiers. All the activities listed redistribute gains and losses among the countries, and intergovernmental and transnational political action at all levels may take place.

At this stage, the economist must make a distinction between two types of common-property problems. If the spillover occurs in discrete units (taking the form, say, of such pollutants as pieces of litter and driftwood that endanger navigation, or of fish that may be caught singly), the information and property problems that normally prevent negotiation and bargaining are not severe. It is conceivable that the source of the spillover can be identified. And, on the receiving side, whatever is enjoyed or suffered by one person comes to him alone (for example, the fish that he catches are not caught by others). Hence, a little institutional ingenuity can devise systems by which common-property resources either become private (or national) property or come under the management of an agency that effectively *internalises* all the activities that affect the property and so prevents the appearance of unconsidered externalities.[2] The commissions that protect and allocate fish between two countries, or that assign rights to withdraw water from boundary rivers and lakes, are dealing with such relatively simple common-property problems.

If, however, the spillover occurs in a way that affects everyone (not only everyone in the victim country but perhaps also everyone in the originating country), there is what the economist calls a *public good* problem. One person experiencing the spillover does not prevent another person having the same experience. For example, the raising of the level of a river affects everyone along it uniformly; one person's gain does not prevent his neighbour's gain (or loss). Again, pollution (or purification) of the air, sea, or rivers may affect everyone who uses them; no institution can assign the enjoyment of the pollution (or purification) to a particular person.

In both types of common property, there may be no direct link between the two parties. The victim suffers (or the beneficiary prospers) because of the general condition of the water or air, and the originator simply contributes to that general condition. There is usually no identifiable party to negotiate with the originator or the victim, even if both may benefit by some bargain. But when the

---

[2] For a discussion of the international options, see Francis T. Christy, Jr., and Anthony Scott, *The Common Wealth in Ocean Fisheries* (Baltimore, Md.: The Johns Hopkins Press, 1965 and 1972).

externality occurs as a public good, the problem of linking the cause and final effect of a particular environmental phenomenon, such as pollution, is greatly complicated. One consequence is that no person feels he need take pains to provide the abatement because he can be a free rider on the coattails of others who do pay for it. Another consequence is that there is no particular *economic* gain of other goods or services from excluding persons from enjoying the public good because such exclusion does not reduce the cost of providing the good. For example, consider a project to reduce a lake's level slightly and thus to lower the storm damage to surrounding wharves and moorages. The changed water level is a public good, affecting all riparians equally in that one person's decision to take advantage of the new level does not affect the benefit that another riparian can achieve. Even if one riparian could in some way be excluded from the benefit, there would be no net economic gain from doing so. When the resource straddles the boundary (or extends beyond it into the high seas), the international common property is the environment for an international public good.

Whether the international externality is simply that of a spillover effect or whether it takes the particular form of a public good, its control and management by people in the two countries are likely to call for transnational organization. Within one country, in the absence of a boundary, one expects to find organizations formed between those immediately interested in the neighborhood. Examples are the oil-field units, range associations, communes, village councils, irrigation districts, and so forth all over the world that manage mineral, land, forest, and water common property. Such organizations, or at least the relationships that motivate them, can also be envisaged along the border. But here our expectations are disappointed. It is noteworthy that, even domestically, few local organizations have been able to manage common-property resources without the backing of governments. And the demand for action by higher government levels is likely to be more vocal as the economic (or other) impact of the transnational spillover increases. This does not mean that unofficial transnational relations cannot still take place; they can and quite frequently do.

As in all jurisdictional choices, there are certain benefits and costs involved in the parties taking their particular transnational relations problem up to higher levels. The benefits are a direct result of economies of scale at the national level. A good example is the radio frequency agreement that sets the frequencies for both the United States and Canada all along the frontier. The costs involved in small groups negotiating their own frequencies every few miles would be very high, and the chances of successfully avoiding interference, very low. There

are also negotiating and bargaining benefits that arise out of the very
large portfolio of relationships the national governments have with
each other. This large scale can bring about a saving in the amounts
of payments or transfers (in money or in kind) that would otherwise
be made between the groups involved in a transnational relationship.
It works by allowing the national government greater freedom to offer
concessions on other matters (which are perhaps not urgent to it but
are important to the other government), rather than depending on
cash offers. The lower the level of the actors, the fewer the number
of matters over which they have jurisdiction, and so the smaller will
be their freedom to make offers to, or accept them from, their oppo-
sites. Firms, individuals, or local jurisdictions will have almost
nothing with which to trade.

EFFECTS ON DOMESTIC POLICIES OF TRANSNATIONAL RELATIONS

Just as in other policy matters, environmental policies do not
emerge full-blown from the minds of Canadian citizen-taxpayers.
There is a long period of inaction while politicians are consulting
technical experts, interested parties, and specialists in public opinion.
My first question here is the extent to which the eventual distillation
of policy has been influenced by ideas or pressures that are transnational in their origin.

As a general matter, it can be confidently stated that popular
concern about the environment and ecology are largely derivative
from the concern in the United States (and to a lesser extent, the
UK). It is true that Canada has more than its share of the world's
concerned professionals (hunters and fishermen, outdoorsmen, rural
recluses, land conservationists, foresters, zoologists, fishery scientists,
medical and public health specialists). And it is true that Canadians
had early taken an independent interest in particular issues that would
subsequently have been labeled environmental: local and industrial
effects of the Trail Smelter case, maintaining forest cover, spraying
for spruce budworm, national subsidization of municipal sewage
works, protection of both freshwater and ocean fish species (utilizing
an unusual domestic expertise in ecology), protection of wilderness,
concern about the popularization of national and provincial parks,
worry about radioactive fallout, mercury, and lead in the environment,
and so on. But no one would claim that many Canadians perceived
these separate concerns (emerging over the past 50 years) as being
instances covered by a single public environmental objective or dogma.

When, however, Canada began to take an interest in air pollution
and water pollution, ecology, and the natural and urban environment,
it did find that on most subjects it had a small nucleus of experts

available. Sanitary engineers and zoologists were no more scarce for public administration (or research) than any other type of professional. As public interest and concern mounted, it was not a scarcity of manpower that prevented governments from learning what was necessary.

The interests most involved have been consulting and government professionals (mostly academic scientists and engineers), industry and business, and a dense fringe of environmental clubs, associations, and ad hoc pressure groups. Working in hearings and demonstrations, through educational and news media, and directly on politicians, they have among them profoundly changed public policy and government budgets. How have transnational relations affected their behaviour and that of their governments?

As for the Canadian scientists and other professional experts (mostly physicians and engineers), there can be little doubt of their almost complete dependence on the international, professional information circuits. They and their research stations are themselves often important elements in these circuits, and their research and administrative experiences are discussed at international conferences and published in international journals, often fairly independently of national allegiance. Thus both Canadians and Americans learned together of prior research and data on mercury pollution from Swedish and Japanese sources, on sulphur oxide air pollution from the UK, and on eutrophication of lakes and rivers from Europe.[3] But, for the most part, the relatively small size of the total Canadian research establishment has given Canadians a passive role. As specialists, they can only contribute to a small part of the relevant professional literature. For the rest, they must remain dependent on American ideas, or sometimes on overseas research or discoveries filtered through American ab-

---

[3] A good example of the conflict that can occur due to the almost instant flow of foreign information and the influence of the media is the recent controversy over automobile emission standards. On 22 March 1973 the *Globe and Mail* (Toronto) reported that the Canadian "Government has not announced its own recent decision [about auto emissions] because of the latest uncertainty in the United States about whether the planned 1975 air emission standards will in fact be adopted" (p. 2, col. 6). On 6 June 1973 the *New York Times* reported that the Environmental Protection Agency in the US had declared that "the 90% reduction of nitrogen oxides in auto emissions . . . is now unnecessary" (p. 23, col. 1). On 14 June the *Toronto Star* reported that "a mechanical engineering professor at the University of Toronto has stated that auto exhaust pollution presents no health hazard in Canada" (p. 14, col. 1). On 15 June the *Globe and Mail* (Toronto) reported that the Canadian "Environment Minister . . . now believes that, while Canada should follow the U.S. lead to toughen automobile emission standards for 1975, it is not necessary to adopt the even more stringent 1976 [nitrogen oxide] auto emissions standards planned by the U.S." (p. 1, col. 2). While the Canadian research establishment is well manned with zoologists and biologists, it has apparently been short of physicians concerned with air pollution and its effects.

stracting services, conference agendas, or official reports. Thus, as with any applied science, the ordering of Canadian environmental thinking, research objectives, and policy priorities is implicitly but inexorably influenced by their ranking and arrangement in the United States, where scientists are largely responding to their own, and their government's, perception of the most serious questions and the most promising strategies. Thus, to revert to an earlier illustration, Canadians were quick to become alerted to the dangers of air pollution from steel mills and automobiles because these had already been chosen for intensive examination in Pennsylvania and California, but were slower to take a vigorous interest in mercury or DDT poisoning (even though both had provoked outspoken protest in Canadian regions) because US research on these problems had lagged.

Parallel to the transnational flow of ideas to scientists, engineers, and administrators has been the popularization of ideas about the environment and the ecology through the mediation of environmental groups. This volunteer fringe, of course, has a shifting membership and quickly changing outlook. Some groups appear to be ad hoc, such as the front that emerged to protest the flooding of the Skagit River valley on the British Columbian border by a Seattle-based utility; it was in effect a temporary coalition of relatively new environmental organizations with older outdoors and nature clubs. A few others appear to be more permanent, such as Pollution Probe, a would-be national organization in Ontario that seems now to have successfully grown into a general clearinghouse for its members. Earlier, it took strong positions on issues, for example, whether Canada and the United States should allow drilling for natural gas in Lake Erie to continue.

The strength of affiliations of these groups with American groups varies. The Sierra Club is only one of several US organizations that have Canadian branches, and these seem most active in western Canada. In eastern Canada, Pollution Probe has been less dependent on American inspiration, stemming instead from an academic group at the University of Toronto. Indeed, in all parts of the country, some of the briefs presented at hearings have revealed a close affinity with radical politics, and hence not only an aversion to the American way of life as the supposed source of environmental decay but also a tinge of explicit anti-Americanism for its own sake.[4]

---

[4] However, while some environmentalists may be radical, most Canadian radicals are not interested in the environment. Even the New Democratic party has not, since 1969, made much of the pollution question in the resolutions of its national conventions, instead laying greatest stress on employment and development issues on the one hand and on nationalism (coupled with socialism) in resource exports on the other. Neither the NDP's Waffle nor its trade union components are

One interesting maverick group, the Greenpeace Foundation, has demonstrated on the high seas against nuclear bomb testing. Gaining its spurs in a campaign against American testing in the Aleutians, it has since shifted its attention to French testing in the South Seas. The former expedition received some support from within the United States and was complementary to agitation against the tests by groups in Alaska, California, and Japan. American groups, however, have not been much interested in the French tests, and foreign support has come chiefly from Australia and New Zealand. In many ways the intensity, sacrifice, and bitterness of these demonstrations have resembled more closely the activities of the British Campaign for Nuclear Disarmament almost twenty years ago than the more light-hearted environmentalism of American youth in the 1970s.

Thus the direct input from the United States varies with the issue, the time, and the region. Canadian nationalism with respect to resource exports and foreign ownership prevents complete harmony, and indeed there may also be a few genuine differences about the seriousness of physical threats to the global environment. For example, Ontario and New York State groups seem to differ on the dangers from nuclear power. But it would be easy to exaggerate this gap. There are important transnational groups steadily at work. And, more important, both Canadian and transnational groups are on a single information-propaganda-research network, much the same as consumer and women's liberation organizations. Through this network are circulated the pronouncements of Ehrlich, Commoner, Hardin, Nader, and Brower, and news about the lawsuits, statutes, and tactics that have proved effective.

Finally, a strong influence on domestic decision making has come from migrants and US citizens with direct interests that are other than commercial. Certainly the long-term effects would appear to be very powerful. Casual observation suggests that the dissatisfied United States citizens who migrate to Canada are frequently sensitive to environmental issues, and thus are more likely to lend their support to groups striving to make or alter Canadian policies. In addition, communication between members of families across the

closely associated with environmental groups. Thomas Burton, in an interesting chapter on the three parties, also finds the federal Conservatives confining their platform to aspects of nationalism and continentalism. Of course, at the provincial level, where most pollution policy is in fact implemented, all three parties have acted almost indistinguishably. See Thomas L. Burton, *Natural Resource Policy in Canada: Issues and Perspectives* (Toronto: McClelland and Stewart, 1972). Burton's brief chronicle of the early days of the conservation movement in Canada can be supplemented by Anthony Scott, *Natural Resources: The Economics of Conservation*, rev. ed. (Toronto: McClelland and Stewart, 1973), chapter 3 and appendix.

border would appear to have influence that is more powerful than, for example, the media. The influence of foreign landowners in places such as Nova Scotia, Vermont, and Washington on the zoning and public service policies of local recreational areas has also been noticed.

An extreme version of this transnational influence is that of an organization known as Ducks Unlimited. Starting in the United States, it has expanded into Canada, supported chiefly by hunters. It is best known for its program of providing feeding and nesting places for waterfowl in farm regions. Since the birds chiefly require ponds or lakes, the investment projects in dugouts and water holes of Ducks Unlimited have been welcomed by farmers and by other outdoorsmen. What makes the example especially interesting is that the benefit in the form of increased game stocks is not only harvested by sportsmen from both countries hunting in both countries but is also migratory between the two countries. Thus the birds (like the lakes and rivers mentioned earlier) are international common property, husbanded by a transnational, nongovernmental organization.[5]

Wildlife preservation provides some examples of the assertions made above, as well as some less general aspects. The annual tourist movement of people into Canada includes a large number of hunters, anglers, and other outdoor enthusiasts who return each summer or open season. Their influence on Canadian game and wilderness management policy has been significant, both negatively and positively.

On the negative side, of course, even though American visitors may be the chief users of Canadian resources, they cannot have a really profound effect on much local policy because their votes cannot be offered to Canadian politicians. Thus their influence is less than extraterritorial.

On the positive side, American recreationists have had and have developed several ways of influencing Canadian policy, as they have purchased licenses, hired guides, joined rod-and-gun clubs, been inspected by rangers and wardens, and patronised lodges, service stations, and stores. This has made it possible for them, indirectly, to influence changes in protection or open-season policies, range-improvement expenditures, roads, and so forth. Their clubs (with Canadian membership also, of course) lobby in the legislatures and meet local game managers. US hunters and fishermen themselves carefully fill out provincial questionnaires about their valuation or expenditures

---

[5] One can only suppose that the strongly entrenched position, since 1917, of the Migratory Birds Protection Act in Canadian law is a consequence of its support not only by Canadian but also by American sportsmen, working through both national governments. (This act is believed by Indians to discriminate against their native rights, and has been the source of much friction.)

while enjoying game resources. They may also actually become proprietors of fishing or grazing areas. (Quebec and the Maritime provinces are tending to repatriate these sites from their club ownership [Canadian or US]).

So far as international unions and foreign-owned corporations are concerned, there seems to have been little important transmission of ideas or policies across the border relating to environmental protection. It would be surprising if organized labour became particularly concerned about pollution, wilderness, or wildlife; thus American links have not been of great significance one way or another. Nor is it possible to detect any particular role that has been played by foreign ownership. The attitude of large corporations to government regulations and their performance in complying with them are of course very similar to those in the United States but, given the similarity of the regulations, quite predictable. Doubtless Canadian subsidiaries have passed on to independent Canadian corporations some head-office tactics useful in delaying and minimising the burden of tough environmental policies, but Canadian-owned corporations may not have had much to learn. And the subsidiaries seem usually to have accepted provincial requirements if they are not more onerous than those already imposed, in the United States, on their parents. On the whole, the environmental record of Canadian business would probably be about the same if the only links were through the trade press and the export market.[6]

Thus, in answer to the question about the extent to which Canadian environmental policies have been influenced by ideas that are transnational in their origin, my answer is that the *unity* and dogmatic nature of Canadian environmentalism is almost entirely an importation from the US. Especially when it is recognised that the provision of environmental policies about pollution, urban-rural conflicts, parks, and wilderness is almost entirely a provincial responsibility, it is remarkable that so much has been accepted. For the provincial governments are traditionally greatly concerned with the heavily capitalised resource industries, especially hydroelectric, wood, mineral, and petroleum services and products. This concern has meant

[6] Of course, because multinational corporations are in a position to pick their foreign locations, they may influence local regulations by choosing or threatening to choose the jurisdiction with the softest standards. See Greenwood's contribution to this volume for remarks on oil refinery location. In general, see Louis T. Wells, Jr., "The Multinational Business Enterprise: What Kind of International Organization?," *International Organization* 25 (Summer 1971): 447-64, for the view that because centralized multinationals can transfer resources across national boundaries they constitute a serious threat to the freedom of action of local jurisdictions.

that in the past within these governments much power and influence has been wielded by the departments that manage and protect resources for exploitation, and comparatively little encouragement has been offered to those concerned with rural preservation, parks, or even hunting and fishing.

This power structure has meant that in ten different provinces, it has been necessary for the environmentalists to divert government attention from resource management for exploitation (largely a civil-engineering approach) to resource management in accordance with the ideas of a relatively small number of enthusiasts for amenity, scenery, ecology, and purity. In one sense, the revisionist task was eventually made simple by the fact that the powerful resource departments were available to be redirected toward the provision of environmental goals. Nevertheless, the accomplishment has been surprising, and it attests to the power of ideas. Even if the energy shortage of 1974 succeeds in blunting and even reversing the environmental thrust of the 1960s, the provincial administration of resources in Canada will have been permanently modified in its technocratic, development-oriented bias.

To conclude this section with a digression, it is interesting to speculate whether the Canadian confrontation of the environmental issue has not merely been an enclave of American activity. The argument might run as follows. On the one hand, transnational actors (investors, manufacturers, exporters) have had a large share in Canadian economic development, and with it a large share in the degradation of the Canadian environment. This environment, furthermore, is in large part shared as common property with the United States, from which has been discharged by far the greatest fraction of its pollutants. Thus, the argument might run, Canadian environmental degradation has been the result of two transnational influences: foreign ownership and operation of Canadian industry plus transfrontier externalities in the common-property environment.

It would then be possible to maintain that the opposition to this degradation has also been implanted in Canada by transnational relationships, especially through the networks supplying ideas to professional administrators and scientists and to the amateurs of the environmental movement. These have already been outlined.

Thus this approach would perceive the whole Canadian environmental "crisis" of the late 1960s as an extension or transplantation of a larger battle within the United States. Nor would this be the first time that conservationists would be taunted with their origins. Opponents of the earlier American conservation movement saw it as a reaction of an East Coast and New England elite to the exploitative development of the American west, itself largely financed and directed by East Coast and New England enterprisers.[7] To a limited extent Harold Innis and A. R. M. Lower may be said to have had similar reservations about the application of US conservationist ideas to Canada (i.e., Ontario) in the 1930s.[8]

Thus the theme of this argument would be that transnational relations of one type (flows of people and ideas) have helped to identify and define the nature of a problem caused by another transnational relationship (pollution and degradation caused by transnational actors plus transfrontier externalities caused by flows of pollutants). The country from which came the disease is the country offering the cure, although the sources were different.

The chief difficulty with this construct is that it requires the reader to imagine a whole alternative epoch of Canadian history in which either the source of the pollution or of the environmental ethic did not come to Canada through transnational flows. We would be asked, for example, to imagine a Canada in which foreign ownership and the drive to export did not play a major role, and then to consider whether environmental policy would have a similar shape and timing to that which we have actually experienced. The assumption is so difficult and unrealistic that it seems hardly possible to consider the question.

The main point of this section is that the Canadian definition of the environmental problem is very similar to that in the United States mainly because the transnational flow of ideas and people has carried the scientific approach and the conservation ethic to Canadian policymakers. In this digression, I have considered whether it is possible to argue that both the problem and its policy reaction are transnational in origin, and concluded that there is no way to confirm this speculation short of trying to reconstruct the history of Canada in the absence of contacts with the United States.

THE MANAGEMENT OF INTERNATIONAL COMMON-PROPERTY AND PUBLIC-GOOD RESOURCES

Joint Canadian and United States management of shared international resources has been provided for in several international agreements between the two countries. Is the prevalence of extensive transnational relations a condition that favors the success of these

[7] For a discussion and bibliography, see Arthur Maass, "Conservation," *Encyclopedia of the Social Sciences* (New York: Macmillan and Free Press, 1968), vol. 3, pp. 271-79.

[8] See Arthur Reginald M. Lower, *The North American Assault on the Canadian Forest* (Toronto: The Ryerson Press, 1938); and Harold A. Innis, "The Economics of Conservation," *Geographical Review* 28 (1938): 137.

agreements? While an exhaustive list would show that many re-sources are at least partly covered by agreements, this section will concentrate on two examples: fisheries [9] conventions, and agreements on water resources environmental management.

To recall part of the argument of the first section of this essay, neither conflicting resource uses, transnational relations between the resource users, nor the economic incentive of mutual gains from end-ing degradation and depletion of the resource are sufficient to bring about nongovernmental international resource management. Even though the actors on both sides of the boundary may be members of the same firm or grouping, their attempts to manage the resource (like a farm or factory) would be frustrated by new entrants. Likewise, a provincial or state government, even if it obtained an agreement with a counterpart government to, say, reduce pollution or conserve fish, would lack powers to prevent free riding by actors under other jurisdictions. Furthermore, because such a lower-level actor may not know with certainty the national source of each unit of the externality he experiences, agreement may be impossible anyway. Thus non-governmental or low-level governmental agreements on the manage-ment of common property are rare (the few that come to mind are informal and impermanent arrangements between adjoining farmers or municipalities near the border).

Instead, the conflicts and frictions, and the opportunities for gain from joint action, tend to get referred to national governments.[10] Thus, as everyone in Canada knows, it was on a fisheries treaty that Canada first asserted its power to sign an international document in its own right (Halibut Treaty, 1923). Such agreements usually pro-vide for an organization to carry out their terms, and Canada and the United States are members of several. These can be divided into two categories. The first may be regarded as being at an early stage, undertaking preparatory research on catch, stock, growth, migration,

[9] There are almost no general discussions of the political aspects of agreements. Christy and Scott, *The Common Wealth in Ocean Fisheries*, and James A. Crutch-field and Giulio Pontecorvo, *The Pacific Salmon Fisheries* (Baltimore, Md.: The Johns Hopkins Press, 1969), chapter 8, are both helpful. Eleanor Barbara John-son has completed a University of Washington Ph.D. dissertation, "The Regula-tion of International Fisheries" (1973), stressing the political role of scientific elites in international fishery organizations. There is an extensive legal literature on fisheries, including fisheries treaties.

[10] The variety of jurisdiction situations is illustrated by west coast fisheries agreements. In the United States, the states of Oregon, Washington, and Alaska administer rules for fisheries, but in Canada the federal government has jurisdic-tion. Conversely, jurisdiction over levels and flows and over pollution around the Great Lakes is exercised more by the central government in the United States than in Canada.

and so forth. The second type provides fishery management for stocks or for regions.

In the first category, Canada and the United States, along with many other nations, are represented not only on the International Council for the Exploration of the Sea (ICES) but also on a number of learned and specialised international organizations, including the fisheries section of the Food and Agriculture Organization (FAO) of the United Nations. They also belong to three bodies charged with making scientific investigations and recommendations concerning measures for stock or catch maintenance, and which are halfway between the two extremes of the research and regulatory agencies. The three organizations are the International Commission for the Northwest Atlantic Fisheries (ICNAF), the Inter-American Tropical Tuna Commission (concerned with the eastern Pacific off Panama and South America), and the commission for the conservation of Atlantic tuna (which makes studies and recommendations about measures to maximize sustainable catch).

In the second type—regulatory—both Canada and the United States are members of the following bodies. The International North Pacific Fisheries Commission, with Japan as the third member, operates to achieve maximum sustained yield in nonterritorial waters by coordinating studies neecssary to determine appropriate application of the treaty's complex abstention principle. The Canadian membership, which is similar for the other countries, consists of a private fisherman, a member of a fishermen's cooperative, a representative from the federal government, and an official from a fishing company. The Great Lakes Fishery Commission coordinates research and recommends programs for the eradication or control of sea lamprey populations. The North Pacific Fur Seal Commission, with Japan and the Soviet Union also as members, undertakes research, recommends enforcement measures, and oversees the apportionment of skins. The International Whaling Commission, including many more members, amends whaling rules and regulations and makes recommendations about proper conservation. The International Pacific Halibut Commission provides for the development and maintenance of maximum sustainable yield of halibut in the North Pacific Ocean and Bering Sea. The Canadian membership consists of a member from a fishermen's cooperative, a representative from the Canadian government, and an official from a fishing company; US membership is similarly distributed, except that fisheries are a state responsibility. The International Pacific Salmon Fisheries Commission is responsible for conducting studies, regulating the sockeye and pink salmon fisheries, and providing for apportioning the catch equally. Canadian membership (again symmetrical for US members) consists of a private citizen, a representative from the Canadian government, and an official from a fishing company.

How might we estimate the effect of transnational relationships on the success of treaty organizations? Conjecture on this question at once suggests the many levels at which an institution's attainments may be judged. If two nations create a body to deal with a problem, and it achieves all that could be expected of it, given the member states' hostility, indifference, sense of urgency, preoccupation with other matters, internal stability, and so forth, is it a success? Clearly this line of inquiry would be fruitless. Instead, I take a less direct approach. I offer a list of conditions (fairly arbitrarily chosen) and ask the extent to which these variables could be predicted to retard or assist the work of the organization. This exercise will be seen to be merely indicative of the need for further research. As nearly 100 years' experience with bilateral fishery and environmental organizations has produced almost no generalizations about them by scholars in the social sciences, we must have recourse to induction and exemplification, but these are no substitutes for real study.

If Canada and the United States set up an organization to reduce their net losses from the neglect or mismanagement of a common resource, it is postulated here that, in given circumstances, a main role of the institution would be to achieve a recognition of the problem and the opportunities for its amelioration in terms that are understandable, familiar, and acceptable to the two countries' policymakers, representatives, or appointed organization members. Thus in fisheries' conventions great care has been taken to establish a factual base trusted by both or all signatories; sometimes the organization even sets up its own in-house research branch; at least it will make strenuous efforts to assure itself that any research, monitoring, or sampling undertaken by its members will be free of the taint of partisanship.

This postulate suggests the first of the conditions that encourage the successful working of a treaty organization—the background of experts. First, the professional advisers to the diplomats and administrators are trained in and accept the same general principles of biological management. Not only as between Canada and the United States, but also when there are several countries involved (especially in ICNAF), the approach to fisheries' science that stems from the applied fisheries population models of R. J. H. Beverton and S. J. Holt has been a unifying influence. This condition sometimes is achieved other ways. As mentioned earlier, some treaty organizations have their own research branches: these provide opportunities for visits, seminars, workshops, and even secondment so that all scientists of the member governments can confidently recommend the acceptance of the same numerical estimates and projections. At least one of the reasons for the 30-year lag in the promulgation of effective whaling protective regulation on the high seas was the absence of this factor. Several of the main whaling nations did not perceive the biological problem in the same terms as the other members.

Common expertise, then, is one condition that makes for success. The postulate that an organization's role is to obtain and present information that national decision makers understand and accept also suggests other conditions.

A second condition is similarity in taste. When people in the two countries have the same tastes for goods and for environmental quality, joint action becomes more acceptable. Each can understand the other's sense of damage when a resource is depleted or degraded, and they may be able to agree sooner on the extent of the damage. Thus, agreement between Canada and the United States on the management of a fishery is probably easier when both seek the same fish than between òne of these and Japan when the countries may place different relative valuations on different species. It is similar for environmental problems: the Trail Smelter case suggested that investigations by joint bodies and arbitrations are accepted when all concerned are capable of putting themselves into the positions of both the injured and the injuring parties.

However, mutual understanding seems more likely to produce agreement on joint resource management or pollution abatement than on the payment of damages to those who have suffered. Cash settlements are made between those who have little in common, as exemplified by the Dutch-French dispute about pollution of the Rhine. The Dutch victims downstream live with different industries, have different recreational patterns, and read different newspapers than the polluters upstream. Sympathy was missing; only cash payments for pollution abatement were effective.

A third condition, parallel to the second, is similarity in technology. If the two countries are using a common resource in the same way (e.g., catching fish with the same gear, dropping pulp-and-paper waste into the same lake), they will find it easier to agree on a joint management program than if their contributions to depletion or degradation are made in the course of different activities. Thus Canada and the United States have found it possible to agree to abolish the use of fish traps and weirs in the northwest sockeye salmon fishery in the interest of conservation.[11] It would have been much more difficult to agree on this step had only one of the countries employed traps.

[11] See Crutchfield and Pontecorvo. The banning of traps illustrates the point in the text, but these authors are, on economic grounds, critical of abandoning this efficient gear.

By the same token, the forbidding of the use of trawl nets by the International Pacific Halibut Commission and the regulation of mesh size under the ICNAF convention have been politically acceptable because their impact on fishing methods did not differ between countries.

It follows that when their technologies are not uniform, the member countries find it difficult to move together. Thus, although the agreement for clearing up the pollution of the lower Great Lakes does contain provision for similar collective treatment facilities to be installed for municipal sewage in both countries, it does not include a suggested federal control of the phosphate content of household detergents. Canada did institute this control but the United States did not. One of the reasons for the American refusal was probably that the phosphate-content approach was technologically direct and effective for Canada, in that most Canadian consumers live in the Great Lakes drainage area, but a wasteful and imprecise national policy for the United States, most of whose households are in drainage areas where eutrophication is not a threat.

These two conditions, taste and technology, tend to blend together and reinforce one another. Distrust and suspicion evaporate when the two parties are not too dissimilar. Each can understand the gains to those who benefit (indeed they may be identical) and the sacrifices by those who must alter their activities. The cordial simultaneous sewage treatment programs on the Great Lakes can be contrasted with the United States–Mexico rancour over scarce boundary waters use and management, where neither experience nor technology lead to sympathy between the two populations.

Another condition that helps the working of an agreement is the pressure of a third party. One of the best examples is the fear of Japanese activity in the north Pacific fisheries. Searching for almost any kind of fish, the Japanese industry uses a distant-water rather than an inshore technology. If anything, its presence has driven Canadian and United States industries to a greater realization of their similarities of interest, and a number of agreements have emerged. To improve their access, the Japanese have, among other strategies, formed transnational relationships by buying into Alaskan and Canadian fishing firms. Similar incentives appear to exist on the East Coast. Lack of this external pressure may be one explanation of the failure of joint action to emerge in the Great Lakes fishery.

Outside parties, the Baltic producers of pulp and paper, have forced Canada and the United States into joining forces in support of the Organization for Economic Cooperation and Development (OECD) pollution policy. The presumed danger is that while the United States and Canada force their own private firms to install expensive abatement equipment, the Scandinavian countries may either demand less of their producers or subsidise them, or both, giving Scandinavian exporters a cost edge over their North American competitors. The two countries have therefore found it politic to support a multinational research project in pulp and paper pollution control, and to advocate the producer-pays-principle for adoption by all member countries.

A final condition is the existence of other transnational relations between the parties using or living around the international common property. This condition seems reasonable: an international organization poised between two countries can manage a resource most easily when the people affected are less divided by the governmental boundary than united by transnational relations.

The difficulty with this condition is that—apart from the links of technology and taste already referred to—it is difficult to find convincing examples from Canada and the United States. Take the fisheries. Concerned because their investment in rearing and protecting salmon stocks was or would be vitiated by the other nation's fishermen harvesting outside the home country's jurisdiction, each has sought an agreement with the other. The agreements call for the imposition of two limitations on each country. The first is a limit on the total catch, which permits escapement and spawning. The second is a limit on the share each country can catch. This sharing provision is always present, though it may not be explicit. No country will sign a treaty that may reduce its future catches. The success of the agreement depends upon the ability of the treaty organization to interpret these two limits and to administer them in a fashion that satisfies the suspicious, individualistic fishermen. How has this been accomplished?

It is possible that transnational relationships have been helpful. Inquiry into the influences at work on members of the various commissions has shown that a complex of interconnections across the borders exists. The fishermen have a comradely relationship with each other, and at various times have talked of linking their unions for price bargaining; it might be argued that such potential connections would make resource management easier. The commission members are also much influenced by the fishing and packing corporations, some of which are multinational. Certainly the head offices of these corporations must be more interested in landings than loyalties, though transfrontier differences in costs, prices, and taxes must also affect their preferences. If they were unconstrained by the border, they would choose where to catch, and land, their combined corporate portion of the total quota. And it might be very difficult for the representative of a large fishing firm, appointed to a treaty commission, to distingiush between national and corporate interest.

The difficulty with these surmises is that in the fishery industry there is at present no evidence for them. Furthermore, in an industry characterised by outspoken denunciations and declarations, there seems never to have been a claim that either the unions or the companies were pursuing anything other than their local interests. Independence and autonomy seem to have been complete so far as the commissions, or their advisory boards, were concerned. More research is certainly necessary to prove or disprove the transnational assumptions, but the results are unlikely to uphold them.

When we turn from fisheries to environmental management, transnational relations do seem a little more evident. It is not difficult to recall examples of utilities, chemical firms, shipowners, and the like that have attempted to join forces across the border to produce a united front with respect to water levels and flows, their seasonal changes, ice cover, and so forth. Similarly, such environmental issues as the flooding of the Skagit River valley have been the occasion for tightening transnational alliances between environmental, public utility groups and second-level government officials concerned with matters like parks, wildlife, and forests. The influences exerted by these groupings mean that the recommendation of the international organization tends to be focused more on the conflict between uses or management decisions than on the conflict between countries. In this sense, the international organization might be said to be more successful when transnational relationships are present. But this impression, like my impression of the fisheries, needs further research.

These observations on the workability of international environmental agreements bring us to the most striking example—the International Joint Commission (IJC). While nominally a creature of the two national governments, its continuing development in response to transnational relationships and spillovers is very relevant to the subject of this volume (see also the article by Holsti and Levy in this volume).

The IJC, created by the Boundary Waters Treaty of 1909, has two national sections (three members each) that work together as one group under their two national chairmen. It has a national office in each country, but its total staff, professional and clerical, is less than twenty. Members are appointed by their governments but are not instructed by them, as is shown by the fact that most IJC decisions have been unanimous.

The IJC has two main roles. The first is semijudicial: to approve applications by citizens or governments of either country to alter the *levels of flows* of boundary waters and rivers that cross the boundary. This fairly technical jurisdiction has been concerned chiefly with the building of dams. The second function is more flexible: to make recommendations to the two governments on problems concerning boundary waters, or anything else, along the common frontier. In fact, such recommendations have dealt chiefly with (1) large projects like the Passamaquoddy Bay tidal power project, the Columbia River Treaty, and the coordination of the levels of all the Great Lakes, and (2) boundary pollution problems of air and water.

It is this pollution activity that is relevant here. In response to references, the IJC has made a number of reports on pollution of such watercourses as the Niagara River, the Detroit River, the Red River of the North, and the St. Croix River, and on air pollution at a number of boundary points, especially in the Windsor-Detroit area. These reports have served as the basis for international agreements, such as the Great Lakes Water Quality Agreement (1972) calling for combined action on Lakes Erie and Ontario.

Because it has no staff of its own, the IJC calls on private citizens, municipal and provincial officers, and especially on federal officers to form expert joint investigatory and control boards to advise it. These board members must wear two hats: for their ordinary work they are responsible to their own government agencies, and for their special inquiries they are responsible to the IJC. Their work, with that of members from the other country, has made it possible to obtain a basis for agreements, for the IJC reports are ultimately based on data that the governments' own servants have helped, as board members, to collect. This system safeguards the IJC reports from being pigeonholed on the basis of inadequate underlying data.

A second important aspect of the IJC's pollution work is its dependence on hearings. On each new question referred to it, the IJC holds preliminary hearings. Next its expert boards study the matter and submit a public, written report to the IJC (this stage may occupy several years). Then the IJC holds hearings on the board report before submitting its own final report to the two governments. In this way the IJC cuts across all the circuits of transnational relations. It hears briefs from companies, unions, volunteer groups, and individual complainants. It may indeed hear from these groups twice, once on each side of the border. Sometimes it is difficult to tell whether a speaker from an oil, soap, or chemical company, from an ecology group, or from a union is an American or Canadian without asking him; he may represent members on both sides of the boundary.

The whole procedure is a continuing activity. For example, the IJC recently heard from both Canadians and Americans at the Duluth-Superior–Thunder Bay end of Lake Superior concerning the dumping of wastes from the iron industry. These hearings were preparatory to an eventual IJC report that should extend the Great Lakes Water Quality Agreement to the upper lakes.

The pattern of technical boards has been augmented by the recent appointment of a Great Lakes water quality board, with its own separate office and full-time staff. This new body, for the coordination of the IJC's lake pollution programs, may become the nucleus of an international agency with a greater, but more localized, autonomy than the IJC itself. Its membership is dominated by state and provincial officers, and it is far from being either a joint arm of the two national governments or independent of the IJC, which is responsible for it and to which it reports.

There are also other examples of growing transnational cooperation and coordination in environmental matters. To list them briefly, I note: (1) the appearance of a Canadian in the action before the United States courts to halt the development of a large tanker route from Alaska to Washington State and California; (2) coordination and cooperation between British Columbia and Washington State on pollution and spills, and between New Brunswick and Maine on other environmental questions; (3) growing working cooperation on the Great Lakes between operating agencies of various levels of government for dealing with the contingencies of unexpected oil and chemical spills; and (4) some consultation and cooperation dealing with parks, beauty spots, and wilderness areas on the frontier (the Gulf Islands, Point Roberts, Skagit River, Waterton Lakes and Glacier National Parks, Niagara frontier, and Campobello Park).

I conclude this section and the essay by speculating about the future of international management organizations. The likelihood of establishing further resource-management agencies seems remote indeed. In the first place, Canada along with a good fraction of the membership of the United Nations are visibly turning away from regional fisheries' conventions in favour of the broadening of coastal zones, giving the coastal state more exclusive fishing rights than would emerge from the limits and quotas of international organizations. In the second place, Canada's nationalistic attitude in surveying its present water and energy commitments (such as the Columbia River Treaty) does not incline it, for whatever reasons, to enter into other long-run commitments, institutionalized or not. Arm's-length, year-to-year bargains would appear to dominate the agenda, rather than commitment to accept future decisions of joint boards or commissions. Kal Holsti, in another article in this volume, suggests that the Boundary Waters Treaty and the IJC survive in acceptability because their rules and procedures were well established before water resource issues became crucial to the two countries. In the third place, the new environmental problem of global air pollution requires an international agency with greater powers and scope than the existing pattern. To be effective, such an agency would, with its mixed membership, have to be empowered to override and overrule the decisions of local, state, and provincial elected bodies with respect to their air pollution regulations. Furthermore, its effectiveness in the long run would depend on the extent to which it had affected industrial and residential location, with attendant effects on employment, transport, roads, and land values. Can one really conceive of either the United States or Canada accepting decision making by a nonelected body with a foreign component in its membership on such politically sensitive subjects?

On the other hand, as population and industrial growth continues, Canada and the United States will have increasing recourse to their shared resources and environment. Already there has been some limited acceptance of the idea that the IJC should take a hand in the planning or administration of border areas such as the St. Croix River, Lake Champlain, the Skagit River valley, and Point Roberts. And even politically aware newspaper editorial writers complain that the IJC's powers do not give it sufficient teeth to deal with Great Lakes pollution or Detroit air pollution. If one can assume that these proponents and complainers know the implications of what they are saying, it may be that residents of border areas, at least, are concerned enough to be willing to concede some political autonomy in the interest of better resource and environmental management.

While it is clear that transnational relations will multiply and intensify with growing environmental concern, much less easy to predict is the political will and capacity of the Canadians and Americans to organize effective agencies for controlling them in the common interest.

PART IV

INTEGRATION, INSTITUTIONS, AND BARGAINING

INTEGRATION AND DISINTEGRATION ON THE NORTH AMERICAN CONTINENT

Robert Gilpin

Although ours is an age of transnational economic and political forces, it is even more an age of intense and intensifying nationalism. In fact, taken as a whole, the twentieth century has been a time of political fragmentation and disintegration. Much of the handiwork of political integration that characterized the nineteenth century has been undone and much else is under severe strain. The empires and multiethnic states that formerly provided order and unity over much of the globe have been destroyed. Once stable societies like Belgium, Canada, and the United States have become subject to severe internal strain. Yet despite the prevalence of this phenomenon, very few political scientists have studied from a systematic perspective the process of political disintegration.[1]

The purpose of this essay is to analyze the processes of integration and disintegration as opposed tendencies. By studying the interaction of transnational economic forces and economic nationalism on the North American continent, this article seeks to contribute both to an understanding of these processes and to the substance of contemporary American-Canadian and English-Canadian–French-Canadian relations. It seeks to do so through the employment of a conceptual model of economic-political integration and disintegration.

While this model emphasizes the role of economic factors, underlying the operation of these economic forces are cultural and political factors that have a reality and importance in their own right. It is in fact the interaction of these economic and nonmaterial factors that ultimately determines whether the integrative or disintegrative process will triumph. The substantive part of this essay begins, then, with

Robert Gilpin is a professor of politics and international affairs at Princeton University.
[1] A notable exception is Karl Deutsch, *Nationalism and Social Communication* (Cambridge, Mass.: The Massachusetts Institute of Technology Press, 1953).

an analysis of the integrative effects of economic growth. It then goes on to show the implications for political integration and disintegration. Subsequently this model is applied to the issue of Canadian-American relations, on the one hand, and to the relationship of anglophone-francophone Canada, on the other. The last part of the essay tries to bring these two sets of relationships into the framework of the triangular relationship composed of the United States, anglophone Canada, and Quebec.

I

The predominant fact on the North American continent has been the emergence in this century and particularly since the end of the Second World War of a highly interdependent continental economy. In economic terms alone, this has been a remarkably successful system. It has contributed to the high rate of economic growth enjoyed by both Canada and the United States. In order to understand the increasing political difficulties between the United States and Canada, as well as the smoldering conflict in Canada itself between anglophone and francophone, one must appreciate the economic and political implications of such an interdependent and rapidly expanding economy.

A major consequence of an interdependent economic system undergoing rapid growth is its impact on the distribution of wealth and economic activities.[2] As economists have observed, economic growth does not take place evenly throughout an economic system but is centered at particular places whose relative importance shifts over time. These so-called growth poles become the nodal points in the system.[3] In the words of the distinguished French economist Francois Perroux, "however basic it may seem, the fact of the matter is that growth does not appear everywhere and all at once; it appears in points or growth poles with varying terminal effects for the whole of the economy." [4]

As a result, economic growth has two opposed consequences for the distribution of wealth, power, and economic activities in an economic system. In the first place, there takes place what Gunnar Myrdal has called the backwash and Albert Hirschman has called the polarization effect; that is, wealth, industry, and economic activities tend to concentrate at the core or initial starting point. In contrast

[2] Mancur Olson, Jr., "Rapid Growth as a Destabilizing Force," *The Journal of Economic History* 23 (December 1963) : 529-52.

[3] Deutsch, p. 39.

[4] Francois Perroux, "Note sur la notion de 'pole de croissance', Matériaux pour une analyse de la croissance économique," *Cahiers de l'Institut de Science Economique Appliquee*, Serie D, 8 (1955), p. 309. Author's translation.

to this agglomeration process, there is an opposed tendency for a spread (Myrdal) or trickling-down (Hirschman) effect also to take place; this is to say, over time wealth and economic activities will tend to diffuse from the center into the periphery and distribute themselves at new nodal points throughout the system.[5]

In the absence of countervailing forces, e.g., war, planning, or depression, the tendency is for polarization effects to predominate over spread effects.[6] The rate of growth of wealth and economic activities at the center will be greater than the spread or diffusion of wealth and economic activities into the periphery. Although economic resources or factors of production are constantly diffused from the center into the periphery, up to a point the counterflow from the periphery into the growth center or core is far greater. As one authority on economic location has written, "the emergence of a polarized structure will normally be accompanied by a series of displacements, from the periphery to the center of the principal factors of production: labor, capital, entrepreneurship, foreign exchange, and raw materials in unprocessed form."[7]

The second and opposite effect of sustained economic growth is to diffuse or spread the process of growth throughout the system. With industrialism and the rise of an interdependent world economy, all the factors of production—labor, capital, technology, and even land itself (i.e., food and raw materials)—have become increasingly mobile. Through the migration of skilled labor, the expansion of trade and investment, and especially the diffusion of technology, the process of growth spreads from the core into what had been the periphery. Even where the diffusion of the more tangible factors of production is not involved, the increasing importance of systematic scientific and technological knowledge for economic growth and industrialization facilitates the spread of industrialization to new industrial cores.

As has already been noted, the diffusion of the growth process does not take place evenly throughout the system. The distribution of raw materials, of transportation networks, and other factors tend to favor one area over another, affecting the patterns of trade, investment, and migration. As a consequence, spread takes place in the form of new concentrations of economic power and wealth arising at par-

---

[5] Albert Hirschman, *The Strategy of Economic Development* (New Haven, Conn.: Yale University Press, 1958), pp. 183-87; Gunnar Myrdal, *Economic Theory and Underdeveloped Regions* (New York: Harper and Row Publishers, 1971), pp. 23-39.

[6] Hirschman, p. 187.

[7] John Friedman, *Regional Development Policy—A Case Study of Venezuela* (Cambridge, Mass.: The Massachusetts Institute of Technology Press, 1966), pp. 12-13.

ticular nodal points in the periphery. In time, what was part of the periphery becomes a growth center in its own right and a center for the further diffusion of growth. While the economics of location provide few guides to forecast the new centers, the basic phenomenon has been described as follows: "Therefore, it will be seen if economic activity were left to itself to spread over the surface of the earth undisturbed by other than economic motives, it would not approximate to a condition of even distribution of marketing and manufacturing centers throughout. On the contrary, there would be certain points of exceptional concentration of commerce or industrial activity or both." [8]

In contemporary writings on international economic relations, there is perhaps no more controversial subject than the tendency of wealth to concentrate and for spread effects to be limited to certain nodal points in the system. With respect to concentration, there are essentially only two alternative explanations. First, one group explains the existence of two great extremes of affluence and poverty by the simple fact of exploitation of the weak by the strong. According to Marxists and economic nationalists, over the past several centuries a transfer of wealth has taken place from the periphery of mankind to the industrial centers. The development of the latter is explained by the exploitation and underdevelopment of the former. This has been accomplished because the economic and military power of the industrial centers has enabled them to create an international division of labor that causes the accumulation of wealth in the initial centers of industrialization and produces underdevelopment elsewhere.[9] While there is undoubtedly some truth in this argument, it explains neither the initial inequalities upon which exploitation is alleged to be based nor the fact that spread *does* take place in varying degrees throughout the system. At the most, exploitation is a marginal explanation; it cannot account for the immense gap between the industrial and lesser-developed powers either today or in the nineteenth century.

The other major explanation of concentration and the limitation of spread effects, equally simple, is that the rate of profit at the growth center is higher, or, there is a more efficient use of resources. This may be due to a large number of circumstances: the availability of resources including skilled labor; the existence of good transportation; the presence of external economies and lower transaction costs; the existing social and technical infrastructure; political stability; a high rate of savings; and economies of scale. It is this higher efficiency

[8] R. G. Hawtrey, *Economic Aspects of Sovereignty* (London: Longmans, Green & Co., 1952), p. 48.

[9] Paul Baran, *The Political Economy of Growth* (New York: Monthly Review Press, 1957).

in urban and industrial centers that attracts and absorbs labor, capital, and resources to the detriment of the periphery. It is, in short, a case of "to them that have shall be given."

The reasons for the concentration of wealth and power in industrial centers is undoubtedly some combination of both explanations. Inequalities in the contemporary world rest on the efficiency advantages and technological supremacy of the existing industrial and urban centers. One may, if he wishes, label these advantages of being first a form of exploitation in order to explain the phenomena of development and underdevelopment. At least it is true that economic inequalities do create the necessary conditions for exploitation however it may be defined. Equally important, there is no doubt that industrial centers frequently seek to prevent the spread of industrialism. Certainly, the immense competitive advantages of the initial industrial centers mean that the spread of industry takes place under formidable disadvantages and usually in opposition to the resistance of the existing centers.[10] Therefore, the later the industrialization of a nation, the greater the effort must be to develop viable industries and to break into world markets. The later the industrialization, the greater the need for centralized national authority to marshal resources, offset centralizing market forces, and overcome the effects of inequalities.[11] For this reason, while the spread of growth, like the concentration of wealth, is to be explained in large part by market forces, a seemingly necessary condition for spread to take place is the existence of some centralized political power that can counteract the economic power of existing centers and the centralizing tendency of market forces. Thus, in nineteenth-century Germany this function was performed largely by the banking institutions, in the United States by corporations protected by high tariffs, and in Japan and Russia by the national government.[12] Once set upon the course of industrialization, however, these late industrializers enjoyed the "advantages of backwardness" which enabled them eventually to surpass the rate of growth of the industrial leader.[13] Utilizing the most modern, efficient machinery and productive know-how, these late starters cut into the lead and overtook the first industrial center, Great Britain, in the latter part of the century and eventually shifted the balance of world industrial power.

---

[10] W. Arthur Lewis, *Theory of Economic Growth* (New York: Harper and Row Publishers, 1965), p. 353.

[11] Alexander Gerschenkron, "Economic Backwardness in Historical Perspective," in *The Progress of Underdeveloped Areas*, ed. Bert Hoselitz (Chicago: University of Chicago Press, 1952), pp. 27-29.

[12] Ibid.

[13] Thorstein Veblen, *Imperial Germany and the Industrial Revolution* (New York: The Macmillan Co., 1915).

Given the natural tendency of economic growth to concentrate wealth and power at particular points in an interdependent economic system, the objective of economic nationalism is to make the process of economic growth operate to the benefit of one's own nation. Through commercial policy, the layout of transportation networks, and other public policies, the objective of economic nationalism is to channel the forces of growth in one's own direction. The nation seeks to accelerate the spread of growth particularly in order to acquire possession of an industrial core.

In effect, economic nationalism arises as a protective measure against market forces.[14] Sharing with preindustrial mercantilism an emphasis on the nation state, economic nationalism as it has developed in our time is a response to the centralizing implications of industrialism and an interdependent world economy: the division of an economic system into industrial core and dependent periphery, the disruptive effects of the expansion of the core on the periphery, and the concentration of wealth in the growth centers.

In the world model of liberal economists, the opposite tendencies of concentration and spread are of relatively little political consequence. In a homogeneous culture and in the absence of political boundaries, the mobility of the factors of production tends to produce an economic-political equilibrium. Thus, the movement of industrial and economic activities to urban centers draws surplus labor from the periphery and thereby moderates the decline of wage rates in potentially overpopulated peripheral areas. As American industry moved west, for example, in response to the discovery of iron and coal, it was followed by some labor migration from the declining mill towns of New England. While this was not a painless and friction-free process, the relative mobility of all factors of production in the United States has been a major source of political stability.

In a situation, however, where cultural differences and political boundaries divide core and periphery, the tendency for wealth, industry, and economic activity to concentrate in the core has profound political implications. Thus, if labor cannot, or will not, move across political or cultural boundaries to the urban core where the industries and jobs are located, then political forces may arise to move the jobs to the periphery—regardless of the economic rationale and consequent loss of economic efficiency.

But the most important political implication of this situation is the dependence of the periphery on the core. The political, cultural, or ethnic group that controls the core is dominant; the periphery

[14] Michael Polanyi, *Primitive, Archaic and Modern Economies—Essays of Karl Polanyi*, ed. George Dalton (Garden City, N.Y.: Doubleday & Co., 1968), p. xxv.

group is subordinate and dependent. It is the *dependency* consequences of economic integration that are most frustrating for the periphery group and are the stimulus to the rise of economic nationalism.

The concept of *dependence* has become one of the most fashionable in contemporary writings on international economic relations. By dependence is meant the loss of alternatives in the sense that there are no perceived acceptable alternatives to integration with the core. The periphery is dependent in that it gains economically from the relationship; the severing of economic ties would cause severe economic damage to the periphery's economy. In short, it is not because the periphery is exploited by the relationship but precisely because it benefits from it that the periphery feels dependent upon the core.

In the situation where political, ethnic, or other boundaries divide core and periphery, this dependency relationship is frustrating for the latter in at least two senses. At the same time that the periphery is incorporated into a larger economic system, the political and career ambitions of its population and particularly its middle class remain limited relative to those in the core. The periphery's middle class cannot aspire to the top. In addition to this source of personal frustration, economic dependence creates a situation of political dependence which is resented by the periphery. The political choices of the periphery are, or at least appear to be, limited and may in fact be made in the core. The political, cultural, or ethnic group that controls the core is politically dominant; the periphery group is subordinate and dependent. Fundamentally, it is these economic and political consequences of increasing economic interdependence across national and cultural-ethnic boundaries that give rise to disintegrating forces of economic nationalism.[15]

Thus, economic nationalism is a response to economic and market forces that create an international division of labor between the high technology of the industrial core and the lower technology industries and raw material producers of the periphery. Economic nationalism reflects the desire of a peripheral political, cultural, or ethnic group to possess and enjoy an industrial core of its own where wealth, attractive careers, and power are located. Its objective is to transform this division of labor through industrialization and to transform its territorial base into a relatively independent industrial core.

Following this analysis of economic nationalism, the argument of this essay is that the rise of economic nationalism in English and

---

[15] For the classical statement of the nationalist argument, see Frederick List, *National System of Political Economy*, trans. G. A. Matile (Philadelphia, Pa.: J. B. Lippincott and Co., 1856).

French Canada is a reaction to the intensification of economic integration on the North American continent; it reflects the ambitions of these groups to possess advanced industrial cores in their own right. In the following section of the essay I deal with the emergence of English-Canadian nationalism which, originating in southern Ontario (Toronto particularly), has spread throughout much of English Canada. Then the essay turns to the Quebec case.

II

In a real sense, Canada has always been a peripheral economy. The concept of the core-periphery model is itself attributed to the analysis of the Canadian economy by the distinguished Canadian economist Harold Innis in his classic, *The Fur Trade in Canada: An Introduction to Canadian Economic History*:

> The economic history of Canada has been dominated by the discrepancy between the centre and the margin of Western civilization . . . agriculture, industry, transportation, trade, finance, and governmental activities tend to become subordinate to the production of the staple for a more highly specialized manufacturing community. These general tendencies may be strengthened by governmental policy as in mercantile systems.[16]

Since the 1930s, and particularly since the end of the Second World War, however, the centre (core) and the margin (periphery) relationship has changed profoundly. The staple is no longer fur but oil, wheat, and iron ore; the relationship is no longer merely one of resource extraction and food stuffs but the extension into the Canadian periphery of branch-plant operations of American corporations. Moreover, the periphery is no longer merely the passive object of economic initiatives from the core but has developed a strength and set of ambitions of its own. The creation of the Canada Development Corporation and its effort to acquire Texas Gulf and other American corporations are a response to the opportunities opened by developing strength and capabilities.

Throughout Canada's history the flow of external capital and the external market have been determinant features of its economic development.[17] As in the case of the United States, foreign capital was

---

[16] "The Importance of Staple Products," in *The Fur Trade in Canada*, reprinted in W. T. Easterbrook and M. H. Watkins, *Approaches to Canadian Economic History* (Toronto: McClelland and Stewart, 1967), p. 18.

[17] This section of the essay relies heavily on Canada, Gray Task Force, *Foreign Direct Investment in Canada* (Ottawa: Information Canada, 1972); also referred to as the Gray report.

instrumental in the development of Canadian natural resources and in the creation of the technical infrastructure of railways, canals, and roads which got these staples and resources to world markets. Prior to World War I, in fact, external capital constituted a higher proportion of capital employed in the Canadian economy than it does today. But the nature of this foreign investment and of Canadian society were such that this heavy dependence, particularly on British capital, did not create the political conflict that American direct investments do at the present time.

British investment in Canada was primarily indirect investment; it took the form of debt securities rather than equities. Thus, despite the heavy reliance upon British capital, apart from the railways there was actually very little foreign control of the Canadian economy. While the Canadians were highly dependent upon the London bond market and upon the British consumer market for their exports, they were in form at least masters in their own house. This situation changed dramatically, however, after the First World War and with the replacement of Great Britain by the United States as the principal supplier of Canadian capital.

In contrast to British investment, American investment in Canada has tended to be direct as well as portfolio investment by American corporations and banks. Both with respect to raw materials and manufactures, American corporations have expanded into the Canadian economy through the take-over of Canadian firms and the establishment of new subsidiaries or branch plants. The difference between these two types of investment is of critical importance with respect both to the economic integration of the two economies and the political implications of economic interdependence.

Between 1914 and 1930, American direct investment in Canada grew rapidly. This investment concentrated in particular sectors of the Canadian economy, including the extractive and processing industries, automobile manufacturing, pulped paper production, electrical manufacturing, and nonferrous mining and refining. At the same time, both the public and private sectors of the Canadian economy shifted their borrowing from the London to the New York money markets. As a consequence, by 1930 American investment in Canada was approximately 57 percent in portfolio and 43 percent in direct investment.

Following a lull throughout the 1930s, American war-related investments expanded in Canada during the Second World War. But the great flood of American direct investment commenced at the end of the war. Between 1945 and 1967, total American investment in Canada increased from $5 billion to $28 billion, direct investment from $2 to $17 billion. About one-half of this direct investment was mainly in manufacturing—the starting up of new enterprises, expansion of existing plants, or the take-over of Canadian firms. Portfolio investment, about half in government bonds, amounted to approximately $8 billion.

As I have already suggested, the difference between the British emphasis on debt securities and the American emphasis on direct investment is of immense economic and political importance. With respect to the former, the motivation is largely financial. Also, as I have already pointed out, management and control continue to rest with the borrower (at least in the Canadian experience); the liabilities incurred can be liquidated through repayment. The motivation behind direct investment and the possession of subsidiaries or branch plants, on the other hand, is primarily the acquisition of control over natural resources, assets, and markets. What is desired by the parent firm is a permanent position in the foreign economy. As a consequence, even though mutual economic benefit may result, direct investment creates economic and political relations of a lasting and significant character between the advanced industrial core and the branch-plant, raw material-producing periphery.

In economic terms, what this flood of American investment has meant is the increasing integration of the Canadian peripheral economy into the American core. In the area of natural resources, American corporations not only own or control a very high percentage of Canadian resources but there has taken place a backward vertical integration—the integration of the earlier stages of the productive process—by American processors and manufacturers. The later stages of processing and manufacturing are located in the American core; extraction and occasionally refining or semiprocessing are located in the Canadian periphery. Thus, because of this vertical integration from extraction to manufacturing to marketing all under American management and control, the peripheral Canadian economy is frequently excluded from the processing and manufacturing of Canadian natural resources.

With respect to manufacturing, American corporations control approximately 50 percent of Canadian industry. In particular sectors such as petroleum, transport, and chemicals, the percentage of American ownership approaches four-fifths or more of the industry. But of greater importance, as in extractive industries, the Canadian subsidiaries and branch plants are highly integrated into the American industrial structure. From the Canadian point of view, these plants are truncated replicas of their American parents; moreover, they are believed increasingly to have deleterious consequences for Canadian economic and political development.

The integration of the Canadian periphery into the American

core has represented a mutuality of interests. For the United States, with the expansion and maturity of its industrial base and the exhaustion of high-grade raw materials, American businessmen looked abroad and initially to America's immediate neighbors. Canada for its own part invited in American investment through favorable tax and related policies as well as by the imposition of tariff barriers. The high Canadian tariff quite deliberately gave American corporations an incentive to invest in Canada in order to have access to the Canadian market and through it to the Commonwealth preference area.

The Canadian strategy for rapid industrialization, then, has been to force the migration of American industry into the Canadian economy. In this effort the Canadian tariff succeeded magnificently, providing the Canadians with one of the highest standards of living in the world. But it did so at the cost of blunting indigenous Canadian entrepreneurship and integrating the Canadian industrial core in southern Ontario with the American industrial and financial heartland surrounding the Great Lakes. But American-Canadian economic relations have changed drastically since a headline in the Canadian *Financial Post* bragged, "Claim Tariff Brings Canada 90 New Plants: Government Points with Pride to Long List." [18]

Parallel with this financial and corporate integration of the two economies, trade between the economies has expanded greatly until today the two economies constitute one another's best customers. This process of intensifying trade relations has accelerated in recent years with the movement of Great Britain toward continental Europe and the creation of the European Common Market. Thus, through investment and trade the American core and Canadian periphery have become increasingly integrated and interdependent. The logic of this economic process, as former Undersecretary of State George Ball told the Canadian House of Commons Standing Committee on External Affairs and National Defense several years ago, was the inevitable economic union between Canada and the United States.[19]

The consequence of economic integration, however, has not been a steady and untroubled evolution toward economic union but the sudden emergence in the mid-1960s of intense economic nationalism and anti-Americanism in English Canada. Not surprisingly, the wellsprings of this nationalist sentiment have been southern Ontario and

---

[18] Quoted in Herbert Marshall and Kenneth Taylor, *Canadian-American Industry; A Study in International Investment* (New Haven, Conn.: Yale University Press, 1936), pp. 274-75.
[19] Quoted in Canadian Institute of International Affairs, *International Canada* (Toronto: Canadian Institute of International Affairs, 1970), pp. 111-12.

particularly Toronto, that sector of Canada that has most benefited from, and been most integrated with, the American industrial core centered in Detroit, Chicago, and the Midwest. Rather rapidly, anti-Americanism subsequently has spread through English Canada until today the doctrine of continentalism is on the defensive throughout English Canada. As a result, today the transnational forces of economic integration and the forces of political disintegration contend against one another as the basic factor in American-Canadian relations.

There are of course no simple explanations for this transformation of American-Canadian relations. One may begin with the simple historic fact that Canadians do not want to become Americans. But the intensification of this sentiment and the pulling back from the United States arise from the growing realization that the logic of economic integration is a continual blurring of cultural and political differences. Moreover, though the loss of Canadian identity has always been a major concern, contemporary developments in American society have reinforced this determination to keep the United States at arm's length.

The Vietnam War, America's internal racial strife, and other domestic problems have acted as centrifugal forces pulling the Canadian periphery away from the American core. The United States no longer is the ideal that it once was for many Canadians; it is increasingly frightening to many others. The jolt to Canadian political thinking caused by these changed perceptions of the United States was undoubtedly a major factor in the sudden emergence of intense nationalism in the 1960s. But of equal or greater importance, the rise of English-Canadian nationalism also reflected the operation of deep, secular forces in Canadian society itself and the economic consequences of integration with the American economy.

The Canadian economy has been undergoing a profound and accelerating structural change. Though industrialization began in earnest in the early decades of this century, due in large part to the stimulus of American investment and trade, the Canadian industrial and financial base has greatly expanded in recent years. In terms of the model of disintegration employed in this study, there has been a significant diffusion of industry to Canada through such mechanisms as American investment, expanded trade, and the automobile agreement. Additionally, Canadian financial resources and the capital market located in Toronto have greatly improved in recent years. Toronto has evolved into an industrial-economic core in its own right. It is this industrial and financial strength that encourages the assertion of English-Canadian nationalism.

While Canadian growth and development were accelerating, the

United States in the late 1960s and early 1970s underwent a relative loss of dynamism. With greater integration between the two economies, the deleterious spillovers from the American core into the Canadian periphery have increased in the form of unemployment, idle plants, and other economic dislocations. Thus, at the same time that Canadians were increasingly vulnerable to American economic disturbances (recession or inflation), the expansion of the Canadian industrial and financial base to the point of self-sufficiency has given Canada the alternative of lessening its dependence on the United States. Therefore, it was seemingly both necessary and possible for Canada to lessen its ties with the American economy in order to reduce Canada's vulnerability to untoward developments south of the border. One may in fact speculate that the emergence of economic nationalism in a peripheral economy is partially the consequence of the loss of dynamism and threat of instability in the core.[20]

Underlying the emergence of (English-Canadian) nationalism then is an important psychological (and economic) transformation. Increasingly Canadians believe that Canada is strong enough to take the necessary measures to reduce its dependence upon the American core and to step away from the political-economic dangers of integration with the United States. The emergent Canadian industrial core and its Canadian periphery are believed to be sufficiently developed now to provide the basis for an assertion of Canadian economic and political independence. In other words, new alternatives to dependence on the American core were opening up at the time that political and economic developments warranted dissociation from the United States. Economic self-sufficiency was held to be a prerequisite for greater political and economic independence from the United States.

Other widely operating and interrelated causes help explain the emergence of nationalism in English Canada and, as we will see, in Quebec as well. Throughout Canada a number of changes have triggered the desire for industrialization and therefore the need to break the vertical integration between Canadian resources and American industries. In the west, in the Prairie provinces, and particularly in Quebec, industrialization has become the keystone of public policy. Behind this desire to industrialize lie the increasing urbanization of Canadian society, a massive expansion of the work force, and especially the emergence of a large, college-educated middle class.

Another element is a new assessment of the costs of foreign direct investment for the Canadian economy. The traditional view in English Canada was that economic nationalism was a luxury that Canadians

<hr>

[20] This interesting idea was suggested to me in a private communication from W. B. Walker of the University of Sussex.

could not afford. The distinguished Canadian economist Harry Johnson, in his influential *The Canadian Quandary* [21] and other studies, made a convincing case that foreign investment brought only benefits to the Canadian economy. Empirical studies, particularly those of A. E. Safarian, confirmed this judgment on the benefits of American investment.[22] The investment issue was thought to be solely a political one; if Canadians followed the lead of Walter Gordon, Melvin Watkins, and other nationalists, they should be prepared to pay a high economic price. In contemporary Canada, however, a new assessment of Canadian interests is emerging.

In order to employ the fastest growing urban work force in the Western world and to provide attractive careers for Canada's expanding college-educated younger generation, Canada, it is believed, must greatly increase its secondary industry. This goal, however, clashes directly with some American interests and the vertically integrated nature of Canada's resource economy. At a time when Americans are pressing Canada for a greater share of its resources in order to feed America's industrial plant, Canada seeks these resources itself to provide the basis for Canadian industrialization. This development as much as the so-called energy crisis explains the anticipated decision of Canada to reduce its export of oil to the United States. The intention to process Canadian raw materials in Canada represents a new industrial strategy on the part of Canada.[23] Like resource-exporting countries the world over, Canada wants real assets in return for its nonrenewable raw materials.

The signal for this new Canadian industrial strategy was the publication of the Gray report on *Foreign Direct Investment in Canada*. While accepting the benefits of and the need for foreign investment, the thrust of the report is a redefinition of the economic and political cost to Canada: the overemphasis on resource development at the expense of an "industrial development policy geared to Canada's own particular growth and employment objectives"; [24] the creation of a high-cost industrial structure that cannot compete internationally; and the establishment of truncated enterprises that do not facilitate the advancement of Canadian capacities and skills, particularly in the area of technological innovation.

This last development is the critical one; it goes to the heart of the matter. Reduced to its essential, the objective of English-Canadian

[21] Harry Johnson, *The Canadian Quandary* (New York: McGraw-Hill Book Co., 1963).

[22] See, for example, A. E. Safarian, *The Performance of Foreign-Owned Firms in Canada* (Washington, D.C.: Canadian-American Committee, 1969).

[23] *Financial Post* (Toronto), 21 July 1973.

[24] Gray report, p. 6.

nationalism is the creation of a high-technology industrial structure. Canada would replace its present subordinate and truncated corporate economy with the type of advanced technological economy possessed by the United States, Japan, and Western Europe. Perhaps the point can best be made by reference once again to the Gray report: "But the essential point—and one that is central to an understanding of this study—is that truncated subsidiary operations usually lack the capacity and opportunity over time to develop the full range of activities normally associated with a mature business enterprise." [25] In other words, Canada must become one of the world's core industrial economies.

This ambition (which is as much political as economic) reflects the emergence of a new, highly educated middle class in English Canada. Nationalism in the modern world is largely a middle-class phenomenon; it arises out of the economic-political ambitions of this emergent, educated class.[26] If these educated Canadians are to have the careers they desire and to be masters in their own house, then they must gain back control of their industrial economy. Then they must go on to create a high-technological economy such as that possessed by the other advanced industrial powers. The encouragement of Canadian entrepreneurship and indigenous technological innovation is undoubtedly one of the foremost objectives of the Canada Development Corporation and other federal agencies.

This desire for an indigenous scientific and technological capability cannot be overstressed. The ambition to innovate new industrial processes and products is one shared by Canadians of nearly all political persuasions. Upon the achievement of this capacity, many Canadians believe, rests an independent Canadian economic and cultural identity. Where the more radical Canadian nationalists and their opponents differ is over the question of whether Canada is now ready to decrease substantially its reliance upon American technology and investment and thereby depend upon Canadian technological and industrial entrepreneurship.

In the last analysis, therefore, the source and success of nationalism rest upon the emergence of a middle class whose interests lie with the severing, or at least the attenuation, of the core-periphery relation and the creation of a nationally controlled industrial economy. A nationalistic elite from this class has now emerged in Canada. This group believes Canada is now strong enough to assert its indepen-

---

[25] Ibid.
[26] This argument, of course, is essentially that of Albert Breton in his influential "The Economics of Nationalism," *Journal of Political Economy* 72, no. 2 (1964): 376-86.

dence from the United States. Thus, a dominant motif of the Gray report and of recent Canadian writings on foreign investment is the fact that internally generated capital can now finance a large fraction of future Canadian development.[27]

Canada has in fact begun the process of buying back the Canadian economy. In 1970, Canadians owned only 31 percent of International Nickel, Canada's largest corporation. Today, Canadian ownership is 51 percent. The assault of the Canada Development Corporation on Texas Gulf and the passage on 25 November 1973 of the first legislation to control foreign direct investment in the Canadian economy signal a more vigorous pursuit of this goal.

But the writers of the Gray report and other Canadians also recognize that industrial independence requires other elements that Canada still lacks or has lacked in the past: technology, entrepreneurship, and economies of scale.[28] There is a limit to the extent that Canada can assert its economic independence from the United States and cut itself off from American technology, investment, and markets. More importantly, there are critical differences of opinion and conflicts of interest that limit Canada's capacity to assert its independence from the United States.

The desire of the western provinces themselves to industrialize places them at odds with the established industrial cores in Ontario and, to a lesser extent, Quebec, on many issues, including that of American investment. Some 80 percent of Canadian manufacturing is located in Ontario and Quebec. The west resents federal policies that are deemed to favor eastern industry and finance. Severe restrictions on foreign investment could place the western provinces at a disadvantage. Like Quebec the western provinces tend to see continued foreign investment as a means to their own industrialization. Regional policies that encourage this foreign investment outside Canada's own industrial core are frequently opposed by forces in Ottawa or Toronto which would restrict further outside investment. In the western view of things, they are the periphery of an eastern core. They would like to lessen their own dependence on the Toronto industrialists and financiers who control so much of the Canadian economy. For example, there is a basic conflict between Alberta and Ottawa over energy policy and exports to the United States. While both Alberta and Ottawa would like to decrease their share of the monopoly rent on oil and natural gas that goes into the coffers of American companies, they are at odds over where in Canada these rents will go—

---

[27] A major point of the Gray report is that the greater part of American investment in Canada is financed from Canadian sources.

[28] *Financial Post* (Toronto), 30 June 1973.

Alberta or Ottawa. Will Alberta be allowed to export oil at high world prices or will that oil be diverted at lower prices to the east and particularly to Quebec?

While these conflicts within English Canada do not suggest a rupture of the country as does the emergence of Quebec nationalism, they do make it more difficult for Canada to develop a unified policy toward the United States and thereby to reduce Canada's economic dependence on the American economy. The more critical problem, however, is the future role and stance of the third leg of the North American triangle—Quebec.

III

What Canada is to the United States both economically and politically French Quebec is to English Canada. Just as the emergence of English-Canadian nationalism is one response to the economic and political forces integrating the Canadian periphery with the American core, so French-Canadian nationalism in Quebec is one response to similar forces within Canada itself which are believed to threaten French-Canadian culture and increasingly have made Quebec part of a Canadian periphery centered upon Toronto, the industrial and financial core of contemporary Canada. Thus, within Canada the integrating forces of economic growth and interdependence have stimulated a powerful disintegrative political movement that threatens to destroy Canadian political unity.

In drastically oversimplified terms, what has been created on this continent is a complex hierarchical division of labor that has integrated the American, Ontario, and Quebec industrial structures into a unified whole. At its apex are the industrial and financial centers of the United States. The strengths of the American economy are its financial, technological, and managerial resources. Within Canada, Toronto has become a secondary financial and industrial center. Its heavy and capital-intensive industry, with a few important exceptions, are extensions of the American industrial heartland. Quebec for its part, although automotive production and heavy industries are developing, is still largely characterized by labor-intensive industries. Lacking sufficiently strong financial, technological, or managerial resources, the French Canadians of Quebec are still at the base of this industrial-financial hierarchy.

Granted their economic situations differ greatly, the same economic and political forces are acting in Quebec as in English Canada. In the first place, like English-Canadian nationalism, French-Canadian nationalism is a response to major changes in society: urbanization, the emergence of a large college-educated middle class, and the need to absorb a rapidly growing labor force. Secondly, the fundamental objective of both nationalisms is the same: the preservation of cultural identity, the assertion of political independence, and the gaining of control over the economy; like their English-Canadian counterparts, French Canadians would like to displace the elite—in this case, English-Canadian and American—that controls the Quebec economy. And, thirdly, both English-Canadian and French-Canadian nationalists believe that the necessary preconditions for the achievement of their long-term political and economic goal is the creation of a modern, high-technology industrial structure. Moreover, like the English-Canadian nationalist, the French-Canadian nationalist now believes Quebec is in a sufficiently strong position to assert its economic independence.

Just as both nationalisms arise from a similar source, they also have a common problem. While this article has stressed the cultural and regional bases of economic nationalism in English and French Canada, nationalism has a class basis as well. As I have argued, in both English and French Canada nationalism is largely a middle-class phenomenon. It is these middle classes that would be the primary beneficiaries of economic nationalism through inheriting control of the industrial and economic structure. Neither of these aspiring middle classes has yet convinced their respective working classes, however, that a shift of masters would be to their economic advantage and that they would not suffer from nationalistic policies. Though both English- and French-Canadian working classes (and especially union leadership) have moved in recent years in the nationalist direction, yet they remain predominantly conservative in the sense of not desiring to disrupt the economic status quo.

The class conflict in the modern world that may be of greatest significance is that of rival middle classes. It is a rivalry that centers on the control of the economy and the hierarchical structure associated with interdependence among advanced industrial societies. It is not merely an issue of the distribution of wealth but of the distribution of career opportunities. What is at stake is the position of particular middle classes in the hierarchically organized international or continental division of labor. Where, in other words, will the functions of higher management, research and development, and such be located? Who will have the professional positions associated with an advanced industrialized economy? It is this intraclass conflict that lies at the heart of the American-Canadian conflict and the conflict within Canada itself.

Thus, it is precisely because they have identical goals and different identities that the English-Canadian and French-Canadian nationalists have come into conflict. Both English and French Canadians desire to command the core of the modernized economy both national-isms desire. It is this fact that has brought them into conflict and which, in particular, causes their attitudes toward the United States and to American investment, for example, to diverge sharply. Thus, whereas English Canada, and especially Toronto, believes Canada can lessen its dependence upon American investment, Quebec in its desire to catch up with Ontario's more advanced industrial structure looks to the United States increasingly for capital, technology, and markets. Thus, the freezing of the status quo by restrictions on foreign invest-ment would, in the eyes of many French Canadians, make permanent Quebec's inferior industrial position vis-à-vis Ontario.

This is not to suggest that there is a convergence of opinion in Quebec with respect to English Canada. Although the movement toward separatism or independence has greatly advanced and many predict the eventual success of the separatist Parti Québécois, the issue still hangs in the balance. The October 1973 Quebec elections certainly did not resolve the issue despite the apparent setback to the Parti Québécois. As in the case of Canada and the United States, the economic integration of English and French Canada has both benefits and costs for Quebec. The problem in both cases is how to decrease the cost and maximize the benefits, and much of the debate over separatism in Quebec centers on this question. The federalists emphasize the benefits of confederation; the séparatistes, its costs.[29]

The basic position of the séparatistes is that unified government is required for effective economic development and industrialization.[30] In contrast to the existing situation where decision making with respect to economic policy is divided between Ottawa and the prov-inces, authority should be centralized. While theoretically the cen-tralization of decision could take place in Ottawa rather than in Que-bec, the price French Canada would have to pay for this political unification, it is argued, would be the eventual loss of its culture and complete absorption into English Canada. Therefore, the séparatistes favor the unification of decision making in an independent Quebec.

In part, the séparatistes argue, the unification of political de-cision is necessary in order to eliminate wasteful duplication between federal and provincial activities. More importantly, economic and

---

[29] For an analysis of the two dominant schools of French-Canadian thought on the future of Quebec, see Gerald Clark, *The United States and Canada* (Cam-bridge, Mass.: Harvard University Press, 1968), pp. 285-96.

[30] The economic position of Le Parti Québécois is spelled out in *La Souveraineté et L'Economie*, Mars 1970; see René Lévesque, *An Option for Quebec* (Toronto: McClelland and Stewart, 1968); *La Solution, Le programme du Parti Québécois presenté par René Lévesque* (Quebec: Edition du Jour, 1970). The most recent statement is Le Parti Québécois, *Quand nous Serons Vraiment chez nous*, October 1972.

social modernization in Quebec in the middle of the twentieth century is said to necessitate a powerful role for the state. The state must not only refashion the institutional framework for economic activity, but in a complex, technological world, the economic role of the state as consumer, producer, and investor is crucial. If Quebec is to become a highly industrialized society and provide attractive careers for the emerging French-Canadian middle class, then the state must use its powers to marshal scarce resources and rationalize Quebec's fragmented economy. In an economy controlled by English Canadians and Americans, the state must become the instrument of French-Canadian ambitions.

Furthermore, the séparatistes argue, a sovereign and independent Quebec would be in a stronger bargaining position vis-à-vis American industry. It could thereby eliminate the truncated industrial structure condemned in the Gray report. Freed from control by Ottawa, it could pursue policies that would encourage foreign investment in Quebec, especially in high-technology industries, and thus reduce the economic gap between Quebec and the richer provinces. In addition, an independent Quebec could use American and other foreign investment as a counterweight to English-Canadian financial power and accelerate the redistribution of wealth and status in Quebec. Thus, in contrast to those who argue that a sovereign Quebec would come under the " 'diktats' de la finance américaine," the séparatistes argue instead it is the only means to preserve French culture and gain control of the Quebec economy.

While French-Canadian proponents of continued federation generally accept the principle of active state intervention in the economy, they do not agree that this necessitates a complete unification of economic decision making in either Ottawa or Quebec. Although the main burden for promoting and managing economic development should rest with the province, this does not require the dissolution of Canada. However, it does mean, these French-Canadian federalists tend to argue, a greater willingness on the part of Ottawa to assist the provinces in carrying out these economic responsibilities.

In the opinion of these profederalist Québécois, separation would cause irreparable damage to the Quebec economy.[31] The great risk of separation, these people argue, would be the loss of Quebec's most important asset—membership in Canada's common market. An economically isolated Quebec could not attract sufficient foreign investment to carry out its ambitious plans for economic development; its

[31] Roma Dauphin, "The Effects of Potential Trade Liberation on Manufacturing Industries of Quebec," p. 6-7. (Mimeographed.)

present economy could not survive. Quebec's present economy is highly labor-intensive and uncompetitive by world standards. According to this position, French Canadians could not afford the luxury of staying at home rather than migrating to Canada's industrial core (Ontario) if it were not for Canada's protective tariff—a form of national subsidy for Quebec.[32] While these profederalist Québécois foresee the day when French Canadians will control the great part of the Quebec economy, the time is not yet ripe. The management of the Quebec economy is dependent upon its English-speaking industrial and financial elite; it is the continuance of this elite that secures Quebec's position in the Canadian economy. Whatever, therefore, the ultimate solution may be to Quebec's desire to create a high-technology economy and to enable French Canadians to be masters in their house, it is not to be found in Québecoisization of the Quebec economy and casting off precipitously the protective mantle of Canadian federation.[33]

In summary, there are two fundamental facts that define the Quebec economic-political situation. The first is the immobility of the Quebec labor force. As French Canadians will not migrate to the jobs, the economic strategy of Quebec is to bring the jobs to Quebec. Here one encounters the second fundamental fact of the Quebec situation: the geographical location of Quebec and its core, Montreal. In contrast to Toronto, Montreal is generally isolated from the American-Canadian industrial heartland. With the movement of the Canadian economy inward and away from Europe, industries and finance have moved from Montreal to Toronto. In terms of economic efficiency and the principles of economic location, the transformation of Montreal into the type of advanced industrial core desired by French Canadians will be difficult indeed. The implications of this ambition for the future of Canadian unity will be dependent upon much larger economic and political forces. It is to them that I now turn.

IV

The argument of this essay is that these issues of integration and disintegration will be and can only be resolved in the context of the triangular relationship of English Canada, Quebec, and the United States. One could even go further and say that the outcomes are dependent upon the larger issues of trade, investment, and monetary relations that are presently being sorted out by the world's industrial

---

[32] Ibid.

[33] For the federalist critique of independence, see Andrew A. Brichart, *Option Canada* (Quebec: The Canada Committee, 1968).

powers. But in this essay the emphasis is mainly upon the significance of the triangular relations on the North American continent itself.

As several observers have pointed out, English Canada is restrained by Quebec in transforming its relations with the United States.[34] The different stages of development of the English-Canadian and Quebec economies and the different interests of English and French Canada with respect to foreign investment and markets place a severe constraint on Canadian unity as Canada attempts to stand up to the United States. We have already seen that English Canada itself is rife with conflicting economic interests: Will, for example, the oil interests of Alberta sell *Canadian* in order to build a petrochemical industry in Canada and supply Quebec and the east with relatively cheap oil when American and world prices are considerably higher? But the critical question will be how to satisfy Quebec's desire to emulate English Canada. Can eastern Canada accommodate two major high-technology, industrial cores?

The second critical relationship is that between English Canada and the United States; the resolution of this issue in part does depend upon the larger arena of world economic relations. In particular, to what extent can Canada diversify its sources of investment and trade relations? How will the United States react to the assertion of greater economic and political independence on the part of Canada? The extent to which English Canada can transform itself from a peripheral position with respect to the American economy and become a relatively independent industrial core is dependent ultimately upon the existence of foreign markets. Will Japan and Western Europe open their markets to Canadian goods? Will the United States take measures to counter the Canadianization of American corporations and the possible withdrawal of Canadian resources for American consumption? As a consequence of Canada's new industrial strategy and its desire to attenuate its peripheral relationship to the American core, Canada and the United States are set on a collision course. The critical question may be how Canada can assert its economic and political independence in a manner that does not produce a costly reaction from its giant southern neighbor.

At this point there enters a further consideration that may be of overwhelming significance for the future of American-Canadian relations. Thus far I have discussed only the economic and political developments within Canada as they affect this relationship. Equally great

[34] See, for example, Kari Levitt, *Silent Surrender: The American Economic Empire in Canada*, reprint ed. (New York: Liveright, 1971) ; see also my "American Direct Investment and Canada's Two Nationalisms," in *The Influence of the United States on Canadian Development*, ed. Richard Preston (Durham, N.C.: Duke University Press, 1972.

transformations appear to be taking place in the United States itself. Profound shifts in the American economy and political system may have an important and perhaps even deleterious effect on the future of American-Canadian relations.

Traditionally, the essence of the special relationship between the United States and Canada has been the economic and cultural ties between eastern Canada and the American industrial-financial cores located along the eastern seaboard and the Great Lakes. It is these two areas that have been most sympathetic to Canada and have bene-fited from the close integration of the two economies. Today these two areas are in relative economic and political decline. Over the past several decades, there has been a rapid and significant shift of indus-trial, financial, and political power to the American south and south-west.[35] The so-called Eastern establishment is in partial eclipse; the center of power in the United States has shifted considerably south-ward and westward to this new industrial-financial core. Mr. Nixon's so-called southern strategy had as much an economic as a racial basis; it was responsive to the new industrial-financial elites of the South, Texas, and southern California.

Moreover, the so-called energy crisis is apt to accentuate this shift as the cost of imported energy rises and the value of southern oil and natural gas and western coal increases. Already the energy shortage and the end of cheap energy are causing the southern state producers to reduce their supplies to the north. This has raised the specter of renewed sectional rivalry within the United States. The bastards referred to on bumper stickers in Alabama and Louisiana, which read "Let the bastards freeze in the dark," are fellow Americans in New England and New Jersey.

It is highly doubtful that this new core of American political and economic power will be very understanding of Canada's new policies. Texas Gulf, the first target of the Canada Development Corporation, is a Texas corporation; Canadian moves in energy strike at the inter-ests of American petroleum corporations headquartered in Texas and Oklahoma. It is perhaps apocalyptic that the American president in Richard Rohmer's best-selling and disturbing novel, *Ultimatum*, is a Texan.[36]

It may very well be the case, as Canadian nationalists assert, that

---

[35] For an excellent analysis of this shift, see Benjamin Higgins, "Regional Inter-actions, the Frontier and Economic Growth," in *Growth Poles and Growth Centres in Regional Planning*, ed. Antoni Kuklinski (The Hague: Mouton, 1972).

[36] (Toronto: Clarke, Irwin and Co., 1973.) Set in 1980, the novel tells of an American-Canadian conflict centering on American demands for Canadian Arctic natural gas. Its climax is the American absorption of Canada.

the threat of American retaliation against Canadian actions Americans dislike is no longer to be taken seriously. Perhaps, as they argue, the relative power balance in the world and on the North American continent is now such that Canadians no longer need fear the "elephant" next door. A United States dependent upon Canadian energy and resources and needing Canadian support against America's rising overseas economic rivals, Western Europe and Japan, may no longer pose a serious threat to Canada. One can only hope that the decision makers on both sides of the border will act with sufficient good sense and mutual respect that such a test of wills never comes to pass.

And lastly, what about the American-Quebec relationship? For Quebec, one possible avenue of development is a more closely integrated relationship with the American northeast. Already economic ties between Quebec and the Boston–New York industrial-financial core have progressed a considerable distance. Evidence suggests a steady turning of Quebec's sights away from English Canada and toward its southern neighbor. Quebec planners hope to further this movement by encouraging Japanese and European direct investments in manufacturing directed at the American market. But the rest of Canada still remains Quebec's best market. The question remains an open one whether American industrial and economic interests would ever permit Quebec to be part of an economic core extending from Montreal down the Boston-Washington corridor.[37] It is very difficult at this juncture to conceive of this relationship in terms that would go very far toward satisfying the ambitions of Quebec nationalists. How the Quebec population can satisfy its longing for a high-technology, industrial economy and yet retain its cultural inheritance is one of the great continental issues yet to be answered.

But the answering of these questions is not the purpose of this essay. Rather it has sought to show how transnational (and within Canada, internal) economic forces and often conflicting political-economic ambitions have set in motion the opposed tendencies of integration and disintegration in both the political and economic spheres. The primary means of doing this has been to argue that economic growth tends toward the creation of core-periphery relationships, and that where core and periphery represent different cultural, ethnic, and political goupings, the consequence is the intensification of economic nationalism and the emergence of powerful movements toward economic and political disintegration.

---

[37] For two different views of this matter, see Rodrigue Tremblay, *Indépendence et marché commun Quebec-Etats-Unis* (Quebec: Edition du Jour, 1970) ; Roma Dauphin, *Les options économiques du Quebec* (Quebec: Editions Commerce, 1971).

BILATERAL INSTITUTIONS AND TRANSGOVERNMENTAL RELATIONS BETWEEN CANADA AND THE UNITED STATES

Kal J. Holsti and Thomas Allen Levy

Preceding essays have documented the dramatic growth of transnational relations between Canadians and Americans and have emphasized the development of new issue areas—private, local, regional, and national—between the two countries. As these relations expand in scope, complexity, and occasionally conflict, we would expect to see a corresponding growth in Canadian-American institutions to provide mechanisms for policy coordination, bargaining, and conflict resolution. The increase in formal governmental institutions between Ottawa and Washington has indeed been notable, but we must not conclude that these institutions constitute the core of the intergovernmental relationship. The informal and formal communications between federal government bureaucracies and between officials of the states and provinces are no less important; hence, the essay will focus not only on the bilateral institutions but also on the phenomenon that Nye and Keohane have called *transgovernmental relations*, that is, the noninstitutionalized relationships between subunits of governments and the activities they undertake that remain reasonably immune from central control (see their preceding essay in this volume).

Kal J. Holsti is a professor of political science at the University of British Columbia in Vancouver. Thomas Allen Levy is a research fellow at the Centre for Foreign Policy Studies, Dalhousie University, Halifax. Mr. Holsti prepared the first three sections of this essay on bilateral national institutions and the fifth section on future institutional development. Some of the material is based on interviews Mr. Holsti conducted with thirteen Canadian officials from four agencies, held on 5 and 6 March and 24 April 1973, and with five Americans in Washington on 12 and 13 March 1973. In addition, Mr. Holsti held talks with Mr. Sperry Lea of the Canadian-American Committee and one retired high-level official of the United States Department of State with extensive knowledge of Canadian-American relations. Mr. Levy prepared the fourth section of this essay on provincial-state relations. The material in this fourth section is based partly on interviews Mr. Levy conducted in seven provinces in 1970.

Some Canadian-American institutions are concerned with issues of high policy, and thus involve the active participation of officials at the cabinet level or those immediately below them. Others, however, are staffed by technical experts and enjoy a wide latitude for policymaking and for establishing and interpreting rules to regulate transnational relations. Indeed, it could be argued that bureaucratic subunits and some bilateral institutions between Washington and Ottawa, as well as between states and provinces, are the prime mechanisms for problem solving, bargaining, and conflict resolution between the two countries once the agenda has been set by private groups, provincial and state officials, or the highest political authorities.

The relationships of subunits of governments and officials working within bilateral institutions are significant from a transnational perspective of international relations where (1) the regulations or agreements the subunits arrive at diverge from established policy, (2) they take the initiative to establish new policies or regulations, and (3) the outcomes or bargaining between the officials in the subunits or institutions substantially alter the distribution of benefits or costs to transnational groups or to the governments of the two countries.

For example, although the International Joint Commission (IJC) was given broad authority in 1964 by the central governments to investigate the problem of pollution in the Great Lakes and to recommend solutions, the proposals of that prestigious institution established important new principles and methods for regulating the Great Lakes environment and for allocating costs between the various federal, state, provincial, and municipal governments (see Scott's article in this volume for further discussion of the role of the IJC in respect to environmental questions). An important bilateral institution, working through its own subunits, such as investigatory boards, was thus able to recommend policies and regulations that would have profound consequences on economic life in the Great Lakes region, on transnational activities, and on the financial commitments of all levels of government in the two countries. It is true that the original commitment to pollution abatement came from authorities at the highest level, and certainly in theory the recommendations and reports of the IJC can be rejected by the central authorities in Ottawa and Washington. But once an impressive conglomerate of boards and commissions has been granted broad authority to investigate a problem, hold public and private hearings, and recommend solutions based on years of research, it is doubtful that its actions could fail to have significant consequences for the central authorities. While an institution like the IJC may not create the political will to cope with a problem, its recommendations pretty well establish the parameters with which policymakers at all levels of government will subsequently operate. In this sense subunits of government agencies and bilateral institutions can develop policy and administer agreements reasonably independently of central control.

BILATERAL NATIONAL INSTITUTIONS

The Boundary Waters Treaty of 1909 established the first permanent US-Canadian institution, the International Joint Commission. This body served as a model for other bilateral agencies created in the interwar period charged with resolving problems and regulating transnational relations dealing with the boundary or with fisheries. It was World War II and the ensuing cold war, however, that gave the impetus to the greatest amount of institutional growth between the two countries. After 1940, some military planning and coordination became centralized under the Permanent Joint Board on Defense. Today in the defense area alone there are eight significant institutions between Canada and the United States, ranging from the North American Air Defense Command (NORAD) to the United States–Canada Civil Emergency Planning Committee.

The list below includes all the presently existing institutions established since 1909 through treaties or agreements. As the reader can see, they range from cabinet-level committees dealing with highly political issues, but meeting sporadically, to technical bodies meeting continuously and endowed with extensive staff, research, and budgetary resources. This list does not include the many subcommissions, committees, and research, monitoring, and regulatory agencies spawned by these eighteen organizations. The bodies are listed in the order in which they were created.

International Joint Commission (1909)
International Boundary Commission (1910)
International Pacific Halibut Commission (1923)
International Salmon Fisheries Commission (1930)
Permanent Joint Board on Defense (1940)
Military Cooperation Committee (1946)
NATO Regional Planning Group (1946)
Canada-U.S.A. Ministerial Committee on Trade and Economic Affairs (1953)
Great Lakes Fishery Commission (1955)
North American Air Defense Command (1957)
Senior Committee on United States/Canadian Defense Production-Development Sharing Programme (1958)

Steering Group of the Canada/U.S. Defence Development and Production Sharing Programme (1958)

Canada–United States Inter-Parliamentary Group (1958)

Canada–United States Ministerial Committee on Joint Defence (1958)

Canada–United States Balance of Payments Committee (1963)

Roosevelt Campobello International Park Commission (1964)

Canada–United States Technical Committee on Agricultural Marketing and Trade Problems (1967)

United States–Canada Civil Emergency Planning Committee (1967)

No particular pattern is found in the dates the institutions were created. For example, there is no tendency toward the creation of more integrated institutions through time. The International Joint Commission and the various fisheries commissions created a half century ago have policymaking and regulatory powers far exceeding those of many committees and boards established after 1945. Decision-making processes in the older commissions could be characterized as joint, concerned with problem solving rather than bargaining; [1] they are technical and nonnational in the sense that differences in the commissions are seldom based on national distinctions. On the other hand, many of the institutions created since World War II contain few integrative features, and decision making tends to be based on bargaining between national teams of negotiators or just consultation.

The largest number of institutions was established in the 1950s (seven), and proportionately the largest number handles defence problems (eight). This list reveals also some important policy areas where there has been no institutional growth. While cooperation, coordination of policy, and joint decision making are notable on defence matters, boundary waters, and fisheries, there are no counterparts for banking, science and technology, energy and resources, health, education, some aspects of fisheries in the Atlantic (although these are covered to a certain extent in multilateral institutions), and transportation. These important policy sectors are handled through the more traditional means of direct contacts and through informal exchanges between different levels of the federal, and sometimes state and provincial, bureaucracies.

Eighteen permanent institutions may appear as a reasonably impressive indicator of the extent to which there is joint policy-

---

[1] Coplin defines problem solving as a situation where two or more governments agree that a common problem confronts them, even though they may offer different solutions and have competing or conflicting interests. In a bargaining situation, the actors "see each other's behavior as the basic problem." William Coplin, *Introduction to International Politics: A Theoretical Overview* (Chicago: Markham, 1971), p. 232.

making, policy coordination, exchange of information, consultation, and bargaining between the two governments. However, a significant proportion of these institutions meet only occasionally, and a few have become moribund. The Ministerial Committee on Joint Defence has not met since 1964, and the senior policy committee to oversee the defense production sharing program has been in limbo since 1965. Despite important differences in the trade sector, the relevant ministerial committee has not met since 1970. In brief, many of the institutions were created to cope with specific problems; once those were resolved, they fell into disuse. Thus, the list indicates no underlying commitment to increased institutionalization by either government, little spillover (except in the regulatory commissions) from institution building in one area to another, and certainly no trend toward increasing the authority and powers of existing institutions.

That there is no underlying thrust in Canadian-American relations toward creating more integrated mechanisms is also revealed by the broad variety of functions seen in the eighteen institutions. Some, like the ministerial committees, are used primarily for exchanges of views and information, casual coordination of policies, ratification of agreements reached at lower levels of government, and general reviews of situations likely to be of interest to each government. Others are used primarily for bargaining or joint research into problems affecting the two countries. The regulatory commissions have important policing functions, in addition to their research and policymaking. Finally, some of the committees seem to work primarily to establish ground rules and procedures for handling or defusing contentious issues that may otherwise lead to conflict at higher levels of government. While having the appearance of agencies for consultation and bargaining, their most important latent function is conflict avoidance, prevention, or resolution.

The most interesting organization of this type is undoubtedly the International Joint Commission. Comprised of three commissioners from each government, its formal task is to find equitable solutions, based on technical studies, to a variety of problems arising in connection with boundary waters. While constitutionally the IJC has the authority to make policy, it normally recommends courses of action or solutions to problems for formal approval at the cabinet and presidential levels. However, because its studies are based on extensive research by technical specialists, its recommendations are influential and are usually acted upon by the senior governments.[2] Also, by tak-

_____

[2] The effective power of the IJC in some problem areas is revealed in the comment of one Canadian official who suggested that more bodies of the IJC type would not be welcome today because they are difficult to control by the central governments.

ing some issues out of the political arena and basing recommendations on highly specialized technical data, the IJC can defuse potentially contentious issues; hence its conflict-avoidance function.

In addition to its research, problem-solving, and conflict-avoiding functions, the IJC has capabilities for monitoring agreements (such as the Great Lakes Water Quality Agreement) and holding hearings on issues it is considering. Altogether the IJC oversees the activities of 27 research, surveillance, and control boards. Policy recommendations are made on the basis of a majority vote. In practice, votes seldom divide according to national lines since the working assumption of the bodies is that professional management of shared resources, within a framework of interests defined as virtually identical, must be based on technical, not national, criteria and information.

Do the various institutional arrangements reflect important differences in handling different issue areas and policy sectors? One general impression is that the institutions featuring the highest degree of integration (as measured by the degree of joint decision making, permanency, staff, research capabilities, and the like) are designed to cope with problems arising directly from geographical contiguity: border monuments and parks, boundary waters, fisheries,[3] pollution, and, to a lesser extent, defence. In contrast, those institutions having the least integrative features are concerned primarily with issue areas and policy sectors where interests seem to diverge strongly along national lines. These would include the institutions dealing with trade matters and balance of payments. Finally, in those areas where there is virtually no area of shared interest— such as the allocation of airline routes and landing rights between the two governments—there is no institutional growth at all. The agreements and treaties that are hammered out result from painstaking bargaining between ad hoc teams of national negotiators, not without bitterness, reproaches, and occasional breaking off of negotiations.

These observations would seem to support the hypothesis that institutional growth and extension of authority are more likely in areas that are technical and politically unimportant and where the exercise of institutional authority has little impact on critical national or regional interests.[4] In the case of Canada and the United States in general and the IJC in particular, an additional explanation seems equally convincing. The problems arising from boundary waters or

---

[3] The case of fisheries is more difficult to classify. The institutions are strong, but interests both converge (preventing depletion of stock) and diverge (allocation of catches to fishermen of each country). See also Scott's article in this volume.

[4] Joseph S. Nye, Jr., *Peace in Parts: Integration and Conflict in Regional Organization* (Boston: Little, Brown & Co., 1971), pp. 23-24.

fisheries are inherently no less difficult than those of trade or airline route allocation. Although the interests affected are often local rather than national, the stakes measured in dollars can be very large indeed. But the Boundary Waters Treaty sets forth some fundamental rules or principles that have guided problem solving ever since 1909.[5] In other words, this treaty and the resulting IJC were created *before* the most serious problems arose, whereas in other issue areas or policy sectors such rules or principles have not been created prior to the establishment of the bilateral institutions.[6] As is obvious to anyone who has followed the tortuous course of monetary and trade relations over the past few years, there is no universal, timeless, much less Canadian-American, criterion that designates what is a fair deal between governments in the areas of international trade, balance of payments, or airline routes and landing rights. Lacking such fundamental principles, it is hard to imagine bilateral institutions operating in the same manner as the IJC. An important key to institutional growth, therefore, may not be so much the type of issue area or the extent to which institutions handle political matters but the degree to which basic principles governing allocation of costs, rewards, and responsibilities between the two countries have been worked out prior to the launching of institutions.

TRANSGOVERNMENTAL RELATIONS AND BUREAUCRATIC NETWORKS

It is clear that the eighteen institutions, some of which remain in a state of suspended inanimation, do not handle the bulk of Canadian-American relations. Indeed, most transactions between Ottawa and Washington are dealt with through direct informal contacts between subunits of the bureaucracies.[7] Hence, the category of transgovernmental relations, more or less under central control, is of interest to us as well.

There are no records of the number of transactions between the two capitals, although we can reasonably assume that it has grown significantly during the past decades. Some figures for 1968 do reveal, however, the extraordinary amount of business that is conducted by direct visits of the officials of both countries. Canadian ministers, heads of agencies, and other officials made 4,687 visits to the United

[5] Some of the rules were already well established in international law; others represented radical departures from accepted practice.

[6] Many of the formulas for allocating NORAD costs were agreed upon prior to the signing of the agreement.

[7] The Merchant-Heeney report lists 49 American and Canadian agencies that deal directly with each other. United States Department of State, "Principles of Partnership," *Department of State Bulletin* 53 (2 August 1965): 193-208.

States.[8] In the same year, American counterparts made 1,843 visits to Canada, discounting travel by personnel from the Department of Defense. One would assume that the number of telephone communications undertaken directly between officials of bureaucratic subunits, without reference to the Department of External Affairs or the Department of State, must be much greater.

It is a matter of conjecture regarding the extent to which the contacts, discussions, exchange of information, consultation, and bargaining reflect bureaucratic interests (transgovernmental relations) as opposed to interstate relations or interests—assuming that the two sets of interests may not always coincide. No official is willing to say that the negotiating position he has adopted, or the agreement he has just made with his counterparts on the other side of the border, represents only an agency foreign policy or is in any way contrary to government policy. Yet the phenomenon of bureaucratic foreign policies inconsistent with general governmental priorities definitely exists. One example will be cited, to be followed by somewhat less concrete evidence which permits us to make the inference of extensive transgovernmental activity lacking centralized control.

The defence production sharing agreement (DPSA) is an arrangement whereby Canadian defence industries (some of which are subsidiaries of American corporations) are able to compete for defence contracts on an equal basis with firms located in the United States. This arrangement has enabled the Canadian defence industry to survive where otherwise it may have died due to limited markets. It has also helped to provide substantial employment for Canadians.[9] Through the arrangement the American defence establishment is able to obtain some materiel at lower costs and high quality. Among other advantages to the United States, when the DPSA was promulgated some American defence officials were concerned about the vulnerability of American defence industries to nuclear attack. To the extent that these industries were dispersed throughout North America,

---

[8] See Canada, House of Commons, Standing Committee on External Affairs and National Defence, *Minutes of Proceedings and Evidence*, 1969-1970, vol. 1, p. 64. The total given in the document is actually 12,900 visits, but this number includes 8,313 visits by staff from the Department of National Defence. Of the 8,313 visits by the military, a large proportion are Candian armed forces personnel sent to the United States for special training. I would not include these visits as an indicator of formal and informal contacts between government officials.

[9] Fifteen thousand persons are directly employed in and another 100,000 are dependent upon defence industries. To get the proper magnitude, American readers should multiply these figures by ten. The figures are cited in John J. Kirton, "The Consequences of Integration: The Case of the Defence Production Sharing Agreements," paper presented at the Inter-University Seminar on International Relations, Ottawa, 8 April 1972, p. 15.

they believed, the greater the chance of maintaining some defence-related industry in the event of nuclear war.[10] From the military point of view, then, the arrangement brings important advantages to the United States. From an American economic point of view, the DPSA is less defensible. Indeed, the Treasury Department can show the agreement has had adverse effects on the American balance-of-payments situation, and the Department of Labor can argue that American purchase of Canadian materiel has had an impact on unemployment levels in certain regions of the United States. Thus, in 1972 when an American firm lost on a production contract bid to a Canadian competitor, the Treasury Department suggested that the DPSA might be "revised." [11] While the priority of the Nixon administration in its trade policy in general and toward Canada in particular has been to reduce American deficits, the Department of Defense has resisted pressures for revision of the agreement by those in other agencies who saw it as contributing to the American trade deficit with Canada in the early 1970s.

One example does not, of course, prove the existence of widespread transgovernmental interests that contradict other national policies or evade central control. However, there is other evidence, though less concrete, that allows us to make inferences about the bureaucratic networks extending between Washington and Ottawa. From interviews conducted in Ottawa in 1969, in was apparent that bureaucrats often felt it was to their advantage not to let all of their problems be resolved at the highest political level. During periods of strained relations at the highest level of government, they tried to isolate their policy sectors and ways of doing things.[12] The diplomatic culture between Washington and Ottawa placed great emphasis on consultation, exchange of information, personal friendship, informal communication, and easy access to points of decision; in such an environment bureaucratic networks transcending national boundaries are likely to flourish. Although these networks have atrophied in certain policy sectors in the 1970s (see below), there is still considerable evidence of persisting efforts by officials to immunize their departments and programs from disrupting influence from the highest political level, from legislative interference, or from some manifestations of public opinion.

Evidence indicating the existence of transgovernmental networks

[10] Interview with US Department of Defense official, 13 March 1973.

[11] Interviews with former Department of State official and Department of Defense official, 12 and 13 March 1973.

[12] See Kal J. Holsti, "Canada and the United States," in Steven Spiegel and Kenneth Waltz, eds., *Conflict in World Politics* (Boston: Winthrop, 1971), pp. 375-96.

comes, secondly, from a prominent characteristic of the relations between Ottawa and Washington: linkages are seldom made between different issue areas or policy sectors. While that ephemeral phenomenon, the political climate between Washington and Ottawa, can help or hinder problem solving, the resolution of conflicts, or the launching of new cooperative programs, there is seldom an effort to determine the outcome in one problem area by manipulating issues in another area. The United States government, for example, will not make concessions on defence matters in order to gain advantages in trade, and despite the fact that the Canadian government may be approaching a position of strength in so far as export of natural resources and energy is concerned, it has not consciously linked its assets in this area to any other issue.[13] Officials in both capitals agree, moreover, that it is virtually impossible to measure gains and losses in bargaining when one is comparing, let us say, the results of the automotive products agreement with Canada's policy toward China.

But the explanation for the absence of linkages between policy sectors or conflict issues lies, in my opinion, more in the bureaucratic networks between the two governments than in carefully reasoned strategies of bargaining: officials in separate agencies find it virtually impossible, given their vested interests, to give up something dear to them so that another agency can obtain something dear to it. The case of defense production sharing is certainly one example. There may have been similar examples of bureaucratic encroachment in Ottawa, but they have not been revealed publicly. Certainly it would be difficult to envisage, let us say, the Department of Industry, Trade and Commerce agreeing to the renegotiation of the automotive products agreement to make it more favorable to the United States in return for an American promise to renegotiate agreements within NORAD that would reduce the costs of the alliance to the Canadian defence establishment.

These comments do not imply, however, that the highest political levels are unaware of relationships between issues. They may very well decide how to treat different sectors in light of their impact on the overall political climate. For example, the Canadian decision in 1973 to renew the NORAD agreement (although only for two years) was probably made, among other reasons, in the expectation that with-

---

[13] Officials in Washington and Ottawa both emphasize that problems between the two countries are dealt with separately and that no strategy involving trade-offs between areas had been, or would be, contemplated. Without being very specific, Canadian officials definitely felt that issue linking is a dangerous strategy for the smaller party in a relationship. See also Greenwood's article in this volume.

drawal could exacerbate Canadian-American relations in other issue areas.[14]

Issue area isolation has not been much studied. It seems to occur much less often in relations between states in which a high level of conflict is characteristic—the subject, of course, of most studies in international politics. One would expect the phenomenon to appear precisely where relations between two governments have become routinized and where there is a tradition of easy communication and access directly between the bureaucracies of the two countries. Canada and the United States maintain what is probably one of the most profuse bureaucratic relationships between any two countries in the world. That transgovernmental relations, whether or not they are conducted through formal bilateral institutions, are an important dimension of the overall relationship between the two countries follows almost inevitably. The evidence outlined above would lend some weight to the assertion.

INTEGRATION THROUGH NONINSTITUTIONALIZED CONTACTS?

We have seen that only a few of the formal bilateral institutions between Canada and the United States have the authority, resources, or decision-making patterns that indicate a reasonably high degree of integration. The question remains whether the informal bureaucratic networks stretching between Washington and Ottawa contain integrative characteristics. I pose this question because some scholars have argued that international integration can be measured by the degree of joint policy development, decision making, and policy application between two or more governments and that formal institutional arrangements may be only of secondary importance.[15]

---

[14] When Lyndon Johnson vetoed a bill that would have been highly detrimental to Canadian lumber exporters, he was reported to have remarked privately to a Canadian official that it was now Canada's turn to make a goodwill gesture to the United States. The famous "shopping list" of grievances held by Washington against Ottawa during the trade crisis of 1971-72 linked a broad set of issues, but they were all basically in the areas of trade and communications. Efforts to resolve the outstanding differences in these two issue areas through a package deal came to nought. Among other reasons, the negotiators found it impossible to weigh or compare gains and losses in problems so different as automobile trade and customs exemptions for Canadian tourists. On the NORAD decision, see Colin S. Gray, "Still on the Team: NORAD in 1973," *Queen's Quarterly* 80 (Autumn 1973): 398-404.

[15] See Nye, p. 41; Leon Lindberg, "The European Community as a Political System," *Journal of Common Market Studies* 5 (1967): 359; Leon Lindberg and Stuart Scheingold, *Europe's Would-Be Polity: Patterns of Change in the*

Using an integration continuum ranging from completely autonomous national action on problem identification, policy proposals, decision making, and rule application to community action in these stages, Lindberg and Scheingold investigated the European Economic Community (EEC), dividing the measurements according to issue area or policy domain. They found, for example, that there has been considerable growth in joint policy development and application (growth of community action as compared to strictly national action) in economic, social, and cultural areas between 1957 and 1968 but no significant increase between 1968 and 1970. Growth of integrative characteristics was far less apparent in the political/constitutional and external relations policy sectors.

Regrettably, no such studies have been completed on the Canadian-American relationship. There are no organized data that allow us to discriminate between degrees of policymaking integration in different issue areas, much less measurements that would indicate trends or tendencies. It is probable, nevertheless, that the degrees of Canadian-American integration—if measured in terms of the concepts and indicators developed by Lindberg and Scheingold—would be greater in defence, pollution control, and perhaps fisheries than in civil rights, education, and many other policy sectors. But given the lack of data and the broad and complicated pattern of informal contacts between Washington and Ottawa, we are not in a position to judge whether there are more integrative characteristics in those policy sectors handled primarily through noninstitutionalized transgovernmental relations than in those handled in formal bilateral institutions. The indicators and categories of Lindberg and Scheingold would be useful tools for conducting research on the IJC or the Permanent Joint Board on Defence, but they would be difficult to apply to the informal and irregular contacts that are so prominent in the Canadian-American relationship.

Another problem rendering generalization on the degrees of integration difficult is the demonstration effect operating between the two countries. This results in the appearance of common policy development, decision making, or policy coordination, even though both governments have acted independently. When one government adopts regulatory measures or new domestic policies to cope with problems, the other may adopt it as well, though perhaps slightly modified to account for local peculiarities. Following President Nixon's wage and

European Community (Englewood Cliffs, N.J.: Prentice-Hall, 1970); and for further discussion of developing integration measures, see Leon Lindberg, "Political Integration as a Multidimensional Phenomenon Requiring Multivariate Measurement," *International Organization* 24 (Autumn 1970): 649-731.

price restraints in 1971, many Canadians demanded that Ottawa follow suit. And, reversing the effect, when the Canadian government developed standards for the allowable amount of phosphates in laundry products, these were relayed to American officials who subsequently sought to have the data and standards incorporated into American legislation on the matter. Some Canadian foreign policy initiatives, such as the establishment of diplomatic relations with China and the conclusion of consultation and scientific exchange treaties with the Soviet Union (prior to Nixon's first visit to Moscow), undoubtedly were looked upon with great interest in Washington. Nevertheless, it must be assumed that the demonstration effect flows basically in a northward direction from the United States.

Finally, the growing importance of provincial-state relationships —a phenomenon not found in the European context—would have to be included in any measurement of noninstitutionalized forms of integration between Canada and the United States.

THE PROVINCE-STATE DIMENSION OF TRANSGOVERNMENTAL RELATIONS

Bilateral contacts between provincial and state governments constitute an increasingly significant aspect of Canadian-American relations. Extensions of these transborder ties include linkages between the provinces and Washington, between the states and Ottawa, and between private groups that attempt to influence provincial and state policies.

Provincial and state governments deal directly with each other because of a felt need to collaborate in policy areas in which they possess legislative authority, because jurisdictional parameters are not clear, or because the respective national governments choose either not to exercise their own authority or to delegate power to the regional governments. American states may legally enter into official contact with Canadian jurisdictions subject to the approval of Congress. Although the Canadian provinces do not have explicit authority to conduct relations across the national frontier, a number of provincial governments have acted as though they had such power.[16] On

---

[16] For a fuller statement of the constitutional issues, see Richard H. Leach, Donald E. Walker, and Thomas Allen Levy, "Province-State Transborder Relations: A Preliminary Assessment," *Canadian Public Administration* 16 (Fall 1973): 470-72. While the foreign relations of the states are confined mostly to Canada and Mexico, provincial external activity is more broadly international, including intergovernmental contact with Britain, France, and Japan. See Thomas Allen Levy, "The Involvement of the Provinces in Foreign Affairs II," in *The Changing Role of the Diplomatic Function in the Making of Foreign Policy*, Occasional Paper of the Centre for Foreign Policy Studies (Halifax: Dalhousie University, June 1973), pp. 57-72.

the whole, the provinces are more actively involved in transnational and transgovernmental relations than are the states, thus complicating the Canadian government's efforts to evolve coherent policies vis-à-vis the United States. In addition to coordinating the interests of numerous federal departments and agencies, Ottawa must also resolve crucial policy differences with those provinces that have their own viewpoints and interests regarding Canadian-American relations.

Interaction between state and provincial governments is a comparatively recent phenomenon. Of 47 selected province-state relationships discovered in 1970, 29—more than one-half—originated since 1960.[17] Province-state cooperation includes a large amount of public activity that can be classified as administrative, cultural, and economic.

Province-state administrative interaction in a number of policy fields closely resembles interprovincial and interstate collaboration. That is, the cooperating parties exchange experience, provide mutual assistance, and attempt to plan and make decisions jointly in some areas. Most provincial-state cultural relations are concerned with particular contacts between French Canadians and Americans of French origin and francophiles generally. Transborder economic ties between Canadian provinces and American groups include efforts to influence or neutralize aspects of the national governments' economic policies that are of central importance in Canadian-American relations, e.g., trade policy, investment flows, and the distribution of energy and other resources.[18]

Administrative Transactions

Administrative collaboration has spawned complex forms of interaction, including informal official contact, joint membership of subnational units in intergovernmental organizations, and formal agreements. In the fields of health, welfare, labor, and agriculture, provincial and state bureaucrats get to know each other, exchange ideas, and render each other mutual assistance via the meetings of such organizations as the Conference of State and Provincial Health Authorities of North America and the International Association of Governmental Labor Officials. Where transnational organizations do not already exist, there are few impediments to provincial participa-

---

[17] Leach, et al., p. 481.

[18] Province-state agricultural cooperation involves the exchange of experience and hence constitutes an administrative relationship. The existence of transborder electricity grids connotes mutual assistance, an administrative link as defined here, while the long-term export of provincially controlled energy resources would constitute an economic linkage. Inasmuch as provincial and state trade offices serve to influence investment flows, they are of economic significance.

tion in such bodies as the American Public Welfare Association, the New England Agricultural Engineering Society, and the Midwestern and Western Associations of State Departments of Agriculture.

In other administrative fields, such as transportation, hydro-electric interties, and forest fire suppression, where the economic benefits and obligations to the respective parties may be quantified, formal agreements commonly record the responsibilities of the contracting states and provinces. The interests of American and Canadian truckers and exporters in seeking the uniformity of highway load limits, license fees, and other regulations have led to numerous province-state vehicle reciprocity agreements. British Columbia and Alberta, for example, are parties to the Uniform Vehicle Proration and Reciprocity Agreement, a compact involving seventeen western states. Sometimes joint planning or at least joint consideration of contiguous highways is undertaken as well. Both types of province-state highway cooperation are often inspired by the meetings of the Committee on Reciprocity and International Relations of the American Association of Motor Vehicle Administrators, a body with membership in 50 states and ten provinces.

Impressive as this pattern of transborder collaboration may be, cost-benefit calculations are rarely lost sight of by the parties. Reciprocity agreements between contiguous provinces and states have more stringent conditions than those between more distant neighbors, so that highways in one province or state would not be overused by truckers licensed in the party directly across the border. Also, jurisdictions such as Manitoba and Maine have proven reluctant to build highways largely for the advantage of cross-border neighbors. Another noteworthy feature of the highway transportation field is the extent to which provincial transportation departments enter into direct relationships with the US Interstate Commerce Commission. Since 1967 the government of Canada has attempted to reduce the authority it had previously delegated to the provinces over the transborder movement of motor carriers, but the ongoing pattern of province-state cooperation has not been noticeably affected.

Mutual interest in suppressing forest fires in border areas has produced yet another type of province-state formal arrangement. As of June 1970, the Provinces of Quebec and New Brunswick were full members of the Northeastern Interstate Forest Fire Protection Commission, an interstate compact between the six New England states and New York. Both provinces required Ottawa's consent expressed through an exchange of notes between the two national governments.

All in all, province-state relations in administrative fields have produced an impressive network of intergovernmental associations, a respectable number of contractual relationships, and a persisting pat-

tern of easygoing, informal contact.[19] Moreover, provinces and states
tend to avoid controversy with each other and with their respective
national governments in the administrative policy area.

Cultural Transactions

As in the case of province-state administrative ties, the maintenance of contact between American and Canadian francophones has
become a governmental responsibility, particularly at the subnational
level. Despite the political overtones of Quebec-France cultural relations, the province's cultural activities in the United States are
relatively uncontroversial.

Established in 1963, the Service du Canada Français d'Outre
Frontières of the Quebec Department of Cultural Affairs ministers to
Americans interested in the French language and culture as well as
to French Canadians in other Canadian provinces. Given Ottawa's
recently expanded cultural support to the French-Canadian minorities,
the Quebec Service is in a position to increase that part of its budget
slated for American operations. As of early 1974 Americans interested in cultural relations with French Canada are concentrated
largely in Louisiana, New England, and northern New York, areas
where there are large numbers of Americans of French, French-
Canadian, or Creole descent.

Contacts between French Canadians and Louisiana Acadians
were sporadic and unofficial for most of this century. As a consequence of the "Quiet Revolution," however, Quebec authorities manifested in the 1960s greater interest in the French-Canadian "dias-
pora." Quebec public figures visited Louisiana in 1963 and 1966, while
a francophone member of the governor's staff called on the Quebec
government in 1965. By 1968, the governor and both legislative houses
had endorsed closer friendly relations with French Canada. Formal
relations with Quebec and New Brunswick would include "exchanges
of visitors having common cultural or linguistic origins." [20]

With the assistance of the director and staff of the Quebec Government Office in Lafayette, Louisiana, the Council for the Development of French in Louisiana (CODOFIL) was established. Autho-

[19] A Great Lakes Environmental Conference, for which Ontario was host and
which was attended by eight states in September 1970, was undoubtedly significant
in hastening the Great Lakes Water Quality Agreement signed by the two national governments in April 1972. A more detailed analysis of province-state
administrative relations may be found in Leach, et al.

[20] Text of House Resolution No. 81 in Québec, Ministère des Affaires Culturelles,
Service du Canada Français d'Outre Frontières, *Québec-Amérique*, January 1969,
p. 30 (author's translation). For the historical background see ibid., October
1967, pp. 13-16.

rized by a 1968 statute, this body may receive gifts "from societies and governments" to promote its objectives. As of 1969, the majority of the 50-member group was of French descent as was its chairman.[21]

In September 1969, the Louisiana governor was officially received by the premier of Quebec which their "Joint Communiqué" described as "the heart and main-stay of North American francophones." The two leaders reviewed progress already made in Quebec-Louisiana cultural ties and resolved to strengthen these relations further. Among the measures envisaged were the dispatch of a Quebec "permanent respresentative" to Louisiana, the establishment of the Quebec-Louisiana Liaison Committee, Quebec assistance in the definition and fulfillment of the state's French education program, youth exchanges, the utilization of Quebec teaching materials in schools and in radio and television stations, and the fostering of tourism.[22]

The Liaison Committee held its first working session in Quebec in March 1970. The state delegation was led by the Louisiana secretary of state who was also a member of CODOFIL. The Quebec section was chaired by the commissioner-general for external cooperation. Subjects reviewed included the loan of Quebec teachers and a specialist in the teaching of French, study sessions for Louisiana students in Quebec, the preparation of programs for French-language nursery schools, the retraining of Louisiana French teachers, and cooperation in the fields of the French language, books, artistic exchanges and in other cultural activities.[23]

Closer to home, Quebec has actively engaged in cultural promotion in the New England states. The Quebec Government Office in Boston, Massachusetts, was helpful in the organization of the Council for the Development of French in New England (CODOFINE) and has made efforts to introduce French television in New England via cable.

In 1968, the Massachusetts legislature established the American and Canadian French Cultural Exchange Commission. This group was to consist of seven members "all of whom shall be American citizens descended from Canadians of French ancestry and residents of the commonwealth to be appointed by the governor for terms of

[21] The text of the act establishing CODOFIL may be found in ibid., January 1969, pp. 35-36. The chairman of the organization is appointed by the governor.
[22] Gouvernement du Québec, Conseil Exécutif, Office de l'Information et Publicité, "Joint Communiqué," n.d.
[23] Gouvernement du Québec, Conseil Exécutif, Office de l'Information et Publicité, "Quebec-Louisiana Liaison Committee," n.d., pp. 1-3. According to former Quebec Intergovernmental Affairs Minister Marcel Masse, the Quebec component included senior officials of the Departments of Cultural Affairs and Education and of the Civil Service Commission. See his speech at the 13 December 1969 meeting of CODOFIL at Nachitoches, Louisiana.

seven years."[24] Other New England states manifest varying degrees of interest in cultural relations with Quebec.

More recently, the Quebec government has attempted to shed the image of being interested exclusively, or even primarily, in cultural relations with Americans of French-Canadian ancestry.[25] Finally, while cultural contacts constitute a significant portion of Quebec's presence in the United States, these activities are sometimes incidental to the provincial interest in north-south transnational economic relations.

Economic Transactions

Transnational economic relationships go beyond the parameters of province-state official contact. The provincial governments are the principal Canadian subnational actors in this issue area, but their opposite numbers tend to be United States federal agencies, American-controlled multinational enterprises, and the principal money markets of the United States. While the state governments are not wholly inactive on the economic scene, the Canadian provinces are the chief subnational governmental actors in transborder economic activity.

Provincial government officials have occasionally expressed interest in free trade with the United States,[26] but the response from the US has been negligible. Even in individual cases, a province's concern for easier access of its products to the American market is hard to impress on the US government. For instance, the premier of Nova Scotia failed in his direct appeal to Washington to rescind the countervailing duty on tire exports from the subsidized Michelin plant in his province (see Litvak and Maule's essay in this volume).

With the possible exception of Ontario, most provincial governments actively search for private American capital. Provincial premiers, industry ministers, and heads of provincial development cor-

[24] State of Massachusetts, Acts, 1968, ch. 681, approved 19 July 1968.

[25] See Georges-Henri Dagneau, "Les Lignes de Conduite du Service du Canada Français d'Outre-Frontières," ACSUS Newsletter 2 (Spring 1972): 81-82. Other writings on Quebec's cultural presence in the United States include Jean-Charles Bonenfant, "Les Relations Extérieures du Québec," Etudes Internationales 1 (February 1970): 83, and 1 (June 1970): 85-86. Cultural activity supported by the French government in Louisiana now surpasses considerably that of Quebec. Moreover, there are unconfirmed reports that the Canadian federal government is paying the salaries of one or two employees of CODOFIL. Whatever the extent of recent French and Canadian cultural involvement in the United States, Quebec's catalytic role in the cultural renaissance among American francophones is undeniable.

[26] For examples, see Canada, Constitutional Conference, Second Meeting, February 1969, Proceedings (Ottawa: Queen's Printer, 1969), pp. 128 (Alberta) and 303 (New Brunswick); and British Columbia, Opening Statement to the Federal-Provincial Conference, Ottawa, November 15, 16, and 17, 1971, pp. 4-5.

porations are often invited by business groups in major American cities to describe the investment climate in their respective provinces. Most provincial finance departments maintain contact with the US Securities and Exchange Commission for the purpose of floating provincial bond issues in the United States. This provincial search for American capital persists in the face of increasing popular sentiment in Canada for controls on foreign investment and federal admonitions to the provinces to concentrate their borrowing on the Canadian capital market. In this respect Quebec does not differ from other provinces. Hence, a number of provincial administrations seem to be allied with those private and governmental interests in the United States that are concerned about an emerging consensus in Ottawa for at least minimal controls on continued American investment.

In order to lure American capital and tourists to Canada, some provinces maintain permanent offices in certain American cities. These bureaus are not accredited by the federal or state governments, but they do register with the Department of Justice as foreign agents. Ontario and Alberta expressed an interest in direct representation in Washington in order to lobby Congress and the executive on behalf of provincial interests. Alberta was concerned about its future in the continental energy trade while Ontario was determined to protect its position in a possible realignment of North American manufacturing. At the end of 1973 neither province had established a Washington office while the Canadian federal government indicated greater willingness than in the past to take account of these provincial concerns.

To deal with some energy and resource questions, American firms and United States and Canadian subnational governmental authorities have made ad hoc alignments. Initiatives taken by Ontario and New York State helped propel the creation of the St. Lawrence Seaway. A meeting in 1945 between the respective governor and the premier led to an agreement in 1950 between the Ontario Hydro-Electric Power Commission and the New York State Power Authority to collaborate in the building of a powerhouse near Cornwall, Ontario. Ottawa's recognition of the provincial government's interest in developing St. Lawrence power in concert with American firms removed the last major obstacle to the signature of the Seaway treaty in 1954.[27]

In the Columbia River negotiations, the combined efforts of the Kaiser interests in the states of the Pacific Northwest, President Kennedy, Secretary of the Interior Udall, the American cochairman of the IJC, and the Bennett administration in British Columbia suc-

[27] See William R. Willoughby, *The St. Lawrence Waterway: A Study in Politics and Diplomacy* (Madison, Wisc.: University of Wisconsin Press, 1961), pp. 181-220 and passim.

ceeded in putting pressure on Ottawa to relax its rules on the export of hydroelectric power as part of the plan of controlling the flow of the Columbia River. The key to the revised 1964 treaty was the purchase agreement between the British Columbia Hydro and Power Authority and a consortium of Pacific Northwest power firms.[28] In contrast, the Province of Saskatchewan failed to secure a share of the water.

Another example of transgovernmental economic coalitions concerns Saskatchewan–New Mexico potash negotiations in late 1969. Production of the mineral in Saskatchewan is largely controlled by affiliates of American energy firms. Concern in the United States that continued "dumping" of Saskatchewan's production would depress prices and employment led to a New Mexico–Saskatchewan agreement according to which the latter agreed to proration production by a system of export licenses, thereby establishing minimum prices. However, direct efforts by the governor and the premier to forestall antidumping duties under consideration in the United States Senate were unsuccessful. For their part, federal officials in Ottawa regarded Saskatchewan's actions as highly irregular and professed disinclination to support the prices of the American-controlled firms.[29]

Subnational transborder economic relationships have not produced much transgovernmental machinery, perhaps because of the serious federal-provincial and Canada–United States disagreements over policy referred to above. However, this situation may change as the habits of cooperation developed in province-state administrative relations make themselves felt at a time when all levels of government are assuming greater responsibilities in economic management. For instance, in August 1973 the governors of the six New England states met with the five eastern premiers to discuss energy and transportation as they affect transborder trade. A follow-up conference was held in June 1974. Whatever the future course of subnational governmental contact in transborder economic relations, the increasing proclivity of provincial administrations to deal directly with leading American firms and with the federal and state levels of government does compromise the ability of the government of Canada to present a unified, rational, and domestically supported bargaining stance to the United States.

Although the pattern of subnational transgovernmental relation-

---

[28] I am grateful to Professor Willoughby of the University of New Brunswick and to Professor Neil A. Swainson of the University of Victoria for making their respective unpublished researches available to me.

[29] Interview conducted at the Department of Industry, Trade and Commerce, Ottawa, 16 June 1971.

ships varies from issue area to issue area, the increased scope of these activities has indicated the need for centralized control within the provincial and state bureaucracies. Earlier, province-state contacts had been conducted on a department-to-department basis. On the Canadian side, Quebec, Ontario, and Alberta have departments devoted to intergovernmental affairs. In other provinces, the practice has been to assign the coordination of transnational departmental relations to an individual in the premier's office or in the cabinet secretariat. State machinery for the conduct of transborder relations is rudimentary by comparison. However, Maine took steps to create an Office of Canadian Affairs in the fall of 1972. Although there is little evidence of spillover from issue area to issue area, these new subnational "foreign ministries" are involved in each of the administrative, cultural, and economic fields.

This brief survey of the interests and activities of subnational actors indicates some differences in political and administrative processes in the three issue areas referred to above. Administrative relations are carried on between most provinces and those states nearest the Canadian border.[30] Many policy areas are the subjects of an extensive network of informal links and formal agreements. In some cases, cooperative administrative ties are facilitated by joint membership in transborder intergovernmental organizations. Cultural contacts are cordial though confined to the Province of Quebec and a handful of states. Quebec's Departments of Cultural Affairs and Education are prominent in transborder cultural ties, while such American groups as CODOFIL and CODOFINE are at the same time semipublic and "penetrated" in varying degree by foreign governments. Provincial and state governments rarely use administrative and cultural relationships to put pressure on their respective national governments to alter national policies vis-à-vis the other country or to claim a greater role in national policymaking.

In contrast, there are few fixed patterns of dealing with transnational economic issues below the federal level. Provincial and state administrations are very active in this area, but transgovernmental relations are of an ad hoc nature. Moreover, the provincial governments exert strong pressure within the Canadian federal system and often act as virtually independent states in their relations with American governmental and private entities. Provinces and states have taken a number of initiatives in all three issue areas. However, the economic field is the only one in which provincial behavior, at least, has tended to diverge from or even run contrary to Canadian federal policy.

[30] See Leach, et al., p. 480, table 3.

Perhaps these types of behavior patterns differ because of the economic stakes. Parallel to developments at the national level, province-state institutionalized relationships appear to have developed the furthest in those policy fields where the economic stakes are relatively slight. On the other hand, regularized contact between provincial governments and American actors regarding vital economic interests is somewhat increasing in the 1970s. On the whole, the instances of harmonious intergovernmental relationships at the subnational level provides an interesting contrast to some recent tendencies toward contention and conflict observable at the top federal echelons in the Canadian-American constellation.

INSTITUTIONAL DEVELOPMENT IN THE FUTURE

To return to the national level, during the 1950s and 1960s it was not uncommon to hear terms such as *good partners, equal partners,* or *the special relationship* used to describe the essence of the relationship between Canada and the United States. Such rhetoric certainly implies an extensive degree of casual and informal communication, broad consultation on new policy initiatives, a reasoned appreciation of each other's sensitivities and interests, some joint ventures that involve pooling of resources (or, as many call it today, with a pejorative connotation, *continentalism*), candor and honesty in negotiations, and, overall, a recognition of both the similarities and differences in the problems facing the two nations.[31] Were these characteristics to develop into formal patterns and institutional mechanisms, we would expect a corresponding tendency toward formal integration or at least common policymaking. Yet, as we have seen, there is no trend toward institutional proliferation, and some of the aspects of the "good partners" relationship have changed perceptibly in recent years.

Most observers agree that the Canadian-American relationship entered a new phase around 1970, and most certainly by August 1971 when the American government imposed import duties on foreign goods and refused to grant an exemption to Canada from the new regulations. Since that time there has been a significant change in the images of each other and in the definition of the relationship. The model of an American-Canadian partnership reflected a perception of

[31] The best-known analysis of the special character of Canadian-American relations is the report by Livingston Merchant and A. D. P. Heeney, "Principles for Partnership," in *Department of State Bulletin* 53 (2 August 1965), pp. 193-208, and printed by the Queen's Printer, Ottawa, 1965. See also John Sloan Dickey's analysis of the decline of the partnership rhetoric: "The Relationship of Rhetoric and Reality: Merchant-Heeney Revisited," *International Journal* 27 (1972): 172-84.

considerable overlapping of interests between the two countries. Trade brought advantages to both countries; American investment in Canada helped to develop resources and a manufacturing capability in Canada while bringing home handsome profits to American investors. The control of fisheries and boundary waters, based on equitable allocation of costs, advantages, and responsibilities,[32] were other areas where joint action could be taken. And perhaps most important, Canadian and American policymakers defined their security problem in roughly the same terms: to Canadians the chief way to contribute to peace was to help secure the American second strike capability by providing the land and airspace for an early warning system against incoming bombers and parts of a tracking system against missiles. The cold war, as well, was defined in roughly the same manner in the two countries.

But during the past decade increasing divergences of interest between the national governments have appeared and images of and assumptions about the relationship have changed notably. Canadian willingness to accept American definitions of international political problems has probably diminished in the face of such foreign policy miscalculations as the Bay of Pigs, the Dominican intervention, and Vietnam. The assumption of mutual advantages to be maximized by increasing the size of the pie through joint endeavors has been replaced in many policy sectors—notably energy and resources—by the view that the gain of one can very easily be at the expense of the other. There is a widespread feeling among sections of the Canadian public that deals with the United States seldom bring to Canada benefits commensurate with the costs. As the awareness of finite resources has grown, old notions of a pool of continental resources, somehow to be developed and allocated between the two countries (although largely owned by Canada), have become anathema north of the 49th parallel. Canadian worries about the high degree of American ownership of Canadian manufacturing and resources (see the preceding essays by Litvak and Maule and by Gilpin in this volume) have made many Canadians critical of suggestions emanating from Washington that smack of integration. The overall tone of Mr. Trudeau's foreign policy statements and the rhetoric of the press and parliamentarians have been to emphasize Canadian interests rather than North American interests, Canadian resources rather than continental resources.

[32] Some of the agreements made with the United States in past years were accepted at the time of negotiations as being reasonable bargains in terms of distribution of costs and benefits. Today, some Canadians question those agreements. They believe that the Columbia River Treaty in particular may have brought disproportionate benefits to the United States.

Perceptions among policymakers in Washington have changed as well. They can be summed up in the comment of one official: "Canada used to be our ally in the Cold War problem; now Canada is part of [our worldwide economic] problem." President Nixon views Canadian-American relations as part of an overall world situation rather than as a separate and distinct area of concern.[33] At least three times during the 1950s and 1960s American administrations had exempted Canada from legislation and regulations that reduced the flow of American investment abroad or restricted foreigners from buying on the American capital market. The restrictions would have had serious consequences for the Canadian economy. In each case, a Canadian delegation hurried to Washington to seek exemption, arguing that the measures would have serious negative consequences on the United States (through a diminution of American exports to Canada) as well as on Canada. But in 1971 the Canadian delegation was rebuffed in a manner that was considerably at odds with the norms of a good partnership. As seen in Washington, Canada had contributed seriously to the American balance-of-payments difficulty, and the unwillingness of the Canadians to help out the United States in its hour of economic trial suggested that they should be dealt with in the same manner as other United States trading partners. And on global problems the independent initiatives of Canada in trading with Cuba, recognizing China, and reducing troop commitments in NATO have led some officials in Washington to question the reliability of Canada as an ally—a question that was seldom raised during the 1950s or 1960s.

No change occurs overnight in the perceptions of policymakers. Some officials in Washington maintain that communication between the two capitals remains unrestricted, consultations go on as before, access to important officials remains open, and personal friendships developed over the years have not eroded. Yet in part a new generation of bureaucrats and higher-level officials dealing with Canadian problems has appeared in Washington, and to a certain extent also in Ottawa. Many of those Americans who had intimate knowledge of Canadian matters and close personal relations with their Canadian counterparts have left the government, to be replaced by those whose basic intellectual perspective is the global character of America's economic difficulties. Many of them have no particular interest in, or knowledge of, Canada. Thus, the norms of diplomatic conduct developed during the special relationship are less in evidence today than previously, although this comment applies to some policy sectors,

[33] Roger Swanson, "The U.S.-Canadian Constellation, I: Washington, D.C.," *International Journal* 27 (1972): 188.

notably trade and resources, much more than to others, such as environmental control or defence, and is contrary to the direction of subnational relations. Access to the highest points of policymaking in the United States is difficult for Canada as for most other governments.[34] No special exemptions will be made to Canada, and Canadian officials will seek none. There is no presumption of advanced consultation on some important domestic policies that have a spillover effect into the other country.[35] Many situations are defined by particpants in zero-sum terms rather than cooperation.[36] Above all, the Nixon administration has put a priority on building with Canada an "equitable" trading relationship. There has not been agreement between the two capitals as to what economic components go into making an equitable relationship.

In Washington, moreover, there has been a notable concentration of decision-making power with regard to economic matters. While transgovernmental relations will continue to be an important aspect of the Canadian-American relationship, on matters of trade, at least, the amount of central control exercised by the White House and the Treasury Department has grown during the Nixon administration.

[34] One reporter has claimed that the Canadian ambassador to Washington has not received an audience with President Nixon in three years. See Walter Stewart, "Our Washington Game Plan," *Maclean's*, August 1973, p. 50. Stewart also notes the more nationalist attitude of younger Canadian diplomats in the Washington embassy.

[35] Officials of both governments admit that they do not engage in advanced consultations when it is not in their interest to do so. They would prefer not to listen to foreign objections when formulating domestic policies. The Michelin tire case and the DISC proposal are two recent cases. The unwillingness to consult on some key issues is a notable departure from the recommendations of the Merchant-Heeney report. Occasionally, of course, transnational coalitions may form to oppose or promote a propsed domestic program. The conferences of state and provincial authorities were an important factor in promoting at the federal levels interest in Great Lakes pollution control.

[36] Barbara Haskel has suggested that in bargaining between states of disparate size, the weaker seeks to ensure adequate payoffs, assuming that the final agreement is in the nature of a fixed sum. It treats the negotiations as an "issue," or "an area of common concern in which the objectives of the two parties are assumed to be in conflict." The stronger party treats the negotiations as a "problem," where a possible solution can benefit both parties. It concentrates on increasing the joint gain. Lacking a required number of case studies, it is difficult to estimate to what extent this hypothesis holds for Canada and the United States. It would seem, however, that in the 1950s and 1960s most negotiations were seen by Washington and Ottawa as problems. Today Ottawa defines many of its relations with Washington as an issue; the American government treats sectors such as resources and defence as problems but trade and airline routes as an issue. See Barbara Haskel, "Disparities, Strategies and Opportunity Costs: The Example of Scandinavian Economic Market Negotiations in the 1950s and 1960s," *International Studies Quarterly* 18 (March 1974) : 3-30.

In many other policy sectors, however, the old patterns of conducting relations persist.

This is not to say that officials of the United States government are unmindful of the positive advantages of consultation, policy coordination, and constructing new institutions—at least in some circumstances. Almost all the officials interviewed agreed that there were inadequate amounts of consultation between Ottawa and Washington on a broad range of matters, and a former assistant secretary of commerce advocated in a 1972 speech in Toronto the creation of an intergovernmental structure for research and study of Canadian and American plans for economic growth during the next decade.[37] Other proposals for creating new bilateral institutions have been made recently, or are currently being considered in Washington. Thus, despite the changing perception of Canada and the toughening stance toward that country in some policy sectors, there are federal officials who still consider that important advantages are to be gained through applying the practices of the special relationship.

In Ottawa there has been little receptivity to American proposals for creating new institutions. Official representations have been politely rejected and trial balloons have been ignored. Reasons for these actions vary. Some officials, wedded to the ad hoc approach to institution building, claim there is no need presently for further structures. Others argue that given the state of public opinion in the country, it would be impolitic to create new agencies which give the appearance of locking Canada further into America's problems. At any rate, they contend, institutions like the IJC function satisfactorily and some new problems can be referred to it. It is argued, in addition, that permanent institutions create rigidities and hamper the flexible arrangements that from a bargaining point of view are more advantageous to a small state vis-à-vis a superpower. Many problems, moreover, have become multinational, so that creating purely bilateral institutions would be inappropriate. Finally, the record of the immediate past has alerted some Canadian officials to the possibilities of embarrassment ensuing from the nonuse of institutions. There are already enough joint committees that have not met for a long time.

The literature on the EEC has shown that however one measures integration, there is no steady trend toward institution building, spillover, or policy coordination. The variations in integration as measured by institution building tend to follow the vicissitudes of more traditional forms of diplomacy; when relations become cool, the thrust

---

[37] The assistant secretary of commerce in question resigned from the government shortly after presenting the proposal.

toward integration declines.[38] There is, of course, no assumption of formal integration between the United States and Canada, either in Washington or in Ottawa. There can be forms of economic free trade, such as in the automotive products agreement, but control over such agreements rests with two sovereign governments. This is equally true for institutions such as the IJC, although they do contain important integrative characteristics if we define the phenomenon in terms of joint policymaking.

Bureaucratic networks and bilateral institutions are very important for an understanding of Canadian-American relations, but the present political climate between Ottawa and Washington does not suggest any luxurious growth of new bodies on the national level; on the contrary, if the two federal governments define their interests in increasingly incompatible terms, there are likely to be higher levels of conflict and presumably, therefore, more distinct efforts by central authorities to maintain some control and supervision over the bureaucratic and diplomatic networks. Ad hoc arrangements will continue to be used extensively. Yet despite provincial-state cooperation, few of the political prerequisites for effective institution building on the national level are to be found in 1974 in Ottawa and Washington.

[38] See Barry B. Hughes and John E. Schwarz, "Dimensions of Political Integration and the Experience of the European Community," *International Studies Quarterly* 16 (September 1972) : 263-94.

THE INFLUENCE OF THE UNITED STATES CONGRESS ON CANADIAN–AMERICAN RELATIONS

Peter C. Dobell

Traditionally relations between nations, including Canada and the United States, have been analyzed in terms of the interaction between the executive branches of the two governments. This approach used to reflect relatively accurately the actual state of affairs. It is still broadly consistent with the constitutional allocation of powers, particularly in Canada. While the president of the United States must seek congressional action in order to declare war and Senate action to ratify treaties and to confirm ambassadorial appointments, these powers in Canada fall within the prerogatives of the crown, and *constitutionally* no parliamentary approval for decisions by the executive branch in any of these areas is required.

But this situation is far from static. In both countries, in quite different ways, the executive and legislative branches are constantly struggling to assert themselves.

The conflict in Canada has been muted by the parliamentary system of government. A government that senses it cannot control an action of Parliament will modify its position, often making quiet compromises. On the surface, the government must appear to be giving leadership, even if in fact it is reluctantly conceding to forces that it cannot control. Two recent instances of this phenomenon occurred when the secretary of state for external affairs submitted motions in the House of Commons protesting on 15 October 1971 the United States decision to explode under Amchitka Island a nuclear device and on 5 January 1973 the bombing of Hanoi and Haiphong. The latter motion very much offended President Nixon, who did not appreciate the argument of the Canadian government that had it not taken the initiative of submitting a moderate resolution, it would have felt obliged to go along with a much stronger condemnatory motion introduced by some opposition members.

Peter C. Dobell is director of the Parliamentary Centre for Foreign Affairs and Foreign Trade in Ottawa.

Mutual misunderstandings by both Canadians and Americans of the influence of each other's legislatures have arisen due to a lack of recognition of the differences in the two systems. This article examines in specific terms only the influence of Congress on Canadian-American relations. Its impact is much greater than that of the Canadian Parliament because of the independent status of Congress, and is also more direct and demonstrable. In neither country does the power of the legislature approximate that of the respective executive branches, but in both countries the legislatures are increasingly—by comparison with their previous activity—becoming forces to be taken into account. Their influence is mainly expressed in modifications to policies sought by the executives, although again more in the United States than in Canada, and the legislatures have also increasingly exercised an innovative influence.

In analyzing the role of Congress, the first phenomenon to be considered is the declining role of the foreign affairs committees of both houses relative to other committees. This illustrates how unimportant have become the traditional constitutional powers accorded to the Senate of ratifying treaties and confirming the appointment of ambassadors. The distinction between domestic and foreign affairs has in a legislative sense become confused as more and more domestic problems are affected by the actions of foreign states, and vice versa. The main part of this article is concerned with examining a broad range of congressional actions affecting Canada, divided somewhat artifically into those cases where the initiative has been taken by the administration, and other cases where the initiative has come from Congress. The article concludes with an examination of instruments open to the Canadian authorities for seeking to communicate concerns and influence the thinking of congressmen.

ROLE OF THE FOREIGN RELATIONS COMMITTEES OF CONGRESS

Coincident with the growth of transnational and transgovernmental relations between Canada and the United States has been the major increase in the number of committees within Congress concerned with some phase of the relationship. In the past, arrangements for cooperation between the two countries were normally expressed in treaty form, which therefore led to the involvement of the Senate Committee on Foreign Relations. But as the range of contacts has grown and the instruments for cooperation have become more informal and varied, matters affecting Canada have decreasingly been examined in the Senate Committee on Foreign Relations and the House Committee on Foreign Affairs and increasingly have come to be discussed in committees dealing with fisheries, energy, defence appropriations, immigration, agriculture, or transportation, to name only a few.

The role of the Senate Subcommittee on Internal Security in the 1950s has to be briefly commented upon, because it had so much to do with the development in Canada of the view that congressional effect on relations between the two countries was essentially malevolent. In 1954 Senators Jenner and McCarran made a much publicized visit to Montreal to interview the Soviet spy Igor Gouzenko as part of their investigations. In 1957 the subcommittee repeated allegations it had first raised in 1951 against a senior Canadian public servant, Herbert Norman. His subsequent suicide caused a storm of protest in Canada against American and, in particular, congressional interference. In 1957 the Canadian government sent an official note via its ambassador in Washington to the US secretary of state protesting "in the strongest terms the action taken by an official body of the Legislative branch of the United States Government in making and publishing allegations about a Canadian official." [1] Also, the leader of the opopsition spoke out strongly when he declared, "Let us once and for all tell the United States that the jurisdiction of these Senate Committees is in the United States. It does not take in Canadians. Let us tell the Americans they have no business condemning Canadians." [2] Resentment was aroused again in 1958 when similar allegations were made and broadened to include the then secretary to the Canadian cabinet.

Distressed by this deterioration in Canadian-American relations, the Senate Foreign Relations Committee in 1958 instituted a study to determine the causes and to try to bring about some improvement in the relationship. One outcome of the study was the Foreign Relations Committee's decision in 1959 to set up the Subcommittee on Canadian Affairs. It proved, however, to be anything but active. In its ten years of existence, the subcommittee gave cursory consideration in 1963 to the question of placing nuclear warheads in Canada and sought unsuccessfully to hold hearings over the proposed automotive products agreement.

In 1969, a decade after its establishment, the Subcommittee on Canadian Affairs was disbanded and responsibility for Canada given to the Subcommittee on Western Hemisphere Affairs. While reflecting the inactivity of the Subcommittee on Canadian Affairs, this move was part of a larger consolidation of subcommittee competences corresponding to the workload of the preceding decade.

[1] Canada, House of Commons, *Debates*, 10 April 1957, pp. 3357-58.
[2] "Hands Off Canadians Diefenbaker Tells US as Vote Drive Opened," *Globe and Mail* (Toronto), 8 April 1957.

The absence of Senate Foreign Relations Committee activity directed to Canadian problems has persisted. Between 1969 and 1971, apart from four minor treaties involving Canada submitted for endorsement by the administration and two bills from the House regarding border bridges, the only initiative affecting Canada of the Senate Foreign Relations Committee was the proposal to establish within the Department of State a post of undersecretary of state for Western Hemisphere affairs, with an assistant secretary for Canadian affairs reporting to him. The year 1973 saw a single hearing devoted to Canadian affairs—the questioning of the deputy assistant secretary for Canadian affairs to inquire whether the Department of State had deliberately held up the transmittal of information from the Canadian government regarding ownership of the possible Mackenzie River valley oil pipeline. Significantly, however, the lengthy substantive hearings relating to the route for moving Alaskan oil to the lower 48 states, which very much involved Canada, were held before the Senate's Interior and Insular Affairs Committee.

The same pattern has been repeated on the House side. The Senate Foreign Relations Committee's examination of Canadian affairs was paralleled by the Hays-Coffin report of 1958, a two-part study showing sensitive understanding of Canadian-American relations, which was largely the personal product of Congressman Frank Coffin of Maine.

Apart from offering sound advice, most of it relevant principally to the administration, the study's main fruit was the push it gave within the House of Representatives to the formation of the Canada–United States Interparliamentary Group. The group's creation, however, would not have been possible without the active advocacy and personal effort on the US side of Senator George Aiken of Vermont. The initiative and interest of both the Senate and House committees in this potentially influential interparliamentary body is reflected in the congressional resolution setting it up, which specifies that out of the twelve members to be appointed from each house, at least four are to be from the Senate Foreign Relations Committee and four from the House Foreign Affairs Committee.

The House Foreign Affairs Committee decided against establishing a subcommittee on Canadian affairs, as the Senate had done in 1959. The decision was tacitly reaffirmed in 1965 after the proposal had been advocated afresh in a report prepared for a Republican study committee chaired by Congressman Stanley Tupper of Maine and including three other members of the House Foreign Affairs Committee. In 1969, the committee reorganized its subcommittee structure and decided to transfer responsibility for Canadian affairs from the Subcommittee on Europe to the Subcommittee on Inter-American

Affairs, thereby bringing its organizational structure into line with that of the Senate Foreign Relations Committee.

Throughout the 1960s no hearings were held in the House Foreign Affairs Committee on a Canadian problem. By this standard the early 1970s have seen frantic activity. In December 1971 Congressman John Culver, chairman of the Foreign Economic Policy Subcommittee, undertook in a series of hearings to review the state of US economic relations with its major trading partners, with the Nixon measures of August 1971 giving particular urgency and focus to the inquiry. A specific hearing was devoted to relations with Canada. In March 1973 the Subcommittee on Inter-American Affairs held hearings to consider the current high water levels in the Great Lakes, and in November 1973 it discussed energy problems between the two countries.

It would be a mistake to conclude that past inactivity reflects lack of interest in Canada on the part of Congress, there being ample evidence to the contrary in the activity of many other congressional committees. But it does indicate something about how Congress regards Canada. Problems between Canada and the United States seem to be considered quasi-domestic in character, to be resolved at the professional or official level, and not to be elevated to the level of interstate relations. Some Canadians react adversely to such analysis, bridling at the implication that American congressmen take Canada for granted. However, I see in this only an indication that members of Congress do not feel the need for foreign affairs expertise in interpreting the minds of Canadians, whereas they do feel such a need with virtually all other countries. The Department of State, no less than the two congressional committees on foreign affairs, has been a victim of this same process of thought. Departments such as Agriculture, Commerce, and Labor, as well as numerous agencies, which are quick to seek Department of State guidance in overseas dealings, normally feel competent to negotiate directly with their opposite numbers in Canada.

If the Department of State is to some extent a victim of this outlook, it has failed to use opportunities to modify congressional attitudes. Every Wednesday morning the Department of State organizes an hour briefing for any member of the House of Representatives who wishes to attend, with the department choosing the topic. The practice is popular, attendance rarely falling below 30 and sometimes being well over 100. These briefings have concentrated on major themes such as China, the USSR, Vietnam, Bangladesh, the Middle East, and troop levels abroad. It is significant that during the four years from 1969 to 1972, not one of these briefings was devoted to United States relations with Canada. Similarly, the department organizes monthly luncheon briefings for the staff of members of Congress, which normally attract 200 participants. This group has shown an interest in concrete problems such as Japan's application of voluntary controls on steel exports. But in the period 1969-72 it had no presentation on Canada. The fact that both sets of briefings are given by assistant secretaries does mean that the director of the Office of Canadian Affairs would not be asked to speak and the responsible assistant secretary for European affairs would normally focus on current problems in Europe.

One initiative of the Senate Foreign Relations Committee remains to be examined before I turn to the work of other committees. The Senate version of the Foreign Relations Appropriations Bill (1972) contained the directive to the Department of State, noted above, that Canada should be transferred from the competence of the West European region, be placed in the Western Hemisphere region, and an assistant secretary for Canadian affairs be appointed under a deputy undersecretary for Western Hemisphere affairs. The Department of State balked at the first part of the directive, arguing that Canada belonged economically, politically, socially, and culturally with the Western European countries. An intervention by the Canadian ambassador, to be described later, clinched the argument, and the Foreign Relations Committee gave way on this point. Indeed, the whole proposal was dropped from the bill in Senate-House conference, although this was only agreed to after the Department of State had given written assurances that it would appoint a deputy assistant secretary for Canadian affairs. Lest it be assumed that Canada is ignored in the Department of State, the Office of Canadian Affairs, set up in response to a suggestion in the Merchant-Heeney report of 1964, was one of only a few offices in the department devoted to the affairs of one country. The appointment of a deputy assistant secretary for Canadian affairs enlarges significantly on the special treatment already accorded to Canada.

THE ADMINISTRATION'S INITIATIVES

Congress often acts in response to proposals submitted by the administration, which therefore has the first opportunity to decide on their form and character. In these instances Congress serves as overseer, responding by altering and modifying. Even this situation is one that an administration tries to avoid by seeking ways of conducting external relations to the greatest extent possible without seeking congressional authority. But when treaties are involved or legislative authority is needed for tariff changes going beyond those already authorized, Congress must give its approval. In this section I examine several typical examples of Congress's response to administration initiatives.

Two major administration initiatives involving Canada came automatically before Congress in the 1960s, the Columbia River Treaty and the automotive products agreement. The first, as a treaty, went to the Senate Foreign Relations Committee. Although negotiating was lengthy and difficult, the benefits on the United States side were so evident that there was no disposition in Congress to press for renegotiation. The treaty was, therefore, approved as presented.

The automobile products agreement was a far more controversial proposal. For Congress, the first issue to be resolved was jurisdiction. Since it was to be put into effect through an exchange of letters, the Senate Foreign Relations Committee could not make an overriding claim based on its treaty-ratifying powers. The requirement for a modification in the United States tariff eventually gave the Senate Finance Committee and the House Ways and Means Committee the decisive argument, and the substantive hearing took place before those two committees.

Since the automotive products agreement involved a major transformation in the marketing arrangements of the largest single manufacturing industry in the United States, the administration's proposal was closely examined. The successful outcome in Congress depended on the strength of the case for rationalizing the automobile industry in North America to meet growing foreign competition, on the support of all sectors of the industry, on the support of the trade union movement, on the full commitment of the Johnson administration and the strong support it had in Congress, especially in the House of Representatives, and finally on the good reputation Canada enjoyed, as well as the evident financial problem facing Canada. Even so, the administration had problems in the Senate. The main opposition came from two quarters: those like Senator Vance Hartke who opposed the agreement without qualification, believing it would damage the interests of American auto-parts manufacturers; and those like Senator Albert Gore who objected to the letters exchanged privately between the Canadian government and the auto manufacturers on the grounds that they constituted a one-sided advantage to Canada which the administration should not have accepted. In spite of this opposition, the administration decided to resist all amendments, an approach that succeeded although the final vote was close.

The automotive products agreement has since been occasionally attacked by individual members of Congress, and some in the American labour movement have pressed for renegotiation of the terms. It is particularly notable that Senator Russell Long, who was floor manager of the bill in 1964, has since become an opponent. While Congress would probably not be prepared to endorse a similar agreement if one were to be presented in the mid-seventies, it ih also unlikely to make a move requiring renegotiation. A fairly widespread feeling in Congress that Canada has done relatively better than the United States out of the agreement would probably be reflected in a more careful scrutiny of any comparable new proposal which an administration might submit to Congress and from which Canada might be expected to derive benefit. This attitude could, of course, change if the US overall balance-of-payments situation continues to improve, if the terms of trade in cars shifted significantly in favour of the United States, or if by one means or another the agreement were to be modified. In the meantime, although the agreement has general support, there is a sense that the administration was bested in the negotiations by the Canadian government.

A comparison of the extended hearings on the automotive products agreement with the cursory consideration the same two committees gave to the administration's proposal in 1963 to grant Canada exemption from the Interest Equalization Tax illustrates how responsive congressmen are to the visible effect of legislation on local employment. With no local impact to take account of, Congress was much readier to respond to the overall merits of the administration's submission and not inclined to seek ways of modifying it.

I turn now to a case where the congressional impact has been greater. The framing of the Immigration and Nationality Act of 1965 involved substantial congressional input, although the administration's determination to modernize United States immigration regulations was the catalyst. The main issue in contention was a quota for Canada and Mexico.

When the 1965 bill was being debated on the Senate floor, Senator Samuel Ervin of North Carolina, floor manager of the bill, accepted an amendment submitted by Senator Philip Hart of Michigan that exempted the Western Hemisphere from the application of the general quota of 20,000 for nonsponsored immigrants from any one country. Stressing the importance of not restricting the flow of immigrants from Canada, Hart argued against a "numerical limitation on each nation." "This," he stated, "would have been, indeed, a jolt to our Canadian neighbours." [3] The administration did not like the amendment but decided it could not be defeated.

The lack of national ceilings in the Americas has had unanticipated results. In the short time since the act came into effect in 1968, Canadian applications to emigrate to the United States have fallen

---

[3] US Congress, Senate, 89th Cong., 1st sess., 22 September 1965, *Congressional Record*, vol. 111, part 18, p. 24758.

below 20,000 for a variety of reasons, while Mexicans have profited from the exemption in the legislation to rise to above 60,000 a year.

To check the flow of Mexican immigrants, most of whom are unskilled, the administration has sought to restore the situation to that intended in the original proposal in the sixties. It introduced a new bill (HR 9409) in July 1973 designed to stem the inflow to some degree, setting a limit of 35,000 for Canada and Mexico and a 20,000 limitation for all other countries. The chairman of the House Judiciary Committee, Congressman Peter Rodino, formerly chairman of the Subcommittee on Immigration and Nationality, represents Jersey City; as his district is not secure he has a particular interest in not offending Spanish-speaking Americans. Anticipating the administration's bill, Mr. Rodino earlier in 1973 introduced his own bill (HR 981) providing for unlimited immigration from Canada and Mexico, the two contiguous countries, and 25,000 per country from all other countries.

In a surprising development, both the chairman's provision for unlimited immigration and the administration's proposal for a 35,000 limit for the two contiguous countries were defeated in subcommittee and in full committee in favour of a proposal to apply a quota of 20,000 to all countries. The reasoning of the majority of committee members was that at present rates Canadian immigration, which was highly desired, would not be restricted by the 20,000 quota, whereas Mexicans, who were less welcome, would take up the full 35,000 places, in addition to the many Mexicans who enter outside the quota as immigrants sponsored by immediate relatives.

Where the president already has the necessary power to act, Congress can only advise and urge. Congress faced such a situation when Richard Nixon announced the New Economic Policy of August 1971. Its application was broad, but the varying levels and character of trade with United States trading partners meant the effect of its application was not uniform. Canada and Mexico, as neighbouring countries with the largest percentage of their trade with the United States, were particularly threatened. Within a couple of months resolutions modifying the measures had been submitted in both houses.

The resolution submitted to the House was sponsored by several congressmen with a long history of interest in Canada who had served together in the Canada–United States Interparliamentary Group. Their version referred only to an exemption for Canada. In the Senate an early resolution was submitted by Senator Mike Gravel of Alaska, who is of French-Canadian origin, also calling for the exemption of Canada only, but this was subsequently amended by Senator James Buckley of New York to include Mexico as well as Canada. Not only was this tactically wise by attracting the potential support of senators from the Southwest, but it could also be expected to be popular with Spanish-speaking Americans in New York City.

Buckley's bill came to a vote without debate on 13 November 1971, and was defeated 36 to 29. The significance of the vote is complex. Among those voting against it were many who were opposed to the whole policy of the surcharge, and who did not want to reduce the pressure for its withdrawal by alleviating its worst effects. Others, knowing that a basis for compromise with the Europeans and Japanese was being worked out and that the surcharges would probably soon be lifted across the board, were opposed to piecemeal settlement. Congressmen also instinctively do not like to make exemptions in the application of legislation if this involves specifically naming countries. Finally, there were those who thought Canada should make adjustments toward the United States. Several senators felt that Canada had profited from earlier agreements, including the automotive products agreement, at the expense of the United States and were hoping that the administration might gain some concessions from Canada. Chief among these was Senator Russell Long of Louisiana, chairman of the Finance Committee, who let it be known that if the bill were to be debated, he would be highly critical of the economic benefits Canada had derived from previous special treatment by the United States. Under the circumstances the sponsors were happy to proceed to an immediate vote.

CONGRESSIONAL INITIATIVES

The most continuous and dramatic instance of congressionally initiated legislation involving Canada concerned Chicago's diversion of water from Lake Michigan. Although bills on this subject had been regularly introduced in every Congress for twenty years, the strongest thrust occurred during the 83rd to the 86th Congresses. In this seven-year period (1953-59), bills were passed by two successive Congresses, failing only as a result of presidential vetoes, and in the two later Congresses bills passed the House easily but did not complete the legislative course before adjournment. During the same period the Canadian government addressed eight notes of protest to the Department of State, and the Canadian ambassador paid a dramatic, unpublicized visit to the Senate majority leader.[4]

---

[4] The story does not need to be recounted in detail because it has been fully described in an excellent monograph by J. Richard Wagner, *Canada's Impact on United States Legislative Processes: The Chicago Diversion Bills*, Research Series #14 (Tucson: University of Arizona, 1973).

These bills sought to approve an increase in the volume of water diverted from Lake Michigan of 1,000 cubic feet of water per second, from the existing level of 1,500 cubic feet per second of water, to facilitate sewage disposal in the Chicago area by flushing it into the Mississippi River system. The principal advocates were congressmen in the Chicago area. However, during the early and mid-1950s high water levels in the Great Lakes also attracted the support of members of Congress along the whole length of the US side of the Great Lakes whose constituents had been adversely affected.

The principal issues in the debate were domestic. Ranged against the bill were Great Lakes and St. Lawrence River power and shipping interests, as well as a less well-organized resistance from those who objected to having Chicago's sewage flushed into the Mississippi River.

Those forces alone were not nearly strong enough to defeat the bill. Faced with the prospect of more unilaterally approved water diversions affecting the whole Great Lakes system, the Canadian government expressed strong opposition. While not fully accepting the legality of the Canadian government's position, the Department of State transmitted the notes to Congress, and when asked for its views, the department counseled against unilateral action by the United States. A precedent for unilateral American action might have weakened the United States bargaining position in the negotiations over the Columbia River Treaty.

After presidential vetoes of bills passed in the two preceding Congresses, a new bill passed through the House swiftly and decisively in the 86th Congress. Passage in the Senate seemed assured, and Senator Everett Dirksen believed he had President Eisenhower's agreement not to veto the bill again. However, some members of the Senate had become aware through the first meeting of the Canada–United States Interparliamentary Group in June 1959 of the strong Canadian resistance; they conceived a tactic by which the bill would be reported *jointly* to the Foreign Relations Committee and to the Public Works Committee. The majority in the Foreign Relations Committee was known to be opposed to the bill. At this juncture the Canadian ambassador sought an appointment with Senator Lyndon Johnson, the key figure if the manoeuvre were to succeed. Mr. Heeney recounted that "a couple of discreet telephone calls . . . brought me quickly into the presence of the majority leader. I explained the basis of Canadian opposition to further diversions at Chicago, and within minutes the crisis was avoided. The bill, he assured me, would not pass." [5] The majority leader subsequently threw his support to the

[5] Arnold Heeney, *The Things That Are Caesar's, Memoirs of a Canadian Public Servant* (Toronto: University of Toronto Press, 1972), p. 127.

joint committee reference, and the bill never emerged from the Foreign Relations Committee. This decision, plus reduced pressure owing to falling water levels in the Great Lakes, effectively ended decisive congressional action on this matter.[6]

The success of Ambassador Heeney's intervention at a critical moment in the congressional process has led some to suggest that the Canadian embassy has close and effective contacts with Congress which were exploited as necessary and that Canadian intervention like Mr. Heeney's were "commonplace." Mr. Heeney, however, believed "that direct recourse to Congressional friends should be reserved for the most critical situations in which no practical alternative was available," and recounted that during his seven years as ambassador to Washington this was the "only . . . occasion upon which I felt justified in going directly, and literally, 'to the Hill.' "[7]

The Chicago Water Diversion Bill was, of course, an exceptional situation in that in Canadian eyes a treaty with the United States, one on boundary waters, was being ignored. It was this consideration that gave standing to Canadian objections and caused the administration's extended resistance to the bill, in spite of the support organized in Congress. It is interesting to compare the long drawn-out battle fought over this proposal to divert 1,000 cubic feet of water per second from the Great Lakes with the lack of an official Canadian response to the North American Water and Power Alliance (NAWAPA) plan which, if enacted, would have had far more drastic implications for Canada. NAWAPA, advocated by Senator Frank Moss of Utah, represented a monumental scheme for diverting water to the arid southwest via a trench formed by parallel ranges of the Rocky Mountains. A large part of the water was to be bought in Canada. Senator Moss put much time and effort into the advocacy of this plan, some of it in Canada where he argued that the export of renewable resources was a more sensible way to earn United States dollars than through the sale of nonrenewable minerals and oil and gas. But in spite of the publicity he attracted and an encouraging report from a subcommittee which he chaired, Senator Moss could arouse no interest among his colleagues, who were alarmed either by the vast cost, the environmental consequences, or both. With the administration opposed to the proposal and Canada showing no interest in it, Senator Moss let it lapse.

The desire of the Department of Transportation for legislation to

---

[6] Mr. Wagner's monograph omits the critical role in providing behind-the-scenes support played by Congressman Thomas O'Brien of Chicago, a friend of Speaker Rayburn and Senator Dirksen and one to whom several southern congressmen were indebted.

[7] Heeney, p. 127.

improve navigational standards and facilities in American ports and along the coastline had the strong support of Senator Warren Magnuson of Washington, chairman of the Commerce Committee. But he exacted a price for his sponsorship of the bill in the form of a requirement for "comprehensive minimum standards of design, construction, alteration, repair, maintenance, and operation of [vessels]." [8] Under this provision, which became Title II, of the Ports and Waterways Safety Act of 1972, the United States Coast Guard is reluctantly drawing up standards relating to vessels to be in force by 1 January 1976, but it is concerned that unilateral United States action may encourage the proliferation of differing national regulatory schemes which could endanger the movement of world commerce.

Canada has been triply affected by this legislation: the standards would apply to Canadian ships entering United States waters; foreign shipping destined for Canadian ports might feel the need to meet US standards whether Canada required them or not; and tankers carrying oil for the Montreal area, which is landed in Portland, Maine, would have to meet US standards. However, there could be no basis for a Canadian complaint, since all vessels, United States and foreign, are being treated equally and the Coast Guard has sought the views of shipping interests in all countries regarding the proposed standards. But unlike Title I of the act regarding navigational arrangements in coastal waters, which has the full support—and even collaboration in adjacent waters—of the Canadian Ministry of Transport, Title II is looked on in Canada as a premature initiative and the standards called for are awaited with some trepidation.

Efforts to regulate water quality for the Great Lakes reveal even more complex interactions between Congress and the administration on the one hand and Canadian interests on the other. While the Great Lakes Water Quality Agreement itself was negotiated by the administration, it was Congress that had originally advocated the establishment of the Environmental Protection Agency (EPA), and it was Congress that pressed for lower levels of phosphates in detergents and for higher levels of federal funding for sewage treatment plants than the administration was prepared to recommend. In this field Congress has consistently prodded the administration.

United States compliance with the terms of the Great Lakes agreement calling for the construction of facilities so as to meet certain water quality standards by 1975 has been endangered by Congress's sharp response to President Nixon's impoundment of one-third of the $18 billion for environmental work. On discovering that the

[8] US Congress, *Ports and Waterways Safety Act*, PL 92-340, Title II, sec. 201 (1972).

balance of those funds that the president was prepared to have the EPA expend were to be allocated on a priority basis to projects involving direct discharge into the Great Lakes, Congress in December 1973 hastily passed an amendment to the Federal Water Pollution Control Act. This amendment seeks to deny to the administration the power to give priority to the funding of the construction of water treatment facilities on the shores of the Great Lakes to the detriment of approved schemes in other localities for protecting the environment. Canada is thus caught involuntarily in the general issue of impoundment.

ROLES AND MOTIVES OF CONGRESSMEN

Although human motivation is difficult to unravel and especially so in the case of the legislators, some attempt to determine the motives and objectives for congressional involvement in Canadian-American relations should be made.

Geographic Considerations

An important source of congressional action naturally derives from the long border linking Canada and the United States, which can sometimes present a dilemma to individual legislators. Many congressmen find themselves forced by President Nixon's impoundment of funds to make a choice between giving priority to a cleanup of the Great Lakes, to which the United States is now committed by international agreement, or breaching it in order to secure funds for their own districts. It is significant that one of the strong defenders for giving priority to obligations toward Canada was Congressman Charles Vanik of Cleveland, whose city would, in fact, have secured priority funding for sewage treatment facilities. But for many other congressmen the only way to avoid the choice was to press the president to release the impounded funds or to seek special additional funding for facilities on the Great Lakes.

Point Roberts provides a particularly intractable example of a difficult border problem. A small peninsula of land jutting southward into Puget Sound from British Columbia, Point Roberts, because it lies south of the 49th parallel, is American territory. While it has some 200 permanent residents who are US citizens, in summer it attracts some ten to twenty times more Canadians who own most of the property. Point Roberts has insufficient water and British Columbia has been unwilling to supply it, arguing that the water should be piped through an underwater pipeline from the United States, a project that would be enormously costly. With only 200 residents, to provide basic medical, police, and fire services is difficult. Unfortunately, this situation has aroused nationalist feelings on both sides.

Given the small number of Americans involved, it is natural that application of pressure on their congressman—since 1964 Lloyd Meeds—has been the main hope of the local residents. Congressman Meeds concluded early that the best course was to secure a reference to the International Joint Commission (IJC). Initially both governments declined to make such a reference, arguing that the IJC's competence was limited to boundary waters, but under his and others' pressure the two governments withdrew their opposition. Mr. Meeds pressed his congressional colleagues on the Appropriations Committee to make no cuts in the IJC budget, and had his staff make a study of all aspects of the problem, which later was used by the IJC. The international study team appointed by the IJC reported its findings in November 1973 and recommended that "Point Roberts should become a part of an international conservation and recreation area set astride the United States and the Canadian border. . . ." [9] The IJC has since organized a series of hearings on the west coast on both sides of the border to ascertain local reactions to the special study prior to attempting to decide on a formal recommendation to the two governments.

Alaska and the "Lower 48"

A surprisingly large number of congressional initiatives involving Canada result from problems caused by the geographic separation of Alaska from the "lower 48" states. Being local or regional in their effects, the initiative for their remedy has often been sought by congressional representatives. Some of these have benefited Americans without really affecting Canada, an example being an act to permit American citizens transiting Canada on the Alaskan highway to recover medical expenses if these were incurred in Canada. Sometimes these United States decisions may even bring benefit to Canada at no cost. This may be the result if a congressional proposal initiated by Senator Ted Stevens of Alaska results in US highway trust funds being used to pay for the paving of the remaining unpaved sections in Canada of the Alaska highway.

The problem of transporting Alaskan oil to the lower 48 states has uncontestedly aroused more feeling in Canada and in the United States Congress about Canada than any other geographic complication in recent times.[10] The initial experiment to determine whether the oil could be moved by reinforced tanker through the Northwest Passage, an initiative undertaken by a single American company, had dramatic

[9] *Globe and Mail* (Toronto), 16 November 1973, p. 2.
[10] See Ted Greenwood's article in this volume for a discussion of the energy question in a wider perspective.

consequences in the Canadian Parliament.[11] Canadian reaction to the congressional authorization for enlarging a right-of-way for the Alyeska [12] pipeline probably has not been so great. The voyage of the reinforced tanker *Manhattan* demonstrated that there was no present alternative to moving the oil overland. This realization provoked a debate within the United States between Midwest interests, who favored the Mackenzie River valley route through Canada, and West Coast interests, who preferred the trans-Alaska route to Valdez with tankers bringing the oil down the west coast. The oil producers opted for the West Coast route because it was cheaper in their judgment, offered broader market flexibility, and could be built more quickly. The administration claimed to have been persuaded by the last consideration. Other arguments that carried weight with some were the boost to the United States maritime industry if the tanker route were chosen and greater control if the route were all-American. Complicating the conflict were the concerns of environmentalists about the risks of building a line in the ecologically fragile northern environment, especially since the proposed route for the Alyeska line passed through seismologically active terrain.

Although the pipeline is to be built by private capital, Congress has been three times centrally involved in the controversy: first, to legislate an Indian land claims settlement agreement of unprecedented generosity to overcome the resistance of the native peoples of Alaska and the legal potential for delaying law suits; second, to legislate exemption from the full legal consequences, with their potential for delay, of Congress's earlier requirements specified under the Environmental Protection Act by asserting that Congress was satisfied with the environmental studies already completed; and third, to increase the right-of-way when it developed that the existing authority to grant a right-of-way was insufficient for the large pipeline that was projected. To this latter legislation, the Congress has attached a broad range of directives regarding ship construction and navigation standards, liability for accident, and the like. In addition, the legislation requested the president to enter into negotiations with the Canadian government to determine its willingness to agree to transport oil and gas via pipeline across Canada, as well as agreeing to the use of tankers by way of the Northwest Passage.

Canadian involvement in this United States internal debate was inevitable. The line favoured by Midwest interests would cross Canadian territory; the line desired by the American consortium and sup-

---

[11] These events are outlined in my book, *Canada's Search for New Roles, Foreign Policy in the Trudeau Era* (London: Oxford University Press, 1972), pp. 69-70.
[12] The Aleyska Pipeline Service Company, which is to build the pipeline.

ported by the US administration would result in heavy tanker traffic off Canada's west coast and into Puget Sound. Fears of a major oil spill in the inland sea off Vancouver alarmed many Canadians across the country, and especially those on the west coast, leading to a general disposition in favour of a route down the Mackenzie River valley. Yet no group of companies could be found that was prepared to build an oil pipeline from Prudhoe Bay through Canada and into the Midwest. The Trudeau government chose to take the legally correct but ambiguous position that it was prepared to "welcome any application" for a Mackenzie River valley line. (It did not emphasize that in 1971 the minister of energy, mines, and resources held talks with United States oil companies during which he learned that they would not consider constructing an oil line through Canada unless they were denied the right to build a line across Alaska.) The effect of the government's position was to convey the impression that it was in some undisclosed way promoting a Canadian oil line.

These repeated offers to welcome any application for a line along the Mackenzie valley were seized on in the United States as evidence of a Canadian desire to build a line through Canada. However, the US advocates of a Canadian pipeline ignored the ambiguity of the government's statements and the political weakness of the Trudeau government after 1972. The United States administration, by contrast, regarded these affirmations at best as a complication to be circumvented and at worst as a misleading intrusion into United States affairs that might delay construction of the Alyeska line.

In the third and crucial debate that raged in Congress during the first six months of 1973 over the right-of-way bill, the intentions of the Canadian government became a major point at issue. In advocating passage, the secretary of the interior attributed certain positions to the Canadian government; advocates of a line to Midwest markets charged him with distortion. The chairman of the Subcommittee on Public Lands of the House Committee on Interior and Insular Affairs privately invited, through the Department of State, a Canadian spokesman to appear as a witness in Washington. When the invitation was declined, he requested further information from the Department of State which, in turn, submitted a series of questions to its embassy in Ottawa. The Canadian Department of Energy, Mines, and Resources transmitted a reply to Washington in late June. Shortly thereafter the Canadian department decided to modify that part of the text concerning ownership of an oil pipeline; but through a series of unfortunate bureaucratic accidents, the corrected text was only available in the Senate on the eve of the day on which the final vote on the Senate's version of the bill was held. Opponents of the Alyeska line were quick to charge the Department of State with a deliberate effort to conceal the true Canadian position on an important objection raised by the administration to the Canadian route. In Canada the hard-pressed government seemed happy to allow the same impression to circulate.

Senate passage of the right-of-way bill produced an immediate reaction in the Canadian Parliament: both houses called for a special meeting of the Canada-US Interparliamentary Group to register Canadian concern over the decision. The United States section responded with speed and courtesy, and a meeting was held four days later in Washington, on 24 July. Accepting that the United States was not to be diverted from the Alyeska route, the Canadian group decided to concentrate on proposals to protect the inland sea between Vancouver Island and mainland British Columbia. Their first choice was to repeat an offer made earlier by the minister of energy, mines, and resources, Mr. Donald Macdonald, by which Canada would supply sufficient oil to enable the Puget Sound refineries, which at the time were using 80 percent Canadian crude, to operate entirely without offshore oil. The second proposal was to encourage the United States to collaborate with Canada in the development of legal and technical arrangements for protecting the inland sea.

The renewal of the offer to supply the Puget Sound refineries with Canadian crude opened a new controversy in Congress between opponents of the right-of-way bill and Secretary of the Interior Morton, who asserted that Canada was only offering to maintain the existing levels of oil export, which would mean diverting Canadian oil now being delivered to the Midwest. The subsequent international oil crisis and the introduction of a new Canadian oil policy have totally closed that option.

As a result of the meeting of the Canada–United States Interparliamentary Group, American advocates of the Mackenzie valley route finally realized that there was, in fact, no Canadian desire to build an oil pipeline, and this revelation hastened the end of the debate in the House of Representatives. On the Canadian side it forced members of Parliament to recognize that the second alternative they had offered, that is, the development of legal and technical arrangements to provide some protection for the west coast, represented the best form of protection available in the circumstances. While the Canadian visitors gained a first-hand appreciation of the gravity of the United States energy problem, the American participants got a feeling of the intensity of Canadian concerns for the inland sea. This latter impression contributed to including in the final bill a provision for a compulsory liability fund of up to $100 million to cover cleanup costs and other damages.

Canadian public interest in and governmental comment on the

Alyeska pipeline probably exceeded concern over the Chicago water diversion bills. Yet the Canadian government did not address notes to the United States government, intended for transmission to Congress. Recognizing it has no legal right to intervene in the legislative process, it confined its public activities to speeches by ministers intended to be noted in Washington and to visits by ministers and officials, the most important being one by Mr. Macdonald to Secretary Morton. The Canadian embassy in Washington merely responded to inquiries with texts of these speeches, carefully refraining from offering interpretative comment. Far from appearing to be a carefully orchestrated Canadian campaign to modify United States policies in directions beneficial to Canada, the Canadian government's response seems to have been primarily intended to win domestic support in its own country.

Defending Constituent Interests

Where pressures from local constituencies for congressional action coincide, they can become a potent political force. High water levels on the Great Lakes produced such a situation in the early 1970s. Congressmen with constituencies from Duluth on Lake Superior to Oswego on Lake Ontario were all being pressed by desperate constituents whose property losses may in aggregate amount to hundreds of millions of dollars. A manifestation of this pressure was the joint letter signed by 34 congressmen addressed in December 1972 to President Nixon appealing to him for help of any kind. In April 1973 these direct pressures led to an insistence on the American side of the International Joint Commission that the flow from Lake Superior be curtailed at Sault Ste. Marie. Reluctantly concurred in at the time by the Canadian section of the IJC, the decision was reversed some months later when the backed-up waters threatened to flood Duluth, the home of John Blatnik, the powerful chairman of the House of Representatives Public Works Committee.

As long as the water levels remain high so will pressure on the IJC to ensure the maximum flows down the St. Lawrence consistent with agreed water levels in Montreal. The water level problem has led to demands in Congress for broader representation on the IJC and for more publicity for its activities. Canadians with properties on the north shores of these lakes are suffering similarly; conceivably this could produce a different Canadian response to the Chicago water diversion, if it could be shown that greater diversion might reduce water levels in the lower lakes.

When domestic manufactured goods lose out to foreign competition, companies are likely to seek support from their congressman who in turn is likely to seek whatever administrative protection may be available. If this is inadequate, he may propose a new bill. A comprehensive example is the strongly protectionist bill sponsored in 1972 by Congressman James Burke and Senator Vance Hartke. Directed against imports in order to protect union jobs, the bill would affect Canada more severely than other countries because more trade is involved.

Congressmen use debate, remarks printed in the *Congressional Record,* and the introduction of bills to demonstrate active support to constituents even when they expect no legislative results. Such measures may induce administrative action or provide leverage to the administration in trade negotiations.

As the United States largest trading partner, it is not surprising that Canada has come in for its fair share of critical comment regarding unfair competition. Typical were complaints by a New Mexico senator about imports of potash from Canada and by a Louisiana senator about imports of Canadian sulphur. The impulse in both cases was local employment, since both industries in Canada are largely in the hands of American companies.[13]

Tendencies to Generalize in Legislation

Legislative remedies are framed in general terms. This can sometimes lead to a wider impact than was intended. Thus, a rider was attached to the Defense Appropriations Act of 1972 largely at the insistence of Pennsylvania representatives to give their steel industry some protection against specialty steels for defence production being imported from Japan. Known as the specialty metals rider, it was passed in spite of the opposition of the administration. Its purport was to require that all special steels used in defence production in the United States should be processed in the United States. Being general in its phraseology, it has excluded all imported specialty steels, including those from Canada which in the previous year had amounted to some $10 million. The effect of this rider runs counter to understandings under the defence production sharing arrangements.[14]

Such legislative practices are difficult for foreign governments to handle. They can make representations to the government department concerned, as Canada did to the Department of Defense with respect to the specialty metals rider. In this instance the department was

[13] The United States Tariff Commission decided in 1973 that US producers were likely to be injured by Canadian imports sold at less than the domestic sales price and the Treasury Department has ordered dumping duties imposed.

[14] See Roger Swanson's article on defense and Kal J. Holsti and Thomas Allen Levy's article on bilateral institutions and transgovernmental relations in this volume.

confident that the rider would be deleted in the Senate-House conference called to reconcile the two texts, where, with proceedings confidential, concessions can be made without explanation. But the Department of Defense was wrong. Perhaps in this particular situation, since the rider was known to be directed against Japan, an informal suggestion to the sponsors that the rider be amended to exclude countries with which the United States has defence production sharing agreements (i.e., only Canada) might have been acceptable to them.

To refrain from mentioning specific countries in legislation can involve dangers for Canada where no harm was intended. In March 1973 Congressman Lionel van Deerlin of San Diego, California, introduced a bill (HR 751) designed to secure reciprocal treatment for Greyhound buses, which are at present being denied under Mexican law the right to carry tours into Mexico while Mexican buses operate freely in southern California. But rather than refer specifically to Mexico, the bill seeks to bar foreign bus companies from crossing into the United States "unless . . . such foreign country grants reciprocal privileges to citizens of the United States." [15] For geographic reasons, this bill, therefore, becomes applicable to Canada, if enacted. Mr. van Deerlin had no interest in or knowledge of the Canadian situation, and has been surprised by the interest aroused in Canadian trucking circles. Even if enacted, however, the bill represents no present threat to Canada. Moreover, it is quite likely that the bill will suffer the fate of the vast majority of bills annually submitted to Congress.

In at least one well-known case, legislation of this kind, although framed in general terms, was designed specifically to inhibit the import of Canadian lumber into the United States. Introduced in 1963 by the late Senator Wayne Morse of Oregon to protect the lumber industry of the northwest, it required the labeling of each piece of lumber imported into the country. Since almost all imported lumber comes from Canada, the general application of the bill was just a legislative convention. Morse's personal standing and his legislative skill secured the passage of his bill through both houses. Only the veto of President Johnson, who feared the inflationary effects of the measure and its effect on relations with Canada, prevented the bill from becoming law.

Unintentional Impact of Congressional Action

Because of the interdependence of the two economies and the similarity of many social conditions in the two countries, Congress

---

[15] US Congress, House, *Bill HR 5751 to Amend Section 202 of the Interstate Commerce Act*, introduced 15 March 1973, p. 2.

may take action for purely domestic reasons that has unintended impact in Canada. Examples in the industrial field are so numerous that one will suffice to make the point. Owing to the integration of the automobile industries in the two countries, the setting of maximum car emission standards by Congress virtually establishes a lower limit for Canada as well (see Scott's essay in this volume). Because of propinquity and social similarities between Alaska, the Yukon, and the Northwest Territories, the Alaskan land claims settlement has been taken as a model by Canadian native people, even though neither of the two considerations that were decisive in the United States— enormous oil discoveries or the felt need for urgency—prevail in the Canadian north.

These influences are not only in one direction. Canada has, along with a number of other fishing nations, adopted the principle of straight baselines for defining fishing zones. The United States government has opposed the concept and in particular its application by Canada. Senator Ted Stevens of Alaska has prepared a bill committing the United States to straight baselines for fisheries protection reasons. He believes that while the administration is still not ready to adopt this approach, the ground will have been prepared for a reversal of the US position at the Caracas Law of the Sea Conference. If that happened, it might remove an irritant which now exists between the two countries.

CONGRESSIONAL ATTITUDES TOWARD CANADA

The information does not exist with which to draw a profile of congressional attitudes toward Canada. However, favorable references to Canada and to Canadian practice and experience far exceed critical statements. Many congressmen, when seeking to persuade their colleagues to adopt given legislation, work on the principle that the most favorable model they can cite is Canada. If the arrangements proposed have been tried and found to work in Canada, they feel this is a powerful example both because of the similarity of social and economic conditions between Canada and the United States and the generally favorable image of Canada which most of them believe prevails in Congress.

This impression derives in part from the fact that Canada is seen as a friendly neighbour, hardly a foreign country at all. Nevertheless, particularly as a result of the debate on the Aleyska pipeline, there is a growing understanding that Canadian and American interests frequently do not coincide.

How these attitudes influence a congressman faced with a vote is difficult to determine. In general, a favorable Canadian image would rarely prevail in a situation where a congressman was under significant local pressure urging him to vote or act in a way that, while protecting a local interest, might do some harm in Canada. He might rationalize his dilemma either by doing the minimum to support his constituency or by persuading himself that his action would be nullified by those of his colleagues who did not have to make the same choice. But as was made clear with the Chicago water diversion bills, in case of a conflict between a clearly perceived domestic interest and that of a foreign country, even one that is favorably regarded, the domestic interest is likely to prevail.

A critical factor is whether a perceived national interest is involved. If the congressman is not receiving significant local representations, he will feel freer to take a broader assessment of the national interest. For example, Representative Henry Reuss of Wisconsin, an influential Democrat on the Joint Economic Committee, had been impressed by Canadian arguments regarding the damage they were suffering from the US Food for Peace program (PL 480). He succeeded in getting an amendment to the legislation to require that the program be modified so as not to harm the markets of traditional friends of the United States. He wished to remove a source of friction between the two countries, and was able to follow his larger sense of United States national interest due to his strong position in Congress and to the absence of pressure from grain growers since Wisconsin is primarily a dairy state.

Congressional views toward Canada may remain friendly, but in recent years attitudes in higher levels of the executive have been less benign than they used to be. From Roosevelt to Eisenhower, the shared experience of wartime collaboration and the building of the postwar security structure gave an intimacy to the relationship that permeated the whole executive branch. The election of President Johnson, a man of the southwestern United States with little previous contact with Canada, coincided with the effective disappearance of Canada as a major actor on the world stage. More recently, Canadian criticisms of the war in Vietnam and the pressure generated within the administration by unfavorable trade balances and oil shortages have introduced new complexities into intergovernmental relations, regardless of congressional views.

Canada—United States Interparliamentary Group

The separate and considerable powers of Congress, the favorable attitude held by most congressmen toward Canada, and the decline in high-level administration concern to maintain friendly relations with

Canada have given a new importance to maintaining contact with Congress. Its neglect in the past was less serious than it has now become.

Unique among such links is the Canada–United States Interparliamentary Group.[16] The group, set up by joint resolution of the two legislatures, brings together delegations representing both houses in each legislature for annual discussions of problems of mutual concern. The group deliberately makes no attempt to reach a consensus of the views of participants, and there are few instances where group meetings have led to specific legislative action. The group's aim in bringing Canadian and American legislators together for private exchanges at least once a year is rather to encourage better understanding of each other's politics and problems. While its structure and working practices have not enabled it to achieve its full potential, it has been a valuable instrument for helping some congressmen to understand Canadian attitudes and concerns, and vice versa.

Examples where congressmen have been sensitized by these meetings include: Canadian sentiments on the Chicago water diversion proposals; Canadian problems in developing the automobile industry and, therefore, the need for the automotive products agreement; complications for Canadians seeking to work in the United States caused by the Immigration and Nationality Act of 1965; the potential effect of the import surcharges of 1971 on Canada as the United States's largest trading partner; and Canadian fears regarding the effects of bringing oil tankers into Puget Sound.

An auspicious and recent development within the Canada–United States Interparliamentary Group has been the holding of special one-day meetings (as compared to the normal three-day meetings) organized at short notice and devoted to a single issue of particular concern. The first such meeting, held on 11 November 1971, was sought by the Canadians to permit them to place their concerns before their American colleagues regarding the potentially heavy impact of the 10 percent import surcharge levied on 15 August 1971 on Canadian exports to the United States and ultimately on Canada's ability to import from the United States. The second meeting was also sought by the Canadian members of Parliament who were alarmed by Senate approval of the Federal Lands Right-of-Way Bill in connection with the Alaska pipeline; it had a valuable educational impact on both

[16] For further details of this group, see Matthew J. Abrams, *The Canada–United States Interparliamentary Group* (Ottawa/Toronto: Parliamentary Centre for Foreign Affairs and Foreign Trade/Canadian Institute of International Affairs, 1973).

countries' legislators. In terms of ground covered, both meetings were probably more effective than the annual meeting of the group.

The Canada–United States Interparliamentary Group has an unrealized potential by comparison with the many interparliamentary groups or conferences developed since the Second World War. Members on both sides speak the same language, share a similar cultural background, and represent countries with closely linked economies and with more transnational links than between any two other major countries. Moreover, legislators are instinctively drawn one to another through having been elected. Therefore, there are few of the normal inhibitions to communication. The obstacles they experience derive from the competing demands on their time, which may limit attendance at the infrequent meetings which take place and which mean that few legislators on either side are adequately prepared for the exchanges. Nevertheless, in spite of the deficiencies, the meetings do promote better understanding between the two countries and have the possibility of playing a larger role in the future in maintaining closer relations.

The Canadian Embassy and Congress

Since the Washington legation was first raised to the status of an embassy in 1944, Canadian governments have considered it wise to make their approaches to the executive branch and leave it to interpret and protect Canadian interests vis-à-vis Congress. The rationale for this practice is twofold: a belief that the executive is better equipped than the embassy to deal with Congress, and a concern not to arouse suspicion that the embassy might be making deals with Congress behind the administration's back. The practice undoubtedly also owes much to Canada's experience with parliamentary government, under which the prime minister and the government are in practice normally able to speak for and commit Parliament. That the separation of powers produces an entirely different situation in Washington is a fact often ignored in Canada. In consequence, while the embassy did not avoid social contact with congressmen, neither did it organize a purposeful program of cultivating influential senators and representatives. Exceptions were made sometimes for contacts with individual congressmen who sought embassy assistance, but only if they had demonstrated their discretion. This attitude was one that the executive branch encouraged; it facilitated the executive's task and increased its leverage with Congress.

Increasing economic interdependence has forced congressmen concerned with trade and economic policy to look abroad and to take more interest in the external world. The Department of State has also begun to look on the local embassies as resources to be used in educating congressmen. Concerned at growing opposition in Congress to the maintenance of large American forces in Europe, it has started encouraging the major West European ambassadors to take their arguments directly to Congress. Similarly, Department of State officials prompted Ambassador Ushiba of Japan to join them in explaining the importance of the US decision to agree to the reversion of Okinawa to Japan. In a similar move, the Department of State recently asked the Canadian ambassador to discuss with members of the Senate Foreign Relations Committee their proposal for shifting responsibility within the Department of State for Canadian affairs from the European affairs office to the inter-American affairs office. Ambassador Cadieux explained to the chief advocates, Senators George Aiken and William Spong, that Canada was satisfied to be grouped with the industrialized nations of Western Europe and was not seeking a change in jurisdiction within the Department of State. The Senate committee subsequently gave way on this point.

A combination of considerations is causing a gradual, yet cautious, change in the attitude of the Canadian embassy toward contact with Congress. A modest program of cultivating powerful members of both houses has been initiated, and a member of the embassy staff has been made responsible for following congressional affairs and for developing contacts among congressmen and their staffs. The embassy is also passing informative material to senators and congressmen if their public statements appear to have been based on inaccuracies. Thus, it is following the practice of the United States embassy in Ottawa, which has for many years designated an officer to follow parliamentary affairs and to develop personal contact with Canadian legislators. Ironically, the US embassy in Ottawa is more active in a situation where the potential benefits are fewer than is the Canadian embassy in Washington in an environment where the potential benefits are relatively much greater.

The risks, however, must be calculated. These are of two main kinds: that congressmen might judge the embassy to be interfering unreasonably; or that the executive branch might think that the embassy (or government) was going behind its back, either publicly or privately. The Canadian embassy has over the years experienced both difficulties.[17]

---

[17] For an example, see US Congress, Senate, 85th Cong., 2d sess., 18 March 1958, *Congressional Record*, vol. 104, part 4, p. 4649.

CONCLUSION

The role of each country's legislature is evolving in response to two distinct developments: increasing governmental involvement in national affairs, which is forcing Canadian governments, for example, to disregard their constitutional prerogatives and seek parliamentary endorsement for many foreign policy decisions; and growing international interdependence. Nowhere has this latter process gone further than in United States relations with Canada, owing to the extraordinarily high degree of transnational and transgovernmental activities. The range and extent of existing connections, the broad cultural, social, and ideological similarities, the contemporary forces of international integration—all these factors have produced a mutual linkage that has multiplied the instances where congressional action has had its effect on Canada and on Canadian-American relations. In some cases congressmen have not even been aware that their actions were having effects in Canada until this was called to their attention. To improve such communication is part of the future agenda of Canadian-American relations.

QUEBEC AND THE NORTH AMERICAN SUBSYSTEM: ONE POSSIBLE SCENARIO

Daniel Latouche

For a majority of Québécois whose mother tongue is French, transnational relations with the United States are like palm trees. They are known to exist elsewhere but are rarely talked about and much less seen.[1] This apparent neglect, which contrasts markedly with the almost frantic attention now accorded to Canadian-American relations in anglophone Canada, does not imply that Québécois are unaware of the economic, cultural, and political proximity of the United States or that significant transactions across the Québec-American border do not take place.[2] They do occur, but they are not always readily apparent.

To show that these transactions really exist I have chosen to examine the possible effects of Québec's independence on the North American subsystem. Why this future-oriented approach and why this particular scenario? First, the likely impact of Québec independence is in itself a valid question. Does Québec, with its small industrial output ($14.9 billion in 1972) and population (6.1 million), constitute such an insignificant economic actor that its political destiny

Daniel Latouche is associated with the Centre d'Etudes Canadiennes-françaises, McGill University, and the Groupe de Recherches sur le Futur, Institut National de la Recherche Scientifique, Université du Québec.

[1] Words are seldom neutral carriers of meanings. In Canada whether one speaks of French Canadians or Québécois, or of separation rather than independence, for instance, serves to define one's political coordinates. In recent years a number of French-speaking Canadians living in Québec have come to define themselves as Québécois, thus stressing their geographic rather than their ethnic affiliation, while French-speaking minorities outside of Québec continue to refer to themselves as French Canadians. In the same way the term *separatist* is most often used by those who wish to stress negative aspects of the independence option. In this article I use the word *independentist,* an anglicized version of the French *indépendentiste,* to refer to those who favor independence for Québec.

[2] This is evidenced by the positive response of English-Canadian scholars to this idea of a special issue of *International Organization* on Canadian-American transnational and transgovernmental relations as contrasted with polite indifference of Québec social scientists who, on the whole, have shown little interest in the United States-Canada-Québec triangle.

will have little consequence for major issue areas, such as trade, investment, energy, and for natural resources, such as asbestos, iron ore, and timber products?[3] Or can it not be argued that Québec, whatever its own objective economic strength, poses a serious problem for the stability of the North American economic system since it could bring about the disintegration of the most important economic partner of the United States?

My second objective in making use of the scenario technique is not to predict the future but to force the phenomena under investigation to reveal themselves by experimenting with one eventual reality.[4] The logic of scenario construction, like that of model building, forces us to focus on some key variables and thus facilitates the post facto reconstruction of phenomena that are not immediately apprehensible by direct investigation techniques.

There is no doubt that instead of independence other equally plausible scenarios could have been posed to achieve this objective. But by looking at one alternative, perhaps extreme, it should prove easier to test the sensitivity of Gilpin's model of Canadian-American and English-Canadian–French-Canadian relations (see his essay in this volume) by examining what could happen when the model is pushed to one of its plausible conclusions.[5] This procedure should enable us to uncover some of the links between the dynamics of Canadian-American relations and the dynamics of Canada's own internal problems.

THE PLAUSIBILITY OF THE INDEPENDENCE SCENARIO

My scenario for Québec's independence rests on four premises: (1) independence has a reasonably high probability of occurrence; (2) independence, if it comes, is likely to be the result of an electoral

---

[3] The dependent character of the Québec economy is well documented in the first comprehensive study of the Québec economic structures: Marcel Saint-Germain, *Une économie à liberer* (Montréal: Les Presses de l'Université de Montréal, 1973). Since 1970 the annual Québec GNP has been more than $4 billion. Its GNP per capita is more than $3,500 per year, surpassed only by the US, Sweden, the rest of Canada, and Switzerland (among Organization for Economic Cooperation and Development countries).

[4] This use of the scenario, which contrasts with that of Herman Khan and the Hudson Institute, was first proposed by a research team working for the planning office of the French government. See Délégation à l'aménagement du territoire et à l'action regionale, *Une image de la France en l'an 2000* (Paris: La documentation française, 1971). Many of the ideas expressed here were first suggested by colleagues at the Future Research Group of the Institut National de la Recherche Scientifique, notably, Pierre Lamonde, Pierre-André Julien, and Edouard Cloutier.

[5] Until now, models of international relations, for example those of Morton Kaplan, have typically been tested by applying them to past historical situations. But it is also possible, as Dennis Meadows has done in his study of *The Limits to Growth* (New York: Universe Books, 1972), to test the internal coherence of a model by projecting the model into the future rather than referring to the past.

victory by an independentist party; (3) independence would be implemented only after a gradual process and a majority vote in a referendum; and (4) the political and economic program of this successful independentist party will be social democratic in its orientation and similar to the one now advocated by the Parti Québécois.[6]

But for many Americans the plausibility of Québec's independence still remains to be demonstrated, especially in the light of the October 1973 electoral performance of the Parti Québécois (30 percent of the votes but only 5 percent of the seats).[7] Is the premise of an electoral victory for an independentist party a reasonable one? Furthermore, what kind of victory can this party expect to win—a majority or only a plurality of seats? Clearly the nature and the strength of the Parti Québécois's (PQ) electoral support will determine the willingness of the United States and Canada to recognize the new state. To answer these questions, I must briefly turn from transnational to electoral considerations.

The Socioeconomic Basis of PQ Support

To what extent is the Parti Québécois, as is so often suggested, a party of the intellectuals, the well off economically, and certain urban Québécois?[8] If such is the case, the party has little chance of attracting the rural and lower-class vote and is thus condemned to remain a minority party.

The strength of the PQ is not equally distributed between all groups (see table 1). For example, a survey analysis of voting in the 1973 provincial election reveals that the PQ was most successful among the francophone elements of Montreal, attracting 63 percent of the francophone voters under 35 years of age. For the PQ this is an encouraging sign since in 1976 close to 70 percent of the total

---

[6] Founded in 1968, the Parti Québécois has rapidly become the major spokesman for Québec's independence, obtaining 23 percent of the vote in the 1970 election, an increase of 17 percent from the 1966 performance of the first independentist party, the Rassemblement pour l'Indépendance Nationale, and 30 percent in the 1973 election. For empirical studies on the support for Québec's independence, see Vincent Lemieux, et al., *Une election de réalignement* (Montréal: Editions de l'Homme, 1970); J. Jenson and P. Regenstreif, "Some Dimensions of Partisan Choice in Québec," *Canadian Journal of Political Science* 3, no. 2 (1970): 308-18; Serge Carlos and Daniel Latouche, "La composition de l'électorat péquiste," in D. Latouche, G. Lord, and J. G. Vaillancourt, *L'élection de 1970* (Montréal: Editions H.M.H., forthcoming).

[7] On 12 March 1974, Dan Int-Hout, president of the American Paper Institute, referred to Prime Minister Robert Bourassa as the "knight who expurgated separatism from the Province of Québec" (*La Press*, 13 March 1974).

[8] See Hubert Guindon, "Social Unrest, Social Class and Québec's Bureaucratic Revolution," in Hugh Thorburn, ed., *Party Politics in Canada* (Scarborough, Ont.: Prentice-Hall of Canada, 1967), pp. 189-200; Pierre E. Trudeau, "Les séparatistes: des contre-révolutionnaires," *Cité Libre* 15 (1964): 2-6.

TABLE 1. PROPENSITY OF SELECTED SOCIAL CATEGORIES TO SUPPORT
EACH PARTY IN THE 1973 PROVINCIAL ELECTION (in percent)

Characteristic [a]	Liberal Party	Parti Québécois	Social Credit Party	National Union Party
High level of education	*	+11.7 [b]	−7.6	*
High revenue	+12.2	*	−10.2	*
White collar	+13.8	*	−9.3	*
Francophone	−46.7	+33.8	+10.4	*
Men	−9.5	+8.8	*	*
Young	−18.3	+18.2	*	*
Montreal	*	+11.3	*	−5.1

SOURCE: Serge Carlos, Edouard Cloutier, and Daniel Latouche, "The 1973
Election," *La Presse*, 19-25 November 1973.

[a] High level of education=10 years of schooling or more
High revenue=$9,000 and more
White collar=professionals, civil servants, service employees, administrators
Young=35 years old and younger
Montreal=Montreal metropolitan region
Francophone=language of the interview is French

[b] The plus sign before a percent figure means that this group is *more* likely to
support the PQ than is the opposite group (e.g., people with a high level of education are 11.7 percent more likely to support the PQ than are people with a low
level of education), and the minus sign means that this groups is *less* likely to
support the PQ than is the opposite group. An asterisk means that the variable
makes no difference in the propensity to support a given party.

Québec population will be under 38 years old. Furthermore, the party
was not without significant support among the anglophone elements
(30 percent of the low revenue, blue-collar anglophone workers), and
among the more educated non-Montrealers (39 percent), a group that
is likely to grow with the spread of secondary and university education in the rural and semirural areas.[9] Considering the fact that the
PQ electorate is very faithful (90 percent of 1970 PQ voters did not
switch parties in the 1973 election), it seems realistic, on the basis of
these data, to assume that the PQ could obtain a plurality of the total
francophone vote in the province and an absolute majority in the
urban centers at the next election.[10]

[9] The strength of attraction of the PQ among selected social groups at the
time of the 1973 election is as follows: francophones-Montreal-young—63 percent;
francophones-Montreal-old—41 percent; francophones-province-high education—
39 percent; anglophones-low revenue-blue collar—30 percent; francophones-prov-
ince-low education—21 percent; anglophones-province-white collar—11 percent;
anglophones-high revenue-blue collar—10 percent. See Serge Carlos, Edouard
Cloutier, and Daniel Latouche, "The 1973 Election," *La Presse*, 19-25 November
1973.

[10] Within greater Montreal, only in the western part of the Montreal region,
where French-speaking voters usually make up less than 30 percent of the electorate, did the PQ not succeed in winning an absolute majority of the French-
speaking vote. But even in western Montreal the PQ obtained a plurality of the
French-speaking vote. See Pierre Drouilly, "Une analyse du vote du 29 octobre à
Montréal," *Le Jour*, 28 February-6 March 1974.

The PQ Support and Its Attitude Toward Independence

But is this electorate attracted to the PQ because of the party's socioeconomic program or because of its proindependence stand? The question is important: If the PQ won a plurality but not a majority of seats in the National Assembly, in such a situation the party would be very reluctant to hold a referendum on the question of independence if a majority of its electorate does not approve of independence.

As revealed by table 2, 77.1 percent of the Parti Québécois electorate in 1973 declared itself in favor of Québec's independence; only 12.5 percent disagreed with this option. Thus there is clearly no empirical base for contending that most PQ voters do not support independence but are merely attracted by the party's socioeconomic program. If the party ever obtained a plurality of seats, it would not object to seeking a popular mandate through a referendum, especially since in such a referendum the PQ could count on a substantial number of electors who did not vote PQ in the election but nevertheless favored independence.[11]

TABLE 2. ATTITUDE TOWARD QUEBEC INDEPENDENCE BY PARTY AFFILIATION IN 1973 (in percent)

	Parti Québécois	Liberal Party	Social Credit Party	National Union Party
Strongly agree	23.8	2.3	6.9	0.0
Agree	53.3	8.8	15.4	21.5
Don't know	10.5	7.1	18.6	13.6
Disagree	8.3	36.4	22.1	27.7
Strongly disagree	4.2	45.4	36.9	37.2
Total (n=508)	100.1	100.0	99.9	100.0

SOURCE: Serge Carlos, Edouard Cloutier, and Daniel Latouche, "The 1973 Election," *La Presse*, 19-25 November 1973.

The Electoral System

But even if PQ support continues to grow so as to provide the party with a majority of the francophone vote and a plurality of the total vote, will this be sufficient to give the party a majority of seats? Under the present electoral system this objective is almost impossible since the PQ is in good position (30 percent of the vote or more) in only 48 percent of the ridings. Yet a plurality of seats (40 to 45) is not an impossible dream, especially if the electoral system is modified

---

[11] This group clearly outnumbers the nonindependentist PQ supporters: 26.1 percent of the independentists did not support the PQ in the 1973 election, while 12.5 percent of the PQ electorate disapproved of independence.

so as to introduce some elements of proportional representation that would not only help the PQ by increasing the size of its parliamentary representation but would also insure the survival of a three-party system and thus facilitate the task of the PQ. Such a reform has been repeatedly promised by the current Liberal government, which with 54 percent of the vote has nevertheless won 92 percent of the seats.

On the basis of these findings I can argue: (1) that the present cohort aged 18 to 35 is likely to maintain, to a very large degree, its independentist sympathies as it grows older and influential, since socioeconomic considerations have little impact on independentist support; (2) that the present cohort will be replaced by voters now in their teens who will be equally or more independentist; (3) that the older cohort, disproportionately federalist in sympathies, will move on to the cemetery; (4) that the present correlation between urbanization in Montreal and independentist sympathies will not only continue as the urban proportion of the Québec population continues to rise but will also extend to other urban areas in the province; [12] and (5) that the present correlation between education and PQ support will result in a substantial number of voters from rural areas supporting the PQ.

In short, I argue that these electoral considerations provide a *sufficient* measure of credibility for my initial assumptions so that I can envisage the following scenario. Having won a majority of the francophone vote (58 percent in Montreal and 45 percent outside of Montreal), a plurality of the total vote (43 percent), but only 55 of the 130 seats in the National Assembly, the Parti Québécois is called upon by the lieutenant governor to form the new Québec government. Because of its minority position in the National Assembly, the PQ agrees to hold a referendum at the appropriate moment, during or after its first term in office, so as to receive a clear mandate to negotiate the terms of independence with the federal government. What would happen then?

THE DIRECT IMPACT OF QUEBEC'S INDEPENDENCE

The effects of Québec's independence on the North American grid of interstate, transgovernmental, and transnational relations will be felt both *directly*, depending on the policies of the new state, and *indirectly*, through the structural changes introduced in North America by the appearance of a third actor. In the rest of this article I argue (1) that the direct impacts of Québec's independence will

[12] In the 1973 election the most spectacular PQ gains were made in the Québec region (from 20.1 to 35.7 percent), the second most urbanized center in Québec. See "Après ce 19 octobre 1973," *Maintenant*, no. 131 (1973), pp. 4-34.

be rather minimal since the policies advocated by the PQ reflect attitudes widespread among the Québec elite (whether or not they support independence), and (2) that the indirect structural effects could be substantial.

Contrary to anglophone Canada, the PQ believes, as does the present Liberal Québec government, that it would be both useless and rather presumptuous to adopt a general policy toward the United States since Québec, independent or not, controls very few of the levers that may bring about fruitful implementation of any such policy. For the Québécois, the United States presence is a geopolitical fact about which little can and should be done. In itself, this presence is not perceived as constituting an immediate danger to Québec's cultural survival. In fact, this American predominance is often seen as beneficial since it has forced anglophone Canada to make numerous concessions to the myth of provincial autonomy in order to differentiate itself from the United States and its (at least until very recently) melting pot policy.

This absence of an "American policy" on the part of the PQ and the similarity between this PQ attitude and the policies followed by the various Québec governments since 1960 can be easily documented both for interstate and transnational levels of Québec-American relations. For example, while it has shown no reluctance in establishing quasi-diplomatic relations with a number of European and African countries, the Québec government has not pressed for similar links with any branch (executive, legislative, or judicial) or any level (White House, department, or other federal agencies) of the United States government.[13] In the case of the United States, Québec has strictly adhered to the principle of a single international voice for Canada.

Two reasons explain this discretion. First, there is the widespread belief in the Québec Department of Intergovernmental Affairs that the size and complexity of the American federal bureaucracy makes it preferable to let federal representatives defend Québec's interests. Secondly, because they have always been underrepresented in those federal departments that most frequently deal with the United States (Departments of National Defence, Industry, Trade and Commerce, External Affairs, and Ministry of Transport), few Québécois have developed an expertise or an interest in those sensitive areas of

---

[13] Québec delegations have been established in Paris (1961), London (1962), Milan (1969), Düsseldorf (1970), Brussels (1973), and Tokyo (1973). In addition to an extensive program of cooperation with France, Québec is a member of the Agence de Cooperation Culturelle et Technique and has signed bilateral agreements with eight African countries—Gabon, Ivory Coast, Madagascar, Zaire, Senegal, Mauritania, Mali, Dahomey—as well as with Lebanon.

Canadian-American relations. Negotiations with and visits to the
United States by Canadian officials are considered to be the special
preserve of anglophones, who are presumed to have developed good
personal relations with their American counterparts due to a simili-
tude of culture and "old school ties." This feeling of impotence and
isolation has been reinforced by the relative lack of success of the six
commercial and cultural offices recently established in selected American cities, largely for the purpose of facilitating contacts with the
American business community.[14] Due to their paucity of resources
and personal contacts, they have yet to establish a distinct, broadly
perceived Québec presence in much of the US. When considering
extending their operations into Québec, American businessmen still
prefer to make use of the facilities offered by the federal Department of Industry, Trade and Commerce rather than their Québec
counterparts.

This feeling of impotence is likely to remain under a PQ government. Although the PQ recognizes that the United States will be its
second major foreign economic partner after Canada, its program
offers no specific suggestions as to how it would seek to organize its
relations with its neighbour to the south.

The PQ leadership shares with most Québec elites a deep admira-
tion for the only North American society that is said to have succeeded in providing itself with an autonomous model of development.
According to Jean LeMoyne, the United States is not only a neighbour
but "it is part of our being, because it constitutes, in front of us and
in us, the only finished form of the North American differentiation.
The language of its culture is the most familiar, intimate and comprehensible language." [15] Consequently the socioeconomic model for the
Québécois is not Canada, for it exists only as an act of will, but the
United States which has succeeded in giving form to the North
American myth. Thus few Québécois are willing to make concessions
to English Canada in order to help the latter recapture its former
relative economic and cultural autonomy from the United States.

In an article written after the 1973 election and appropriately
titled "Meanwhile Back in Washington," psychiatrist Claude St-
Laurent summarized in the following terms the attitude of the
Québécois toward the United States: "We share the same aspira-

[14]In Boston, New York, Chicago, Lafayette (Louisiana), Dallas, and Los
Angeles, a series of interviews I carried out in 1970, for a study of Québec commercial offices in the United States confirmed this feeling of impotence and
frustration of Québec representatives. The Louisiana office includes commercial
concerns, but the major part of its activities is in the cultural and educational
field.

[15] Jean LeMoyne, "L'indentité culturelle," in Le Canada au seuil du siècle de
l'abondance (Montréal: Editions H.M.H., 1969), p. 27.

tions which led to the American Revolution. We envy them and have helped them occasionally despite threats from our clergy and our British administrators. In time of economic depression we seek refuge in the US. On a Sunday afternoon, we drive across the border. We study in Boston, shop in New York and take our vacations in Miami." [16]

As revealed by a 1965 survey, a considerable percentage of francophone Québécois (25 percent versus 19 percent for anglophone Canadians) would prefer an outright political assimilation of Québec with the United States to the present status quo.[17] This percentage would undoubtedly rise if the alternative were cultural assimilation with anglophone Canada. If we are to lose our cultural identity, writes St-Laurent, "we will choose to become Americans since the Canadian identity is only a poor image of the Homo Americanus." [18]

According to the PQ leadership, this community of aspirations should make it possible for the Québécois to win the respect of the Americans in the same way as "the Finns have succeeded in winning the respect and confidence of the Russians [for] it is essentially a question of self-respect, of defining a collective project and of expressing a collective desire to live up to its self-expectations." [19] For the PQ it is clear that the United States "could have remained in the British Empire, but it had the courage to choose political independence." [20] Consequently, the PQ leadership believes Americans will

[16] Claude Saint-Laurent, "Pendant ce temps à Washington," *Maintenant*, no. 131 (1973), p. 16.

[17] Social Research Group, "A Study of Interethnic Relations in Canada," a study prepared for the Royal Commission on Bilingualism and Biculturalism, Ottawa 1967. (Mimeographed.) The survey does not differentiate between francophone Québécois and French-speaking minorities living outside of Québec, although very few of the latter group were included in the sample. In their article in this volume, Sigler and Goresky reported that 12 percent of Québec respondents (anglophone and francophone) in 1972 favored "joining the US even though this meant losing Canadian independence." The correspondig figure for all of Canada was 5 percent.

[18] The love-hate attitude of Quebec intellectuals toward the United States is well described in Gérard Bergeron, *Le Canada français après deux siècles de patience* (Paris: Seuil, 1967); and Guy Rocher, *Le Québec en mutation* (Montréal: Editions H.M.H., 1973), pp. 91-106.

[19] Saint-Laurent, "Pendant ce temps à Washington," p. 16.

[20] This section is primarily derived from official PQ documents: René Lévesque, *Option-Québec* (Montréal: Editions de l'Homme, 1968); Parti Québécois, *La Souveraineté et l'économie* (Montréal: Editions du Jour, 1970); Parti Québécois, *La Solution: la programme du Parti Québécois* (Montréal: Editions du Jour, 1970); Parti Québécois, *Quand nous serons vraiment chez-nous* (Montréal: Editions du Parti Québécois, 1972); Parti Québécois, *Les dossiers du 4e Congrès* (Montréal: Editions du Parti Québécois, 1972); Parti Québécois, *Un gouvernement du Parti Québécois s'engage* (Montréal: Editions du Parti Québécois, 1973); Parti Québécois, *C'est pas sorcier* (Montréal: Editions du Parti Québécois, 1973). Personal interviews supplemented these public sources.

accept, regard with indifference, or even sympathize with the idea of Québec independence.[21]

As does the present provincial government, the PQ hopes to make the most of the more tense climate now prevaling in Canadian-American relations by putting forward the image of a "good and comprehensive" francophone neighbour without any trace of the anti-Americanism so common in English-speaking Canada. The promotion of this image would be enhanced by the lack of any outstanding disagreements between the American and Québec governments.

Since the Ashburton-Webster Treaty of 1842 and the International Boundary Treaty of 1908, the Québec-American border has not been marked by disputes similar to the Point Roberts controversy in British Columbia.[22] Contrary to the situation in Nova Scotia, New Brunswick, and British Columbia, the fishing, maritime, and underwater jurisdictions of Québec and the United States do not meet and thus do not give rise to conflicting interests and claims.[23] Because the Québec-American border is largely uninhabited, problems of pollution have not reached the same acuity as those of the Great Lakes region. In fact, there have been only three issues where Québec and American interests have recently diverged: pollution of Memphremagog Lake, permits for Québec forest workers who seasonally migrate to Maine, and a Québec–New Brunswick highway across northern Maine. The first two issues have been rapidly settled, while it is New Brunswick and not Québec that has been unsuccessfully pressing for a Maine highway.[24] Because of this absence of outstanding conflicts of interests, Québec officials have not felt the need, nor have they found the occasion, to develop any extensive network of transgovern-

[21] This expectation is naive if we consider the results of a 1971 survey conducted by the American Institute of Public Opinion for the Canadian embassy in Washington: 96.3 percent of the American public had no opinion as to whether or not the United States should support an independent Québec. See Murray Goldblatt, "Ce qu'Oncle Sam pense du Canada: Les résultats d'un sondage," *Perspectives Internationales*, May-June 1972, pp. 14-16.

[22] Paradoxically, the Québec-American border is the only one of the five maritime and land borders of Québec that has been definitely settled. The borders with Ontario, New Brunswick, Newfoundland, and the Northwest Territories are still subjected to claims and counterclaims. See N. L. Nicolson, *The Boundaries of Canada* (Ottawa: Queen's Printer, 1964).

[23] However, it has recently been argued by a research team from the Bedford Oceanographic Institute that 65 percent of the variation of the fish catch in the Gulf of St. Lawrence can be attributed to the water level in the American Great Lakes (*Le Devoir*, November 1972).

[24] In the case of Lake Memphremagog an ad hoc meeting was held in November 1973 between Québec and Vermont officials. All participants agreed that the American city of Newport was the sole culprit and that remedial measures should be taken by Vermont and Newport.

mental relations with their American counterparts in the American border states.[25]

In addition to this lack of conflicting interests, there has been an evident lack of enthusiasm on the part of the Québec government to support actively the US minorities of francophone origins or to enter into formal agreements with American states (see also Holsti and Levy in this volume). In the case of the Louisiana, Massachusetts, and Maine-Québec agreements, the initiative rested entirely with American state officials.[26] Québec's decision to go along in these areas was in a large part dictated by its desire to prevent the Canadian federal government from doing so in its place. Similarly, Québec's participation in the conference of New England governors and eastern Canada premiers held for the first time in June 1973 had little to do with a desire to establish closer ties with American states. Rather, it was part of the new governmental strategy of enlisting the support of Canada's Atlantic provinces to break the traditional isolation in which Québec has found itself in recent federal-provincial conferences. The hope is to trade Québec's support for the Maritimes' claims on underwater resources for the latter's support in the areas of communications and social affairs.

This situation is not likely to change under a PQ government. It is well understood within the PQ that if the Franco-Americans of Maine, New Hampshire, and Vermont were actively encouraged to join an independent Québec, this would bring an immediate reaction from the American government. There has never been any suggestion within the PQ leadership of a special Québec responsibility toward the North American "francophonie." For Claude Morin, the former deputy minister of intergovernmental affairs and now a member of the PQ National Council, the survival of these minorities "depends solely on their own will and on their own internal dynamism. Furthermore, there are no reasons to believe that Québec's indepen-

---

[25] Labrador, now part of Newfoundland but claimed by Québec, could possibly give rise to Québec-US disagreements on questions of extent of territorial seas, economic zones, and passage rights. But although a PQ government would seek a ruling on the matter by the International Court of Justice, it is not expected that an independent Québec would press its claim in a vigorous way.

[26] The Maine-Québec agreement, signed in August 1973, includes the following provisions: an exchange of civil servants; a Québec cultural week in Augusta; an exchange of popular music groups; a tour by Québec artists; the financial participation of Québec in a research program on Madawaska folklore; an exchange of secondary school teachers; 30 Québec scholarships to a French summer school. Except for discussions on energy matters and on the perennial question of a Québec–New Brunswick highway across northern Maine, the agreement has no commercial or financial provisions.

dence would deprive them of their newly acquired rights." [27] For the PQ leadership, as for most Québécois, Americans of francophone ancestry (including those whose forebears came from Canada) and Franco-Canadians (from outside Québec) are a lost cause who should be provided only with sympathy and quite limited cultural aid.[28] As for the anglophone minority (either Canadian born or already settled immigrants) in an independent Québec, it would retain all of its rights, including that of voting in a referendum and the right to a distinct schooling system, publicly financed, so that its position in an independent Quebec would remain considerably superior to that of the francophone minorities now dispersed across Canada.[29] Thus there would be, in the views of the PQ leadership, little occasion for the Canadian government (and certainly no need for the American government) to intervene to ensure the survival of this anglophone minority.[30]

In short, at the interstate level a PQ government would probably adopt a low profile in keeping with the general belief among Québécois elites that Québec has little to gain in adopting a detailed ideological stand, since there will not only be few controversial issues between the two countries but also little hope for Québec ultimately to succeed in imposing its views on the United States. Thus, not unlike Canada before 1960, an independent Québec would seek to play down formal interstate relations and try to avoid politicizing relations with the United States since such would only underscore the wide discrepancy in the political and economic strength of the two countries. This does

---

[27] "Le Québec et les minorités: attentes et intérêts réciproques," *Le Devoir*, 4 October 1972. As a symbolic gesture, the PQ program suggests that an independent Québec would welcome the immigration of French-speaking Canadians from other provinces. No mention is made of French-speaking immigrants from the US. Presumably they will be treated in the same way as other American immigrants.

[28] Except for British Columbia and Newfoundland, the percentage of Canadians who declared French as their mother tongue has declined in all Canadian provinces between the 1961 and 1971 censuses. Outside of Ontario and New Brunswick the assimilation rate—those with one (or more) francophone bilingual parent whose offsprings no longer speak or understand spoken French—has been estimated at close to 50 percent.

[29] As soon as the anglophone population in a given Québec census district reaches the figure of 5 percent of the total population in that district, it does not suffer significant transfer to the other linguistic group. The equivalent figure for the French population is 88 percent. In other words, only when there are 88 percent francophones in a district is this population in no danger of assimilation. See C. Castonguay and J. Marion, "L'anglicisation du Canada," *Le Devoir*, 8 and 9 January, 1974.

[30] However, new American (and other anglophone) immigrants would not be granted any special status and their children would have to attend the French school system, at least until university level. On the other hand, the PQ has no plan to restrict, as in Nova Scotia, foreign ownership of summer (or other part-time) residences.

not mean that the PQ would refuse to participate in such bilateral intergovernmental organizations as the International Joint Commission. On the contrary, the PQ budget includes a Québec contribution to the Commission and similar organizations (like the St. Lawrence Seaway) equivalent to one-third of the present Canadian contribution.

A similar attitude on the part of the PQ applies with regard to transnational relations in the areas of foreign direct and portfolio investments, bonds, energy, labour, and defense matters.

Foreign Investments

In foreign investments the present Québec government wants as few restrictions as possible on the flow of US capital into Québec and on its own access to the American financial market. In a 1972 speech to the Canadian Manufacturers' Association, Raymond Garneau, Québec's minister of finance, summarized the Québec position toward foreign investments in these terms: "Until now the Canadian government has favored the entry of foreign capital to maintain a rapid economic growth and a high consumption level. We hope that this policy will be maintained. Any drastic modification would be contradictory to the two fundamental objectives of Québec's economic development: maintenance of a high standard of living and a diminution of unemployment." [31] When the bill on screening of foreign ownership was first submitted to the federal Parliament in May 1972, the reaction of Québec officials was one of relief; it was felt that the procedure proposed in the bill allowed for flexibility in application of screening so that certain underdeveloped regions like Québec could continue to maintain an open-door policy toward needed direct foreign investments. Similar relief was expressed in the private sector. Charles Perreault, president of the Conseil du Patronat du Québec, said the bill would have little effect on American investors since the latter, in contrast to the British, prefer to invest in new ventures rather than acquire established enterprises.[32]

This attitude of relief contrasted markedly with the critical reactions of the prime minister of Ontario, William G. Davis, who immediately attacked the bill for the absence of an aggressive policy of

[31] *Le Devoir*, 28 March 1972. This Québec view is typified by a 1973 interview of Québec's minister of commerce and industry: *Question:* "You have certainly discussed the Gray report with your federal counterpart." *Answer:* "Beg your pardon . . ." *Question:* "You know, the Gray report . . ." *Answer:* "Ah, yes. You should understand that this is not the sort of thing that we discuss when there are so many urgent and important tasks to meet." See *Le Devoir*, 12 January 1972.

[32] *Le Devoir*, 4 May 1972. According to the president of the Montreal and the Canadian Stock Exchange, the federal bill simply amounts to a reiteration of the guidelines for corporate "good behaviour" in Canada.

economic and cultural nationalism.[33] According to Premier Davis, the bill should have included both provisions to discourage foreign investors from buying shares in Canadian industries and measures to regulate the behaviour of foreign firms operating in Canada.

This negative reaction of Ontario's premier only confirmed the widespread impression among Québec officials that this new Canadian economic nationalism is a conspiracy between Ontario businessmen, anxious to preserve their economic domination of Canada, and a federal Liberal party that is only too willing to appease anglophone economic nationalist sentiments in order to regain some of its electoral strength outside Québec. No one would deny that Canada is economically dependent on the United States, but at the same time it is believed that Québec should not be called upon to pay the price to modify this situation. According to Michel van Schendel, a Québec economist, the effects of this dependence are not similar across all Canadian regions.[34] He claims that certain provinces, notably Ontario, can compensate the draining of their savings and the repatriations of profits by American subsidiaries by draining the savings and the profits from the poorer Canadian provinces. Ontario's production is believed to be diversified enough to compensate for its deficit with the United States by surpluses everywhere else. The Québec economy, on the other hand, is neither strong enough to act in the same way nor poor enough to benefit from the massive subsidies paid by the federal government to the Atlantic provinces.[35] In other words, Ontario is considered by Van Schendel to have prospered by organizing, to its own profit and with federal complicity, Canadian economic dependence. It has monopolized most of the benefits of this dependence

[33] Le Devoir, 9 May 1972. Contrary to Québec, Ontario has established its own study groups (Parliamentary Commission, Inter-Ministerial Working Group, Conference on Economic and Cultural Nationalism) to deal with the question of foreign investors.

[34] Michel Van Schendel, "Dépendance économique et souveraineté canadienne," in La dualité canadienne à l'heure des Estats Unis (Québec: Les Pressés de l'Université Laval, 1965), pp. 111-20. Another economist, Roland Parenteau, president of the Conseil d'Orientation Économique du Québec, has made substantially the same point: "Instead of an economic policy which has served to specialize each region of Canada through a subsidized national transportation system, it would have been possible to diversify the economy of each region in order to increase its autonomy" ("Crise de l'unité nationale, crise du régime économique," in Le Canada face à son avenir [Montréal: Editions du Jour, 1964], p. 87).

[35] In 1971-72, 16.1 percent ($814 million) of the total revenue of the Québec government was in the form of unconditional fiscal transfers from the federal government, and 9.1 percent ($459 million) in the form of conditional transfers (i.e., for specific programs). No statistically comparable figures are available for the Maritime provinces but the federal contribution is usually estimated at 50 percent of the provincial revenues. See Statistiques financières du Gouvernement du Québec (Québec: Bureau de la statistique, 1973).

while passing out the costs to the other regions of Canada.

The present PQ leadership not only accepts this claim but has stated repeatedly that American investments will continue to be required if Québec is to become a development center in its own right. These investments, it is assumed, will be easily available and will not be scared away by independence since the behaviour of American corporations is presumed to be guided primarily by economic considerations. According to the PQ program, "American enterprises now operate in dozens of countries. For the last 25 years they have seen almost every possible situation and are now accustomed to operating under a variety of political regimes." As a result, they are unlikely to be upset by a series of events that "will appear spectacular to us but are only incidental to them." International business competition is so intense that no American firm will think of leaving Québec unless "contradictory legislation and unreasonable taxes" force it out.[36] The feeling among the PQ is that as long as there is "money to be made in Québec, foreign capital will be interested. After all, why would Coke leave if this meant abandoning its market to Pepsi." [37]

If American investors continue "to invest in the Middle East, it is not an independence legally achieved through the electoral process which will frighten them away." In fact, it is assumed that a stable, independent Québec would be more appealing to American investors than the instability and anti-Americanism now prevailing across Canada. Consequently, there are no reasons why an independent Québec could not continue to buy and sell to the United States "if we have the good sense of not engaging in a suicidal economic war" with either Canada or the US.[38]

In the climate of economic nationalism now prevailing in English Canada, the PQ attitude toward foreign investments, particularly those of American origins, appears somewhat overprudent.[39] But to

[36] PQ, *C'est pas sorcier*, p. 16.

[37] Naively the PQ assumes that the promulgation of French as the official and working language in Québec will have no impact on investment decisions since American firms are already used to operating in non-English-speaking countries. Obviously the PQ leadership is not aware of a recent study that shows the variable "American ownership" to be one of the most important factors explaining the necessity of French-speaking employees to work in English in Quebec. See Robert N. Morrisson, *Corporate Ability at Bilingualism and Biculturalism* (Ottawa: Queen's Printer, 1970). All quotations are from official PQ documents. For an analysis of the PQ economic doctrine, see J. M. Treddenick, "Quebec and Canada: The Economics of Independence," *Journal of Canadian Studies* 8, no. 4 (1973): 16-31.

[38] PQ, *La Solution*, p. 39.

[39] Already in a 1969 symposium one leading Québec economist, Bernard Bonin, argued vigorously in favor of the multinational firm. See Bernard Bonin, "La firme plurinationale comme véhicule de transmission internationale de technologie," *Actualité Economique* 46, no. 4 (1971): 707-25. When the Gray report on

what extent is this carefree PQ attitude representative of the opinion of francophone Québécois on this question of Canadian-American relations? According to the Canadian Institute of Public Opinion (CIPO) polls analyzed by Sigler and Goresky, the proportion of Québécois with no opinion is consistently higher than the equivalent percentage for respondents from the rest of Canada (table 3).[40]

Québec respondents are clearly less interested in most Canadian-American issues than their Canadian counterparts, although the difference between the two groups has steadily decreased over the years. The percentages of Québec respondents expressing attitudes favorable to US investments are, on the whole, slightly higher than the percentages of other Canadian respondents. But on the cultural impacts of the United States on Canada, it would seem that at least in 1961 (CIPO 291) the Québécois were more critical of the US cultural influence than were respondents from outside Québec. An examination of the correlation coefficients between Québec respondents (or other Canadian respondents) and pro-American attitudes reveals that the association between being a Québécois, rather than being elsewhere in Canada, and having a pro-US attitude is neither very high nor very consistent and has tended to decrease with the more recent polls (table 3).

The PQ has promulgated an investment code as the most important element of its economic program. Applicable to all foreign firms, including those of American or Canadian origin, operating or planning to operate in Québec, this code will include the following provisions:

1. No foreign investments will be tolerated in certain key cultural sectors such as radio, television, mass media, and publishing (coedition will be permitted). This situation is similar to the one now existing in Canada.[41]

---

foreign investments was published, Québec economists were the first to point out its weaknesses and contradictions. See Velg Leroy, "Le Rapport Gray: prelude d'un nouveau testament," *Actualité Economique* 48, no. 2 (1972): 211-25; and Rodrigue Tremblay, "Investissements directs étrangers et stratégies industrielles et commerciales: le dilemme canadien," *Actualité Economique* 48, no. 2 (1972): 226-53.

[40] See Sigler and Goresky in this volume. The Québec respondents included also anglophone respondents, but it is unlikely that their weight was sufficient to modify significantly the findings. Their exclusion would have probably reinforced the trends noticed here.

[41] An exception will probably be made for *Time* which has only an English edition. In the case of *Reader's Digest*, which publishes a widely distributed French edition, an exception is less certain since this magazine is viewed by the Québec intellectual and cultural elite as the epitome of propaganda for the American way of life.

TABLE 3. A COMPARISON OF QUEBEC AND OTHER CANADIAN
ATTITUDES ON CERTAIN CANADIAN-AMERICAN ISSUES

	Percent of No Opinion		Pro-US Presence		
CIPO Polls	QUEBEC	REST OF CANADA	REST OF CANADA	QUEBEC	CORRE-LATION COEFFI-CIENTS [a]
CIPO 275 (1959)	40	11	68	77	.22
CIPO 303 (1973)	24	13	76	77	.03
CIPO 323 (1967) [b]	17	12	69	65	−.10
CIPO 286 (1961)	25	11	35	48	.55
CIPO 305 (1963)	32	18	42	43	.01
CIPO 323 (1967) [b]	20	14	30	20	−.20
CIPO 343 (1970)	19	11	25	41	.35
CIPO 351 (1972)	11	12	24	35	.27
CIPO 343 (1970)	24	20	59	62	.07
CIPO 351 (1972)	17	15	81	81	−.05
CIPO 354 (1972)	37	21	44	52	−.16
CIPO 291 (1961)	30	6	62	29	−.52
CIPO 318 (1966)	14	10	42	35	−.13

SOURCE: Sigler and Goresky's essay and data in this volume.

[a] These are Yule Q. correlation coefficients. Respondents were divided according to their place of residence (Quebec/Canada) and their attitudes on the specific issue covered by the poll. A positive coefficient reveals a positive association between a pro-US position and being a Quebec respondent.

[b] Two different questions but the same poll.

2. The steel industry (excluding mining) will have to be entirely Québec controlled either through private companies or through the government-owned steel complex SIDBEC.[42]

3. Minority participation (up to 49 percent) will be accepted in the fields of banking, transportation, insurance, mining, electronics, communications, and forestry. In the case where shares are distributed between a large number of shareholders, no foreign shareholder will be allowed to control more shares than the most important Québec shareholder.

4. Majority participation (up to 99 percent) will be accepted only in those sectors that have no real importance in the determination of the Québec economic policy. The Coca-Cola Company is an example of a firm where the degree of foreign control is said to be of no importance.

5. Majority participation (up to 99 percent) will also be accepted in those few sectors "which depend heavily on external markets for the sale of their products, in which Québec is not in any competing position economically or in which the necessary technology does not exist in Québec." Presumably Inter-

[42] SIDBEC has recently announced plans for a joint venture.

national Business Machines (IBM), Xerox Corperation, and various pharmaceutical industries are to be included in this category. Certain mining industries, iron for instance, are examples of firms that would rapidly move out of Québec if a majority foreign participation is not allowed, since equivalent, if not better, alternatives exist in other countries. Note that even in this category, foreign investors will not be allowed to control 100 percent of an enterprise. In this way it will be possible for the government to be at least informed of the inner workings of the enterprise, its relations with its head office, the amount of royalties and fees paid outside of Québec, and the export of profits.

In addition to this investment code, some guidelines will also be introduced. Commercial and financial operations will have to be conducted in French. Antitrust laws will be tightened in order to prevent foreign firms from dividing up the Québec market between themselves. Profits and dividends will also be closely watched. In the case of a firm controlled by foreign investors (more than 50 percent), dividends should not represent more than 50 percent of profits after taxes. Foreign firms will have to hire a majority of Québécois at their management level. Every firm will need to obtain a Québec incorporation and maintain a Québec-based headquarters. Finally, the assent of the National Assembly will be required in the case of every acquisition of a Québec firm by foreign interests.

What this investment code and this set of guidelines amount to is a new set of rules, not a restructuring of the Québec economy. It is argued that these rules will be accepted by foreign investors who are not so much worried by the existence of rules as by the insecurity that accompanies constant changes or the absence of clear rules. As with the present Québec government, the PQ attitude toward foreign capital is motivated by a desire to control the social and cultural impact of this capital and not by a desire to control its ownership per se, which is judged to be of secondary importance.[43] As pointed out by Kari Levitt, the PQ sees little danger in "liberating Québec from the domination by the English Canadian financial elite with the help of more powerful American capital." [44]

[43] PQ economic thinking borrows heavily from G. Adler-Karlsson, *Reclaiming the Canadian Economy: A Swedish Approach through Functional Socialism* (Toronto: House of Anansi Press, 1970).

[44] Kari Levitt, *Silent Surrender: The Multinational Corporation in Canada* (Toronto: Macmillan of Canada, 1970), p. 147.

Bonds and Capital

Late in the 1973 electoral campaign it was revealed by the Québec Department of Industry and Commerce that for the last twenty years (with the exception of 1965) Québec has been a net exporter of capital, which has presumably served to finance American and Canadian development. Furthermore, since 1966 the Québec commercial balance (trade and services), contrary to all expectations, has run an annual surplus of $750 million. With the support of these figures and with the knowledge that the private savings of Québécois amount to $25 billion, the PQ has repeatedly stressed the feasibility of raising within its own territory the monies needed for its social and economic development. "When General Motors invests X million in a new plant, it does not find these millions in the United States, but in the pockets of the Québec consumers to whom it sells automobiles. Profits and reserves are always the main sources of investments. Our development has never come and it will never come from others. Economic Santa Clauses do not exist." [45]

To achieve this objective of capital autonomy, the PQ puts high hopes in the continued performance of the Caisse de Dépôt et Placement (CDP) which canalized all contributions to the Québec Pension Plan. Already the CDP with its $2.6 billion has become one of the main sources of short-term and long-term financing for the Québec government ($1,300 million), the municipalities ($151 million), and school boards ($87 million).[46] The CDP has partially succeeded in liberating the Québec government from a group of brokerage houses that until 1965 had exclusive control of all government bonds. It is difficult to see how it would provide the $1,142 million borrowed in the United States during the 1968-72 period as well as the $573 million floated in Europe.[47] No PQ government could afford to pay higher interest rates for the simple pleasure of floating its bonds in Québec. Nor has the PQ specified how it would prevent the export of capital by US-owned Québec corporations. With a public debt of more than $8 billion, in addition to 25 percent of the Canadian debt that the PQ has promised to take over, there is no doubt that the American market will continue for a long time to play an important role. And this could

---

[45] PQ, *C'est pas sorcier*, p. 15. One is struck by the frequent allusions to General Motors in the PQ program as if this economic giant were representative of economic success.

[46] Department of Trade and Commerce, *La situation économique au Québec*, (Québec: Ministry of Industry and Commerce, 1973), p. 49.

[47] Jacques Parizeau, the leading PQ economic spokesman, was the main force behind the dismantling of this brokers club headed by the Bank of Montreal and the A. E. Ames Corporation. See his "Les Dessous de l'Histoire, 1963-70," *Le Devoir*, 2 February 1970.

even prompt a future PQ government to accept a monetary union with Canada since Québec bonds would then present less of a risk.[48]

Energy and Other Natural Resources

In the area of energy the PQ does not foresee problems arising in future Québec-American relations. For the past few years Hydro-Québec has been only too willing to sell its surplus production to Consolidated Edison Company of New York. No opposition, even from the most radical independentist elements, has been raised against such transactions, which are expected to continue after independence. For the period 1977-96, Hydro-Québec has further agreed to sell all surplus energy produced by the James Bay project to the New York power pool. Calling for the delivery of 14.1 billion kilowatt hours during the first five years, this contract can be abrogated unilaterally if emergency needs ever arise in Québec. Since the United States is expected to have developed an extensive nuclear capacity by 1990, it is not expected that the termination of these contracts at that time will have a serious adverse effect on the American economy. Although the specific content of the proposed North American energy grid has yet to be spelled out, the PQ has not rejected the possibility of participating in such a pooling of resources. According to the PQ, the Québec energy situation is relatively straightforward: Québec has an overabundance of one source, hydroelectricity, while it is completely dependent on the outside for its oil and coal supplies. Furthermore, as the Québec territory is vast and sparsely inhabited, it could accommodate an impressive network of nuclear plants. As a result Québec could readily expand its hydro and nuclear production of electricity in return for assured oil (and coal) supplies from Canada or the United States.

On the question of renewable (particularly forest) and nonrenewable (especially mineral) resources, the PQ has been slow, as has the present Québec government, to identify the strengths and weaknesses of the Québec situation. According to the PQ leadership, Québec's bargaining leverage is not as strong as is often believed.[49]

With 18 percent of the world production of pulp and paper and a 30 percent share of the American market, it appears that Québec is in a favorable position to profit from the projected doubling of world needs in pulp in the next ten years. But, claims the PQ, this picture is a distorted one. Québec's shares in world and US markets have declined—for example, in 1951 Québec provided more than

---

[48] See J. M. Treddenick, "Québec and Canada: Some Economic Aspects of Independence," *Journal of Canadian Studies* 7, no. 4 (1974): 16-31.

30 percent of world production and 41 percent of the American market. Furthermore, although it now exploits only 46 percent of its potential of 1,960 million cubic feet of lumber, starting in 1985 the annual cuts are projected to equal the possibilities for self-renewal (at least under known technology). Convinced that the major companies operating in this field, most of which are American owned, have deliberately let the Québec position deteriorate, but also convinced of their indispensability, the PQ program proposes a $308 million nationalization of all privately owned forest land so as to achieve at least a limited measure of control over its development.[50]

In the mining sector the PQ program suggests that the one area where Québec accounts for more than 50 percent of the world production—asbestos—should be under exclusive Québec control (either private or public), especially since the largely US-controlled asbestos companies have been particularly slow in making maximum use of their relatively favorable position.[51] In other minerals where Quebec production is substantial (zinc, titanium, copper, and iron), the PQ program seeks to nationalize production primarily to prevent underexploitation or nonexploitation of known deposits by foreign-owned companies.

In both the forest and mining sectors, the major PQ preoccupation has not been to extract the optimum financial resources but to increase as much as possible the transformation within Québec of these resources into finished or semifinished products. This objective, of course, raises the critical issue of the US tariff pattern that permits import of unprocessed raw materials likely to be in increasingly short supply in the United States while maintaining often virtually prohibitive protectionist barriers against more processed versions of the same materials.

Labor

The principal area of Québec-American transnational relations where there have already been major conflicts between American and Québec interests is the labor scene (see also Cox and Jamieson in this volume). In Québec close to 40 percent of union members belong to Canadian locals of American international unions. Until 1950 this international membership generated major controversies with political and religious overtones since American unions were alternatively

---

[49] *Les dossiers du 4e Congrès National du PQ*, pp. 77-150.

[50] The five major companies are Canadian International Paper, Consolidated-Bathurst Ltd., Bathurst Power and Paper Company Ltd., Price Company Ltd., and Domtar Ltd.

[51] According to a government report, asbestos companies have not created a single new job since 1945 (*Le Devoir*, 19 March 1974).

suspected of being Protestant or Communist dominated.[52]

However, in recent years international unions affiliated with the Québec Federation of Labour (QFL) and with the Canadian Labour Congress (CLC) have proven about as militant both on the socio-economic and Québec francophone nationalist fronts as those unions belonging to the rival Confederation of National Trade Unions and thus independent of United States unions. This increased militancy by the QFL has increased tensions between the CLC and what it considers its "Québec affiliate." In February 1972 Donald McDonald, president of the CLC, declared that Marxism would not be tolerated among the CLC ranks. Since then the two organizations have been engaged in verbal warfare, culminating in the 1973 decision of the QFL to permit the affiliation of locals directly and solely to the Québec central. So far there has been no reaction by American labor officials, who in the case of the Québec Electricians Union have accepted without much overt reluctance the creation of an autonomous Québec union to replace Local 568 of the International Brotherhood of Electrical Workers. The process of Québecisation of international unions appears to be so well along that it is unlikely that a PQ government would feel obligated to legislate much further to prevent American or Canadian control over Québec unions.

Defense

Defense is an area where the PQ program could apparently upset significantly the existing North American situation and raise serious concerns among influential elites in the United States. In 1973-74 the Canadian government spent $2.2 billion (12 percent of the federal budget) to support a total armed force of 82,400 men. The present Québec share of this budget is estimated by the PQ at $550 million. A PQ government would reduce this amount to $230.8 million by opting out of NATO and NORAD.[53] NATO, it is argued, is no longer needed in the light of the Soviet-American rapprochement and the climate of détente that now seems to prevail in Europe. Furthermore, the PQ believes NATO is incapable of successfully resisting a full-

[52] On international unions in Québec, Louis-Marie Tremblay, *Idéologie de la CSN et de la FTQ, 1940-1970* (Montréal: Presses de l'Université de Montréal, 1972); Jacques Dofny et Paul Bernard, *Le syndicalisme au Québec: structure et mouvement* (Ottawa: Imprimeur de la Reine, 1970); Jean-Guy Loranger, "L'impérialisme américain au Québec: analyse de donnés récentes," *Socialisme 68*, 14 (1968): 26-52.

[53] These figures are taken from the 1974-75 budget proposed to the electorate by the PQ during the 1973 campaign. These figures were obtained by the PQ from a confidential Québec government document on the costs of federalism to which the PQ had access.

scale classical attack without the use of nuclear weapons. In other words, NATO is judged by the PQ to be incapable of performing a task that is *depassé* in any case. An independent Québec would seek to remain in the political and cultural structures of NATO while officially staying out of the military ones. The same reasoning is applied to NORAD (North American Air Defense Command), where the only Canadian contribution on Québec territory has been one squadron of CF-101 Voodoo interceptors based at Bagotville.[54]

Largely due to a lack of expertise in this field, there has been little discussion within the PQ as to the attitude to be adopted toward the two new American proposals for North American defense: the over-the-horizon radar (OTH) and the airborne warning and control system (AWACS). The OTH system, now being tested at Hall Beach on the Melville Peninsula south of Baffin Island, will eventually replace some of the existing fixed radars in the NORAD system but will require no installation on Québec territory. AWACS, on the other hand, would require overpass and refueling rights for its fleet of Boeing 707s. On this question and on related issues, such as permission for Strategic Air Command (SAC) bombers to overfly Québec on airborne alert in time of crisis or the use of Québec airfields for dispersal of aircraft, it can probably be presumed that an independent Québec will seek to coordinate its policy with that of Canada. Consequently, permissions and facilities that could prove politically embarrassing to give to the United States could more easily be given if both Canada and Québec could develop common or parallel policies to acquiesce to them. Thus, although an independent Québec would not actively participate in the destruction function of NORAD by acquiring the new IMI interceptor, it would nevertheless participate indirectly in its identification and control mission by allowing the use of its territory for communication relays (such as the one at Senneterre), training, landing, and satellite detection facilities.

Savings could also come from transforming the new Québec armed forces into a Costa Rican-type territorial force without such extravagant armaments as submarines, destroyers, aircraft carriers, and supersonic interceptors. Even with such sophisticated equipment, Québec (or Canada for that matter) could not by itself resist an attack by a major power (USSR) while the probability of an attack from a middle power (e.g., Australia, Brazil, or Canada) is almost nonexistent. The major tasks of this Québec army would include these

---

[54] The mid-Canada radar line was abandoned in 1965 and the Pine Tree installations have either been dismantled or integrated in a larger radar network. There are no DEW (Distant Early Warning) Line installations on Québec territory. The headquarters of the fifth NORAD region are in North Bay (Ontario) where the SAGE control centre is also located.

twelve: air surveillance, detection of marine and Arctic pollution, surveillance of the coastal fishing zones, aerial cartography, surveillance of animal migration in the Arctic, custom duties in isolated outposts, logistical support in the case of natural catastrophes, air and sea rescue, transport of urgently needed medical facilities, civil defense in case of war, support of police forces in case of civil disturbances, and road police and fire fighting.

The new Québec armed force, approximately 15,000 men, would be made up in great part from the 14,450 francophones, mostly from Québec, now serving in the Canadian military forces (17 percent of its total strength). No involuntary military service is envisaged, and because of the well-known antipathy of the Québécois for compulsory military duties, it is highly unlikely that any such service could be implemented with more than minimal success.

Since the PQ program mentions the conversion of the few defense industries now operating in Québec into civilian-oriented enterprises, it can be presumed that Québec will do without a defense industry. As a result, Québec, having nothing to share, will opt out of the existing Canadian-American defense sharing agreements and purchase all of its military hardware (insofar as it has no relatively close civilian counterpart, e.g., trucks) from outside furnishers, presumably Canadian, American, and French sources. Nevertheless, academic institutions and business enterprises will not be prevented from receiving grants or doing business with the United States and the Canadian defense departments.[55]

It can be hypothesized that a Québec government, although hesitant about transgovernmental and transnational transactions in the defense area, would not have the political resources to control and monitor such transactions. The new defense bureaucracy, which will be imported almost entirely from the current Canadian armed forces, will want to maintain its privileged relationships with Canadian and American defense officials, and it will be left free to do so as long as these relationships are not formalized into institutional agreements that would prove politically embarrassing to a Québec government anxious to preserve the appearance of military neutrality. If the United States and Canada are unwilling to accept a Québec participation in the Joint Board on Defence or the Ministerial Committee on Joint Defence, it is probable that Québec's integration within the

---

[55] During the 1967-71 period, 45 Québec companies had received defense contracts totalling $200 million from the Canadian government while one Québec university, McGill, received close to 25 percent of the $35 million attributed directly by American defense authorities to Canadian universities. See Sam Noumoff, "How to Make a Killing," McGill University, 1972. (Mimeograph.)

North American defense grid will be carried out mostly through trans-governmental transactions between Canadian and Québec defense establishments, since transactions between these two actors will be easier to achieve and less sensitive politically than direct Québec-American linkages at the policymaking level.

From the preceding description it would seem that Québec's independence would have little immediate effect in the areas of foreign direct investment, energy, and labor. In all of these areas, the PQ program is either similar to the one followed by the present Québec administration (energy, labor) or parallel to the direction recently taken by the Canadian government (direct investments). In the field of defense, although changes may appear more fundamental, the PQ argues that they would not entail any basic reorganization of the North American defense system since Québec is not in any case a crucial component of that system and since an independent Québec would hope to continue to cooperate closely with Canada in defense matters. Not unlike the government of France, a PQ government would be more concerned with the formal than with the de facto aspects of North American defense cooperation and would not object to informal and in-the-field cooperation as long as it did not have to support the financial costs.

Although the direct effect of Québec's independence should not modify substantially intra-North American relations and politics, I suggest that in the medium and long term things will never quite be the same in North America. It is to the indirect effect of Québec's independence on the structure and dynamics of the North American subsystem that I now turn.

SOME INDIRECT IMPACTS OF QUEBEC'S INDEPENDENCE

In terms of international relations, North America is in a somewhat peculiar situation. First, it is considered by other actors in the international system as a nonregion. For example, Canada and the United States are both founding members of NATO, which is basically oriented toward the defense of Europe. Both countries have asked for and have been given full membership status in the Conference on European Security. Except on defense matters, Canadians and Americans do not see themselves as constituting a region in the same sense as Africa, Latin America, or Western Europe are said to constitute regions. Until recently both countries used to take each other so much for granted that there was little to think out or say at the political level about their relations. One could almost say that the level of transnational and transgovernmental relations between the two countries has been so high that their mutual recognition as two independent states (especially on the American side) has been somewhat eroded.

Second, although they do not see themselves as a region, both countries have in the past had a somewhat mystical vision of their closeness and of the underlying unity of their world vision. North America has been seen since the early twentieth century as something different from the other regions: an area free of conflict and of the trappings of international politics, in short, a region where the peoples understand one another so well and share so many things that their respective governments do not need specific institutional apparatus to deal with each other. It could be said that until recently, transnational and transgovernmental rather than interstate relations were the major form of transactions across the Canadian-US border. It is almost as if the relations between the two countries were of the non-zero sum variety, i.e., where both countries could benefit from agreeing on most matters. Until recently the foreign affairs of both countries were conducted under the umbrella of messianism: in one case the mission was grandiose, to bring progress and democracy to the world; in the other, the mission was more limited but as important in that it served to prevent serious misunderstandings from arising between the Western allies. In foreign affairs the United States and Canada (especially from the point of view of Canada) complemented one another; they formed a team somewhat along the line of the Lone Ranger and Tonto, with the United States as the all powerful ally and Canada the small but devoted and resourceful ally who could be counted upon to extricate the giant from major difficulties.

A third unique characteristic of the North American continent is that it comprises only two countries,[56] thus transforming all the international relations within this region into bilateral relations. With only two countries there can be no state coalitions and no subgroupings of state members. Consequently, the relations of the two countries are apparently more simple, less secretive, and less "political." The fact that one of the two actors is an immensely powerful state while the other is only a third-rate power has also accentuated the apparent straightforward character of their relationships.

A last characteristic of the North American region is that it is made up of two federal states. From the end of the American Civil War until the present, there have been relatively few problems in the internal functioning of these two federal states, but this should not obscure the complexity of the system with over sixty subunits, each with rather extensive autonomy of their federal governments (particularly on the Canadian side).

[53] Excluding Mexico, of course.

How could Québec's independence affect the structure of this complex North American political subsystem?

For one thing, the creation of a new state actor could considerably alter the picture of interstate relations in North America. Instead of only one possible transaction pair (Canada–United States) there would now be one three-member grouping (Canada/United States/ Québec) and six possible dual groupings: US-Canada, US-Québec, Québec-Canada, US/Canada-Québec, US/Québec-Canada, and Québec/Canada-US. While in the actual North American environment there is no possibility for coalition, such coalitions would naturally become the order of the day whenever a new state actor is introduced.

In terms of interstate relations, the potential consequences are considerable. First, interstate politics could become much more important than it has been so far. With the appearance of a new actor whose policies represent a less-known factor and with the numerous possibilities for bilateral transactions and coalitions, the other two state actors would tend to pay more attention to their relations as states. Furthermore, it can be expected that in a time of uncertainty, decision making in regard to Québec-US and Canada-US relations could be centralized in the US Department of State and the Canadian Department of External Affairs. Similarly, the international transactions which until now were the responsibility of such departments as transportation, immigration, commerce, and defense will be recuperated by the foreign affairs decision-making apparatus. Already this recuperation is in process as witnessed by the recent Canada– United States negotiation on air routes.

Second, the atmosphere in which North American international relations will take place could also move away from a non-zero-sum toward a zero-sum game situation. With a new state actor it will become more difficult to find solutions that are equally beneficial to all parties involved. Compromises will be more difficult to reach when three actors are involved. Relations between the three state actors may become more formal and official. Old school ties and informal meetings could become less important since one of the actors will be relatively new at this game and of a different cultural tradition from the two others. On the other hand, it could equally be argued that the new Québec elite, now in power and fully bilingual, would attempt to integrate itself into this North American network of transgovernmental relations so as to consolidate its own position within Québec. Furthermore, since the proposed Québec Department of Foreign Affairs will have neither the capacity nor the interest to regulate all of Québec–North American relations, the bureaucratic elites, even now so powerful in Québec, will succeed in taking over these relations.[57]

It is conceivable that with the coming of a third state actor and the increased complexity of issues, Canadian, American, and Québécois political leaders will come to pay more than lip service to North America as a region, albeit with the United States continuing to be the major force shaping the destiny of the area. In fact, the secession of Québec may very well consolidate even further US domination of North America, for facing a nation of 220 million there will now be two nations, one of 16 million, and the other of 6 million, rather than a single nation of 22 million. On the other hand, it may also be argued that free from the necessity of maintaining an appearance of binationalism, Canada may move more dynamically toward asserting its own individuality—thus making possible a more aggressive foreign policy, more divergent from that of the United States. Moreover, it could also be argued that Québec's independence could trigger the disintegration of the rest of the Canadian federation with each region going its own way.

In fact, with Québec no longer a member of the Canadian confederation, it is quite conceivable that the provincial divisions in English Canada will give way to a process of regional consolidation in a north-south direction. In the case of the Maritimes, cut off from the rest of Canada by an independent Québec, this process of consolidation could become a necessity. These regions—Maritimes, Ontario, Prairies, and British Columbia—may increasingly look toward their American counterparts immediately to the south for economic and commercial ties and further increase the difficulties of keeping a workable federal system in the rest of Canada. Thus, the secession of Québec could result in the emergence of such north-south regions as distinct political actors in the North American continent, or perhaps even in their political integration into the United States.

The PQ has not yet made it clear what kind of international system it would prefer. Until now PQ leadership has not systematically examined the spectrum of possibilities, which range from the creation of a North American customs and monetary union to the unilateral erection of its own tariff structure. So far the discussions within the party have focused on two closely related issues: the nature of the future economic agreements between Canada and Québec, and the possibilities of a common market agreement or free-trade area, with or without Canada, with the United States. On the first question the 1973 PQ program makes clear that although a monetary union with the rest of Canada still makes sense, such a union

---

[57] The internal situation of Québec after independence is obviously an important variable that is not considered here.

would probably be impossible to achieve in the short run. As for the question of a Québec-US common market, although the PQ has officially rejected this possibility, the debate has been given new vitality with what is thought to be a rising dependency of the United States on outside sources for energy and other natural resources.

The appearance of a new state actor would not create new issue areas. There would still be problems of defense, natural resources, trade, and commerce to discuss. What would be different is that while there has been a single Canadian official position on these issues, there would now be two—one for Québec and one for Canada. Since the latter will no longer include Québec, it is likely that its position on some issues (electricity export, foreign capital) will be significantly different from what it now is.

Because of this increased complexity of the context in which issues would be discussed, it should not be surprising if we witnessed increased linkages between issues, a tendency that could prove disastrous for Québec. In order to put together a winning coalition at home and prevent the formation of any such coalition by the other two actors, each state actor may resort to the technique of package deals that would be negotiated on a take-it-or-leave-it basis. As issues become more complex and as solutions become increasingly elusive, there would be a tendency to introduce new issues in the discussion in the hope of finding a common denominator. For example, if three countries could not agree on a common policy for the sharing of electric power, there would be strong pressures to try to resolve the deadlock by bringing in the question of oil, then of coal, and then of access to the St. Lawrence Seaway in order that each actor would find itself in a good bargaining position (i.e., a situation where the actor is willing to give something in order to receive something else). The result would be that even if this proved to be dangerous for the smaller states, issues would be increasingly tied together for tactical purposes but not necessarily in any substantively coherent way. In addition, once a package deal were struck, it would be an almost insurmountable task to modify it in a way satisfactory to all.

CONCLUSIONS

As I have attempted to show, the PQ has not worked out a detailed United States policy or even thought in systematic fashion about its future relations—intergovernmental or transnational—with the United States. The fact that the PQ has made detailed propositions regarding a number of secondary aspects of the internal workings of an independent Québec suggests that this absence of a US policy is not the result of an exclusive preoccupation with electoral considerations but of a more general lack of concern with this specific question and with foreign relations generally (e.g., with France) except with Canada. For example, during the 1973 campaign the PQ published a 40-page program budget with separate provisions for the more than 400 programs now supported by the Québec and Canadian governments.[58] But nowhere in its budget or in its program has the PQ indicated the objectives it would seek to achieve in its relations with the United States. The other Québec political parties, usually so quick in their attacks on the PQ, apparently did not consider this shortcoming a worthwhile electoral target for their criticism.

Nor is the absence of a PQ American policy a sign that the PQ does not consider future Québec-American relations to be an important element of its foreign policy. On the contrary, the PQ leadership is well aware of the results of a 1973 survey that revealed 64.5 percent of the Québécois believed that Québec-American relations should have priority in Québec's foreign relations, while only 19.7 percent believed the priority should go to Québec-French relations.[59]

As I have tried to show, this absence of a United States policy is a symptom of a widespread belief among the PQ leadership that it should be easier to work out mutually satisfactory arrangements with Americans than with Canadians. But this may of course prove to be a naive illusion. By nationalizing certain critical raw material production, such as asbestos, iron, and others in increasing demand in the United States, and by insisting, possibly in conjunction with Canada, on greater United States acceptance of these resources in processed rather than in raw form, along with liberalized entry into the United States market for semifinished and secondary manufactured goods, an independent Québec could probably win important United States concessions. However, such policies, depending on how Québec attempted to implement them, would undoubtedly result in heated controversy in the United States Congress and executive, and in the articulate United States body politic generally.

[58] The PQ budget calls for spending $11.08 billion for 1974-75. The similarity of outlook between the PQ and the actual Liberal government leadership in the province is best illustrated by the fact that there is a .94 correlation between the PQ budget and the 1973-74 budget of the Québec government.

[59] *Quebec International* 1, no. 4 (1973) : 3.

TRANSNATIONAL RELATIONS AND INTERSTATE CONFLICTS: AN EMPIRICAL ANALYSIS

Joseph S. Nye, Jr.

Canadian-American relations have tended to bore statesmen and scholars who long to be where the action is. According to one scholar, "study of Canadian-American relations tells one almost nothing about the big problems facing the world," while in a classic essay Arnold Wolfers used the unguarded border as an example of "indifference to power." [1] If we view world politics with "realist" assumptions that unified states are the only actors, force is the major source of power, and solving the military security dilemma is their overwhelming objective, then Canadian-American relations are indeed dull.

There are large areas of world politics, however, in which economic objectives are more salient than military security objectives, force is not very useful in achieving positive objectives, and unified governments are not the only significant actors. [2] As these areas are perceived to be important, the Canadian-American case becomes more relevant. Economic and social issues have dominated the agenda for some 50 years, accounting for some 80 percent of the references to Canada in President Roosevelt's prewar public papers (1933-39) and from 55 to 63 percent of the references in the public papers of the

Joseph S. Nye is a professor of political science at Harvard University and a member of the Board of Editors of *International Organization*. The author is indebted to Carl Beigie, Robert Bowie, Annette Fox, Ted Greenwood, Barbara Haskel, Samuel Huntington, Robert Keohane, Sperry Lea, Kari Levitt, Peyton Lyon, Edward L. Miles, Wynne Plumptre, Roger Swanson, and John Yochelson for comments on an earlier draft of this article. He is also grateful to the Ford and Rockefeller Foundations for financial support of this research.

[1] David Baldwin, "The Myths of the Special Relationship," in Stephen Clarkson, ed., *An Independent Foreign Policy for Canada?* (Toronto: McClelland and Stewart, 1968), p. 5; Arnold Wolfers, *Discord and Collaboration* (Baltimore, Md.: The Johns Hopkins Press, 1962), p. 97.

[2] This assertion is developed in Robert O. Keohane and Joseph S. Nye, "International Interdependence and Integration," to be published in Fred Greenstein and Nelson Polsby, eds., *The Handbook of Political Science* (Reading, Mass.: Addison-Wesley, 1974).

postwar presidents (1950-70).[3] Threats of force have not been instruments for the achievement of government objectives for an even longer period.[4] But mutual enjoyment of a sense of security community did not end political conflicts or create an indifference to power. Uneven vulnerability and subtle suggestion of potential retaliation in situations of economic interdependence became a significant source of power. Another source has been the ability to use the cross-border activities of nongovernmental organizations and contacts among government agencies acting autonomously. The fact that a third (by value) of all corporations in Canada (58 percent in manufacturing) are foreign owned has led some observers to coin the term *Canadianization* for a situation that they assume to mean transnational restriction of the host government's power.[5] In other words, Canadian-American relations may not be such a unique situation in world politics among advanced industrial societies. Or to be more accurate, the uniqueness may be in the extent, rather than in the type, of relations. As such, it is a limiting case, and limiting cases can be fruitful points of focus for testing hypotheses and exploring trends.[6]

In an earlier volume, Robert Keohane and I argued that attention must be paid to transnational and transgovernmental actors as well as state actors if we are adequately to understand political processes and outcomes in many areas of world politics.[7] We argued that actors and outcomes vary by issue area, and that greater attention should be paid to linkage among issue areas. We also argued that while transnational and transgovernmental relations have long existed, they have probably increased in importance over time. Finally, we speculated about the ways in which transnational relations may redistribute influence among governments. These hypotheses could be quickly rejected if they can be falsified in the limiting case of Canadian-American relations. While the converse is obviously not

[3] I calculated this from all references that were not purely pro forma or goodwill statements in *Public Papers of the Presidents of the United States* (Washington, D.C.: Office of the *Federal Register*, National Archives and Records Service.)

[4] Canada's Defense Scheme #1 against the US was formally cancelled in 1931, but the political sense of security community predated the demise of the military contingency plan. James Eayrs, *In Defence of Canada*, vol. 1 (Toronto: University of Toronto Press, 1964), p. 77.

[5] See, for example, Theo Sommer, "The Community Is Working," *Foreign Affairs* 51 (July 1973) : 753.

[6] Harry Eckstein, "Case Study and Theory in Political Science," in Greenstein and Polsby, eds., *The Handbook of Political Science*.

[7] Robert O. Keohane and Joseph S. Nye, eds., *Transnational Relations and World Politics* (Cambridge: Harvard University Press, 1972). The theoretical work and hypotheses underlying the present article were developed in collaboration with Professor Keohane. In addition, I am indebted to Professor Keohane for part of the research on the prewar period and for comments on the article.

true, the following analysis may stimulate replications needed before the hypotheses can be sustained with full confidence. In the hope of providing a basis for cumulative works, I have tried to use procedures that are explicit and that make the cases accesssible for others to compare and reinterpret.

It may at first seem paradoxical to some readers of our earlier volume that the analysis in this essay focuses so heavily on state-to-state interaction. This focus was chosen because state-to-state interaction remains one (though not the only) important dependent variable in political analysis and because this focus meets state-centric skeptics on their own ground. Obviously there is another range of dependent variables concerned with which groups benefit from transnational interactions (even though they may never reach the interstate agenda). These questions are important but they are not the focus of this essay. In the following analysis, I distingiush the role of transnational relations in agenda formation and in the political process of decision making in interstate conflicts. In the conclusion, I speculate about the implications for integration and Canadian autonomy. First I must lay the basis for the empirical analysis.

IDENTIFYING CASES

One of the greatest obstacles to clear analysis of Canadian-American interstate bargaining is the well-selected anecdote. Each side has its preferred illustrations. Canadians tend to focus on a few specific incidents such as the magazine tax while Americans often emphasize the auto pact. It is almost as if the proverbial blindfold'ed men trying to describe an elephant peeked from under their blindfolds in order to seize the part most useful to their different purposes. It is not unusual to hear Canadians claim that they do poorly in bilateral bargaining with the United States, or to hear American officials complain that Canadians get away with too much. Such myths are resilient because they are politically useful. But what is useful for statesmen can be obstructive for analysts.

How can we avoid the myths and obtain a more accurate portrayal of interstate agendas between the two countries? For the earlier years, it is a relatively simple matter to go through the published diplomatic documents and identify those subjects placed on the agendas of the governments by a formal or informal communication from the other government. Counting interstate interactions with Canada in the annual volumes of *Foreign Relations of the United States* gives the picture of the intergovernmental agenda shown in table 1.

TABLE 1. INTERSTATE INTERACTIONS WITH CANADA,

By Issue Area (Government Objectives)

	MILITARY	POLITICAL	SOCIAL	ECONOMIC
1920s (n=4)	3	8	16	72
1930s (n=92)	5	10	20	65
1940-46 (n=119)	44	20	6	30

SOURCE: *Foreign Relations of the United States*

What the published documents show is a high preponderance of economic issues on the interstate agenda (except for the war years), and a tripling in the average number of annual interactions from 6.4 per year in the 1920s through 9.2 per year in the 1930s to 17 per year in the early 1940s. It is interesting to note that as the agenda became more complex, the proportion of issues coming before the president increased somewhat; but the most dramatic change was the decline in the proportion of issues handled by cabinet officials (primarily the secretary of state) and the rise in the proportion handled by the bureaucracy.

While it seems likely that this trend continues, it is virtually impossible to ascertain the entire agenda of interstate interactions for the current period when the diplomatic documents have not been published.[8] In 1968, for example, there were some 6,500 visits back and forth across the border by Canadian and American officials from and to some 30 Canadian agencies outside the defense field.[9] Much of this total agenda involves minor matters and is not centrally monitored. The Department of External Affairs sent and received only 139 of the 6,500 visits. Getting an accurate picture of the total intergovernmental agenda poses an enormous problem for statesmen as well as researchers.[10]

My solution to the research dilemma was to focus on significant interstate conflicts that reached the attention of the US president. While this solution has the disadvantage of focusing on only part of the total interstate agenda, it has several redeeming advantages. First, and most important, the presidential conflict agenda offers the

[8] At the time this research began, 1947 was the most recent volume.

[9] The total is 18,000, but among the 11,500 visits involving national defence are a number of visits for military training. Canada, Department of External Affairs, "Canadian Governmental Instruments for Conducting Relations with the United States," 1969, Appendix B.

[10] Indeed, the Departments of State and External Affairs often cooperate in helping each other to monitor the flows.

1920-46 (in percentages)

| By Level of Attention in US | | |
PRESIDENT	CABINET OFFICERS	OTHER OFFICIALS
12.5	75	12.5
15	34	50
16	20	64

best prospect of presenting a universe of like cases. Conflictual behavior at the top tends to be better reported by observers and better
remembered by participants. While complete discovery is unlikely,
it is probably possible to approach a reasonably complete universe of
significant cases. In addition, there are substantive justifications for
focusing on the presidential conflict agenda. Since conflicts that reach
presidential attention tend to be more important than others, there
is an implicit weighting of cases. It is true that summit meetings
sometimes produce agenda-filler items.[11] Moreover, unlike total
bureaucratic resources, presidential attention is a physically restricted
and very scarce resource. Since I am interested in how transnational
and transgovernmental interactions have affected interstate relations
over time, it is useful to see their relationship to a fixed resource.
Moreover, by focusing at the level of high politics, the bias I introduce
is *against* my hypothesis of an important role of transnational and
transgovernmental relations. Finally, because the president has the
broadest jurisdiction over issues of any governmental actor, it is at
the presidential level that there is the greatest probability of discov-
ering the linkages among issues that are commonly held not to exist
in Canadian-American interactions.

One of the difficulties in identifying cases concerns the boundaries
and outcomes of conflicts. By a significant interstate conflict I mean
a situation where one government communicates a request to the other
and there is sufficient incompatibility of objectives or costliness of
means that the request is not easily fulfilled. Conflict in this sense is
not necessarily dramatic. The conflict may be treated as a problem
within a continuing cooperative relationship, and the resolution may

[11] One US official, for example, described how he and a Canadian counterpart
took the initiative in working out a new approach to a problem of Great Lakes
pollution. By the hazards of timing of a summit meeting and the need for
"friendly" items for the communiqué, his venture reached presidential attention.
It is hard to discover examples where conflictual issues need to be deliberately
added to the agenda.

leave both countries better off.[12] There may be large areas of mutual compatibility of government objectives; and the major area of incompatibility need not arise out of the preferences or actions of the chief executives. What *is* necessary for a significant interstate conflict to exist, however, is some incompatibility of objectives between groups in different countries that becomes expressed in an interstate request that cannot be easily or costlessly complied with by the recipient government. The request need not take a particular diplomatic form, but there must be communication of a mutually understood preference for (or against) a particular course of action.

A conflict begins at the time of the first intergovernmental request and ends when there are no further requests or the conflict has been depoliticized. A conflict can involve one or many requests. I treat a set of requests as a single conflict if the government objectives remain largely unchanged and subsequent requests largely repeat the major objectives stated in the first request. Thus the magazine tax case, for example, recurred during three Canadian administrations, but the nature of the American requests (nondiscriminatory treatment of *Time* and *Reader's Digest*) remained essentially the same. On the other hand, Canadian exports of oil to the United States became a different case in the 1970s from what it was in the 1960s because the governments' objectives (and requests) changed from US limitation to United States encouragement of imports from Canada.

Scoring the outcome of conflicts also poses certain problems. The approach taken in table 2 is to examine the range of incompatibility of initially held objectives and to ask whether the general outcome was, for whatever reason, closer to the objectives held by one or the other government at the time of the first request or was roughly equidistant between them. Where a conflict is not solved by the end of the period under study, or where there is a major delay during which government objectives change, the delaying country is regarded as having achieved its objectives. For example, though the US eventually changed its treatment of the People's Republic of China, it did not do so until some fifteen years after St. Laurent first raised the question with Eisenhower. This approach admits the possibility that the winning side may have made some concessions and that both sides

---

[12] There are often Pareto optimal solutions to conflict that make both countries better off. This is the joint gain component of the solution. But the exact location on the curve of Pareto optimality is indeterminate. This is the question of distribution of gain on which I focus in this essay. In some cases, the joint gain may be in some ways more significant than the distribution of gain, but it is the latter that tests hypotheses about interstate bargaining in a situation of asymmetrical penetration by transnational actors.

may gain from the resolution of the conflict. The approach does not try to judge whether decision makers held the "right" objectives.[13] In retrospect, for example, two observers may argue over whether the auto pact was good or bad for Canada depending on their relative preferences for autonomy or employment. The argument may be impossible to settle. But even two observers with disparate ideological preferences should be able to say which government got more of the objectives it then (perhaps unwisely) held.

Quite obviously these procedures for identifying and scoring a set of conflicts address only part of the Canadian-American relationship. The focus is on conflicts at the pinnacle of the intergovernmental process rather than throughout the government. During the 1920s and 1930s, however, the pattern of outcomes of eighteen conflicts that did not reach the presidential level (9 US, 5 equal, 4 Canada) was remarkably similar to the pattern at the presidential level.[14] For the 1950s and 1960s it is impossible to make careful comparisons, but impressionistic evidence does not suggest a great difference in patterns of outcomes at different levels.

Another problem is that the approach divides a continuous process into discrete parts and scores the relationship as a sum of parts rather than as a whole. While this objection has a certain validity worth bearing in mind when drawing conclusions about the whole relationship, it is interesting to note that many diplomats and politicians themselves often have a rough scoring system in their heads.[15] As one official put it, "there is a general sense of who has been making more concessions over the past few years." This vague awareness of who has overdrawn their credit in political bank balances that statesmen carry in their heads is a subtle but important background link

[13] One Canadian official argued that certain cases were not really conflicts because the American officials did not correctly perceive their own interests. Even if true, however, the problem of interstate conflict cannot be so easily defined away.

[14] The eighteen conflicts were: 1920s—Great Lakes naval limitations, Great Lakes water diversion, Missisquoi Bay fishing, Roseau River drainage, Canadian peach embargo, US dairy embargo, St. Mary and Milk River diversion, US sinking of *I'm Alone* liquor ship, border crossing privileges, Passamaquoddy Bay power; 1930s—Canadian discrimination against US tugboats, US seizure of Canadian ship, St. Clair River dredging, Canadian seizure of four US fishing boats, consular visits to criminals, Great Lakes cargo, income tax agreements, arms for Spanish Civil War. I am indebted to Alison Young for research assistance on these cases.

[15] Some 30 present and former officials were asked to comment and correct the description and scoring of conflicts in tables 2, 3, and 4. Only one (Canadian) objected to the procedure of trying to score discrete conflicts (on the grounds that it misrepresented a continuous process).

among issues.[16] If issues are closely linked, then an unfavorable outcome for a government on one issue may simply be the price it is paying for a favorable outcome on another. Generally speaking, however,
the linkages are not this close. In the words of a high Canadian official, "marginally you shade a deal because of timing and goodwill, but
basically each deal is on its own."

Finally, it is important to remember that generalizations about
the entire Canadian-American relationship made on the basis of a set
of high-level conflicts do not include "nonconflicts" that fail to arise
because of anticipated reaction or because of societal or transgovernmental contacts that lead to a statement of government objectives
which diminish the range of conflict. For example, some Canadian
subsidiaries of American firms probably shunned Chinese orders so as
not to run afoul of extraterritorial restrictions on their trade.[17] A
glance at the following tables quickly shows, however, that it is not
true that Canada never raises big issues. And one must beware of
spurious causation in considering why certain conflicts were muted.
For example, Canada's delay in recognizing the People's Republic of
China was partly in deference to the United States, but also because
of domestic politics.[18] In other words, one must be careful neither to
read too much nor too little into the following cases. With these
caveats in mind, I summarize the 31 postwar cases in tables 2, 3, 4
and eight prewar cases in table 5 before analyzing them in terms of
agenda formation and political process.[19]

[16] Different bureaucracies in the same country may keep different scores. US
Treasury officials tended to complain more frequently in the early 1970s that
Canadians always came out ahead. As one State Department official observed, "In
the 1960s the relations among financial officials were so close that we were often
shut out of policy. Now, their relations are so poor that they complicate policy."
[17] David Leyton-Brown, "Governments of Developed Countries as Hosts to Multinational Enterprise" (PH.D. dissertation, Department of Government, Harvard
University, 1973).
[18] F. Conrad Raabe, "Canada's Decision to Recognize the Communist Government of China," *Association for Canadian Studies in the U.S. Newsletter* 2
(Spring 1972) : 12-20. Also, *Mike: The Memoirs of the Right Honourable Lester
B. Pearson*, vol. 2 (Toronto: University of Toronto Press, 1973), p. 195.
[19] The procedure for constructing tables 2, 3, and 4 was as follows: A long list
of interactions was constructed from all references to Canada in *Public Papers
of the Presidents of the United States*, presidential references in the *Department
of State Bulletin*, and the Council of Foreign Relations clippings files (primarily
New York Times, New York Herald Tribune, Financial Post [Toronto], *Globe
and Mail* [Toronto]). Further references were added and interactions not involving significant conflict were removed from the list on the basis of secondary accounts. Particularly useful for 1950 to 1963 were the Canadian Institute of International Affairs volumes on *Canada in World Affairs;* and for the 1960s, the *Canadian Annual Review*. The list was then further refined through interviews with
30 current and former officials and observers. Certain issues (such as DEW Line,
ABM, bunkering facilities, Laos) have been excluded as not involving sufficient
incompatibility of objectives. Others (such as Cuban trade, Mercantile Bank)
have been excluded as lacking direct presidential involvement.

TABLE 2. DYADIC CONFLICTS, 1950s

First Government Action	Interstate Request	Outcome Closer to Objectives of:	
Canada	Canada	Equal	*1. St. Lawrence Seaway, 1945-58 (49, 51, 53). Canada threatened to build alone if United States failed to speed decision.
United States	Canada	United States	2. United States agricultural import quotas, 1953–mid-1960s (53, 54, 55, 56, 57). Canada repeatedly protested United States protection. United States made minor concessions but did not meet basic request.
United States	United States	United States	3. Gouzenko interview (1953). United States requested that Canada arrange interview for Senate subcommittee. Canada initially declined but agreed to a second request under certain conditions.
United States	Canada	Canada	*4. Chicago water diversion, 1954-59 (54, 56). Canada repeatedly and successfully protested pending United States legislation to permit Chicago to divert water from Lake Michigan.
United States	Canada	United States	5. United States quotas on lead and zinc imports, 1954- (54, 58). Canada unsuccessfully protested United States restrictions.
United States	United States	Equal	†6. Columbia River development, 1944-64 (56, 61, 63). United States requested development of Columbia as a system. Canada delayed until compensated for downstream benefits, and until it reconciled internal dispute with British Columbia.
United States (state)	Canada	Canada	*7. Carlings Brewery (1956). Canada protested Maryland discrimination against Canadian corporation. Eisenhower persuaded Maryland to change.
Canada	United States	United States	†8. Magazine Tax, 1956-65 (56, 58). United States repeatedly protested discriminatory tax treatment of Canadian editions of United States magazines. A 1956 law was repealed; and in 1965, *Time* and *Reader's Digest* were exempted.
United States	Canada	Canada	*9. Security information guarantees (1957). Canada protested Senate subcommittee disclosures that led to suicide of Canadian official. United States acceded to Canadian request for guarantees against future misuse of information.

(Continued on next page)

TABLE 2 (continued)

First Government Action	Request Interstate	Outcome Closer to of: Objectives		
United States	Canada	Canada	†10.	Exemption from oil import quotas, 1955-70 (58, 59, 62). Canada successfully protested the illogic of import restrictions against it based on national security grounds, and threatened to pipe western Canadian oil to Quebec and thus exclude Venezuelan oil.
United States	Canada	United States	†11.	Extraterritorial control of corporations, 1956- (58). Canada requested United State to forego extraterritorial restrictions on freedom of subsidiaries in Canada. United States refused to give up principle, but agreed to consultation procedure for exemptions in specific cases.

Dates in parentheses indicate some major dates of presidential attention.

† Indicates cases in which transnational organizations played a significant role in the political process.

* Indicates cases in which transgovernmental relations played a significant role in the political process.

TABLE 3. DYADIC CONFLICTS, 1960s

First Government Action	Interstate Request	Outcome Closer to Objectives of:	
United States	Canada	Canada	*1. BOMARC procurement, 1959-60 (60). Diefenbaker asked Eisenhower to continue development of the BOMARC missile threatened by Department of Defense and congressional cutbacks. The funds were restored.
Canada	United States	United States	*2. Nuclear arming of Canadian weapons, 1961-63 (61, 62, 63). United States requested that Canada arm its weapons systems in NORAD and NATO. Diefenbaker's government split and fell. The Pearson government armed the systems.
United States	Canada	Canada	†3. United States restriction of lumber imports, 1961-64 (61, 64). Canada requested relaxation of administrative restrictions and later veto of a highly protective congressional bill. Johnson vetoed the bill.
Canada	Canada	United States	†4. Seafarers' International Union, 1962-64 (63, 64). Canada requested that the United States government restrain AFL-CIO support of the Seafarers' International Union and disruptive boycotts of Canadian shipping. Presidential efforts to influence the AFL-CIO were insufficient and the disruption ended only when the Canadian government trustees came to terms with the SIU. United States government objectives were to be helpful but without antagonizing the AFL-CIO.
Canada	Canada	Equal	5. Renegotiation of civil air routes, 1962-65 (63). Canada requested renegotiation to permit deeper penetration of United States by Canadian airlines. Agreement was reached on basis of Galbraith plan treating continent as a unit.
Canada	United States	Canada	6. Extended fishing zones, 1963- (63, 66). Canada unilaterally declared extended fishing zones and straight baselines. United States protested. Canada made provision for historic fishing rights but was not deterred from extension.
United States	Canada	Equal	7. Interest Equalization Tax (1963). Canada requested exemption from tax on grounds that an integrated capital market existed. United States granted exemption for new issues on condition that Canada not increase its reserves through borrowing in United States. United States objectives were to improve its balance-of-payments position.

(Continued on next page)

TABLE 3 (continued)

First Government Action	Inter-state Request	Outcome Closer to Objectives of:		
United States	Canada	Equal	†8.	United States balance-of-payments guidelines, 1965-68 (65). Canada requested exemptions from United States guidelines, voluntary in 1965 and mandatory in 1968, encouraging American corporations to restrict outflows and increase repatriation of capital. Exemptions were granted in return for restrictions on the pass-through of United States funds and on the level and form of Canadian reserves.
Canada	United States	Canada	†9.	Auto pact, 1962- (64, 65). United States threatened retaliation over Canadian export subsidy designed to achieve Canadian objective of increased production in Canada. Pact integrating automobile trade led to joint gain but Canada achieved more of the gain.
Canada	United States	Canada	†10.	Arctic pollution zone, 1969- (69). United States protested and asked Canada to defer extension of jurisdiction to 100 miles following the 1969 voyage of the tanker *Manhattan*. Canada refused.

Dates in parentheses indicate some major dates of presidential attention.
† Indicates cases in which transnational organizations played a significant role in the political process.
* Indicates cases in which transgovernmental relations played a significant role in the political process.

TABLE 4. CONFLICTS INVOLVING RELATIONS WITH THIRD COUNTRIES, 1950-69

Inter-state Request	Outcome Closer to Objectives of:	
Canada	United States	1. Conduct of Korean War, 1950-53 (50). Canada repeatedly requested United States restraint, but without great effect.
United States	Canada	2. Defense of Quemoy and Matsu, 1954-55 (55). United States requested Canadian support, but Canada disassociated itself from defense of the islands.
Canada	United States	3. Recognition of People's Republic of China, 1954-70 (54, 56, 58). Canada raised the possibility of recognition three times in 1950s but was deterred, in part, by United States inflexibility.
Canada	Canada	*4. Wheat sales to third countries, 1954-64 (56, 57, 58). Canada repeatedly requested that United States restrict dumping of surplus wheat. Agreement was reached on consultation and avoidance of dumping in Canadian overseas markets.
United States	Canada	5. Canada and the Organization of American States, 1961-63 (61). United States requested that Canada join as part of strengthening Latin America against Cuba and Communism. Canada did not join.
United States	Canada	6. British entry into the EEC, 1961-63 (61, 62). United States requested Canadian support for British entry to strengthen Atlantic world. Canada did not support at that stage.
United States	Canada	7. Aid to less developed countries, 1961-63 (61). United States requested increased Canadian assistance in strengthening poor countries. Canadian aid declined.
Canada	United States	8. Disarmament and nuclear test ban (1962). Canada opposed United States atmospheric tests and requested quicker US agreement to a test ban. Little effect on United States policy.
United States	Equidistant	*9. Cuban Missile Crisis (1962). United States informed Canada of its actions and expected diplomatic support and military mobilization. Diefenbaker delayed full support, but military mobilization went faster than he authorized.
Canada	United States	10. Conduct of Vietnam War, 1964-73 (64, 65). Canada requested United States restraint but had little impact on policy.

Dates in parentheses indicate some dates of presidential attention to the Canada–United States dimension of the issue.

* Indicates transgovernmental relations played a significant role in the political process.

TABLE 5. CONFLICTS ON PRESIDENTIAL AGENDA, 1920-39

First Government Action	Inter-state Request	Outcome Closer to Objectives of:	
Both	Canada	United States	1. Regulation of fisheries, 1918-37 (19, 21, 23). Canada pressed United States for ratification of treaty on fisheries issues, particularly salmon. United States delayed on salmon treaty until 1930s when a threat developed from Japanese salmon fishing.
Canada	United States	United States	2. Canadian restriction of pulpwood exports, 1920-23 (21). United States successfully protested by threatening "far-reaching retaliation." Canadian objective was to encourage processing in Canada.
United States	United States	Equal	†3. St. Lawrence Seaway, 1918-41 (24, 30, 31, 32, 34, 37, 39). United States pressed for joint navigation and hydroelectric development. Canada reluctant, but agreed to 1932 treaty which then failed in United States Senate. United States pressed for new agreement. Canada still reluctant but signed in 1941.
United States	United States	United States	4. Control of liquor smuggling, 1922-30 (25). United States successfully pressed Canada to take internal measures that would make United States enforcement of prohibition laws easier and cheaper.
United States	Canada	United States	5. United States tariffs, 1928-38 (28, 33, 35, 37). Canada unsuccessfully sought to deter 1930 rise in United States tariffs. Canada retaliated and sought alternative trade patterns. By 1933, Canada pressed for trade agreement. United States delayed, but signed agreements in 1935 and 1938. Canada gave somewhat greater concessions.
United States	United States	United States	6. Trail Smelter pollution, 1927-35 (34, 35). United States protested damage done to Washington farmers by fumes from British Columbia smelter and requested referral to IJC. Under pressure from farmers, United States rejected IJC recommendations and successfully pressed Canada to set up a special arbitral tribunal.

(Continued on next page)

TABLE 5 (continued)

First Government Action	Interstate Request	Outcome Closer to Objectives of:	
United States	Canada	Canada	*7. Liquor tax bill (1936). Canada successfully protested a proposed punitive tax designed to force Canadian distillers to come to an agreement with United States Treasury. Department of State sympathized with Canada, and Roosevelt backed State Department.
United States	United States	Canada	8. Construction of Alaska highway, 1930-38 (37). United States proposed joint construction of a highway through British Columbia. Canada feared the "penetration" and successfully resisted until 1942 when war changed its objectives.

SOURCE: *Foreign Relations of the United States.*
Dates in parentheses indicate major dates of presidential attention.
† Indicates cases in which transnational organizations played a significant role in the political process.
* Indicates cases in which transgovernmental relations played a significant role in the political process.

AGENDA FORMATION

Agenda formation is an aspect of interstate politics that is too often neglected by analysts. Allocating the scarce resource of presidential attention toward certain issues to the exclusion of others is sometimes as significant as influence in the making of decisions. Influence over agendas is a hidden but important face of power.[20]

The Scope of the Agenda

Comparing the presidential agendas of two interwar and two postwar decades, one sees a fourfold increase (from 8 to 31) in the number of conflicts that involved presidential attention. While nearly all the conflicts that reached the president in the interwar years concerned economic objectives (the Alaska highway being a partial exception), half the postwar agenda involved conflicts concerning military (7) and political (9) objectives. The world outside North America played a larger part in the postwar agenda. While the interwar agenda consisted entirely of dyadic problems, a third of the postwar agenda consisted of conflicts over relations with third countries. This difference reflects changes from the isolationist policies followed

[20] Peter Bachrach and Morton Baratz, "Two Faces of Power," *American Political Science Review* 56 (December 1962): 947-52.

by both countries for most of the interwar period.[21] Moreover, nearly all the postwar conflicts over relations with third countries could be said to reflect cold-war alliance policies. Transnational relations played little part in such conflicts, as one can see from table 4. Only two (wheat sales, Britain and the EEC) were concerned in part with the organization of transnational markets.

Whose Agenda?

James Eayrs has hypothesized that in an asymmetrical relationship, it is the smaller state that sets the agenda.[22] The hypothesis is somewhat ambiguous, since initiative can refer to first state action or to first interstate request. If it is the latter, one assumes that the smaller state concentrates a greater portion of its attention on the larger and addresses more requests to it. The beaver sleeping with the elephant must remind the giant to be careful when it moves. This seems to be true, but not dramatically so. Table 6 indicates that Canada raised half again as many of the disputes as the United States did.[23] And the US raised half the conflicts over relations with third countries (see table 4).

TABLE 6. AGENDA SETTING IN DYADIC CONFLICTS

	1920-39		1950s		1960s		Totals	
	CANADA	UNITED STATES	CANADA	UNITED STATES	CANADA	UNITED STATES	CANADA	UNITED STATES
Interstate request	3	5	8	3	6	4	17	12
First government action *	1	6	2	9	6	4	9	19

SOURCE: Tables 2, 3, 5.
* The 1920s fishery conflict arose from joint action.

[21] See G. P. de T. Glazebrook, *A History of Canadian External Relations*, vol. 2 (Toronto: McClelland and Stewart, 1966), chapters 17 and 18; John B. Brebner, *North Atlantic Triangle* (Toronto: McClelland and Stewart, 1968), chapter 15.
[22] "Sharing a Continent: The Hard Issues," in John S. Dickey, ed., *The United States and Canada* (Englewood Cliffs, N.J.: Prentice-Hall, 1964), p. 60.
[23] Determining the *first* interstate request is often difficult for the recent period when the documents are not available; so I have used the source of the *basic* request underlying the conflict. This is sometimes not the same as the first request. For example, in cases where the US requested voluntary export controls but Canada requested better access to the American market, it is the US action that generates the issue but the basic request is Canadian.

If, however, we ask in which country the first governmental action occurred that led to the dyadic interstate conflict, it is somewhat more clearly the elephant's agenda. The United States was the source of twice as many conflicts as Canada. But the striking aspect of table 6 is that this pattern is true of the 1920s, 1930s, and 1950s, but is not true in the 1960s. During the last decade, Canada increasingly set the interstate agenda. This may be a reflection in part of the diversion of presidential attention to problems elsewhere, such as Vietnam. The change can also be seen as indication, however, of a rising Canadian nationalism and dissatisfaction with the earlier established status quo.

Transnational Influences on the Agenda

What role have transnational interactions played in structuring the agenda of high-level conflicts? In six of the eight prewar cases and in 16 of the 31 postwar cases, transnational relations played a major role. If we take only the dyadic cases, transnational interactions played a major role in structuring the agenda in 15 of 21 cases. In other words, in the dyadic cases transnational interactions were as important in agenda formation in the 1920s and 1930s as they were in the 1950s and 1960s. When we include cases involving relations with third countries, transnational relations were more important in the earlier than in the later period. On the basis of high-level Canadian-American conflicts, it is not possible to sustain a hypothesis of increased importance over time for all types of transnational interactions in agenda formation.

There are many types of private interactions across national frontiers. One important distinction is between transnational interactions among a number of otherwise unrelated actors and those in which the same large bureaucratic organization is involved on both sides of the border. The former arm's-length interactions I will refer to as *general transnational flows;* the latter interactions involving the same organization on both sides of the border I will refer to as *transnational organization.* Trade carried out through arm's-length market mechanisms is a prime example of a general transnational flow that has long been a matter of governmental concern, particularly when one or another government attempts to manipulate the flow by policies such as tariffs, quotas, or export subsidies. A case can be made, however, that what has changed in the last half century is not the overall role of transnational interactions in agenda formation but the increased organization of such transnational interactions.[24] The cases

[24] This conforms with Huntington's argument in "Transnational Organizations in World Politics," *World Politics* 25 (April 1973) : 333-68.

presented here sustain the hypothesis of increased importance of transnational *organizations* over time. Whereas only one (the liquor tax case) of the earlier cases involved the activities of large transnational organizations, seven of the sixteen postwar cases in which transnational relations played a major part in agenda formation involved such organizations (see table 7).

TABLE 7. SEVEN CONFLICTS IN WHICH TRANSNATIONAL ORGANIZATIONS PLAYED MAJOR ROLE IN AGENDA FORMATION, 1950-69

Conflict	Transnational Organization	Initiatory Activity	Locus of Activity	First Government to Act
Carlings Brewery	Carlings	Investment in Maryland	United States	Maryland
Magazine tax	*Time, Reader's Digest*	Large share of Canadian market	Canada	Canada
Extraterritorial control	United States subsidiaries	Compliance with US law	Canada	United States
BOMARC procurement	Boeing	Lobby for BOMARC	Canada, United States	United States
Seafarers' International Union	SIU	Labor violence	Canada	Canada
Guidelines	United States subsidiaries	Compliance with US law	Canada	United States
Arctic pollution zone	Humble Oil	Tanker voyage	Canada	Canada

Six of the seven cases in table 7 involved corporations; one involved a labor union. Three of the cases (magazine tax, SIU, Carlings) were politicized as a result of domestic groups appealing to their home government for protection against the activities of the transnational organization. One (Arctic pollution) was politicized because the Canadian public perceived the tanker voyage as a threat to symbols of Canadian sovereignty.[25] The initial politicization in two cases (extraterritorial controls, guidelines) came through US government manipulation of corporate subsidiaries. The first case became an

[25] Walter Stewart, *Trudeau in Power* (New York: Outerbridge and Dienstfrey, 1971), p. 153. Also Bruce Thordarson, *Trudeau and Foreign Policy* (Toronto: Oxford University Press, 1972), p. 186.

issue for Diefenbaker in Canadian electoral politics in 1957,[26] and the
second was politicized in Canada through transgovernmental conflict
when Eric Kierans, a provincial minister, prodded the Ottawa government out of a complacent acceptance by sending (and publicizing)
a letter of protest to the US Department of Commerce.[27]

Canada was the locus of the transnational organizations' activity
in six of seven cases, reflecting the asymmetrical role of Canada as
host more than home state. It is also worth noting, however, that at
least five of the cases were widely politicized in Canada and thus had
the effect of helping to arouse feelings of Canadian nationalism.

Government efforts at regulating transnational flows and markets
are a more traditional source of interstate conflicts. Here in table 8
we find essentially similar patterns in the prewar and postwar periods.
The majority of cases in both periods involve governmental interventions in transnational trade flows. In general, the pressure for

TABLE 8. GOVERNMENT EFFORTS TO REGULATE TRANSNATIONAL FLOWS

Date	Total	Trade	Capital	Pollutants	Other
1920-39					
Canadian gov- ernment	2	Pulpwood	—	—	Fishing *
US government	4	Liquor smuggling Tariff Liquor tax	—	Trail Smelter	—
Total	6	4	—	1	1
1950-69					
Canadian gov- ernment	3	Auto pact	—	—	Fishing Air routes
US government	6	Agriculture Lead and zinc Oil Lumber	I.E. Tax Guidelines	—	—
Total	9	5	2	—	2

* Raised by both.

[26] In 1957, Diefenbaker charged that the Liberals would make Canada "a virtual
49th economic state." James Eayrs, *Canada in World Affairs, 1955-57* (Toronto:
Oxford University Press, 1959), p. 125. In the 1958 election, an alleged refusal by
Ford of Canada to sell trucks to China was widely publicized. Trevor Lloyd,
Canada in World Affairs, 1957-59 (Toronto: Oxford University Press, 1968),
p. 93.
[27] See John Saywell, ed., *Canadian Annual Review for 1966* (Toronto: University of Toronto Press, 1967), pp. 209, 298.

politicization comes from a domestic group seeking its government's protection against the effects of transnational flows. Exceptions to this pattern in the prewar period were the pulpwood case where the Canadian government tried to use export quotas to locate more of the employment benefits in Canada [28] and the liquor smuggling case where the United States pressed the Canadian government to intervene domestically in an illegal transnational system so as to make US domestic policy more effective.[29] In the postwar period, the auto pact developed out of a Canadian export subsidy scheme designed to increase production in Canada. In the regulation of capital markets, the efforts to curb capital outflows were initially politicized at high levels rather than from below. By and large, these conflicts over regulation of transnational flows tended to be concerned more with access to the larger American rather than to the smaller Canadian market. Perhaps for this reason such conflicts tended to have less of an effect on increasing Canadian nationalism than did the cases that involved large transnational organizations.

PROCESS AND OUTCOMES

When we look at whether the outcomes of high-level conflicts are closer to the objectives of one or the other government, we notice in table 9 a striking change over time. The outcomes were closer to the Canadian government's objectives in only a quarter of the prewar cases but in nearly half the postwar cases. Outcomes were closer to American government objectives in five-eighths of the prewar cases, and nearly half the cases in the 1950s, but in only a quarter of the cases in the 1960s. Canada has done better in the postwar than prewar period, and better in the 1960s than in the 1950s.

TABLE 9. PATTERNS OF OUTCOMES IN HIGH-LEVEL CONFLICTS

	United States	Canada	Equal	Total
1920-39	5	2	1	8
1950s	7	6	2	15
1960s	4	8	4	16
Total	16	16	7	39

SOURCE: Tables 2, 3, 4, 5.

[28] See *Foreign Relations of the United States, 1921* (henceforth, FRUS), vol. 1, p. 307. Also *FRUS, 1923*, vol. 1, pp. 494-98.

[29] Richard Kottman, "Volstead Violated: Prohibition as a Factor in Canadian-American Relations," *The Canadian Historical Review* 43 (June 1962): 106-26.

Issue Areas

There is significant variation, however, in the pattern of outcomes by issue areas.[30] The United States does better in the area of its military objectives; Canada does better in the area of its economic objectives (see table 10). To some extent this variation by issue area may

TABLE 10. CONFLICTS BY ISSUE AREA, 1950-69

	Military (n=7)	Political (n=9)	Economic (n=15)
Outcomes closer to US government objectives	* Korean War Nuclear arms * Disarmament * Vietnam War	Gouzenko * China Extraterritoriality Seafarers' Union	Agricultural imports Lead and zinc imports Magazine tax
Cases with equidistant outcomes	* Cuban Missile	—	St. Lawrence Columbia River Air routes Interest tax Guidelines
Outcomes closer to Canadian government objectives	* Quemoy-Matsu BOMARC procurement	Security information * OAS * GB and EEC * Aid Arctic zone	Chicago water Carlings * Wheat sales Oil Lumber Fishing zones Auto pact

* Conflicts involving relations with third countries.

reflect the greater disproportion in military resources (37 to 1) than in economic size (12 to 1); but it also reflects the fact that a majority of the conflicts over military objectives involved relations with third countries. As table 5 shows, neither Canada nor the United States is very successful in getting the other to change its policy toward third countries. The two exceptions (wheat sales, Cuban Missile Crisis) in the list of ten cases are instructive. Both involved transgovernmental coalitions (one tacit and one explicit). In the case of the wheat sales, the US Department of State took the Canadian side against the US Department of Agriculture because it felt that Agriculture's policies of dumping grain supplied under public law 480 were destructive of the liberal world-trade structure that the State Department was trying to build.[31] In the Cuban Missile Crisis, the close relations between

[30] Issue areas are defined in terms of dominant objectives of the US government. *Political* refers to objectives of autonomy, sovereignty, and relations with third countries. *Economic* refers to material welfare. In one case (magazine tax) the American government's objectives were more economic while the Canadian's were more political.

[31] Interview with former State Department official, 1973; see also James Eayrs, *Canada in World Affairs, 1955-57*, pp. 112-27.

Canadian and United States defense officials in the North American
Air Defense Command (NORAD) led the Canadians to bring Canadian forces to a de facto level of alert close to the American government's objectives nearly 48 hours before Prime Minister Diefenbaker
finally decided to authorize it.[32]

Causes of Outcomes

It is impossible to do full justice in such brief form to the causes
of the outcomes of these cases. Nonetheless, it helps to place the role
of transnational and transgovernmental relations in perspective if we
look at certain other factors associated with outcomes, such as relative intensity, the locus of jurisdiction, the generally low salience of
Canadian issues to the American president, and specific or general
(linked) fears of retaliation.

In contrast with conflicts over relations with third countries, the
general patterns of outcomes in dyadic conflicts indicate that outcomes
tend to be closer to the objectives of the government that initiated the
interstate request. If initiation of an interstate request can be taken
as an index, albeit an imperfect one, of relative intensity, this indicates a certain degree of reciprocity in the pattern, with states tending
to win when they care more. But this does not hold in about a fifth
of the cases, three raised by Canada (agriculture, extraterritoriality,
SIU), and three by the United States (fishing zone, auto pact, Arctic
zone).

Another way of looking at the relationship is to see how the two
governments do when conflicts involve decisions that are within the
domestic (or joint) jurisdiction of the other state. Table 11 presents
five such cases from the prewar period with some possible explanations. The Americans prevailed in four that were in Canadian or joint
jurisdiction because they successfully threatened economic retaliation
in three; and in the fourth (fisheries), where the Canadians sought
American action, a variety of threatened linkages by Canada proved
insufficient to move the American position.[33] The one case within

---

[32] Peyton Lyon, *Canada in World Affairs, 1961-63* (Toronto: Oxford University
Press, 1968), pp. 42-45; also Peter C. Newman, *Renegade in Power* (Toronto:
McClelland and Stewart, 1963), pp. 336-39.

[33] In the pulpwood case, Secretary of State Hughes threatened "retaliation of a
far-reaching nature" (*FRUS, 1923*, vol. 1, p. 496). For the Canadian concern
about impending US tariff changes in the liquor smuggling case, see Richard Kottman. In the Trail Smelter case, the US "stressed the relationship between a trade
agreement and the pollution settlement"; see D. H. Dinwoodie, "The Politics of
International Pollution Control: The Trail Smelter Case," *International Journal*
27 (Spring 1972): 232. It is interesting that US companies fearing similar suits
helped the Canadian company during the 1937 hearings, but this transnational
alliance was at the implementation, not the political process, stage.

TABLE 11. SOME CAUSES OF OUTCOMES OF CONFLICTS IN 1920s AND 1930s

	Jurisdiction	Losing Government Split?	Low Cost or Salience to Loser?	Fear of Specific Retaliation	Fear of Link	De Facto Transnational Ally	Transnational Organization Role?	Transgovernmental Role?
US Outcomes (4)								
Fisheries	joint	no	no	—	—	—	—	—
Pulpwood	Canada	no	no	—	trade	—	—	—
Smuggling	Canada	no	no	—	trade	—	—	—
Trail Smelter	joint	no	no	—	trade	—	—	—
Canadian Outcomes (1)								
Liquor tax	United States	yes	no	no	general climate	—	Canadian distillers	State Department

United States jurisdiction in which Canadian objectives prevailed
(liquor tax) can be accounted for by the fact that the US government
was split and the Department of State was a transgovernmental ally
of Canada against the Treasury Department.[34]

The postwar picture is quite different. Table 12 presents five
cases involving matters within Canadian jurisdiction in which the
outcomes were closer to United States government objectives. Whereas
American success in the prewar cases was related to linking issues to
Canadian desire for access to the American market, the sources of
postwar success were more diverse. In only one case (magazine tax),
and that only in part, was fear of linkage to other trade issues a significant factor.[35] Political lobbying in Canada by *Time* and *Reader's
Digest* was important in the magazine tax case; and political pressure
in Canada by international unions was important in the Seafarers'
Union case.[36] Transnational and transgovernmental elite networks
contributed to the split and fall of the Diefenbaker government in the
nuclear weapons case.[37] In the final two cases, Gouzenko and extraterritoriality, Canada extracted some concessions but seems to have
indulged American objectives out of concern for the general climate
of relationship with the alliance leader.[38]

There are seven postwar cases involving matters within United
States or joint jurisdiction in which the outcomes are closer to the
objectives of the Canadian government (table 13). In four of these
cases the United States government (or governments, because the
state of Maryland was involved) was divided and Canada benefited
from having transgovernmental allies. In addition, three of these
cases could be solved by the president at relatively low cost. In the
fourth case (Chicago water), American concern with the possibility

[34] Secretary of the Treasury Morgenthau told Canadian officials that the Treasury Department was handling the case, not the State Department, but Undersecretary of State William Phillips told Department of External Affairs officials
that the State Department was trying to kill the tax and Canada should hold off
its appeal to Roosevelt until the right moment. *FRUS 1936*, vol. 1, p. 801.

[35] Denis Smith, *Gentle Patriot: A Political Biography of Walter Gordon* (Ed-
monton: Hurtig, 1973), p. 232. Also A. F. W. Plumptre and Pauline Jewett in
Stephen Clarkson, ed., *An Independent Foreign Policy for Canada?*, pp. 47, 52.
Peter C. Newman, *The Distemper of Our Times* (Toronto: McClelland and
Stewart, 1968), p. 225, cites a 1961 US linkage to defense contracts, but this was
difficult to confirm in interviews.

[36] David Kwavnick, *Organized Labour and Pressure Politics* (Montreal: McGill-
Queens University Press, 1972), chapter 6. Also, John Crispo, *The Role of International Unionism in Canada* (Washington: National Planning Association,
1967), p. 47.

[37] Peyton Lyon; Peter C. Newman, *Renegade in Power*.

[38] See James R. Wagner, "Partnership: American Foreign Policy toward
Canada, 1953-1957" (Ph.D. dissertation, University of Denver, 1966).

TABLE 12. CASES WITH OUTCOMES CLOSER TO UNITED STATES GOVERNMENT'S OBJECTIVES, 1950-69

	Jurisdiction	Canadian Government Split?	Low Cost or Salience to Prime Minister?	Canada Fear Specific Retaliation?	Canada Fear Link?	De Facto Transnational Ally in Canada	Transnational Organization Role?	Transgovernmental Role?
Military/Political (4)								
Gouzenko	Canada	no	no	no	—	no	—	—
Extraterritoriality	Canada	no	no	no	—	no	Corporations	—
Nuclear weapons	Canada	yes	no	no	—	yes	—	military
Seafarers' Union	Canada	no	no	no	—	yes	SIU	—
Economic (1)								
Magazine tax	Canada	yes	no	yes	Auto pact	yes	*Time, Reader's Digest*	—
Totals (5)		2	0	2	1	3	3	1

TABLE 13. CASES WITH OUTCOMES CLOSER TO CANADIAN GOVERNMENT OBJECTIVES, 1950-69

	Juris-diction	US Gov-ernment Split?	Low Cost or Sa-lience to President	Fear Specific Retalia-tion?	Fear Link?	De Facto Transna-tional Ally	Transna-tional Organi-zation Role?	Transgov-ernmental Role?
Military/Political (2)								
BOMARC	United States	yes	yes	—	—	Boeing	Boeing	military
Security information	United States	yes	yes	security information	—	—	—	State Department
Economic (5)								
Chicago water	joint	yes	no	Columbia River	DEW Line	hydro	—	State Department
Carlings	United States	yes	yes	US invest.	—	—	—	State Department
Oil	United States	no	no	pipeline	defense	northern oil refiners	—	—
Lumber	United States	no	no	—	—	—	IWA, Crown Zellerbach	—
Auto Pact	joint	no	no	auto tariff	—	auto companies	auto companies	—
Totals (7)	4	3	5	2	4	3	4	

of Canadian linkage to higher priority objectives such as the Columbia River and construction of the DEW Line seems to have played a role.[39] In addition, there were domestic interests in the United States pressing for the same outcome that Canada preferred. Indeed, such de facto allies played a role in four of the cases. In three cases (BOMARC, lumber, auto pact) lobbying inside the United States by Boeing, International Woodworkers Association, Crown Zellerbach, and the auto companies strengthened the Canadian position.[40] Perhaps most striking, however, is the existence of a Canadian capability to subtly hint at possible retaliation and linkage. Unless guarantees were received, Canada threatened to cut off cooperation in security information.[41] The possibility of Canada diverting the Columbia River played a role in the Chicago water case. Possible retaliation against US corporations in Canada played a role in the Carlings case.[42] The possibility of building a cross-country pipeline that would result in the exclusion of Venezuelan oil from eastern Canada was part of the bargaining over exemption from oil quotas; and the possibility of a highly protected automobile industry was hinted at during negotiations on the auto pact.[43] Credible threats helped to redress the asymmetry in resources. Sometimes beavers bite.

Table 14 summarizes the cases in which transnational organizations were either a necessary condition in determining the outcome of the political process or were a major contributory factor. Transnational organizations played an active role in the political process in six of the ten cases, two primarily in Canada, two primarily in the United States, and two in both countries. In four other cases, the transnational organization was less an actor in the political process than an instrument of governments, used twice by the United States and twice by Canada.

Important Cases and Transnational Politics

It can be argued, however, that the Canadian government does well in unimportant cases but not in those of major importance.

---

[39] Ibid., pp. 157-58.

[40] On Boeing's lobbying, see Jon B. McLin, *Canada's Changing Defense Policy, 1957-63* (Baltimore, Md.: The Johns Hopkins Press, 1957), p. 91ff.; on the International Woodworkers, see Crispo, p. 33. Also based on interviews.

[41] Eayrs, *Canada in World Affairs*, pp. 153-60; Wagner, chapter 7.

[42] Eayrs, p. 128.

[43] On replacing Venezuelan oil, see Lloyd, p. 86. During the auto negotiations the Canadians hinted at the possibility of a highly protected market like that of Mexico. As one participant put it in an interview, "we could occasionally point to our sombrero under the table."

TABLE 14. TEN CASES IN WHICH TRANSNATIONAL ORGANIZATIONS
PLAYED MAJOR ROLE IN PROCESS, 1950-69

OUTCOME CLOSER TO OB- JECTIVES OF :	IMPORTANCE OF TRANS- NATIONAL ORGANIZA- TION TO OUTCOME	CASE	TRANSNATIONAL ORGANIZATION LOBBIED	Political Role
				TRANS- NATIONAL ORGANIZA- TION USED BY GOVERNMENT
Equal	contributory	1. Columbia River	Kaiser and Brit- ish Columbia	—
United States	necessary	2. Magazine tax	*Time, Reader's Digest* in both	—
Canada	contributory	3. Oil import quotas	Oil companies in US	—
United States	necessary	4. Extraterritorial controls	—	United States
Canada	necessary	5. BOMARC pro- curement	Boeing in both	—
Canada	contributory	6. Lumber imports	Union and corp. in US	—
United States	necessary	7. Seafarers' Union	Union in Canada	—
Equal	necessary	8. Payments guide- lines	—	United States
Canada	necessary	9. Auto pact	—	Canada
Canada	contributory	10. Artic zone	—	Canada

NOTE: This is a minimal list; transnational organizations played some part in
several other cases but did not meet these levels of causal importance.

Table 15 presents cases selected because of their long-run importance
to Canada's autonomy as a nation.[44] The United States did better in
these cases than it has done generally in the postwar period. Nonetheless, the difference is not dramatic, with the United States coming out
ahead in four cases, Canada ahead in three, and three equal. More
telling about asymmetry is that while Canada came out ahead in two
cases that were in US or joint jurisdiction, the United States came out
ahead in four cases that were in Canadian jurisdiction. In two of
these cases (magazine tax and SIU), one could argue that US-based
transnational organizations were the real winners. In two others
(extraterritoriality, nuclear weapons), the United States government's objectives were served by its ability to influence transnational

[44] I am grateful to Peyton Lyon and Garth Stevenson of Carleton University and
John Trent of the University of Ottawa for helping me to select the cases in
table 14.

TABLE 15. TEN MAJOR CONFLICTS AFFECTING CANADIAN AUTONOMY

Jurisdiction	Outcome Closer to Objectives		Transnational/ Transgovernmental Agenda	Transnational/ Transgovernmental Process	Transnational Organization/ Transgovernmental Win/Lose	Government Use of Transnational Organization/ Transgovernmental
		1950s				
Joint	equal	Columbia River	—	transnational organization	lose (Kaiser)	—
Canada	United States	Magazine tax	transnational organization	transnational organization	win (*Time*)	—
United States	Canada	Oil imports	transnational flow	transnational organization	—	Canada
Canada	United States	Extraterritoriality	transnational organization	transnational organization	—	United States
		1960s				
Canada	United States	Nuclear arms	transgovernmental	transgovernmental	[win (pronuclear)]	United States
Canada	United States	Seafarers' Union	transnational organization	transnational organization	win (SIU)	—
United States	equal	Interest tax	transnational flow	—	—	—
United States	equal	Guidelines	transnational organization	transnational organization	—	United States
Joint	Canada	Auto pact	transnational flow	transnational organization	win (auto companies)	Canada
Canada	Canada	Arctic zone	transnational organization	transnational organization	—	Canada

and transgovernmental actors.[45] On the other hand, it is also clear from table 14 that the Canadian government is able to use transnational organizations to achieve its objectives as well. In the oil case, lobbying in the United States by large northern refiners helped Canada.[46] In the auto pact, the letters of undertaking that Canada solicited from the auto companies [47] were a significant factor in ensuring its larger share of the joint gains. And in the Arctic pollution zone case, the fact that Humble Oil needed Canadian approval and support before it could undertake a second voyage greatly strengthened the de facto nature of Canadian claims.[48] In summary, transnational organizations prevented the Canadian government from obtaining its objectives in two important cases and served US objectives in another, but it is equally true that transnational organizations greatly enhanced the Canadian government's ability to achieve its objectives in three other cases.

If we compare the prewar and postwar conflicts that reached the presidential level, it is clear that transnational and transgovernmental interactions played a more important role in the postwar period. In the prewar period, transgovernmental interactions were important in the liquor tax case.[49] A transnational political role was that of US-owned power companies in Quebec in delaying the St. Lawrence Seaway. Roosevelt publicly warned Canadians against them.[50] This

[45] The pronuclear group in the Progressive Conservative party was reinforced by official and unofficial visits and communications with NATO and NORAD officials (from interviews in Ottawa).

[46] Lloyd says that the international oil companies provided "mild support," p. 86. Lobbying by northern US refiners was more important (from interviews in Washington).

[47] Carl Beigie, "The Automotive Agreement of 1965: A Case Study in Canadian-American Economic Affairs," in Richard A. Preston, ed., The Influence of the United States on Canadian Development (Durham, N.C.: Duke University Press, 1972), p. 118. A Canadian minister went over the head of GM Canada to negotiate directly with General Motors officials in New York. It is said that without the separate side agreements Canada would not have signed the intergovernmental agreement (from interviews in Ottawa). See also testimony in US Congress, Senate, Committee on Finance, United States–Canadian Automobile Agreement, Hearings Before the Committee on Finance on H.R. 9042, 89th Cong., 1st sess., September 1965, pp. 153-56.

[48] Richard B. Bilder, "The Canadian Arctic Waters Pollution Prevention Act: New Stresses on the Law of the Sea," Michigan Law Review 69 (November 1970): 4.

[49] In addition, transnational organizations played a very minor role in the political process. Seagrams gave a party for congressional employees. Phillips told Hume Wrong that such an effort to influence legislation was "not a pleasant thought," and Wrong replied that he was "frankly horrified" (FRUS 1936, vol. 1, p. 819).

[50] For Roosevelt's accusation and warning, see R. N. Kottman, "The Diplomatic Relations of the United States and Canada, 1927-1941" (Ph.D. dissertation, Vanderbilt University, 1958), pp. 364-66. There were also direct transgovernmental contacts between a New York congressman and Ontario Premier Hepburn in 1937. William R. Willoughby, The Saint Lawrence Seaway (Madison, Wis.: University of Wisconsin Press, 1961), chapter 12.

amounts to two of the eight cases in table 5. In the postwar period transnational organizations played a significant role in ten cases and transgovernmental relations played a major role in seven additional cases, adding up to more than half the total of 31 cases listed in tables 2, 3, and 4. And it is clear from table 15 that transnational relations played a significant role in all the most important postwar cases. The hypothesis of increased importance of transnational and transgovernmental relations in the political process is clearly sustained.

CONCLUSIONS

In summary, the cases indicate that transnational relations have increased in importance over time, but it is useful to distinguish between transnational flows and transnational organizations, and between importance at the stage of agenda formation and in the political decision-making process. In agenda formation, transnational *flows* were a relatively more important source of all the conflicts that reached the presidential level in the prewar period. This is partly a reflection of the isolationist policies of the two countries during that period. In the two postwar decades under examination, transnational relations contributed to placing half the cases on the agenda. The interesting change in a predicted direction was the increased importance of transnational *organizations* in the postwar period. At the political process stage, I found a clear increase in the importance of transnational organizations and of transgovernmental relations in the postwar period.[51]

Somewhat more surprising is that these cases do not support the hypothesis that transnational organizations strengthen the ability of the US government to achieve its objectives in bargaining with Canada (see table 16). Canada actually did better in cases in which transnational organizations played a significant role than in cases where they played no role in the political process. In a number of the cases inspected, transnational organizations proved to be entities with interests of their own that did not always coincide with the interests of the US government. This differentiation meant that in some cases the transnational organization improved rather than weakened the

[51] In an indirect sense, transnational organizations may have been more important in the prewar period than the cases indicate. I noted that the US was able to achieve its objectives in several instances through linking issues to the greater Canadian concern with access to the US market. President Hoover seemed quite unconcerned with the possibility of Canadian retaliation on tariffs. Part of the explanation may have been that American-based transnational corporations easily jumped Canadian tariff walls by direct investment. See Stephen Scheinberg, "Invitation to Empire: Tariffs and American Economic Expansion in Canada," *Business History Review* 47 (Summer 1973) : 233.

TABLE 16. PATTERNS OF OUTCOMES BY TRANSNATIONAL
AND TRANSGOVERNMENTAL ROLE

| | Outcomes Closer to Objectives | | |
	CANADA	UNITED STATES	EQUAL
1920-39			
Cases without transnational or transgovernmental role (6)	1	5	—
Cases with transnational organization role (1)	—	—	1
Cases with transgovernmental role (1)	1	—	—
Total (8)	2	5	1
1950-69			
Cases without transnational or transgovernmental role (14)	5	7	2
Cases with transnational organization role (10)	5	3	2
Cases with transgovernmental role (7)	4	1	2
Total (31)	14	11	6

SOURCE: Tables 2, 3, 4, 5.

position of the Canadian government in bargaining with the United States government. As one American official said of the role of the companies in the auto pact, "We knew about the Canadian plan to blackjack the companies, but we expected the companies to be harder bargainers. They didn't have to give away so much. It must have been profitable to them."

Canada did even better in cases involving transgovernmental relations, coming out ahead in five of eight cases in which transgovernmental relations played an important role, whereas the United States came out ahead in only one such case. Relative governmental cohesion plays an important part in determining outcomes. In the cases inspected, the United States proved to be less cohesive than Canada. In part this is a function of sheer size and of presidential as contrasted with parliamentary government, but it is also a function of the asymmetry of attention. The United States government does not focus on Canada the way the Canadian government focuses on the United States. Greater cohesion and concentration help to redress the Canadian disadvantage in size. The Cuban Missile Crisis and nuclear arms cases are informative exceptions to this rule, in that the ideology of an interdependent defense community faced with a common threat helped to legitimize the transgovernmental defense coalition.

One must be careful not to read more into these conclusions than the data justify. It does not follow, for example, that transgovernmental relations benefit the smaller country overall. On the contrary, close contact among relatively autonomous agencies may lead to avoidance of interstate conflict by understating Canadian objectives. This may have been true of the Columbia River; and a transgovernmental military coalition pressed Diefenbaker into the early acceptance of nuclear weapons that he later came to regret.[52] Canadian dependence on transgovernmental communication of relevant information can limit Canadian government options.[53] Similarly, while the bargaining position of the Canadian government may have been strengthened rather than weakened in somewhat more cases, it is often more costly to the more penetrated nation to sustain even a few major losses. Indeed, the costs of losses in the SIU and magazine tax cases are regarded as very heavy by Canadian nationalists. Such losses sustain a structure that encourages transnational coalitions that affect Canadian society even though they may not lead to intergovernmental conflict.[54] With these caveats in mind, however, it is worth repeating the conclusion derived from table 16 that transnational and transgovernmental relations on the average improved rather than weakened the bargaining position of the Canadian government in achieving its objectives in high-level conflicts.

The argument at the outset of this essay was that interstate politics among highly interdependent advanced industrial societies may be characterized by the absence of force, but there is not an indifference to power. Replacing the classical recourse to force, one finds more subtle sources of power such as, in some cases, the ability to use the activities of transnational and transgovernmental actors, as well as veiled suggestions of possible retaliation in situations of uneven interdependence. Canada's success in governmental bargaining under conditions of great asymmetry stemmed partly from greater

[52] See Larratt Higgins's argument in Ian Lumsden, ed., *Close the 49th Parallel* (Toronto: University of Toronto Press, 1970); but compare with John V. Krutilla, *The Columbia River Treaty* (Baltimore, Md.: The Johns Hopkins Press, 1967), chapter 10. On nuclear weapons, see McLin.

[53] See General Foulkes, "The Complications of Continental Defence," in Livingston Merchant, ed., *Neighbors Taken for Granted* (New York: Praeger, 1966), p. 101, where he states: "In the assessment of the threat Canada is dependent upon the United States for virtually all principal intelligence estimates."

[54] It is interesting to note that in the sequel to the magazine tax case, major Canadian magazine publishers formed an alliance with *Time* and *Reader's Digest* to compete for advertising against the television media. See Abraham Rotstein and Gary Lax, eds., *Independence—the Canadian Challenge* (Toronto: Committee for an Independent Canada, 1972), p. 218.

concentration and cohesion, but also from the fact that on many issues it had sufficient resources (and credibility) to deter American actions (see table 13). Canada is smaller, but not powerless. On many issues, particularly economic ones, it is large enough to be able to threaten significant retaliation. In an analogy to the interstate politics of force, Canada has sufficient deterrence in a number of economic issue areas.

Deterrence is successful, however, insofar as such weapons are not used. When a major weapon is used, there is a high risk that a relationship involving joint gains may be transformed into one where the joint gains are destroyed or joint losses ensue. The diplomatic norms that have characterized the postwar Canadian-American relationship ("Thou shalt not openly threaten; thou shalt not link extraneous issues")[55] have played an important role in ensuring that the relationship did not deteriorate into one involving joint losses, as it did for example on the trade issue in the 1920s and early 1930s.

One of the striking contrasts between the prewar and the postwar periods is the frequency of linkage of extraneous issues in the prewar era and the relative absence of such linkages (so far as I can tell without the documents) in the postwar period. In the 1920s and 1930s, the United States quite frequently linked extraneous issues in order to exert the leverage of its overall preponderance, particularly in trade, against Canada (see table 11). Canada also tried linking issues (usually linking subissues within issues such as salmon and halibut fisheries, or Trail Smelter pollution and Detroit air pollution), but without success. In the postwar period up to 1970, explicit linkages for bargaining purposes have generally been taboo, thus restraining the United States from using this means of redressing Canadian advantages in particular issues.

The norms that helped preserve the joint gain structure of the postwar relationship arose out of a sense of common interest developed during a close wartime and cold-war alliance. Both sides were interested in preserving the alliance and the general structure of the relationship. As the leader of a global alliance, however, the United States devoted less attention to the Canadian-American component of the relationship than Canada did and more attention to the overall structure. Maintenance of an overall structure of relationships is a task of leadership, and one of the costs of leadership is acceptance of some sacrifices in the distribution of gains in order to preserve the structure that maintains joint gains. It is interesting that in the 1950s Canada seems to have made equal or greater sacrifices to preserve the overall structure of relations but that this pattern changed in the 1960s. In any case, while not the direct cause of the outcomes in many

---

[55] See the discussion in the "Introduction" to this volume.

of the particular cases of high-level conflict that I inspected, this general question of structure and leadership helps to account for the difference in linkage norms and behavior before and after World War II, and thus helps to explain the striking improvement in the number of outcomes favorable to Canada in the postwar as contrasted with the prewar period.

By the early 1970s, however, a number of frictions had contributed to the erosion of the sense of political-military alliance both in Canada and in the United States, and a number of Americans felt that the US could not (or should not) continue to pay the costs of alliance leadership.[56] One of the indications of this greater American nationalism was a tendency toward linkage of issues, particularly by the Treasury Department.

A critical question for the future is whether the norms that have helped to preserve the joint gain nature of the relationship will survive the decline of a sense of political-security alliance and continue as the basis for the economic relationship. This depends also on patterns of Canadian nationalism, and it is interesting to speculate about what effect transnational flows and organizations will have on Canadian national identity, the integration of the two countries, and Canada's autonomy as a nation. George Ball has speculated, for example, that a high degree of political integration will follow economic integration.[57] And economic integration has been increasing. Exports to the United States rose from half to over two-thirds of Canada's total exports between 1948 and the present. Each country is the other's largest trading partner, and exports to each other as a percent of total US and Canadian exports rose from 26 percent to 36 percent during the decade of the 1960s. This is a level of trade integration approaching that of the European Common Market, and greater than in several free-trade areas.[58]

Will political integration follow? It is useful to distinguish three types of political integration: (1) the creation of common institutions; (2) coordination of policies (with or without institutions); (3) development of attitudes of common identity and loyalty. For voluntary assimilation to occur, all three types must develop. Yet when we look at the Canadian-American case, there is a striking absence of the first and third types. Indeed, one could argue that while

---

[56] See Canadian-American Committee, *The New Environment for Canadian-American Relations* (Washington, D.C.: Canadian-American Committee, 1972).

[57] George Ball, *The Discipine of Power* (Boston: Little, Brown & Co., 1968), p. 113.

[58] The analogous figure for the European Common Market in 1966 was 43 percent; European Free Trade Association, 25 percent; Latin American Free Trade Association, 10 percent.

there has been some increase in the second type, there has been a *decrease* in the third type. The relationship to the growth of transnational interactions may not be coincidental. Indeed, some integration theorists have hypothesized that under conditions of asymmetry, the effect of rapidly rising transnational interactions may be to stimulate nationalism.[59] One is tempted to go a step further and speculate that highly visible transnational corporations accentuate this effect. It is intriguing that the growing intensity of English-Canadian nationalism as shown in public opinion polls [60] and the gradual development of government programs for greater control of transnational organizations and communications follow the great economic boom of the early 1950s, when direct investment grew to exceed portfolio investment (1950) and nonresident control grew to more than 50 percent of Canadian manufacturing (1956).[61] If transnational interactions have such effects under conditions of great asymmetry, then the Canadian-American case illustrates an important problem involved in structuring norms and institutions to cope with interdependence among advanced industrial societies.

Whatever the causal role of the transnational corporation, the argument that changing nationalist attitudes affected Canadian government policies seems to be borne out in patterns visible in the high-level conflicts examined here. As noted above, the agenda switched from one primarily set by American government actions in the 1950s to one reflecting more Canadian government actions in the 1960s. Over the same period, there was also an increase in outcomes closer to the Canadian government's objectives. Perhaps even more indicative is the fact that while there were a number of solutions to high-level conflicts in the late 1950s and early 1960s that could be termed integrative in their effects (oil import exemption, balance-of-payments measures, air routes, auto pact), these types of solution have been notably absent in more recent years.[62] Increasing transnational interactions create societal interdependence and policy interdependence, but they do not by themselves create a transnational sense of political community. The advanced industrial world may be a world of transnational relations, but so far the transnational world in North America is not a postnationalist world. The eagle may soar; beavers build dams.

[59] See Joseph S. Nye, *Peace in Parts: Integration and Conflict in Regional Organizations* (Boston: Little, Brown & Co., 1971), chapters 2 and 3.

[60] See the article by John Sigler and Dennis Goresky in this volume.

[61] See Isaiah A. Litvak, Christopher Maule, R. Robinson, *Dual Loyalty: Canadian-U.S. Business Arrangements* (Toronto: McGraw-Hill, 1971), chapter 1.

[62] This has not been for lack of opportunity. For example, a Canadian regional subsidy to a Michelin tire factory was treated as an export subsidy by the US which imposed countervailing duties. A decade earlier one might have seen an integrative response to this situation of policy interdependence.

PART V
CONCLUSIONS

CANADA AND THE UNITED STATES: THEIR BINDING FRONTIER

Annette Baker Fox and Alfred O. Hero, Jr.

Without a counterpart for any other country there is in the United States government a deputy assistant secretary of state for Canadian affairs, a post created in December 1972. This, like the lower-level Office of Canadian Affairs established in 1965, was an institutional recognition of the increasing importance of Canadian-American relations.[1] Were these offices also harbingers of increased state-centric attention to relations between the two countries, which until then had been subject primarily to transnational and transgovernmental management of affairs? Or were they rather recognition that in addition to the uniquely complex web of transborder relationships outside of or at levels below those dealt with by high political authorities, state-centric relations were increasing because of the importance of and increase in unofficial and bureaucratic transactions?[2]

Many of the preceding articles, in fact most of them, comment on the emergence of a "new era" in Canadian-American relations marked by alienation and unilateral action. Most do not suggest that it is part of a recurring cycle of easy and difficult relations, although farsighted John Holmes did refer to times past when "the game was exceedingly rough." Reading the memoirs of a former Canadian ambassador to Washington, Arnold Heeney, one sees 1960-62 as a

Annette Baker Fox is a research associate in the Institute of War and Peace Studies at Columbia University, and Alfred O. Hero, Jr., is director and secretary of the World Peace Foundation in Boston. Together with Joseph S. Nye, Jr., they are the editors of this volume.

[1] Another was the appointment as ambassador to Canada in February 1974 of a career diplomat who had been undersecretary of state for political affairs, the third highest post in the Department of State.

[2] As the first occupant of the new State Department position commented, all the while a " 'so-called impasse on trade issues' " was being discussed by the media, " 'trade worth $23,000,000,000 has crossed the border' " (interview with Mr. Rufus Smith in *Chronicle-Herald* [Halifax], 27 January 1972, quoted in *International Canada*, December 1972, p. 227).

decidely low point, and notes its coincidence with the premiership of
a Canadian politician who had his troubles with other countries too.[3]
Many of the contributors to this volume pointed to August 1971 and
President Nixon's New Economic Policy as the watershed for the era
they have noted. With somewhat less justification other allies of the
United States were at least equally traumatized by the president's
actions. In seeking trends and the explanation for them, we should
not overlook the impact of particular leaders who set the tone for
their administration. As John Sigler and Dennis Goresky noted, the
acerbities and affronts attributed to high-level politicians and underscored in the media were not much reflected in public opinion polls of
Canadians, while the Americans polled have continued to reveal their
usual ignorance of things Canadian.

STATE-CENTRIC VS. TRANSNATIONAL RELATIONS

The articles in Part III address themselves by design to issue
areas; by definition this emphasizes interactions in which the two
national governments are not in agreement. Given the official governmental sources on which the contributors often relied, they necessarily
highlighted governmental actions and almost involuntarily concentrated on state-centric behavior. The very nature of the transnational
relationship presents great difficulties to researchers, preventing them
from easily identifying, much less appraising, events that go un-
marked because they are so natural and so taken for granted. Such
events are also unlikely to appear in the other major information
source, newspaper accounts, which tend to report mainly controversial
matters.

Thus the authors could not, or at any rate did not, pay as much
attention as may be desirable to interactions that took the form of
transnational problem solving rather than intergovernmental bargaining over disagreements. (Some exceptions to these observations
appear in the Holsti-Levy, Scott, and Swanson essays.) Furthermore,
they were writing in the heat of a particular political climate that is
set more by state-centric actions than transnational behavior. In the
conduct of Canadian-American relations, the atmosphere is created
by high government officials. On the American side, these leaders are

[3] Arnold Heeney, *The Things That Are Caesar's, Memoirs of a Canadian Public
Servant* (Toronto: University of Toronto Press, 1972), pp. 163 ff. As one of the
prestigious authors of the report that was to point to ways to improve Canadian-
American relations, and one who was appalled at widespread Canadian misrepre-
sentation of one recommendation about "quiet diplomacy," he wondered if "spasms
of emotional outburst among Canadians against their big neighbor were not
endemic, an inevitable aspect of our national psychology" (p. 198).

usually unconversant with Canadian affairs and often make decisions intended for general application without much consideration for their specific impact on the smaller Canadian neighbor. This is one way a transnational issue becomes politicized.

Joseph Nye's examination of interstate conflicts that arose out of transnational relations does in fact cover a half century. To stress the importance of the latter he turned to diplomatic exchanges, which are essentially state-centric acts. Nevertheless, this method does reveal the prevalence of economic and social issues. These issues touch individuals and specific interest groups directly, and the immediacy of their effects helps to account for their frequency and intensity in comparison with defense and foreign policy matters related more to world politics than to bilateral concerns. Perhaps for this reason, in his article on defense Roger Swanson could concentrate on transgovernmental relations that were not high politics. In the same vein John Holmes commented that the North American Air Defense Command (NORAD), once a somewhat political issue for Canadians, had taken on the appearance of a convenient and practical mechanism.

Attention in this volume has focused on both nongovernmental interactions and those involving officials below the highest policy-making levels, in addition to the normal relations between central governments. For some issue areas, such as defense and the law of the sea, the role of central governments has been very large, because of the nature of the activity. In others the central governments' role has been minimal, as in labor and until recently in most environmental questions. Although monetary regulation is inevitably a state function, the role of central governments in matters of capital flows and foreign investment is also of recent origin and not dominating. The same is true for energy questions. Sometimes national governments become involved as a necessary response to new requirements for regulation of increased transnational relations. On other occasions transnational relations are affected because national governments take initiatives in a broader policy arena, such as general efforts to alter the balance of payments or military strategy. Yet the capacity of the highest policy levels in Canada and the United States to regulate or counteract transnational and transgovernmental relations between the two countries has never kept up with changes in the pattern of these relationships. It falls further behind with new areas of interaction opening up, as Anthony Scott pointed out in his discussion of environmental and fisheries questions.

POLITICIZATION

Although national government involvement does not by itself

politicize an issue, many of the cases dealt with in this volume represent efforts by private groups to expand their influence by bringing the matter to the attention of the highest decision makers.[4] On other occasions the central governments have initiated the controversial action. Several contributors put their fingers on a basic source of tension between Canada and the United States, the center-periphery relationship in which the smaller power is regarded as dependent on the greater power, a situation complicated by center-periphery relationships inside each of the two countries.[5] This tension is unlikely to disappear but instead will probably grow as Canadians gain increasing confidence, already observable, in controlling their own affairs. Where there was a confrontation with the United States government in recent years, as Joseph Nye and David Leyton-Brown among others noted, the Canadian government usually achieved its objective if it chose to press hard enough and to incur whatever costs might be exacted. When it did not succeed in altering American actions to suit Canadian desires, the reason might have been uncertainty and ambiguity of intention, as in the case of the Alaska pipeline (described by both Messrs. Greenwood and Dobell).

Sometimes the Canadian government has been pushed by Canadian groups into taking a political stand, as in the case of the Seafarers' International Union conflicts on the Great Lakes. The Trudeau government's dependence on the more nationalistic New Democratic party to stay in power from after the 1972 elections until election of a Liberal majority Parliament in July 1974 ensured a more politically aggressive stand during this period on some transnational issues. Sometimes, as in the case of unilaterally asserting some kind of jurisdiction over large expanses of coastal waters, the Canadian government finds an issue so popular that it cannot avoid confrontation with the United States government, which is often looking to the global implications if the Canadian government's position is accepted. The tendency for interest groups to organize, both nationally and transnationally, has also helped to politicize some issues formerly hardly articulated, as Joseph Nye pointed out. Sometimes, as indicated by Litvak and Maule and by Leyton-Brown, the Canadian government itself has taken a hand in purposely politicizing an issue. It may sponsor an investigation and report on a matter such as science in Canada or otherwise publicize a position, thus making more difficult—even unlikely—much concession to Americans when conflict develops. In

---

[4] Examples are the Mercantile Bank, the *Time* and *Reader's Digest* tax exemption, and the Michelin tire exports to the United States.

[5] In particular, John Holmes, Robert Gilpin, Robert Cox and Stuart Jamieson, Isaiah A. Litvak and Christopher J. Maule, and Anthony Scott.

other cases, as Holsti noted, the bureaucrats who had jurisdiction over some issue area worked with their counterparts across the border to *prevent* politicization.

In those cases involving overlapping jurisdictions within the Canadian federation, as in the areas of energy and foreign investment, issues became politicized for domestic reasons. While the effect might seem to weaken the Canadian government in confronting Americans, government or private, John Holmes pointed out that this very "looseness" in the Canadian constitutional system is a source of strength for genuine Canadian nationalism. Thus an internal Canadian center-periphery relationship in which the periphery enjoys much freedom of action may satisfy the desire for self-determination among many in the provinces, similar to that which nationalists seek in relationships between Canada and the United States. Thomas Levy's examination of provincial-state relations indicated that below the national level politicization was uncommon, although he noted that some provincial governments are making efforts to centralize what were formerly department-to-department relations with some American states.

Usually it was the Canadian government that politicized an issue; but this does not mean that the United States government was passive, only that the Canadians were not passive when the United States was attempting to expand its control. This was most noted in several touchy types of incidents involving multinational corporations. Through export controls (trading-with-the-enemy regulations), antitrust regulations, and capital outflow controls, the American-owned corporation in Canada was to be one instrument for furthering some wider American policy, usually with little effect except to irritate Canadians. On both sides of the border, though more publicly on the American side due to the role of Congress, domestic economic groups have sought protection against trade competition from the other country. This tendency attracted notoriety because of the inconsistency in United States policy in the cases of Michelin Tire and the Domestic International Sales Corporation (DISC); a political issue was bound to develop due to differing national interpretations of what constituted a legitimate subsidy.

Several authors found transnational coalitions that formed either to politicize an issue or to help resolve it once politicized. Among the more recent are environmental groups, which sometimes join forces across the border. Earlier the fact that such a large proportion of the oil industry in Canada was American owned helped to bring about exemption of Canada from import quotas imposed by the United States. Anthony Scott speculated about why such coalitions have not formed between American and Canadian fisheries. We might speculate about the contrast with transnational coalitions of banking and finance and treasury officials, which Gerald Wright and Maureen Molot described and evaluated in the successive settlements of the capital guidelines issue. Even more intriguing is the evidence provided by Cox and Jamieson that organized coalitions in the field of labor are beginning to lose their legitimacy in the eyes of some workers; the very fact of coalition has become politicized, though not through national government action. Peter Dobell pointed out some instances where the coalition included congressmen who supported some Canadian interest before their own body. Lobbying by interests from across the border is one method employed.

As indicated in the introductory chapter, deliberately linking issues as a means of political strategy does not characterize Canadian-American negotiations. Succeeding articles failed to establish evidence of such linkage. Opportunities may have arisen since actions in one issue area sometimes have by-product effects in another. For example, Cox and Jamieson explained that foreign investment and international unionism in Canada are intertwined because they have derived from a transnational economy, and Litvak and Maule showed how the practice of switching funds engaged in by multinational corporations has created problems for Canadian monetary and exchange-rate policy. However, it is neither in the interest of bureaucrats where they are involved in an issue to do anything but ensure that it is strictly channeled nor in the interest of the weaker country to permit any packaging of issues. The attempts by some high United States officials to link issues for bargaining purposes, made very infrequently, reveal that they know much less than subordinates about the way Canadians react.[6]

TRANSBORDER COOPERATION

Instances of transnational cooperation in a Canadian-American political controversy have been noted in this volume, but there are also other forms of transnational or transgovernmental cooperation on a more technical plane that are worthy of attention. Thomas Levy referred to a unique cultural example—Quebec-Louisiana cooperation in developing the French language in Louisiana. He also mentioned provincial-state collaboration in matters dealing with forest fire suppression, public health, transportation, and other welfare activities. Roger Swanson described ways in which Canadian and American defense officials have worked together to forward some common

[6] As the control over scarce resources increases Canadian bargaining power in the future, it is conceivable that linkages will no longer be eschewed.

interest or to help each other out. He pointed out how such trans-governmental relationships help to formulate some defense policy, facilitate its implementation, and resolve problems arising under it. Anthony Scott referred to several examples of formally organized collaboration in the management of fisheries and water resources. Holsti noted that the largest degree of "jointness" is to be found in bilateral activities that arise from geographical contiguity.

These authors suggested possible explanations for the success of certain kinds of transgovernmental collaboration, particularly if it is based on some kind of bilateral agreement. Cooperation between state and provincial officials has been facilitated by membership in the same professional associations, according to Levy. Professional identifica-tion is cited by Swanson as an important ingredient in defense offi-cials' cooperation, and Scott emphasized this in discussing the impor-tance of a common information network and of the experts' similarity of background and techniques in the case of fisheries and water man-agement. He also cited certain aspects of the milieu in which they operate as other conditions for success, e.g., similarities in taste in the populations affected, the pressure of third parties, and the existence of other kinds of transnational relations. Swanson also stressed the structure in which defense collaboration takes place, including the relatively small numbers of actors involved and their multiple roles, in their own system and in a bilateral organization. Both Swanson and Holsti noted the high technological content (as opposed to politi-cal) in the most successful cooperative activities.

This last condition is one emphasized both by Scott and by Holsti in their examination of the outstandingly successful bilateral organi-zation—the International Joint Commission. Although this organiza-tion remains with few counterparts elsewhere despite earlier Cana-dian and American enthusiasm to see it copied around the world, its functioning is of more than North American interest. The fact that under its aegis studies and recommendations are made by some of the very officials who will later be responsible for implementing policies accepted by the two governments is regarded as one ingredient in its success. The way in which hearings are conducted on the spot, thus folding in various local interest groups, is another. That the basic principles it is supposed to uphold were accepted prior to its function-ing is regarded as important by Holsti in explaining its success. In any case, the long tradition of the IJC has developed an esprit in which those associated with it point proudly to their record of problem solving without marked reference to the nationality of the actors.

The foregoing conditions for successful cooperation apply pri-marily to organized transgovernmental relations for some common interest. Yet the same conditions would surely help to explain the existence of transnational (unofficial) relations as well, especially since some of the cooperative arrangements between governments have included private members. One instance, however, where the transnational relations are unofficial—international labor unions—raises the question of who is cooperating against whom. Cox and Jamieson agreed that membership in such unions in Canada places some Canadian workers in an advantageous position relative to others. Similar criticism is often heard in Canada of Canadian affiliates of American-based multinational corporations, where some Canadians are presumed to benefit at the expense of others by their collaboration with Americans. Scott cited examples of transnational cooperation among private citizens concerned with the preservation of wildlife. In pointing out that with respect to environmental concerns the interest and expertise have flowed northward from the United States, he denied that the Americans were merely helping to clean up their own pollution; Canadians can also threaten the environment.

Why has transnational or transgovernmental cooperation been lacking in some issue areas? In the intriguing case of the uses of the sea, where the Canadian and American positions began to diverge in the late 1960s, Ann Hollick suggested one answer. She pointed out that the differences in decision-making processes prevented an effective collaboration between bureaucrats with their counterparts on the other side of the border. The Department of External Affairs very closely controlled Canadian policy, and private interests were more or less shut out, in contrast to the loose American system where major political controversies had to be ironed out nationally and when thus resolved made the United States position rigid. She also indicated the political weakness of marine scientists in Canada. Thus there were few chances for Americans to collaborate with those of like mind on the Canadian side. In his examination of the role of Congress in Canadian-American relations, Peter Dobell stressed the difference in the legislative systems and practices of the two countries as an impediment to understanding and appreciating the Canadian position as well as to cooperation. He believes that the Interparliamentary Group has nevertheless aided in communicating Canadian interests to those in Congress who could affect policy of concern to Canada. Here the American separation of powers may be an advantage: if Canada's interests are not being considered by high administrative officials, Congress provides another point of access.

On the administrative side, Wright and Molot commented that even though a transgovernmental association existed for capital movements, the joint Balance of Payments Committee, it was not composed of sufficiently high-level officials to affect United States policy in the late 1960s. In this issue area as in many others, cooperation may not

be forthcoming from officials who have other bureaucratic and substantive policy interests, whether or not they receive reminders of the
Canadian-American angle. Even the prestigious International Joint
Commission's early studies of water pollution warning of the dangers
for the Great Lakes (1915-18) were ignored, and in the 1960s it had
to start again to prepare for the Great Lakes Water Quality Agreement. This "idea whose time had come" was eventually embodied in
an agreement signed by the president and the prime minister in 1972.

Holsti and Greenwood, among others, mentioned issue areas in
which no Canadian-American intergovernmental organizations of note
exist, such as science and technology, transport, energy, and education. They could have named health, agriculture, and many others.
Neither they nor Scott envisioned that the existing list of institutions
is likely to be expanded in the near future, especially in view of the
fears of Canadian politicians to be linked with the United States in
any more formal organizations, their traditional preference for the
ad hoc approach to cooperation, and the tendency, noted by others as
well, for the Canadian government to continue its efforts to break out
of the continental mold and form cooperative arrangements with other
countries.

COMPETITION

Some transnational relations represent neither cooperation nor
conflict but are essentially competitive. Despite persistent effort to
include in this volume an article devoted to trade, a separate discussion of this vital transnational activity is glaringly absent. Yet the
buyers and sellers across the border of these two countries engage in
more cross-border business than anywhere else in the world through
a competitive free enterprise system, even if the competition is regulated. Perhaps the very complexity, pervasiveness, and size of this
trade impede succinct appraisal, just as the Trudeau government's
six-part *Foreign Policy for Canadians* review omitted a study of relations with the United States until the secretary of state for external
affairs was pressed into providing such an overview two years after
the original studies were published.[7] A few aspects of this transnational trade are touched on in some of the foregoing articles, including petroleum, the automobile pact, the defense production sharing
program, and the exchange of electric power through transborder
power grids. Robert Gilpin started with the basic factor that Canada

[7] To be found in *International Perspectives*, Autumn 1972.

and the US together form a highly interdependent economy in which production and sales are intertwined so intimately that a strong political thrust is necessary to break the transnational links between the two countries or even to alter them significantly. What has become a political issue in Canada, foreign direct investment, was rooted in this continental trade system, since only a portion of it crosses the border without customs duties. Once foreign-controlled multinational corporations became so strong in Canada, Litvak and Maule pointed out, the already weaker Canadian capacity for entrepreneurship was further debilitated in the competitive struggle. John Holmes observed that the more prosperous Canada becomes from its increasing economic power based on trade, the more vulnerable it is, especially to American competitive moves. He added that this dependency is probably more basic than that complained of concerning American direct investment in Canada. One of the transgovernmental organizations listed by Holsti, the joint Ministerial Committee on Trade and Economic Affairs, was created in 1953, a time of particular acrimony, to discuss matters in this issue area. But no amount of organizational consultation can do more than moderate and regulate what is essentially a competitive relationship between private enterprises.

Beginning in the 1960s this relationship between the two countries has changed qualitatively as well as quantitatively. Thus the customary deficit in Canada's trade balance with the United States shifted to a surplus at the end of the decade and was one factor in United States leaders' refusal to grant the usual exemption to its best trading partner when the New Economic Policy was adopted in August 1971. Noteworthy was the major source of the Canadian trade surplus, since it was produced by a kind of modified free-trade arrangement, the automobile pact. The balance has shifted back, but experts disagree on how long the United States will not be in deficit. In any case, the new scarcities in natural resources, especially energy sources and increasingly industrial raw materials, will be additional causes of competition—and political conflict—between the two countries. Canada is rich in many of these highly valued commodities and is the principal foreign supplier to the United States. Thus the old controversies over Canadian access to American markets for sellers of such commodities are likely to be replaced by new ones concerning access for American buyers. These will probably be reinforced by Canadian claims for access for manufactured goods. The growing Canadian interest in processing more of the raw material before export is likely to run up against United States tariff barriers, which for the most part do not exist for the unprocessed commodities. Meanwhile Canada's bargaining position will be strengthened, as would competition as well as United States demand for industrial raw materials continue to grow.

Trade inevitably raises the questions of costs and gains. Some of the authors tackled the elusive question of the distribution of benefits in examining transnational relations in their issue area. So subjective an evaluation is difficult under any circumstances, even when broken down into specific class and interest groups, as was done by Cox and Jamieson, and by Sigler and Goresky, or by kinds of values, only one of which is economic, as recognized by John Holmes and Robert Gilpin among others. Such an appraisal is even more hazardous when the element of time is introduced.

Ted Greenwood's tentative judgment about costs and gains in the energy field emphasizes this important factor. He wrote of the difference in discount rates: American corporations operating in the energy field in Canada are anxious to make their profits in the short run while many Canadian interests are looking to long-run benefits that run counter to the current objectives of the multinational corporations. Since in many respects Canada is still a developing country, the time lag is basic to a number of issues arising between that country and its more advanced neighbor, especially in the field of natural resources, including water. Canadians need time to catch up in the competition. Their efforts to protect a future interest by controlling the flow of energy resources southward may be the precursor of restraints on the export of other raw materials, especially nonrenewable ones they would like to process themselves either for the Canadian market or for export in more finished form.

Another manifestation of the importance of time is the lag in perception as information reaches the Canadian side, a chronic source of misunderstanding. More than one Canadian author in this volume referred to a bill before Congress that would be injurious to Canadian competitors as though it were about to be passed, whereas knowledgeable Americans believe it to be moribund. The same lag in perception may be seen on the American side, as political leaders are only now realizing that, as John Holmes pointed out, Canada has become one of the world's major commercial powers. A few of those who did awake to this fact began to talk in late 1971 as if the competition with Canada was a zero-sum game, contrary to the way it has usually been played and will always have to be played if there is to be a game. Time is unlikely to alter the basic fact that Canada and the United States will continue for the foreseeable future to be each other's most important trading partner even if some diversification with other countries cuts down the proportions to some extent. Sigler and Goresky found a remarkable amount of public support for more liberalized trade between the two countries.

QUEBEC

A time bomb may be ticking on the Canadian side in the province whose existence perceptive Canadian elites have usually been obliged to consider when dealing with the United States. As Sigler and Goresky commented, on many questions of Canadian politics Quebec tends to influence Canada's agenda and limit its freedom of action. Americans, on the other hand, usually forget Quebec when contemplating Canadian matters. Cox and Jamieson made clear that this is a serious mistake when dealing with labor unions. These like many other aspects of Quebec life have evolved along different lines, alien not only to English Canada but also to the United States, while Quebec opinion on many different issues varies significantly from that in the rest of Canada, as suggested by survey findings cited by Sigler and Goresky. Daniel Latouche sketched for his readers one scenario if the present moderate independentist leadership of the Parti Québécois should come to power in Quebec; it contains sanguine views regarding future relations between an independent Quebec and the United States. Others less friendly to private enterprise and foreign direct investment can be imagined, especially if more leftist-inclined factions in the independentist movement should increase their influence. One nightmare of Canadians opposed to an independent Quebec is that such a change might bring in its wake fatal dismemberment of the rest of Canada, or at least greatly strengthen the regional interdependence of adjacent areas north and south of the border which already are sensing and responding to common concerns, as against trans-Canadian, east-west unity.

However, a less than completely separate but politically more autonomous Quebec, within the current federal system or a revised constitution, can also be conceived for the future.[8] Many influential Quebec opinion leaders and intellectuals do so in terms of greater provincial control over education, the mass media and cultural phenomena generally, industry and commerce, disbursement of federal funds for social welfare and the like, and more influence over immigration and foreign policy issues of particular interest to Quebec. Under these circumstances there could be substantial changes in relations with both governmental and private groups south of the frontier. But very few Quebec elites—political leaders, senior civil servants, intellectuals, or others of any political persuasion—have yet pondered this last question systematically; rather, they tend to concentrate on prob-

---

[8] See, for example, François Bouvier and André Donneur, "Relations Québec–Etats Unis: Perspectives d'Avenir" (tentative title), in *Choix* (Spring 1975), Centre Québécois des relations internationales, Québec, Canada.

lems of Quebec per se and its relations with Ottawa and (to a lesser degree) with the other Canadian provinces.

THE REST OF THE WORLD

Among the lacunae in this volume is the consideration of Canadian-American relations where other countries are also involved, especially in a global context. The major exception is Joseph Nye's tabulation of some foreign policy issues arising between Canada and the United States. Scott mentioned some transgovernmental organizations that include officials from other states as members. Litvak and Maule pointed out that some of the Canadian-American conflict arising over varying applications of antitrust rules requires a multilateral solution, a matter that is under study by the Organization for Economic Cooperation and Development. Yet in general each contributor dealt with his or her issue area in isolation in North America alone. Further research would be desirable on the roles of transnational and transgovernmental relations between Canada and the United States regarding issues outside North America, in formal multilateral institutions (including nongovernmental organizations) and in multilateral transnational and transgovernmental networks in which Canada and the United States are only two of the participants.

Had trade been covered in a separate article it would have been necessary to consider not only such bilateral transnational organizations as the Canadian-American Committee but also multilateral transnational and intergovernmental organizations. In such institutions as GATT, OECD, and UNCTAD, Canadian and American bureaucrats concerned with common problems have developed kinds of relationships that need further study. Whatever the trade conflicts between Canada and the United States, leaders in both countries who are interested in trade questions are inclined to agree that with respect to the rest of the world they should "speak with one voice" on the general rules of conduct.[9] This is likely to be especially true since they face the European Community as outsiders.

Only Ann Hollick dealt in this volume with Canada and the United States in the United Nations. Her article raises the question of whether or not having this international forum has accentuated differences in policy between the two countries with respect to the law of the sea. It is a place where Canada has found it politically useful to line up with countries not so well developed 'to call for very exten-

[9] As it was put in the Report on the Fifteenth Meeting, 4-8 April 1973, Canada–United States Interparliamentary Group, by Senator Yale W. McGee, chairman of the Senate delegation, US Senate, Committee Print, 93d Cong., 1st sess., 1973, p. 4.

sive jurisdiction out to sea. Yet in gathering allies in a multilateral context, Canada may lose an advantage enjoyed in such bilateral organizations as the International Joint Commission and the Permanent Joint Board on Defense, where it faces the United States in a working arrangement that reduces its inequality to a minimum.[10] Ann Hollick did mention that experts for different aspects of the uses of the sea have developed significant transgovernmental contacts on a personal basis during the many meetings on this subject, but here the Canadians and Americans associate with each other in the company of other experts from countries far away. Whether the same kinds of relations develop between other Canadian and American officials in different areas of United Nations activity needs further research.

CONCLUSIONS

Due partly to the gaps in its presentation, this volume has given a somewhat one-sided and incomplete view of transnational and transgovernmental relations between Canada and the United States. Besides the omission of those issue areas already noted, nothing has been presented on such subjects as culture, the mass media, education, population migration, and agriculture—to say nothing of sport. John Holmes and Anthony Soott touched briefly on different political aspects of the movement of people across the border, but no full-scale study appears. Some of the authors noted areas where much more information and study are desirable. These include comparisons with European experience in integrative types of behavior along the whole gamut of governmental concerns and the measurement of trends in such behavior (Holsti). More comparison with other pairs of neighboring countries would be useful. Also needed is more research on the conditions for successful transgovernmental organizations in areas such as Scott dealt with, fisheries, environment concern, and the like, and whether or not transnational relations in the same field enhance the effectiveness of such bilateral organizations. Swanson would like to see further work done on how transnational relations are transformed into transgovernmental relations and vice versa. And the complex questions of future Quebec relations with not only the United States but also *la francophonie* and the rest of the world require further intellectual attention.

Because of the inevitably fragmentary and noninclusive nature of this volume, it is hazardous to draw general themes from what has

---

[10] From his own experience Arnold Heeney made this judgment of the joint commissions (p. 201). However, a number of other Canadians do not accept the one-to-one personal relationships as ameliorating differences in bargaining power.

gone before. However, the contributors would probably all agree that transnational relations are increasing and so are state-centric issues between Canada and the United States. In some areas the very expansion of transnational relations has influenced the behavior of the central governments. The marked growth of both anglophone and francophone Canadian nationalism suggests the pull of politics against the tug of economics—though this is not a new phenomenon in the history of the two countries. What is novel is the attack by both countries on the traditional continental capital market which they have shared to mutual benefit. Canadians still sense a divergence of interests from some of those upheld on the other side of the border. Regardless of differences, however, they have an overriding concern that these be handled in an orderly fashion, with minimum recourse to unilateral action along beggar-thy-neighbor lines.[10] To deal systematically with issues inevitably arising from closer and closer ties is likely to require more negotiation between those in the higher levels of the two governments. To perform this task effectively, the leaders on both sides will need to be better informed of the perspectives obtaining on the other than they have sometimes been in the past.

Some of these observations apply equally well to other countries considered either from a bilateral or multilateral perspective. One rationale for this volume has been to seek knowledge that may hold for relationships among other developed countries as well. In particular, the role of the multinational corporation and of foreign direct investment in general as it appears in Canada may have portents for others, although there are few developed countries that have such rich natural resources so greatly in demand by other wealthy countries close by. There are no firm answers given as to the applicability of Canadian-American relations elsewhere, and much room for doubt remains.

What other two friendly countries share 4,000 miles of border? (Alaska adds another dimension, as Peter Dobell pointed out.) Where else is there such informality of official contacts? Where else does a country of modest influence share a continent virtually alone with a superpower, lacking realistic counterweights in alternative relationships with third powers? The problems presented by a bicultural and bilingual Canada, or even an autonomous province, make for a distinctive relationship with the giant neighbor, which shares the principal characteristics of only one of these Canadian cultures. And it is

[11] For example, on law of the sea issues Donald E. Milsten has pointed out that Canada and the United States have a joint interest in a stable international regime, whatever its rules ("The Law of the Sea: Implications for North American Neighbors," *American Review of Canadian Studies*, Autumn 1973, pp. 9-10). This observation is generally applicable to other issue areas as well.

sobering for regional (or international) integrationists to consider
that the strains visible in Canadian-American relations today are
due to a considerable extent to efforts to fragment a continental economic system, not to construct one.

So we end where we start. State-centric relations represent only
a very small aspect of the total relationship of Canada and the United
States, two countries that are held together by personal ties and
mutual concerns as much as any two other countries in the world.
Though bringing out some of the tensions, we hope this volume will
not threaten these bonds while shedding light on them. At least for
the authors they were strengthened in this transnational endeavor.

SELECTED BIBLIOGRAPHY OF LITERATURE ON CANADIAN–AMERICAN RELATIONS

The following bibliography is a selection of the major books, articles, government reports, and other documents to which the authors in this volume referred. It is by no means exhaustive. For example, newspaper articles, Canadian and United States bills and acts, legislative debates, some general works on theory, and many government reports are not included here. The reader should refer to the footnotes of the individual articles in this volume for further reference material on a particular aspect of Canadian-American relations.

BOOKS

Abrams, Matthew J. *The Canada–United States Interparliamentary Group*. Ottawa/Toronto: Parliamentary Centre for Foreign Affairs and Foreign Trade/Canadian Institute of International Affairs, 1973.

Adler-Karlsson, G. *Reclaiming the Canadian Economy: A Swedish Approach through Functional Socialism*. Toronto: House of Anansi Press, 1970.

Ball, George. *The Discipline of Power*. Boston: Little, Brown & Co., 1968.

Behrman, J. N. *National Interests and the Multinational Enterprise*. Englewood Cliffs, N.J.: Prentice-Hall, 1970.

Bergeron, Gérard. *Le Canada français après deux siècles de patience*. Paris: Seuil, 1967.

Bourgault, P. L. *Innovation and the Structure of Canadian Industry*. Ottawa: Information Canada, 1972.

Brebner, John B. *North Atlantic Triangle*. Toronto: McClelland and Stewart, 1968.

Brewster, Kingman, Jr. *Antitrust and American Business Abroad*. New York: McGraw-Hill, 1958.

——————. *Law and United States Business in Canada*. Montreal: Canadian-American Committee, 1960.

Brichart, Andrew A. *Option Canada*. Quebec: The Canada Committee, 1968.

Bryden, Kenneth. *Old Age Pensions and Policy Making in Canada*. Montreal: McGill-Queens University Press, 1974.

Burton, Thomas L. *Natural Resource Policy in Canada: Issues and Perspectives*. Toronto: McClelland and Stewart, 1972.

Canadian Institute of International Affairs. *International Canada*. Toronto: Canadian Institute of International Affairs, 1970.

Chandler, Alfred D. *Strategy and Structure*. Cambridge, Mass.: M.I.T. Press, 1962.

Christy, Francis T., Jr., and Scott, Anthony. *The Common Wealth in Ocean Fisheries*. Baltimore, Md.: The Johns Hopkins Press, 1965 and 1972.

Clarkson, Stephen, ed. *An Independent Foreign Policy For Canada?* Toronto: McClelland and Stewart, 1968.

Craig, Gerald M. *The United States and Canada*. Cambridge, Mass.: Harvard University Press, 1968.

Cox, Robert W., Harrod, Jeffrey, et al. *Future Industrial Relations: An Interim Report*. Geneva: International Institute for Labour Studies, 1972.
Crispo, John. *International Unionism—A Study in Canadian-American Relations*. Toronto: McGraw-Hill, 1967.
———. *The Role of International Unionism in Canada*. Washington, D.C.: National Planning Association, 1967.
Crutchfield, James A., and Pontecorvo, Giulio. *The Pacific Salmon Fisheries*. Baltimore, Md.: The Johns Hopkins Press, 1969.
Dauphin, Roma. *Les Options Économiques du Québec*. Québec: Editions Commerce, 1971.
de T. Glazebrook, G. P. *A History of Canadian External Relations*. 2 vols. Toronto: McClelland and Stewart, 1966.
Deutsch, Karl. *Nationalism and Social Communication*. Cambridge, Mass.: M.I.T. Press, 1953.
Dickey, John S., ed. *The United States and Canada*. Englewood Cliffs, N.J.: Prentice-Hall, 1964.
Dobell, Peter C. *Canada's Search for New Roles, Foreign Policy in the Trudeau Era*. London: Oxford University Press, 1972.
Doeringer, Peter B., and Piore, Michael J. *Internal Labor Markets and Manpower Analysis*. Lexington, Mass.: D. C. Heath, 1971.
Dofny, Jacques, et Bernard, Paul. *Le syndicalisme au Quebec: structure et mouvement*. Ottawa: Imprimeur de la Reine, 1970.
Easterbrook, W. T., and Watkins, M. H. *Approaches to Canadian Economic History*. Toronto: McClelland and Stewart, 1967.
Eayrs, James. *The Art of the Possible*. Toronto: University of Toronto Press, 1961.
———. *Canada in World Affairs, 1955-57*. Toronto: Oxford University Press, 1959.
———. *In Defence of Canada*. Vol. 1. Toronto: University of Toronto Press, 1964.
English, H. E. *Industrial Structure in Canada's International Competitive Position*. Montreal: Canadian-American Committee, 1964.
Gallup, George H. *The Gallup Poll: Public Opinion, 1935-71*. Vol. 3: *1959-1971*. New York: Random House, 1972.
Godfrey, David, and Watkins, Melvin, eds. *Gordon to Watkins to You*. Toronto: New Press, 1970.
Gordon, Walter L. *A Choice For Canada*. Toronto: McClelland and Stewart, 1966.
Hawtrey, R. G. *Economic Aspects of Sovereignty*. London: Longmans, Green & Co., 1952.
Heeney, Arnold. *The Things That Are Caesar's, Memoirs of a Canadian Public Servant*. Toronto: University of Toronto Press, 1972.
Innis, Harold A. *The Cod Fisheries*. Toronto: Ryerson Press, 1940.
Jamieson, Stuart M. *Times of Trouble: Labour Unrest and Industrial Conflict in Canada 1900-66*. Task Force on Labour Relations, Study No. 22. Ottawa: Information Canada, 1968.
Johnson, Harry. *The Canadian Quandary*. New York: McGraw-Hill, 1963.
Keohane, Robert O., and Nye, Joseph S., eds. *Transnational Relations and World Politics*. Cambridge, Mass.: Harvard University Press, 1972.
Kilbourn, William. *Pipeline*. Toronto: Clark, Irwin and Co., 1970.
Krutilla, John V. *The Columbia River Treaty*. Baltimore, Md.: The John Hopkins Press, 1967.
Kwavnick, David. *Organized Labour and Pressure Politics*. Montreal: McGill-Queens University Press, 1972.
Lasswell, Harold D., et al. *Language of Politics*. Cambridge, Mass.: M.I.T. Press, 1965.
Latouche, Daniel; Lord, G.; and Vaillancourt, J. G. *L'élection de 1970*. Montréal: Editions H.M.H., forthcoming.
Lea, Sperry. *A Canada-US Free Trade Arrangement*. Montreal: Canadian-American Committee, 1963.

Lemieux, Vincent, et al. *Une élection de réalignement*. Montréal: Editions de l'Homme, 1970.

Lévesque, René. *An Option for Quebec*. Toronto: McClelland and Stewart, 1968.

Levin, Malcolm, and Sylvester, Christine. *Foreign Ownership*. Don Mills, Ont.: Paperjacks, General Publishing Co., 1972.

Levitt, Kari. *Silent Surrender: The Multinational Corporation in Canada*. Toronto: Macmillan of Canada, 1970.

————. *Silent Surrender: The American Economic Empire in Canada*. Reprint edition. New York: Liveright, 1971.

Litvak, Isaiah A., and Maule, Christopher J. *Canadian Cultural Sovereignty: The "Time–Reader's Digest" Case Study*. New York: Praeger, 1974.

Litvak, Isaiah A.; Maule, Christopher J.; and Robinson, R. D. *Dual Loyalty: Canadian-U.S. Business Arrangements*. Toronto: McGraw-Hill, 1971.

Lloyd, Trevor. *Canada in World Affairs, 1957-59*. Toronto: Oxford University Press, 1968.

Logan, Harold A.; Ware, Norman J.; and Innis, Harold A. *Labour in Canadian-American Relations*. Toronto: Ryerson Press, 1937.

Lower, Arthur R. M. *The North American Assault on the Canadian Forest*. Toronto: Ryerson Press, 1938.

Lumsden, Ian, ed. *Close the 49th Parallel*. Toronto: University of Toronto Press, 1970.

Lyon, Peyton. *Canada in World Affairs, 1961-63*. Toronto: Oxford University Press, 1968.

McLin, Jon B. *Canada's Changing Defense Policy, 1957-1963*. Baltimore, Md.: The Johns Hopkins Press, 1967.

Marshall, Herbert, and Taylor, Kenneth. *Canadian-American Industry: A Study in International Investment*. New Haven, Conn.: Yale University Press, 1936.

Meadows, Dennis. *The Limits to Growth*. New York: Universe Books, 1972.

Merchant, Livingston, ed. *Neighbors Taken For Granted*. New York: Praeger, 1966.

Molot, Maureen Appel. *The Role of Institutions in Canada-U.S. Relations: The Case of North American Financial Ties*. Ottawa: Carleton University School of International Affairs Occasional Papers, No. 24, November 1972.

Morrisson, Robert N. *Corporate Ability at Bilingualism and Biculturalism*. Ottawa: Queen's Printer, 1970.

Munro, William B. *Seignorial System in Canada: A Study in French Colonial Policy*. New York: Russell and Russell, 1974.

Nelles, H. V. *Politics of Development: Forests, Mines and Hydro-Electro Power in Ontario*. Hamden, Conn.: Shoe String Press, 1974.

Newman, Peter C. *The Distemper of Our Times*. Toronto: McClelland and Stewart, 1968.

————. *Renegade in Power*. Toronto: McClelland and Stewart, 1963.

Nicolson, N. L. *The Boundaries of Canada*. Ottawa: Queen's Printer, 1964.

Nye, Joseph S., Jr. *Peace in Parts: Integration and Conflict in Regional Organization*. Boston: Little, Brown & Co., 1971.

Pearson, Lester B. *Mike: The Memoirs of the Right Honourable Lester B. Pearson*. Toronto: University of Toronto Press, 1973.

Preston, Richard A., ed. *The Influence of the United States on Canadian Development*. Durham, N.C.: Duke University Press, 1972.

Richardson, Boyce. *James Bay: The Plot to Drown the North Woods*. Toronto: Clark, Irwin and Co., 1972.

Rocher, Guy. *Le Québec en mutation*. Montréal: Editions H.M.H., 1973.

Rohmer, Richard. *Ultimatum*. Toronto: Clark, Irwin and Co., 1973.

Rosenberg, Milton J.; Verba, Sidney; and Converse, Philip E. *Vietnam and the Silent Majority*. New York: Harper and Row, 1970.

Ross, Arthur M., and Hartman, Paul T. *Changing Patterns of Industrial Conflict*. New York: Wiley, 1960.

Rotstein, Abraham, and Lax, Gary. *Independence—the Canadian Challenge*. Toronto: Committee for an Independent Canada, 1972.

Safarian, A. E. *The Performance of Foreign-Owned Firms in Canada.* Washington, D.C.: Canadian-American Committee, 1969.

Saint-Germain, Marcel. *Une économie à libérer.* Montréal: Les Presses de l'Université de Montréal, 1973.

Saywell, John, ed. *Canadian Annual Review for 1966.* Toronto: University of Toronto Press, 1967.

Schwartz, Mildred A. *Politics and Territory: The Sociology of Regional Persistence in Canada.* Montreal: McGill-Queens University Press, 1974.

Scott, Anthony. *Natural Resources: The Economics of Conservation.* Rev. ed. Toronto: McClelland and Stewart, 1973.

Skilling, H. Gordon. *Canadian Representation Abroad.* Toronto: Ryerson Press, 1945.

Smith, Denis. *Gentle Patriot: A Political Biography of Walter Gordon.* Edmonton, Alberta: Hurtig Publishers, 1973.

Stewart, Walter. *Trudeau in Power.* New York: Outerbridge and Dienstfrey, 1971.

Swanson, Roger Frank. *Canadian-American Summit Diplomacy: 1923-1973.* Toronto: McClelland and Stewart, forthcoming.

Thordarson, Bruce. *Trudeau and Foreign Policy.* Toronto: Oxford University Press, 1972.

Tremblay, Louis-Marie. *Idéologie de la CSN et de la FTQ, 1940-1970.* Montréal: Presses de l'Université de Montréal, 1972.

Tremblay, Rodrigue. *Indépendence et marché commun Québec–Etats Unis.* Montréal: Editions du Jour, 1970.

Wagner, Richard J. *Canada's Impact on United States Legislative Processes: The Chicago Diversion Bills.* Research Series #14. Tucson: University of Arizona, 1973.

Waterfield, Donald. *Continental Waterboy: The Columbia River Controversy.* Toronto : Clark, Irwin and Co., 1970.

Willoughby, William R. *The St. Lawrence Seaway: A Study in Politics and Diplomacy.* Madison, Wis.: The University of Wisconsin Press, 1961.

Wolfers, Arnold. *Discord and Collaboration.* Baltimore, Md.: The Johns Hopkins Press, 1962.

Wonnacott, Ronald J., and Wannacott, Paul. *Free Trade Between the United States and Canada: The Potential Economic Effects.* Cambridge, Mass.: Harvard University Press, 1967.

ARTICLES, AND ESSAYS CONTAINED IN LARGER WORKS

Bachrach, Peter, and Baratz, Morton. "Two Faces of Power." *American Political Science Review* 56 (December 1962) : 947-52.

Baldwin, David. "The Myths of the Special Relationship." In *An Independent Foreign Policy for Canada?* Edited by Stephen Clarkson. Toronto: McClelland and Stewart, 1968.

Beesley, J. A. "Rights and Responsibilities of Arctic Coastal States: The Canadian View." *Journal of Maritime Law and Commerce* 3 (October 1971).

Beigie, Carl. "The Automotive Agreement of 1965: A Case Study in Canadian-American Economic Affairs." In *The Influence of the United States on Canadian Development.* Edited by Richard A. Preston. Durham, N.C.: Duke University Press, 1972.

Bilder, Richard B. "The Canadian Arctic Waters Pollution Prevention Act: New Stresses on the Law of the Sea." *Michigan Law Review* 69 (November 1970).

Bonin, Bernard. "La firme plurinationale comme véhicule de transmission internationale de technologie." *Actualité Economique* 46, no. 4 (1971) : 707-25.

Breton, Albert. "The Economics of Nationalism." *Journal of Political Economy* 72, no. 2 (1964) : 376-86.

Caves, Richard E., and Reuber, Grant L. "International Capital Markets and Canadian Economic Policy under Flexible and Fixed Exchange Rates, 1951-1970." In Federal Reserve Bank of Boston, *Canadian–United States Financial Relationships* (proceedings of a conference held in September 1971), pp. 9-36.

Dickey, John S. "The Relationship of Rhetoric and Reality: Merchant-Heeney Revisited." *International Journal* 27 (Spring 1972): 172-84.

Dinwoodie, D. H. "The Politics of International Pollution Control: The Trail Smelter Case." *International Journal* 27 (Spring 1972).

Eaton, William J. "The Battle of the Great Lakes." *The Reporter* (New York), 21 November 1963, pp. 38-40.

Eckstein, Harry. "Case Study and Theory in Political Science." In *The Handbook of Political Science*. Edited by Fred Greenstein and Nelson Polsby. Reading, Mass.: Addison-Wesley, 1974.

Fayerweather, John. "The Mercantile Bank Affair." *Columbia Journal of World Business* 6 (November-December 1971): 41-50.

Galtung, Johan. "A Structural Theory of Imperialism." *Journal of Peace Research* (Oslo), 8 (1971).

Gilpin, Robert. "American Direct Investment and Canada's Two Nationalisms." In *The Influence of the United States on Canadian Development*. Edited by Richard Preston. Durham, N.C.: Duke University Press, 1972.

Gotlieb, Allan, and Dalfen, Charles. "National Jurisdiction and International Responsibility: New Canadian Approaches to International Law." *American Journal of International Law* 67 (July 1973): 229-58.

Gray, Colin S. "Still on the Team: NORAD in 1973." *Queen's Quarterly* 80 (Autumn 1973): 398-404.

Guindon, Hubert. "Social Unrest, Social Class and Quebec's Bureaucratic Revolution." In *Party Politics in Canada*, pp. 189-200. Edited by Hugh Thorburn. Scarborough, Ont.: Prentice-Hall of Canada, 1967.

Higgins, Benjamin. "Regional Interactions, the Frontier and Economic Growth." In *Growth Poles and Growth Centres in Regional Planning*. Edited by Antoni Kuklinski. The Hague: Mouton, 1972.

Hoffmann, Stanley. "International Organization and the International System." *International Organization* 24 (Summer 1970): 389-413.

Hollick, Ann L. "Seabeds 'Make Strange Politics." *Foreign Policy* 9 (Winter 1972-73): 148-70.

Holsti, K. J. "Canada and the United States." In *Conflict in World Politics*. Edited by Steven Spiegel and Kenneth Waltz. Boston: Winthrop, 1971.

Innis, Harold A. "The Economics of Conservation." *Geographical Review* 28 (1938).

Jenson, J., and Regenstreif, P. "Some Dimensions of Partisan Choice in Québec." *Canadian Journal of Political Science* 3, no. 2 (1970): 308-18.

Keenleyside, H. L. "The Canada-U.S. PJBD." *International Journal* 16 (Winter 1960-61).

Keohane, Robert O., and Nye, Joseph S. "Transgovernmental Relations and International Organization." *World Politics* (October 1974).

Keohane, Robert O., and Nye, Joseph S., eds. "Transnational Relations and World Politics." *International Organization* 25 (Summer 1971): entire issue.

Kottman, Richard. "Volstead Violated: Prohibition as a Factor in Canadian-American Relations." *The Canadian Historical Review* 43 (June 1962): 106-26.

Leach, Richard H.; Walker, Donald E.; and Levy, Thomas Allen. "Province-State Transborder Relations: A Preliminary Assessment." *Canadian Public Administration* 16 (Fall 1973): 470-72.

LeMoyne, Jean. "L'identité culturelle." In *Le Canada au seuil du siècle de l'abondance*. Montréal: Editions H.M.H., 1969.

Leroy, Velg. "Le Rapport Gray: prelude d'un nouveau testament." *Actualité Economique* 48, no. 2 (1972): 211-25.

Levy, Thomas Allen. "The Involvement of the Provinces in Foreign Affairs II." In *The Changing Role of the Diplomatic Function in the Making of Foreign Policy*. Occasional Paper of the Center for Foreign Policy Studies. Halifax: Dalhousie University, June 1973.

Litvak, Isaiah A., and Maule, Christopher J. "Branch Plant Entrepreneurship." *The Business Quarterly* 37 (Spring 1972) : 45-53.

————. "Extraterritoriality and Conflict Resolution." *Journal of Conflict Resolution* 13 (September 1969) : 305-19.

————. "Marketing and Good Corporate Behavior: The Case of the U.S. Subsidiary." In *Canadian Marketing: Problems and Prospects*. Edited by D. N. Thompson and D. S. R. Leighton. Toronto: Wiley Publishers, 1973.

————. "U.S. Domination of Canadian Labour." *Columbia Journal of World Business* 7 (May-June 1972) : 57-63.

Loranger, Jean-Guy. "L'impérialisme américain au Québec: analyse de données récentes." *Socialisme 68*, 14 (1968) : 26-52.

Lyon, Peyton. "The Norstad Press Conference." In *Canadian Foreign Policy Since 1945*. Edited by J. L. Granatstein. Toronto: The Copp Clark Publishing Co., 1970.

MacDonald, R. St. J. "The New Canadian Declaration of Acceptance of the Compulsory Jurisdiction of the International Court of Justice." *Canadian Yearbook of International Law*, vol. 8. Vancouver: The Publications Centre, The University of British Columbia, 1970.

Merchant, Livingston, and Heeney, A. D. P. "Principles for Partnership." *US Department of State Bulletin* 53 (2 August 1965) : 193-208. Also printed by the Queen's Printer, Ottawa, 1965.

Miles, Edward. "Transnationalism in Space: Inner and Outer." *International Organization* 25 (Summer 1971) : 602-25.

Milsten, Donald E. "The Law of the Sea: Implications for North American Neighbors." *American Review of Canadian Studies*, Autumn 1973.

Molot, Maureen Appel. "The Role of Institutions in Canada–United States Relations: The Case of North American Financial Ties." In *Continental Community? Independence and Integration in North America*. Edited by W. Andrew Axline, James Hyndman, Peyton Lyon, and Maureen Molot. Toronto: McClelland and Stewart, forthcoming.

Murray, J. Alex, and Gerace, Mary C. "Canadian Attitudes toward the US Presence." *Public Opinion Quarterly* 36 (Fall 1972).

Murray, J. Alex, and Kubota, A. "What Canadians Think of U.S. Investment." *The International Review*, 12 February 1973, pp. 35-41.

Olson, Mancur, Jr. "Rapid Growth as a Destabilizing Force." *The Journal of Economic History* 23 (December 1963) : 529-52.

Parenteau, Roland. "Crise de l'unité nationale, crise du régime économique." In *Le Canada face à son avenir*. Montréal: Editions du Jour, 1964.

Raabe, F. Conrad. "Canada's Decision to Recognize the Communist Government of China." *Association for Canadian Studies in the U.S. Newsletter* 2 (Spring 1972) : 12-20.

Ratiner, Leigh S. "United States Ocean Policy." *Journal of Maritime Law and Commerce* 2 (January 1971) : 249-59.

Russell, Robert W. "Transgovernmental Interactions in the International Monetary System." *International Organization* 27 (Autumn 1973) : 431-64.

Scheinberg, Stephen. "Invitation to Empire: Tariffs and American Economic Expansion in Canada." *Business History Review* 47 (Summer 1973).

Scott, William A. "Psychological and Social Correlates of International Images." In *International Behavior*. Edited by Herbert Kelman. New York: Holt, Rinehart, and Winston, 1965.

Stacey, C. P. "The Canadian-American PJBD: 1940-1945." *International Journal* 9 (Spring 1954).

Stewart, Walter. "Our Washington Game Plan." *Maclean's*, August 1973.

Swanson, Roger. "The U.S.-Canadian Constellation, I: Washington, D.C." *International Journal* 27 (1972).

Tai, Chong-Soo; Peterson, Erick J.; and Gurr, Ted Robert. "Internal Versus External Sources of Anti-Americanism: Two Comparative Studies." *Journal of Conflict Resolution* 17 (September 1973): 455-88.

Treddenick, J. M. "Québec and Canada: The Economics of Independence." *Journal of Canadian Studies* 8 (1973): 16-31.

Tremblay, Rodrigue. "Investissements directs étrangers et stratégies industrielles et commerciales: le dilemme canadien." *Actualité Economique* 48 (1972): 226-53.

Trudeau, Pierre E. "Les séparatistes: des contre-révolutionnaires." *Cité Libre* 15 (1964): 2-6.

Van Cise, Jerrold G. "Antitrust Guides to Foreign Acquisitions." *Harvard Business Review,* November-December 1972.

Van Schendel, Michel. "Dépendance économique et souveraineté canadienne." In *La dualité canadienne à l'heure des Etats Unis.* Québec: Les Presses de l'Université Laval, 1965. Pp. 111-20.

Watkins, Melville H. "A Staple Theory of Economic Growth." *The Canadian Journal of Economics and Political Science* 29 (May 1963): 144-58.

Wells, Louis T., Jr. "The Multinational Business Enterprise: What Kind of International Organization?" *International Organization* 25 (Summer 1971): 447-64.

Wright, Gerald. "Persuasive Influence: The Case of the Interest Equalization Tax." In *Continental Community? Independence and Integration in North America.* Edited by W. Andrew Axline, James Hyndman, Peyton Lyon, and Maureen Molot. Toronto: McClelland and Stewart, 1974.

Young, Oran R. "Interdependencies in World Politics." *International Journal* 24 (Autumn 1969): 726-50.

GOVERNMENT REPORTS AND RELATED DOCUMENTS

Bank of Canada. *Annual Report of the Governor To The Minister of Finance For The Year 1964.* Ottawa, 1965.

————. *Annual Report of the Governor To The Minister of Finance For The Year 1965.* Ottawa, 1966.

————. *Annual Report of the Governor To The Minister of Finance For The Year 1968.* Ottawa, 1968.

Canada. Department of Energy, Mines and Resources. *An Energy Policy for Canada, Phase 1.* 2 vols. Ottawa: Information Canada, 1973.

Canada. Department of Industry, Trade and Commerce. *Foreign-Owned Subsidiaries in Canada.* Ottawa: Queen's Printer, 1967.

Canada. Department of Industry, Trade and Commerce, Foreign Investment Division, Office of Economics. *Selected Readings in Laws and Regulations Affecting Foreign Investment in Canada.* March 1972.

Canada. Department of Regional Economic Expansion. *Atlantic Region: Economic Circumstances and Opportunities.* April 1973.

Canada. Gray Task Force. *Foreign Direct Investment in Canada.* Ottawa: Information Canada, 1972.

Canada. House of Commons. Standing Committee on External Affairs and National Defence. *Report No. 33.* 28th Parl., 2d sess., 1969-70.

Canada. Library of Parliament, Research Branch. "Laws and Regulations Preventing Undue United States Influence on Canadian Financial Institutions, Transportation, Communications, and Energy Industries." Ottawa, 2 March 1970.

Canada. National Energy Board. *Report to the Governor in Council in the Matter of the Applications under the National Energy Board Act of Alberta and Southern Gas Co. Ltd., Alberta Natural Gas Company, Canadian-Montana Pipe Line Co., Consolidated Natural Gas Ltd., Consolidated Pipe Line Co., Trans-Canada Pipe Lines Ltd. and Westcoast Transmission Co. Ltd.* Ottawa: National Energy Board, August 1970.

—————. *Reasons for Decision in the Matter of the Applications under the National Energy Board Act of Alberta and Southern Gas Co. Ltd., Alberta Natural Gas Co., Canadian-Montana Pipe Line Company, Consolidated Natural Gas Ltd., Consolidated Pipe Line Co. and Trans-Canada Pipe Lines Ltd.* Ottawa: National Energy Board, November 1971.

Canada. Prime Minister's Task Force on Labour Relations. *Report* on "Canadian Industrial Relations." Ottawa, 1968.

Canada. *Royal Commission on Canada's Economic Prospects.* Ottawa: Queen's Printer, 1957.

Canada. Senate. Special Committee on Science Policy. *Science Policy for Canada.* Vol. 1 (1970). Vol. 2 (1972). Vol. 3 (1973).

Canada. Task Force on the Structure of Canadian Industry. *Foreign Ownership and the Structure of Canadian Industry.* Ottawa: Queen's Printer, 1968.

Canada. "Third United Nations Conference on the Law of the Sea." Paper submitted by the government to the Standing Committee on External Affairs and National Defence, House of Commons, 2 November 1973.

Canadian-American Committee. *The New Environment for Canadian-American Relations.* Washington, D.C.: Canadian-American Committee, 1972.

—————. *Recent Canadian and US Government Actions Affecting US Investment in Canada.* Washington: National Planning Association; and Montreal: Private Planning Association of Canada, 1964.

Dominion Bureau of Statistics. *The Canadian Balance of International Payments, A Compendium of Statistics from 1946 to 1965.* Ottawa: Queen's Printer, 1967.

Parti Québécois. *C'est pas sorcier.* Montréal: Editions du Parti Québécois, 1973.

—————. *La Solution: la programme du Parti Québécois.* Montréal: Editions du Jour, 1970.

—————. *La Souveraineté et l'économie.* Montréal: Editions du Jour, 1970.

—————. *Les dossiers du 4e Congrès.* Montréal: Editions du Parti Québécois, 1972.

—————. *Quand nous serons vraiment chez-nous.* Montréal: Editions du Parti Québécois, 1972.

—————. *Un gouvernement du Parti Québécois s'enage.* Montréal: Editions du Parti Québécois, 1973.

Québec. Bureau de la statistique. *Statistiques financières du Gouvernement du Québec.* 1973.

Québec. Department of Trade and Commerce. *La situation économique au Québec.* Québec: Ministry of Industry and Commerce, 1973.

Sharp, Mitchell. "Canada-US Relations: Options for the Future." *International Perspectives* (bimonthly publication of the Department of External Affairs), special issue (Autumn 1972).

Statistics Canada. *Canada's International Investment Position.* Ottawa: Information Canada, 1971.

United States. Congress. Senate. Committee on Finance. *United States–Canadian Automobile Agreement, Hearings Before the Committee on Finance on H.R. 9042.* 89th Cong., 1st sess., 1965.

United States. Department of State. *Foreign Relations of the United States 1948.* Vol. 9: *The Western Hemisphere.* Washington, D.C.: US Government Printing Office, 1972.

United States. Department of State, Office of the Geographer. *Limits in the Seas.* Series A, No. 46, 12 August 1972.

PAPERS, ADDRESSES, UNPUBLISHED REPORTS

Ball, George W. "Interdependence: The Basis of US-Canada Relations." Address to the American Assembly, Arden House, New York, 25 April 1964.

Doeringer, Peter B. "Low Pay, Labor Market Dualism, and Industrial Relations Systems." Discussion Paper No. 271 of the Harvard Institute of Economic Research, 1973. (Mimeographed.)

Johnson, Eleanor Barbara. "The Regulation of International Fisheries." Ph.D. dissertation, University of Washington, 1973.

Kash, Don E., et al. "Energy Under the Oceans: A Technology Assessment of Outer Continental Shelf Oil and Gas Operations." National Science Foundation, Washington, D. C., September 1973.

Kottman, R. N. "The Diplomatic Relations of the United States and Canada, 1927-1941." Ph.D. dissertation, Vanderbilt University, 1958.

Leyton-Brown, David. "Governments of Developed Countries as Hosts to Multinational Enterprise: The Canadian, British, and French Policy Experience." Ph.D. dissertation, Harvard University, 1973.

Lyon, Peyton V. "Canada-US Free Trade (CUFTA) and Canadian Independence." Carleton University School of International Affairs, 1973. (Mimeographed.)

Murray, J. Alex. "An Analysis of Public Attitudes on the Question of US Investment in Canada." University of Windsor International Business Research Unit, 1973. (Mimeographed.)

Noumoff, Sam. "How to Make a Killing." McGill-Queen's University, 1972. (Mimeographed.)

Rasminsky, Louis. "Monetary Policy and the Defence of the Canadian Dollar." Speech given to the Canadian Club of Victoria, 17 October 1968.

Scanlon, Joseph. "Canada Sees the World through U.S. Eyes: One Case Study in Cultural Domination." Carleton University School of Journalism, 1973. (Mimeographed.)

Sharp, Mitchell, Secretary of State for External Affairs. "Canada Extends its Territorial Sea." Statement to the House of Commons, 17 April 1970. (Mimeographed.)

Stevenson, Garth. "Foreign Direct Investment and the Provinces: A Study of Elite Attitudes." Carleton University Department of Political Science, 1973. (Mimeographed.)

Wagner, James R. "Partnership: American Foreign Policy toward Canada, 1953-1957." Ph.D. dissertation, University of Denver, 1966.

INDEX